The
immortal
Warrior

For Robin
with best wishes

John Wells
August 1989

The immortal Warrior

BRITAIN'S FIRST AND LAST BATTLESHIP

by Captain John Wells RN

Illustrated by Gary Cook
Bournemouth and Poole College of Art and Design

KENNETH MASON

Published by Kenneth Mason
The old harbourmasters', Emsworth, Hampshire
© Captain John Wells 1987
Line illustrations © Gary Cook and Bournemouth
and Poole College of Art and Design 1987
Printed in Great Britain and designed by Gary
Cook under the direction of Phil Jones with
assistance from students of Technical Illustration,
Bournemouth and Poole College of Art and Design

British Library Cataloguing in Publication Data

Wells, John
    The immortal Warrior: Britain's first and last
    battleship.
    1. Great Britain, Royal Navy – History
    2. Warrior (Ship)
    I. Title
    623.8'225 VA458.W3/

ISBN 0-85937-333-9

Contents

Preface

CAPTAIN JOHN WELLS has indeed a tale to tell – of the toughness and spirit of the Victorian Navy; and of the vision, determination and staying power of those who have lately brought this great ship back from the graveyard to her rightful place in Portsmouth, the base from which she once exercised her deterrent power. What he does not do is tell us much about himself. At a time of life when most people would be taking a long and well-earned rest, he went back to work and has devoted himself to research into the history and other aspects of *Warrior*. In so doing he has also rediscovered much of importance that had been forgotten about our Navy in the nineteenth century. Like most novel and original projects, the restoration of *Warrior* has been carried through by quite a small band of people, of which he is a member; and one of the pleasures and encouragements of tackling such a desperate enterprise has been that people like him appear out of the blue, give of their best, and turn out to be indispensable.

In return for his labours he shares in a great achievement. *Warrior* is not only one of the most influential warships ever built; she is also the sole surviving nineteenth-century capital ship in the world, the Royal Navy's first – and last – battleship, forerunner and survivor of all her kind. She is also very beautiful; no one who comes on board and first sees the sheer of her enormous deck, her rigging and her masts and yards against the sky, will remain unmoved. We aim to show her without modern alterations or additions of any sort, without notices or concessions to comfort which would break the spell, but exactly like a modern warship on a Navy Day, functional and purposeful in every detail. In this way we hope that she will now have a long and useful future, not just as one more tourist attraction, but as a permanent reminder to all who see her of the virtues of endurance, courage and service.

John Smith

Author's foreword

A love of the sea and of naval history was a paternal inheritance; my first impression on tackling the *Warrior* epoch was its marked resemblance to the navy I joined half a century ago. In those days subordinate officers slept in hammocks, kept a journal, secured boats to the lower (stun'sail) boom and at gun drill dipped the sponge-and-rammer in a tub of water before ramming to 'quench smouldering residue'. All that, of course, has changed now but a naval background certainly helped to interpret *Warrior's* deck and signal logs and hence life on board; certainly the familiar style of official correspondence and regulations made it that much easier to read between the lines of research papers. Another early but understandable impression was the almost total public ignorance of *Warrior* and her significance as a warship. This book is designed to help stake her place in history, although words and photographs cannot properly convey the grandeur and unique character of a vessel that linked the sailing frigates of the Napoleonic wars with their modern counterparts. Only a conducted tour of ship above and below decks is likely to satisfy nautically minded visitors, many of whom will come back for more.

Essentially the *Warrior* story is about people – the admirals and politicians who ordered her construction, the naval architects who designed her, the craftsmen who built her, the generations of officers and men who trod her decks, those who cared for her in solitude and finally the people who brought her back to life. *To assist recapture contemporary atmosphere the text includes dialogue as well as description of certain events in italics; here imagination has been combined with supportive evidence to illustrate what might have occurred.* The story of the ship is complemented by twelve technical appendices to whet the appetite of those wishing to dig deeper into archival material. There can be no apology for employing Imperial measures since *Warrior* was built in feet and inches; her crew communicated in fathoms, ounces and points of the compass.

I must express my warmest thanks to the many people who have given their advice and help especially Vice Admiral Sir Patrick Bayly, Deputy Chief Naval Constructor David Brown, Brian Dolley, Maldwin Drummond, Dr Nicholas Rodger and not least Richard Tomlin.

Research has been no single-handed task and I am indebted to the unremitting efforts of Antonia MacArthur, Bob Ridding, Morin Scott, Ernest Slaymaker and John Warsop; to the generous assistance afforded by Alan Francis and Philip Wilton of the Naval Historical Library; to the staff of the National Maritime Museum, in particular Peter Ince of the Department of Astromony and Navigation; to Commander John Guard, former Queen's Harbour Master at Pembroke Dock; to Captain Ray Parsons and staff of the Royal Naval Museum, Portsmouth; to Frank Sainsbury, former Deputy Librarian of West Ham; to Surgeon Vice Admiral Sir James Watt; to the staff of the Maritime Trust and of Portsmouth City Council; to the late John Moore and to members of the Warrior Association who contributed records of their forebears who served in the ship.

The outstanding quality of Gary Cook's technical illustrations has done much, in my view, to enhance the text and I shall always be grateful to Michael Leek of the Bournemouth and Pool College of Art and Technical Design for allowing him to undertake this task and for giving his advice.

My thanks to Walter Brownlee, Keith Johnson and Jim Wilson of Hartlepool whose knowledge of the ship has been of immense assistance. As one whose manuscript is not unlike an advertisement for buying a word processor I am fortunate to have had it typed so admirably by Amanda and Kathy.

For the past five years I have been under the *Warrior* spell in company with those involved in her restoration and display. Not even the vicissitudes of British Rail could dampen the excitement of each visit to the Coal Dock in Hartlepool to see the changes brought about by reconstruction, particularly in the final stages. It has been a privilege to contribute to such a rewarding project, if only in a small way. As with most sailors the last ship in which one serves is always the best – *Warrior* is just that.

The photograph of HRH Princess of Wales on p119 is reproduced by gracious permission of Her Majesty the Queen from an original in the Royal Archives, Windsor; that of *HMS Warrior* on the front of the dust jacket is by Frederick Tudgay and reproduced by kind permission of Richard Pease; that on the back the work of Stephen Ortega by kind permission of the Bournemouth School of Art and Technical Design.

Permission to reproduce other photographs including those of pictures is gratefully acknowledged to Tim Ashworth for photograph p39; J L Barber Editor of Rutland Record p90; John Bickford Smith p174; Captain K N Bishop p150; Captain J K Douglas-Morris p82; Dr J R George p134; Edward Grove p13; The Rt Hon Lord Hampton p17; Keith Kissack pp85, 112, 151; Mrs I Millest p108; Keith Perkins p162; The Rt Hon The Earl of Perth p20; Commander J R Phillimore pp13, 101, 114, 117, 121, 123-4; Roger Richardson p161; Robert Selby pp159, 165; Mrs Jennifer Towey p177; Lieut Cdr C Wake-Walker p14; Captain C G Walker p160; the late Capt W R Wells p57; Michael Wetherall p170; John Wigston p120.

Also to BBC p187; Devon County Library p21; HMS *Excellent*, Portsmouth p139; Imperial War Museum pp88, 110, 159, 167-8, Malcolm Innes Gallery p118; National Maritime Museum pp142, 163 also silhouettes pp94, 109, 134, 154; RN Air Station Yeovilton p200, RN Museum, Portsmouth pp76, 99, 122; Science Museum p50, 93; HMS *Vernon*, Portsmouth p173; Warrior Preservation Trust pp184, 186, 190-1, 195-6, 203, 204-5.

J G Wells
Liss, Hampshire.

Illustrations

The illustrations in this book have been specially prepared by Gary Cook while a student of Technical Illustration at the Bournemouth and Poole College of Art and Design from 1983 to 1986. They were completed as part of his Higher National Diploma studies following discussions between author, publisher and the undersigned. The aim has been to produce illustrations reflecting a high degree of technical skill and also as accurate a representation of HMS *Warrior* as available reference material allowed. With the exception of the orthographic drawings of the ship, which have been based on the ship herself and the original Admiralty draughts, no illustration has been copied from other works.

The reproduction in colour on the dust jacket of the longitudinal sectioned elevation of the ship was drawn by Stephen Ortega, also a former student at Bournemouth. It was completed in June 1980, after four years work, including research, and measures 9ft x 5ft overall. On completion of the restoration of the ship it will be displayed as a permanent visual record of the ship during her first commission.

Illustrations of the type reproduced here require a great deal of preliminary background work and without the assistance of others it would be impossible to portray the accuracy demanded by the text. To all those who offered their assistance, be it with research, advice or encouragement, I would like to extend, on behalf of the College, my thanks and appreciation. In particular the following must be mentioned; Vice-Admiral Sir Patrick Bayly, Director of the Maritime Trust; the late Ray Hockey and Bill Stevenson, , the Warrior Preservation Trust, Hartlepool; the late John Moore; James Lees, David Lyon and the late George Osbon, all of the National Maritime Museum; Thomas Wright of the Science Museum; Richard Tomlin; Portsmouth City Council; and of course the author himself.

Finally, my thanks to my colleagues; Peter Jarvis and Phil Jones; Alan Hogg and Iris Peters, College Librarians; and James Howe, College photographic technician. The abilities of Gary Cook and Stephen Ortega, I am sure, will speak for themselves.

Michael E Leek MCSD FISTC FRSA
Bournemouth and Poole College of Art and Design
Dorset, 1987

CHAPTER ONE
Concept

JUST BEFORE DAWN on Friday, September 20, 1861 the paddle vessel Pigmy, at anchor in St Helens Roads off the eastern end of the Isle of Wight, showed signs of getting under way. Anchor hove in, the stout little craft steamed out on an easterly course, black smoke belching from her tall thin funnel. No sooner clear of the land than a fresh westerly breeze came up astern, white horses appearing on the crests of waves; as dawn broke Pigmy came abreast the Nab lightvessel.

Turning head to wind and reducing speed to dead slow the Pigmy's master stationed a man at the wheelhouse before joining Senior Admiralty Pilot William Jones who was already scanning the eastern horizon with a small telescope. They did not have long to wait. Shortly after six o'clock Jones spotted the tops of masts coming over the skyline, silhouetted against the rising sun. Within minutes pilot and master could make out first the foretopsail, then the foretopmast staysail of a full rigged ship. Smoke from the funnels indicated that she was also under steam. Gradually a warship's dark hull came into view and they could see waves gently parted by a clipper bow. Back on the helm the Pigmy's master made to intercept while the pilot went below to collect his gear.

By the time he returned the vessel was beam on, a mile or so away. Although her lines were those of a frigate her size was vast. For months the ship had been the talk of Portsmouth but her length! A puff of smoke followed by the dull boom of a gun drew attention to the pilot jack hoisted at the foremast, announcing her readiness to take him aboard.

Jones nodded to the master who brought the Pigmy round a point to approach from the port quarter, aiming for the ladder amidships. As the warship lay head to wind, almost stopped, Jones could see men moving about aloft while a frock-coated officer watched from the side of the after bridge. Pigmy pitched to the short seas, throwing spray over her bows, but the ship herself remained steady with only an occasional swirl of stern wash from the slowly moving propeller. Jones wondered how she would handle, how long the helm would take to answer, what sort of windage she would make as they steamed up harbour later that day.

As Pigmy approached the vessel's stern a port lid opened to reveal the muzzle of a gun being run out ready to salute on anchoring at Spithead. Red patches marred the black of the ship's side but the roman numerals on the stern post were plain enough. Draught marks read 25 feet, as Jones expected which would mean watching the tide once inside the dockyard. He glanced up at the ship's name outlined in gold below the stern windows – WARRIOR. In less than a minute he had clambered aboard.

* * * * * * * *

Even after the banishment of Bonaparte to St Helena in 1815 at the end of the Napoleonic wars, England rightly kept a watchful eye on French naval revival. The balance of power was already threatened by Russian expansionism while inventions of the Industrial Revolution appealing to Gallic imagination and ambitions posed other problems. Time would soon be ripe for Britain's old adversary to mount another challenge.

Few had objected when the British government ruthlessly cut back defence expenditure, laying up most of the fleet in reserve and reducing manpower from 130,000 to 23,000 in four years. For this was the age of *Pax Britannica* in which the navy was seen by Parliament as an instrument of power politics, to show the flag and protect imperial trade even if it meant stretching its limited strength to the far corners of the world.

Warship design has always been a compromise between weapons, protection and speed and in both Britain and France fighting ship characteristics had changed little in 100 years – steam had yet to arrive in fleets content to sail at four knots. Layout and design were dominated by armament to the extent that ships were rated by the number of guns carried, the most heavily armed and largest forming line-of-battle; while smaller, faster vessels with a single gun deck were designated frigates and corvettes. Because of its robust timbering a two- or three-decker line-of-battle ship (liner) could absorb heavy punishment from solid shot; cast-iron smooth-bore muzzle-loaders mounted in broadsides were still the battle winners, designed as they were to disable enemy ships and crews. It needed only a change in projectile to upset the balance between offence and defence.

Due to their inaccuracy and instability explosive shells were distrusted by the Royal Navy. Not so in France, eager to exploit a weapon that might ultimately neutralise British numerical superiority, especially after Colonel Paixhans had demonstrated how a wooden hull could be damaged by time-fused shells. To his proposal for a fleet of small steamers encased in armour-plate which could concentrate their fire on helpless liners, official reaction was cool. But the Ministry of Marine did accept his *canon obusier* (1824) and eventually agreed to gun standardization while continuing to build big wooden two-deckers.

With large numbers in reserve, Britain had little apparent need to build new warships during the first 20 years of peace. Responsibility for design and construction was vested in the Surveyor of the Navy; to Robert Seppings (1813-1832) goes the credit for constructional innovations on a scientific basis, enabling ships to carry more guns and last longer. With a variety of armament a liner of 1830 packed three times the weight of *Victory's* broadside, her hull greatly strengthened by iron beam brackets, diagonals and stringers. Chain cables, iron water tanks and copper containers for gunpowder charges were also common features.

By the mid 1830s post-Napoleonic retrenchment was over and defence budgets again began to increase. As the only foreign navies of importance were French, Russian and American it was Britain's declared policy 'to keep up a navy equal to the navies of any two Powers that can be brought against us.' [1]

Despite diehard prejudice the navy was an early and enthusiastic employer of steam power. First came paddle-wheel machinery which had its drawbacks – the real breakthrough came with the propeller. When Seppings was succeeded by Symonds, a sailing protagonist, steam propulsion went through a critical stage in its evolution. Following successful trials the Admiralty ignored Symonds's protests and directed the building of the prototype screw warship *Rattler*. Eventually the propeller relegated the paddle to coastal and harbour craft – the Royal Navy's last operational paddle tug bowing out in 1981. Problems with early steam plants, fuel storage limitations and lack of coaling stations overseas combined to offset the tactical and strategical freedom of independence from wind. And because steam might interfere with sail propellers were later made hoistable and funnels telescopic, the former evolution neither simple nor speedy. Nevertheless, as the world's leading industrial power, British steam machinery afloat was in the forefront of development.

For some time gunnery training had left much to be desired, needing the concerted efforts of powerful critics, including the artillerist Sir Howard Douglas, to persuade the Admiralty to establish a gunnery school aboard the old three-decker *Excellent* in Portsmouth. [2] The influence of

as soon as Astronomer Royal Sir George Airy had reduced the latter handicap to practical proportions Brunel redesigned *Great Britain* to have an iron hull and the Admiralty bought a small iron ship. Credit for the first iron warship goes to East India Company's *Nemesis* whose performance under gunfire in the First China War sufficiently impressed the Admiralty to order five frigates of different tonnages in the mid 1840s. [3] Doubts as to the effect of gunfire on iron plates then manufactured led to trials on which the *Excellent* reported unfavourably, in particular the splinter effect and that large jagged holes would be difficult to plug. The publicity caused France and America to conduct their own trials and then – like Britain – abandon iron for warship hulls.

After the French occupation of Algeria their fleet's activities in the eastern Mediterranean alarmed the British government. Skilful diplomacy on the part of Palmerston, then foreign secretary, paid off with a well-conducted bombardment of Acre (1840) by an Anglo-Austrian-Turkish squadron, to the mortification of France. Anglophobia then made it easier for Prince de Joinville, son of King Louis Phillipe, to convince his government of the need to expand their navy with a strong steam element. Inclusion of this policy in a well-publicised building programme was sufficient to cause an invasion scare in England.

Early in 1848 Captain Sir Baldwin Wake Walker

her commanding officers on naval gunnery policy became considerable; as well as training officers and men to follow a common doctrine, they evaluated gun and material performance. In response to French standardization, the Royal Navy settled for the 32 pounder of varying lengths and the 8 inch shell gun to which was later added a 10 in shell gun and 68 pdr, initially mounted as a pivot or chase gun on upper decks to augment broadside guns with arcs of fire forward and aft.

Iron shipbuilding in Britain was a significant product of the Industrial Revolution, its advantage over timber being that it made for larger, lighter and more durable hulls. Marine growth fouling of iron bottoms and abnormal compass deviation were justifiable objections but

succeeded Symonds as Surveyor. Walker had been loaned to command the Turkish navy for seven years, leading their squadron at the bombardment of Acre for which he was awarded a KCB. When Walker's new appointment was announced his commander-in-chief in the Pacific reported, 'I never saw a man so distressed when he heard; . . . he imagined there was some error about his appointment.' The admiral showed him the letter from the First Lord (Lord Auckland) which 'gave reasons for the nomination; that he thought a man who had had considerable experience in regulating ships . . . and was a man of judgement and a good sailor, was about the best head to be appointed for the surveying department, without having any particular

● Rear Admiral Sir
Baldwin Wake Walker
(left, in the uniform of
a Turkish admiral)
Surveyor and Controller
of the Navy 1848-61

● Stanislas Depuy de
Lôme, French naval
architect and directeur
de material

found 45-year-old Thomas Lloyd as the Admiralty's third Chief Engineer and Inspector of Steam Machinery. An outstanding engineer Lloyd was not only an influential advocate of the screw propeller but he had helped design the propulsion system for the *Rattler* including the stern configuration. The next arrival was Isaac Watts who had spent much of his early years in Portsmouth dockyard and, like Lloyd, had studied at the School of Naval Architecture for seven years. He joined Walker as first assistant, responsible for ship design, later to become Chief Constructor. In 1851 Watts and Lloyd visited French dockyards, especially to look at *Napoleon*, launched as a 90 gun line-of-battle ship to the design of the up-and-coming naval architect Stanislas Dupuy de Lôme. They would have noted that steam machinery had been given priority over sails – 13 knots was expected – and their report to the Surveyor led to a greater effort in completing Britain's response – *Agamemnon*. Of comparable armament but slightly slower her well-balanced performance under sail and steam was the result of careful planning. The race for supremacy in screw line-of-battle ships had started. Both countries augmented new construction by fitting engines and boilers to recently completed ships or those on the stocks.

When Napoleon III seized power from Louis Phillipe and announced the Second Empire, Anglo-French antagonism intensified which

crotchets of his own about shipbuilding.'[4] In contrast to his predecessor the Board intimated 'that they should not expect him to originate the lines of vessels to be built but these should be designed by naval architects attached to his office'.[5] A wise and experienced administrator, Walker proved the right choice for a difficult job, especially in handling successive Boards of Admiralty during his 12 years of office.

On arrival at Somerset House Baldwin Walker

● La Gloire, world's first
ocean going ironclad,
launched 1858

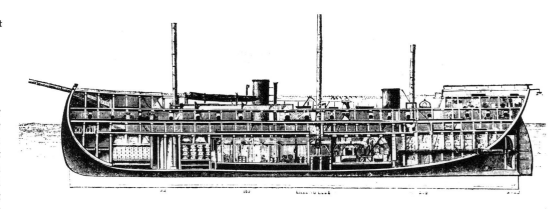

caused a war scare in England during the winter of 1851-52. Not only the two- but one-power standard appeared to be slipping, although with hindsight it is hard to avoid the conclusion that the French threat was again overrated. British confidence, however, was restored by a Spithead review when only three of the 40 ships present lacked steam power. The Royal Navy was now more efficient than it had been for many years but timber was still felt to be best for hulls; the rude test of war forced a change. First came the action at Sinope in the Black Sea late in 1853 when a superior Russian force, armed with French shell guns, destroyed an unprepared Turkish squadron of wooden frigates. Within a year Britain and France were at war with Russia.

Since the Russian all-sailing fleet declined action both in the Crimea – after which the war was named – and the Baltic, allied fleet operations were confined to blockade and army support. Nevertheless the lessons learned influenced future design of ships and armaments as well as the manning of the fleet. First, steam line-of-battle ships, unaffected by calms or contrary winds, confirmed their superiority over sailing vessels, even those aided by paddle tugs. Secondly, bombardments of shore fortifications exposed the vulnerability of wooden hulls to shells and red-hot shot, which led to the construction of small shallow draft, steam-propelled armoured batteries Initiated by the French but planned as a

joint project involving Anglo-French collaboration in design and production, it was Thomas Lloyd who suggested that four and a half inch iron plate with wooden backing was the best protection.[6] In the event only the first three French ironclads arrived in time to spearhead the attack on the Russian defences at Kinburn. Not only did they withstand enemy shot and shell with negligible casualties but their guns assisted in pounding the forts into surrender from 1200 yards.

Entente with France and the unrestricted exchange of information began to diminish even before the Peace of Paris was signed in 1856. Kinburn justified Paixhan's argument for shell guns and France lost no time in applying this lesson. Armour trials were initiated, rifled gun barrels investigated and in January 1857 Depuy de Lôme was made Directeur de Matérial for the whole navy. Instead of competing with Britain in building wooden liners the government switched to a programme of fast ocean-going armoured frigates – to be called ironclads – of which *Gloire*

was laid down in March 1858. Depuy de Lôme's concept was that in an action between two evenly-matched adversaries the smaller, handier ship would have the edge. Thus the smallest practicable dimensions dictated a design based on that of *Napoleon* but slightly longer and larger displacing 5630 tons. Although *Gloire* had a considerable amount of iron in her structure, including an upper deck and about four and a half inches of armour from stem to stern, the hull was wooden. Her main gun deck was planned for 30 rifled muzzle-loading 50 pdrs capable of firing shot and shell, with six more on the upper deck; further she would have powerful steam machinery. Had the French possessed foundry capacity to manufacture plating as well as armour all four ironclads would have had iron hulls. As it was, only the last, *Couronne*, fulfilled her designer's ambition.

Despite material handicaps the influence of Napoleon III on his government and the genius of Depuy de Lôme – perhaps the greatest naval architect of the mid-19th century[7] – changed the concept of major warship design.

In England a different state of affairs existed. The aftermath of the Russian war led to criticism of the navy, that the French had performed better than their allies and were now superior in screw line-of-battle ships. Although untrue, such claims were believed. Money was tight and after the First Lord (Sir Charles Wood) announced that 'sailing vessels . . . would never be employed again in war'[8] the Surveyor introduced a building and conversion programme of large liners such as *Duncan, Victoria* and *Marlborough*. Then Watts was ordered to design a second pair of huge frigates, *Mersey* and *Orlando*, partially intended to counter the American *Merrimack* class. Displacing 5643 tons, a speed of 13 knots and mounting a broadside of 10in and 68 pdrs, their 300 ft wooden hulls, strengthened with iron, had been stretched to the limit. Subsequent performance was disappointing but provided Walker and his assistant Watts with useful data on large frigate construction and armament.

The Russian war gave an immeasurable impetus to the development of naval science particularly in projectiles where experience proved that red-hot shot was more effective than explosive shell; later experiments led to the *Excellent* reporting favourably on Mr Martin's shell that could be filled with molten iron to burst with devastating effect.[9] Arguments continued

over the merits of long- versus close-range gun action – with special reference to the role of large frigates in battle – and whether iron or wood was best for hull construction. The influential Sir Howard Douglas was implacably opposed to iron hulls arguing that armour would cause a ship to lose both speed and the advantage of choosing the range at which to fight. His opinions were shared in Admiralty circles but not by the naval architect and engineer, John Scott Russell, an intelligent and eloquent Scotsman whose whole interest centred on ship design, especially the movement of a hull through water. After initial success in Greenock he moved to London where he designed the hull and paddle engines for Brunel's

Great Eastern, and then secured the contract to build her at his Millwall yard. The venture was a disaster. Fires destroyed his shipyard, post-war inflation caused the money to run out, the ship stuck on the launching ways and the partnership with Brunel dissolved in acrimonious argument. His shipbuilding business survived, but only just.

For some years Scott Russell had toyed with the idea of an iron-hulled, armoured steam warship. It happened that one of the casualties of his shipyard fire in May 1855 was an iron-plated wooden floating battery destined for the Russian war. He decided the navy needed something better and from his drawing board came a shot-proof corvette with an iron hull and an outer skin of thick armour backed by wood. In November 1855 a model and plans were submitted to Baldwin Walker who gave it a sympathetic hearing but kept it in storage, judging that its time was not ripe for putting to the Board.[10]

Various other plans for ironclads arrived on the Surveyor's desk but all were rejected. Then a proposal from a gunnery specialist, Captain William Moorsom, interested the Board sufficiently to ask the War Department at Woolwich to assess the relative merits of hammered and rolled four inch iron plates. They reported that there was little to choose between the two processes, that both would keep out 68 pdr shot at 600 yards and that they could only be penetrated at less if repeatedly struck in the same spot. Moreover such armour could be fitted to ships' sides then considered to be the only protection needed. Receiving grave reports from agents in France, Walker felt it was time to act and with the Board's approval initiated a design for a corvette of 5,600 tons, four inch armour and a speed of 10 knots. There were apprehensions on two counts, first the need for frequent docking to remove fouling – he had an iron hull in mind – and secondly that a 68 pdr might be superseded by a more powerful gun.[11] At any rate the proposals reached the First Lord in February 1858.

Almost simultaneously an Italian exile attempted to assassinate Emperor Napoleon III on a visit to England. Anglo-French relations plummeted, Lord Palmerston's ministry fell and Lord Derby's Conservative government took office. As rumours of French intentions to build an ironclad fleet began to filter through a state of near panic developed in England, whose newspapers attributed exaggerated capabilities to the ironclads, describing them as 'huge polished steel frigates'. Undoubtedly Napoleon III was credited with greater abilities and more sinister designs than he possessed. Although responsible people took the news calmly it left government and Admiralty in a dilemma – whether or not to include ironclads in the building programme that was bound to come. To allay fears and play for time Parliament set up a committee to investigate the increase in naval estimates in the last six years and

enquire into Britain's naval strength vis-à-vis other countries, notably France.[12] 1858 was to be a crucial year.

Early in March a new First Lord of the Admiralty, 59-year-old Sir John Pakington, started his political assignment by despatching a memorandum on the state of the navy to the Prime Minister who commented, 'qui donner à penser . . . If we are in office this time next year we will have, please God, a more satisfactory statement.'[13] In steam liners afloat and building France was rapidly approaching equality, the situation made all the more grave by the threat of support from Russia; as the person responsible for naval policy Pakington was in the hot seat. He

attended the guns-versus-armour trials in Portsmouth, gave ready ear to Scott Russell and was in frequent communication with Baldwin Walker whose opinion he valued[14]

Not least of his undertakings was to keep Buckingham Palace informed on naval affairs. Writing in her own hand in April 1858 Queen Victoria pointed out, 'On the state of naval preparations in the event of war the Queen expects thorough consideration from the Board of Admiralty . . . She does not wish for the opinion of this or that person given without any responsibility attaching to it, but for the collective opinions of Sir John Pakington and his Board . . . a subject on which the safety of the Empire depends . . .' On the question of a Royal Commission to enquire into the navy she commented, '. . . if old First Lords shall be upon it they will stifle the enquiry. We want practical men who are not yet compromised.'

Even more forthright was Prince Albert, who frequently wrote in 'a penetrating and practical manner' to ask why gunboats were allowed to rot in Haslar Creek, '. . . why was the depth of water in Portsmouth docks so shallow that many ships could get in only when lightened or at spring tides?' Above all, what was being done about the French iron sided frigates, '. . . what have we got to meet this new engine of war?'[13]

Pakington's first task had been to choose a Board of Admiralty who were both proficient and

17

of suitable political complexion, quite a problem since promotion after captain was by seniority and flag lists were swollen with ageing officers who had virtually lost touch with active service. Selection was either through nepotism or political influence; the system whereby a number of naval lords changed with the government was a serious hindrance to continuity. Between 1830 and 1861 there were 16 changes in the office of First Naval (Sea) Lord. Since the Board was a passport to promotion most naval members went on to become commanders-in-chief at home or overseas where, by virtue of seniority and location away from Whitehall, the real power often lay.

Pakington, however, was fortunate in retaining the services of three preceding Board members;[15] on getting down to business they drafted a minute 'specifying the number of ships . . . which England should have' if navies of France and Russia were combined against her.[16] On June 22 Walker declared the construction of sea-going ironclads to be 'of the highest importance not only as regards the supremacy of the British Navy but even the safety of the country.' He pointed out that it was not in Britain's interests to introduce new and costly warships until forced upon her by foreign powers when, 'it becomes a matter not only of expediency but of absolute necessity . . . This time had arrived. France has now commenced to build frigates of great speed but with their sides protected by thick metal plates,

and this renders it imperative for this country to do the same without delay.'

Appreciating that a new type of ship required an adequate development period, which was not available, Walker submitted a design 'prepared several months ago . . . on a principle similar to that adopted in the iron floating batteries built during the last war but with fine lines and speed.' His proposal was to build six ironclads, two with wooden hulls at Chatham and Pembroke dockyards and four with iron hulls in private yards. By basing the iron ships at home docking facilities would be easily available. The latest design came out as a 26 gun frigate of 6,096 tons displacement, 1,000hp engines giving more than 12kts and armoured with four inch plates to below the waterline. Estimated cost of hull and engines would be under £200,000 for either type.[17]

Confronted with his first crisis Pakington expressed himself as 'very anxious . . . mortified and vexed'. After discussions on July 29 the Board were persuaded by Corry, the Political Secretary, that appropriations for 1859 should be devoted to 'at least two wooden frigates coated in iron.'[18]

To restore better relations with France, the Queen and Prince Consort visited Cherbourg arsenal and dockyard to be greeted with a fleet of new ships at anchor. 'The war preparations of the French are immense,' wrote the Prince, 'ours despicable. Our ministers use fine phrases but they do nothing.'

In August Captain Hewlett of the *Excellent* reported on a series of successful trials of four and a half inch iron plate mounted on the side of the old 74 gun hulk *Alfred*. Results showed the superiority of wrought iron over 'homogenous metal or steel' as then made. Further trials with the floating batteries *Erebus* (wooden hull) and *Meteor* (iron hull) appeared to demonstrate the value of oak backing to iron plating.[19]

In mid-September Joseph Large and Eugene Sweeney of the Surveyor's department returned from France to report that the French had laid down no wooden line of battleships since 1855 and that they had three ironclads under construction with two to four more projected. 'So convinced do naval men in France seem to be of the irresistible qualities of these ships that they are of the opinion that no more ships of the line will be laid down and that in ten years that class of vessels will have become obsolete.[20] At that time Britain possessed more screw liners but fewer screw frigates than France which of course posed a threat to commerce.

Then came the Admiralty Board meeting of November 26. No records exist of the minutes but since the day was a turning point it is worth reconstructing the discussions that might have taken place.

* * * * * * * *

● Sir John Briggs,
Clerk and Chief Clerk
of the Admiralty 1835-70

● Vice Admiral Sir
Richard Dundas, Lord
Commissioner of the
Admiralty 1852-61

Well before ten o'clock John Henry Briggs, chief clerk and William Govett Romaine, Permanent Secretary entered the Admiralty boardroom, their duty to ensure that papers were in order. They were joined by the First or Political Secretary, the Rt Hon Henry Thomas Lowry Corry MP, a capable, ambitious and influential politician. His arrival coincided with Lord Lovaine, the Civil Lord. A rumble of voices echoing along the corridor signalled the arrival of the first two sea lords wearing the customary frock coat and tall hat of the period. Aged 58, Admiral William Fanshaw Martin, the First Sea Lord, was an impressive looking man. Son of Admiral Sir Byam Martin, a former Controller, he held decided views on ships and weapons, was an authority on steam tactics and had been Admiral Superintendant of Portsmouth dockyard throughout the Russian war. A hard-working, dour and totally dedicated officer, he had the reputation as a strict disciplinarian. While his administrative reforms were first class there were those who questioned his judgement and believed him unsure of himself.

A year younger, Vice Admiral Richard Saunders Dundas was the second son of Lord Melville and a captain at 22. Handsomely featured with an upright figure, he was rather reserved. As a whig he had recentlly been First Sea Lord thereby earning criticism for agreeing to serve a tory administration. Others paid him respect for

putting duty above politics, remembering his KCB awarded for services in the Baltic. Although he had acquitted himself reasonably well it was evident that he was no fire eater. Rear Admiral Alexander Milne at 53 had served for ten years on previous Boards. A progressively-minded officer destined to go to the top he did not always see eye to eye with Martin and was rated by a contemporary as an 'able and hard headed Scotsman'. Last to arrive was Captain the Hon James Drummond, son of Viscount Strathallan, who had Russian war experience and more recently had been secretary to the previous First Lord, Sir Charles Wood. On paper a strong team.[22]

The chimes of Big Ben had already struck the hour when the First Lord arrived slightly breathless, apologising for modest unpunctuality. All present stood until Sir John Pakington had sat down at the head of the table. The main point of the agenda was the Surveyor's report of November 13 in which Baldwin Walker had pointed out that if the Excellent *trials of armour plates led to ironclad construction then '. . . they must be regarded as an addition to our force as a balance to those of France and not calculated to supersede any existing class of ship. Indeed no prudent man would at present consider it safe to risk, upon the*

performance of ships of this novel character, the naval supremacy of Great Britain.'[22] *The Prime Minister, Pakington reported, was delighted to learn of the programme to increase the strength of the navy but was increasingly concerned about feelings in the House that the Admiralty should take demonstrable action to allay fears about the French ironclads. 'Well, admiral,' said Sir John, 'what do you say to that?'* All eyes turned to the First Naval Lord.

Speaking deliberately Martin mentioned that he had read the Surveyor's report, agreed with his conclusions to some extent and was well aware of the concern in the House and press. He was not yet convinced of the value of protection afforded by armour, although he admitted that trials at Portsmouth were encouraging. He preferred to see an increase in the calibre of guns carried by line-of-battle ships, arguing that 'they may possibly have to deal with iron plated ships and to such encounter their present hollow shot guns are quite unequal.' *In regard to the magnitude of the threat from an invasion force he referred to his recent conversation with Sir Howard Douglas who asserted that 'Gloire was a ruse, a decoy to frighten us into discontinuing building any more timber ships of the line . . .' This confirmed his own theory that Napoleon III was bluffing –* 'he had the reputation for doing so' – *and he could not see how France with her industrial handicaps could possibly build all the ironclads they claimed would join the fleet. 'Was Gloire as formidable as their newspapers pretended?' He doubted it. Better to wait a little longer until more was*

●Captain, later Admiral,
the Hon James
Drummond

known about this ship and her sisters. The First Lord thanked him and turned to Dundas.

The Second Sea Lord spoke about British wooden line-of-battle ships. For more than half a century they had maintained the country's supremacy at sea and represented the best investment the navy could ever have. 'Would it not be better to convert some steam ships of the line into iron cased vessels capable of seven or eight knots and each armed with 30 heavy guns?' he asked.[23] 'And could the country afford the great cost of iron ships?' Although in favour of armour protection he was inclined to agree with the First Sea Lord and did not think the navy was yet ready to build an armour-plated ship. Almost before he had finished Milne intervened to say

that while he supported every effort to build a more powerful navy, converting our ships to screw propulsion had not been entirely without problems. Hulls used to last for many years. Now ships were coming in for costly refits after a single commission. Boilers and bearings were causing trouble. He agreed that wooden hulls could resist solid shot but bombardments against Russian fortifications were unsuccessful because our ships were vulnerable to shell fire. 'How would they fare against the French with heavier shell guns if they did not have armour protection? Kinburn proved that armour could resist shell fire.' Argument followed, occasionally contentious – Martin, and to a lesser extent Dundas, ranged against Milne with Drummond wavering between support of Milne and loyalty to his senior officers. Half an hour later Pakington glanced at his watch and invited the First Sea Lord to summarise.

Martin reiterated his assessment of the threat from across the Channel, arguing that 'we shall not be safe until our absolute naval means greatly exceed those of France. We must remember that a combination against us is highly probable, that we have many remote dependencies to defend, the force of France is concentrated and that our existence depends on success.'[24] He wanted to hear further news of the Excellent trials before committing the fleet to an armoured ship, when the matter would again be considered.

Until then Corry has said little but now he felt he must make his point. 'Really, admiral, I do not see

how you can relegate this problem to one for future discussion when it appears to demand immediate attention and is, in some degree, ripe for decision. Of course we cannot hazard the country's supremacy at sea on expectations from a novel vessel of war. But Hewlett's reports are already favourable. He tells us that iron plate backed by wood gives complete protection against ordinary guns and is penetrable only by a description of shot not now in use by any navy. From behind the protection afforded by such armour a single broadside would suffice to sink a ship unprotected. Why must France be the exclusive possessor of this formidable arm? I am in favour of delaying no longer. I propose the immediate order of two wooden ships to be coated with iron to guard in some degree against the advantage that France would have if we didn't.'[25] There was silence as Corry sat back in his chair. Civilian members of the Board were not usually so outspoken and in an atmosphere charged with tension the First Lord rustled his paper and glanced around the table. Milne was nodding his head vigorously, Dundas and Drummond murmuring words that signified acquiescence. Sensing that this forthright statement and proposal had majority support Martin conceded, 'very well, First Lord, I will instruct the Surveyor accordingly.'

* * * * * * * *

●An early impression of
Warrior as originally built,
September 20, 1861

Immediately after the meeting a confidential letter was addressed to Walker requesting him to 'prepare a submission stating the armament and other conditions . . . desirable for the construction of a wooden steam man of war to be cased with wrought iron four and a half inches thick to enable their Lordships to call for plans for building of such ships.'[26]

Although an important decision had been taken the battle was not quite won. Having secured approval for an armoured ship Pakington suspected that the proposed design did not go far enough in meeting the challenge of *Gloire* and that only an iron hull would suffice. Walker was quick to confirm this fact in his submission of December 1.[27] Out of courtesy the First Lord wrote to Sir Howard Douglas expressing his doubts over the use of wood. Now in his 83rd year the old general, who had done so much for naval fighting efficiency, had lost the last round; just before his death in 1861 he insisted, 'all I have said about armoured ships will prove correct – how little do they know of the undeveloped power of artillery' – a remarkable prescience.[28]

In mid-December the Board approved the Surveyor's latest proposal for an iron-hulled frigate, armoured on the sides with timber backing to displace more than 8,000 tons, 34 guns on the main deck, engines of 1000 horsepower and a speed of 14 knots.

On January 18, 1859 with cabinet approval Pakington announced the 'reconstruction of the navy' in an emergency programme that included iron frigates. In his speech on February 25 on the state of the navy, he assured Parliament that the progress of the French ships and the results of the armour tests had convinced the Admiralty that 'whatever the cost, we have no option, in the discharge of our duty but to commence the construction of iron-cased ships . . . we have resolved that it is our duty to build at least two of these vessels.'

Among naval powers it is fundamental that the weaker have a more obvious interest in revolutionizing naval warfare. But when a dominant power can build ships faster and overtake its weaker rivals even if a lead be momentarily conceded, then the argument for conservatism in construction policy becomes stronger. Reluctance to accept change is a characteristic often levelled at senior officers of the mid-Victorian navy but in 1858 the Board had been in office only eight months, barely time to formulate policy or adjust themselves to rapidly changing developments. And because Britain owed command of the sea to a large force of capital ships, which a revolution in naval construction might render obsolete overnight, the admirals were understandably cautious of Walker's proposals even after assurance that the problem of fixing armour to a ship's side by means

of timber backing had been solved.

In response to the threat posed by *Gloire* the Board realized that an iron-hulled armoured ship would have to come sooner or later. What had to be resolved was the timing of its introduction. Faced with the facts and subjected to public and parliamentary pressure the lords commissioners showed commendable perception in making the right decision at the right time to what became a superior yet more costly vessel than *Gloire*. Although reasonably confident of Walker's design they knew that if anything went wrong with the ship there would have been repercussions that might have split the navy. Pakington was prepared to take the risk and the admirals put their professional reputations on the block. Far from being reactionary their outlook was bold and far-sighted.

CHAPTER TWO
Characteristics

WHAT SORT OF NAVY would the new frigate join? At the end of 1858 the Royal Navy claimed to have some 425 effective steam vessels, including 29 screw line-of-battle ships, 26 screw and paddle frigates and 73 screw and paddle corvettes. Although only half the effective strength, except for very minor war vessels, were in full commission in the active fleet there were 21 liners and eight frigates among the 39 ships building, converting or receiving engines.[1]

On overseas stations flag officers commanded squadrons in the Mediterranean – where it was called a fleet – in North America and West Indies, South East coast of America, East Indies and China, Cape of Good Hope, West Africa and Australia. A few ships were assigned to Particular Service. The task of keeping the peace and protecting trade was unending; there were never enough ships.

Closer to home commanders-in-chief in naval bases at Portsmouth, Devonport and the Nore flew their flags in old ships of the line such as *Victory* and *Impregnable,* lesser commands being set up at Cork and Woolwich. To restore public confidence the Channel squadron was formed in 1858 to show the flag on the home station, which not only covered the British Isles but stretched along the coast of Europe from Scandinavia as far south as Gibraltar and the Canaries. Since the 1820s the ancient alliance with Portugal had been implemented to exercise British seapower in the shape of a small Tagus squadron based periodically at Lisbon.

There were no shore establishments so almost all the 5,000 officers and 55,000 seamen, boys and steam department worked and lived afloat in the active fleet or ships in port. The navy was operationally directed and administered by the Lords Commissioners of the Admiralty and some 300 civil servants from its headquarters in London. As well as the secretariat, the Admiralty building in Whitehall, overlooking the Horse Guards Parade, housed the Hydrographer, the Surveyor and the Comptroller General of the Coastguard, while down the Strand in Somerset House were the Accountant General, the Comptroller of Victualling and Transport Services and the Medical Director General.

Naval base dockyards and factories employed 16,000 men refitting and building new ships for the fleet, victualling yards at Deptford, Gosport and Plymouth supplied food, rum and clothing, while hospitals at Haslar and Plymouth cared for the sick. Royal Marines were separately administered from a small office in Whitehall, the corps based on home ports with their own barracks and infirmaries.

By 1859 the navy's personnel had almost recovered from a long stagnation, the process of reform accelerated by lessons learned in the Crimean war which in turn further loosened the shackles of rigid professional conservatism.

Following the 1820 rundown in ships there was no corresponding reduction in officers all of whom had entered on a long term career basis. Having no pension, those unable to get to sea faced half pay ashore. Through compulsory retirements of senior officers the number of unemployed commanders and lieutenants had been reduced to more acceptable proportions; against resistance the Admiralty had overhauled officer recruitment and entrance examinations, as well as establishing the hulk *Britannia* to train 13-year-old cadets. However, the caste of naval officers remained upper class in character, wardroom atmosphere was snobbish and there was no question of an officer not being a gentleman. Not even exceptional men were promoted from the lower deck.

Until 1860 a lieutenant was appointed to a ship for a commission of, say, three years; when the ship paid off the commission ended too, As there were no shore jobs it was half pay for him until he could find another ship. Sea time being a prerequisite for advancement meant an officer aspiring to reach the top needed almost continual employment. Promotion to commander and later captain depended on influence – the patronage of senior officers to ask for an officer's appointment or recommend his promotion. Even so an enterprising officer without family or political connections could also succeed by catching the eye of a superior. Having acquired an 'interest' the admiral or captain concerned would hopefully back his protégé if he happened to be in the right place. Luck played a major part and many a deserving officer languished ashore while his less able contemporaries – known as carpet men – went to sea.

Keeping watch in all weathers at sea and in harbour as well as normal duties the average lieutenant led a strenuous life and although some had private means pay only just covered mess bills and uniform maintenance. Most wardrooms were properly run and provided decent fare cooked in the ship's galley but there were ships where lax discipline allowed drinking and gambling to get out of hand despite Queen's Regulations instructing captains to 'prevent officers from extravagant living.'.

If one of the misfortunes of the early Victorian navy was having too many officers the opposite was true of the ships' companies of the fleet. They suffered from drastic reductions in manpower. Keenly aware that there were no reserves except pensioners and no means of rapidly expanding the navy, the Admiralty decided to attract a better class of volunteer. Inducements to enlist men for up to seven years with incentives to re-engage were followed by increases in basic pay, extra money for seamen gunners and awards of good conduct badges. In 1852 the Continuous Service Act went a long way towards establishing a proper career structure by encouraging youngsters of 14 or 15 to enter as boys for a short spell in a training ship before joining the fleet. The act introduced a ten-year engagement from 18, an intermediate rate of leading seaman and a higher rate of chief petty officer: all too late because when war broke out in 1854 the Baltic and Black Sea fleets were desperately short of crews. No sooner had peace been declared and men discharged, came a general recall to meet further contingencies. Recourse had to be made to the bounty system of inducement which let in a number of undesirable characters with objections to naval discipline. These and the infrequency of shore leave led to disturbances, in reality minor mutinies, in which some commanding officers showed up badly.[2]

The Royal Navy's character had always been reflected in the social life of the country then undergoing violent change because of the movement of industry and population. It was also an age both of great affluence and great poverty. Life for the underprivileged was a struggle; the worst of the Industrial Revolution had yet to be ameliorated by reformers. At least the critical manning situation brought home to Admiralty the need for a more enlightened and humane approach to service life and one of the many sensible recommendations of the Commissioners' Report on Manning (1859)[3] exposed the wretched state of the receiving (accommodation) hulks. There were always vessels in port being built, refitted or brought forward, necessitating crews being temporarily housed in hulks where conditions were little short of scandalous. When the commander-in-chief at Portsmouth produced the model hulk *Bellerophon*, properly equipped and organised, other ports followed suit.

In the autonomous regime of an 1859 man-o-war, life for the sailor was exacting, repetitive and strictly regulated. Every half hour the ship's bell was sounded below decks while the pipes of the boatswain's mates periodically interspersed with beats from a marine drum announced the routine of a day starting at dawn and finishing after dusk seven days a week. Whether aloft or on deck men moved at the rush; in moments of relaxation their thoughts turned to food, rum and leave.

The current victualling scale entitled the crew to a daily allowance of one pound of meat, half a pound of vegetables and a ration of biscuits – soft bread if in port – sugar, chocolate, tea and rice. Fresh meat from victualling yards or cattle pens on deck when available made a welcome change to salt beef or pork and although men were credited with savings on rations not taken up, either due to their inferior quality or because they bought provisions ashore privately, the system was unsatisfactory. Meals remained dull, monotonous, barely adequate for growing youngsters and hardly improved by the method of preparation and cooking that lasted into the next century.

Every morning a 'cook' from each broadside mess was detailed to draw the daily rations, mostly from the issuing room but also from the butcher at the beef screen. Back in the mess he cut the meat into portions, put the vegetables into a net with a metal tally bearing the mess number and prepared the soup. These were then taken to the galley amidships on the main deck where the ship's cooks took over, piling the meat dishes in the ovens and putting the vegetables into an enormous copper of boiling water. 'Cooks of the mess' were later sent below so that when the men came down to the mess decks at noon dinner had been carefully apportioned onto metal plates laid on the tables. Biscuits, salt and vinegar were to hand and thick oatmeal soup in each man's metal bowl. The ritual seldom varied. Main meals were eaten with knives that also did duty on deck, together with spoon or fingers. After the meal the 'cooks' washed plates, bowls and spoons in the vegetable water and returned them to the mess shelf (on the ship's side at the end of the table). Breakfast and supper were little more than biscuits with tea or cocoa but the dinner hour was sacrosanct and officers kept it so.

Rum, the sailor's solace for more than 200 years, was the cause of much crime and its resultant punishment. To reduce drunkenness – not confined to the lower deck – the ration was halved to one eighth of a pint in 1850, the evening issue stopped and a compensating allowance paid to teetotallers. When 'up spirits' was piped at 11.15am, rum in casks was brought up from below under an officer's supervision. Quantities for each mess were measured out on deck, diluted with two parts water and issued from the tub either individually or in mess 'fannies' at 12.30. For those who drank it – the majority – it was the supreme moment of the day as the equivalent of two double whiskies tingled down the throat to warm and comfort. Hardships were momentarily forgotten and for those coming off watch it was the prelude to peaceful slumber. The trouble was that men saved it up for drinking bouts or contrived extra supplies. As a form of currency it stood up well.

Regarded by regulations as a privilege, leave ashore had been restricted traditionally to 48 hours following monthly payment when the average libertyman had but two aims – to get drunk and find a woman. Public houses and prostitutes, readily available in naval ports, meant glorious intoxication that did no good for the image of Jack ashore and often led to cases of syphilis – 'lady's fever' in lower deck jargon. But changes were on the way and ships classified men for leave as well as for conduct so that the well-behaved could get ashore more frequently.

An abundance of fresh air and strenuous exercise when working on deck or aloft compared unfavourably with the foetid, candle-lit atmosphere below decks. Dampness and condensation mixed with the stench of human bodies living in overcrowded, insanitary conditions contributed to infectious diseases, bronchial disorders, ulcers and rheumatic pains. Strenuous manual labour caused ruptures or muscular sprains. From a lack of toothbrushes many suffered dental decay. However, by the 1850s better ventilation systems had been built into ships and commanding officers directed to attend to washing and laundering arrangements, medical inspections and medical comforts. The standard of naval surgeons, whose dedication to the sick and wounded in the Crimean War saved many lives, had risen appreciably and with the assistance of trained staff had cut down numbers on the sick list. Special arrangements were made for the schooling and education of boys, the introduction of libraries was popular and, subject to fire precautions, men were permitted to smoke their pipes although many preferred to chew tobacco as a panacea to discomfort. The establishment of canteens on board was not far off.

In matters of clothing the mid-Victorian navy paid less attention to uniformity than is the case today. The typical officer was a picture of sartorial inelegance with an ill-fitting frock coat, wrinkled trousers and a variety of neckties largely influenced by contemporary civilian fashion. Unlike the crew, officers had no practical working clothes and to perform their duties were required to wear formal dress or modifications of it. Only at sea or at night was relaxation permitted, except the officer of the watch who invariably wore a frock coat.

On the lower deck men dressed more functionally yet contrived to look smart in best clothes. Promulgation of the 1857 uniform regulations confirmed what was becoming the accepted pattern in larger warships, the essential feature of seaman's clothing being suitability for working aloft and on deck. Trowsers (sic) and frocks in white duck or blue cloth were loose fitting yet could be worn under blue jackets. As they had no pockets men kept small personal belongings in soft blue cloth caps; clasp knives were worn round the waist on a lanyard, sheath knives forbidden. One suit was kept for inspections and going ashore, complete with a hat plaited sennit-fashion from straw or palm. While dress material and several articles of clothing could be bought as paymaster's slops the majority of clothes were made aboard. Ships' complements included tailors, shoemaker and barber.[4]

The navy has always been fond of music and the ship's fiddler in great demand, whether to stimulate men to greater effort at the capstan or when hands were piped to 'dance and skylark'. And so the introduction of ship's bands in the 1850s must have been a great morale booster. The average unit comprised a dozen performers able to play wind or string instruments with a repertoire of marches, waltzes, sea shanties and even topical tunes from the music halls.

In 1859 the service was conscious of the need for good order and naval discipline. A whole chapter of Queen's Regulations devoted to the subject was applicable to the conduct of officers as well as men, much of it commonsense welfare, such as the investigation of complaints. Public and parliamentary outcry against corporal punishment had reduced but not abolished its infliction; lower down the scale the Naval Discipline Act listed the less heinous offences such as returning from leave drunk, neglect of duty and smoking out of hours, for which the summary punishments might be deprivation of good conduct badges, confinement in a cell on board, six water grog (one part of rum to six parts of water) and stoppage of leave or pay or both. In most ships justice was fairly and impartially administered as officers came to realize the growing potential in the men they commanded.

This was the navy with its unique social structure as the fleet was about to enter a period of far-reaching technological change. Although steam was used for battle manoeuvres, entering or leaving harbour and increasingly for short passages, sails remained the principal motive power in a navy with world-wide functions, the art of seamanship the prime attribute to be cultivated by executive officers and seamen. But the French challenge had alerted the country to the need for building a stronger fleet. With the scent of war in the air the outlook for the new frigate and those who would form her company

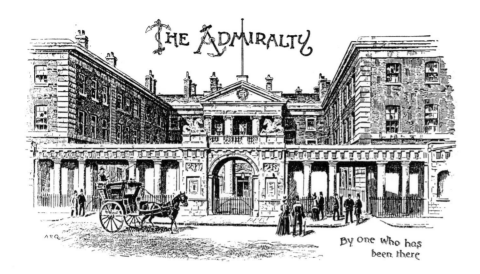

THE ADMIRALTY

By one who has been there

●The Admiralty entrance
from Whitehall in
Victorian times

was exciting.

Events leading up to the decision early in December 1858 to proceed with an iron-hulled armoured frigate had moved swiftly; in view of the forthcoming announcement to Parliament it is probable that the First Lord and the Board would have wished further information from the Surveyor. The following description envisages a day early in January 1859.

First to arrive at the Admiralty was Sir Baldwin Walker, followed by Isaac Watts and Thomas Lloyd each carrying drawings and documents; a cross-section model of a ship being brought in by a doorkeeper. Minutes later they were joined by Sir John Pakington, Thomas Corry, Admirals Martin and Milne and Captain Drummond. Dundas was indisposed with a heavy cold while Lovaine was otherwise engaged. As the size and shape of the vessel began to sink in the lords' commissioners *started to talk at once until called to silence. Turning to the Surveyor the First Lord said,* 'now, Sir Baldwin, please be so good as to tell us about the new frigate. When you have done so we shall be asking questions.' *The Board took their seats and awaited expectantly.*

Flanked by his assistants the Surveyor opened the impromptu presentation, 'Your Lordships, I need hardly tell you that over the past year a great deal of thought has been given to the nature of service for which this ship is intended. When confidential information was first received of the French ironclads my department considered how best to defeat such vessels and their challenge to our fleet. As you are already aware the purpose behind the design you see here is to break away from the notion of a three-decker towards the low hull of a frigate that can not only keep the sea but can outrun and overwhelm any adversary afloat. Speed is therefore of utmost importance and to meet fighting requirements I must emphasise that only a large iron hull can accommodate the necessary weight of powerful engines, coal, guns and armour protection.[5] To achieve the correct balance I have sought the advice of my own assistants, as well as that of Mr Scott Russell, a well known advocate of iron ships.' *From the assembled company came audible grunts that might have meant anything.* 'Needless to say the choice of the 68-pounder was a foregone conclusion. As your Lordships are aware it is not only the heaviest gun in general use capable of firing shot or shell, but having all guns of one calibre mounted on the main deck, you will perceive, has obvious advantages. To furnish the desired weight of broadside a figure of 40 guns has been proposed, of which two would be mounted on the upper deck as pivot guns.' *Pointing to the elevation drawing and the cross-section model he continued,* 'To protect the guns and vital parts of the ship an armoured belt of iron backed by timber and bolted to the ship's side will rest on the first longitudinal, that is to say from the upper deck to five feet below the waterline. The armoured belt will extend for some 213 ft and at each end will be an armoured bulkhead to form a citadel that extends down to the hold. Thus the citadel protects 26 guns of the main deck battery, both magazines, boilers and engine room.

'In consequence my department have determined a total length between perpendiculars of 380 ft, a beam of 58 ft, a draught of 26 ft and a tonnage of more than 6,000 by builders old measurement. I should add that the bow will be especially strengthened for ramming and there will be a partial double bottom under the machinery spaces to afford protection against grounding. Turning now to the engines, we intend to install the latest machinery that would ensure a speed of at least 13½ knots and bunkers capable of providing coal at full steam for seven days. Broadside messing for the ship's company will be on the main deck with cabins for the captain, commander and master in the after part. Wardroom, gunroom and wardroom officers' cabins will be aft on the lower deck.

'As regards masts and rigging there has been more debate on this aspect than almost any other, not only in my department but also in the coffee room of the United Service Club where gratuitous advice is seldom lacking.' *This brought a few smiles and he went on,* 'Indeed, it is of paramount importance that her sailing qualities be of a superior nature and I propose that she be rigged as an 80-gun ship.' *There was a brief pause.* 'And now, your Lordships, these are the salient features of the new frigate, a ship capable of taking her place in line-of-battle and which I am confident will be more than a match for the Gloire. My colleagues and I will answer questions.'

Almost immediately the First Sea Lord rose.
Martin: *'I appreciate we have discussed this previously but is it necessary to construct the hull of iron?'*
Walker: *'In our opinion, sir, yes. Only iron can guarantee the essential longitudinal strength and durability for a hull of such dimensions. If a wooden hull be employed it would be impracticable to construct bulkheads and divisions that make up watertight compartments. Then there are the problems of vibration emanating from the functioning of her engines which are to be in excess of 1,000 horsepower. And you will be aware, sir, of the shortage of seasoned timber.'*
Martin: *'I accept that. Now is it not possible to extend the plating to cover the bow and stern?'*
Walker: *'In a wooden ship, sir, this would be mandatory. In the hull you see before you the casing covers the vital parts and forms the sides of the citadel, the ends of which are also protected by four and a half inches of iron plate, both forward and aft.'*
Milne: *'Then what protection has the bow and stern?'*
The Surveyor turned to Watts.
Watts: *'It is our firm belief, sir, that loading the extremities of the ship with armour plating would make her very uneasy in a seaway.' Pointing to a drawing he continued, 'in the unprotected portions there is a watertight deck 8ft below the waterline. Between the stem and the foremost armoured bulkhead there are four transverse bulkheads as well as a fore-and-aft watertight bulkhead running through the foremost two divisions. Thus, below the waterline there are seven compartments and the whole of them together could hold 400 tons of* water. *The corresponding space aft with four compartments could hold 670 tons. Should both ends of the unprotected parts be riddled with shot near the waterline, only 1,070 tons would be lost from the buoyancy of the ship and she would sink only 26 inches below the waterline, a state in which she would be far from unseaworthy. Finally sir, I should emphasise that with her armoured bulkheads it would be impossible for her to be raked.'*[6]
Milne: *'Thank you, Mr Watts, for a capital explanation.'*
A flush of pleasure marked the first assistant's normally staid expression.
Drummond: *'Is the casing shotproof?'*
Walker: *'In the model you will observe that the iron plating is backed by substantial woodwork 18 inches thick. This will afford the same resistance to the passage of shot, independent of iron plates, as would obtain in a wooden-built vessel. The Excellent trials indicate that such armour will resist 68 pounder shot at 600 yards and probably at closer range.'*
Corry: *'With such a large ship are you confident of obtaining the speed you claim?'*
Lloyd: *'Yes, sir. From the drawings you will note the fine lines and transverse section in the shape of a Vee which we have adopted for a considerable length forward. Then there is her length compared with her beam. With engines of 1200 horsepower it is probable that the ship might attain 14 knots per hour.'*

There were more questions put to Lloyd about dry docking (a dock in Portsmouth was about to be

"BEGGAR MY NEIGHBOUR."

"BEGGAR MY NEIGHBOUR."

An International Duet.

LOUIS.

"COME, MR. BULL, your purse is full,
    Let's have a friendly game :
See, here I play you my *La Gloire*,
    Now what's the card you name ? "

JOHN.

"I play my *Warrior*, a good card,
    And one I'll freely back :
Then follow suit with my *Black Prince*,
    The king of all the pack.

" And so for every card you play,
    You'll find that I'll play two :
My purse *is* heavy, as you say—
    Who'll tire first, I or you ?

" Throw up your cards, I'll throw up mine,
    And cease this fruitless labour :
There's better work for each to do
    Than Beggaring his Neighbour ! "

lengthened), coaling arrangements and lowering the funnels when sailing. Finally the First Lord rose to his feet and asked how much she would cost.

Walker: *'At this stage I cannot be sure of the total amount but we would estimate the hull and engines would cost £250,000.'*

Gasps of astonishment greeted this statement and there was much shaking of heads. The presentation broke up as their lordships scrutinized the drawings more closely, putting further questions to the Surveyor and his assistants. Finally the First Lord made a brief speech of congratulation, thanked the Board for their attendance at short notice and asked Walker if he had anything to add. The Surveyor pointed out that there might well be better designs available for such an important ship and proposed that the royal dockyards and private shipyards be invited to submit their own drawings and suggestions which could be studied and compared with his own office design. The Board agreed.

For as long as the admirals could remember the cost per ton of wooden liners and frigates had increased only marginally over the years, even when iron fittings were used to strengthen the hull. Prior to steam propulsion the construction of a 36 gun frigate cost about £30,000. Fitting engines and boilers brought the figure to about £90,000 but now this enormous iron-hulled frigate would be three times as expensive, enough to absorb a large slice of a year's building programme. Obsessed with the need to maintain numerical superiority over the French the consequence of adding one iron-cased frigate to the overall strength of the fleet caused misgivings. Was it worth the risk?

A letter to potential designers despatched on January 28[7] listed the characteristics to be incorporated while encouraging recipients to present their own designs and suggestions. For the benefit of royal dockyards with no experience of iron shipbuilding, 'a plan with particulars of a wooden ship may be forwarded . . . observing that armour plates must extend from stem to stern.' The necessary payload was to be 1,161 tons, the tender was to state the weights of the hull, armour, engines etc and, most important of all, an estimate was required of cost and time to build. A time limit of one month to complete designs with the prospect of landing a valuable building contract later must have spurred the private shipyards to considerable effort. Thames Ironworks and Shipbuilding Company, for example, called 'a meeting of directors . . . immediately set to work . . . and on 1st March . . . submitted our design, specifications, model of midship section and of the ram bow; the general mode of framing vessels of the mercantile marine being adhered to . . .'[8]

At the end of February came the debate on the Navy Estimates when both sides of the House approved an increase in the shipbuilding vote of £1m, of which £252,000 was to be expended on ironclads. Britain had accepted the challenge and was determined to strengthen the fleet whatever the cost.

Fifteen designs were submitted, six from master shipwrights at the royal yards, the remainder from two private yards at Blackwall, four at Millwall and one each at Birkenhead, Yarrow-on-Tyne and Glasgow. In his covering letter Charles Mare of Millwall Iron and Shipbuilding Works recommended Lowmoor or Bowling scrap iron for armour 'as the power to resist shot must depend on the fibrous quality of the iron', adding that they had the necessary machinery and tools following the building of the *Great Eastern*.[9]

Assessment of plans took seven weeks and in his letter to the Board on April 28 the Surveyor indicated that the shipyard constructors differed widely in their views as to dimensions required: the design of Thames Ironworks was too big, that of Samuda too narrow in the beam. The main point was to include the design, prepared in 1858, 'for the purpose of making an estimate of probable cost' and to ensure 'that the proposed conditions were practical'. Moreover, if accepted 'tenders might immediately be called for.' One suspects that behind this statement was the forceful influence of Isaac Watts who, having scrutinized the efforts of other constructors, had every reason to believe that his was the best, especially as two private yards had endeavoured to bribe his draughtsmen for design information.[10] On April 29 the Board approved the Surveyor's design and his proposal to call for tenders to build the ship.

Commenting on the Admiralty design prepared previously the *Mechanics Magazine* noted that it was 'as nearly as possible a mean of all the other designs' and complimented the Chief Constructor. Other critics were less well informed and months later Walker had to make it clear – it was obviously a touchy point – that the office design was not influenced by submissions. 'The design now being built was shown to the Board with all details before the drawings called for were received' he wrote, thus refuting the implied charge that the plans of the private builders and master shipwrights '. . . supplied the element of the design.'[11]

Then occurred a minor drama. Although instructions had been given to despatch letters to potential builders – all of whom had submitted designs – the Board succumbed to misgivings. They were so 'startled and astonished' at the great size and cost of the vessel that they reconsidered the whole question. Walker was informed that due to the great cost the armour plating would have to be reduced from four and a half to two and a half inches. Walker sent for Captain Hewlett of the *Excellent* who brought evidence to prove that two and a half inches of plating would render the ship highly vulnerable to shot and probably defenceless to shell fire from French guns.[12] It was not until the end of the week that the Board was dissuaded from changing their minds. But in view of the expense involved Pakington decided to restrict the programme to no more than two ironclads until the first could be properly tested, a policy later abandoned. All this meant that builders had less than a week to tender.

On May 11 the tender of Thames Ironworks and Shipbuilding Company was accepted at a cost of £31 10s per ton Builders Old Measurement, a total of £190,225. The contract stipulated that the ship be launched within 11 months from date of acceptance – April 11, 1860 – and be ready for completion, except masting, three months later. Payments were to be made in five instalments, the first when the ship was 'in frame' and the final when 'delivered up complete.' There was a penalty clause of £50,000.[13]

It is important at this stage to disprove the story sometimes put forward that Watts and Scott Russell were co-designers of the new ironclad or indeed that the latter was principally responsible. Neither theory carries supportive evidence nor do their personalities suggest that close partnership was feasible. Watts had advanced by unspectacular solid worth to become – like most successful designers – an autocrat who disliked criticism of his work but, being no innovator, sought advice when needed. Describing his methods to a parliamentary commission in 1861 he stated, 'when a drawing is . . . being prepared I have frequent communications with the Controller (Surveyor). I consult him many times during the course of construction and also . . . with my fellow constructor (Large) and . . . with the Chief Engineer (Lloyd). In building *Warrior* . . . it was a novel character, and very frequent communications took place between the Controller of the Navy, the Chief Engineer and myself with regards to carrying it into practical execution.'[14] After designing the largest wooden warships (*Marlborough* and *Orlando*) he tackled Walker's 1857 armoured corvette project and subsequent designs in planned evolutionary stages. In contrast Scott Russell was ambitious, gregarious and a self publicist whose forceful personality made him a difficult partner. As a naval architect he possessed flair yet his response to the 1858 design competition was criticized for inadequate displacement and hull strength.

Arising out of the allocation of contract was a protest from Scott Russell that his own company's bid had been turned down on account of price and time. His pioneering role with ironclads entitled him to special consideration, he claimed. The Surveyor did not agree. Advising their lordships that although Scott Russell's contributions had been valuable and imaginative, none of the main features adopted had originated with him, with the exception of omitting the protecting plates from bow and stern and introducing transverse shot-proof bulkheads for the protection of the midship part of the vessel. All other features such as fine lines for speed, general arrangements for the skin of the iron hull 'were in such general use that any constructor would, it is believed, consider himself free to adopt them.'[15] Scott Russell's work was not protected by patent, the Admiralty felt no obligation and his building yard may not have been up to the capacity of the successful contractor. A month or so later he received an order for four wooden gunboats, an ironic twist for the advocate of ironclads.

There can be no argument, therefore, as to who designed the *Warrior*. Watts was the navy's senior professional architect and thus totally responsible. Had he not incorporated the best features of contemporary design – including proposals from Scott Russell – he would have failed in his duty. So it must have irked him six months or so after her launch to hear his *Warrior* described as a 'Scott Russell ship'. To his credit Scott Russell had the good sense to acknowledge the Chief Constructor's achievement publicly, although later he wrote a paper pouring scorn on the abilities of both Walker and Watts.[16]

Among the designs and tenders referred to the Admiralty the private yards of the Thames were well represented, concentrated as they were on both banks of the river between London Bridge and Woolwich. Throughout most of the 19th century there were some 50 enterprises constructing ships for the Royal and Merchant Navies, many of them intimately connected by family ties. Their competence was demonstrated when the 27,000-ton *Great Eastern* was launched from Millwall in 1858, the largest vessel of all time, and this when cattle grazed near Chelsea and duck were shot over the marshes of Pimlico.

As ships grew larger and the unceasing flow of passenger and freight traffic demanded better facilities, the Thames Conservancy was set up to keep the river dredged and the several navigable reaches clear. By the 1850s a vast complex of docks had sprung up to make London the world's greatest seaport and commercial centre. When steam came on the scene and iron replaced timber it was the Thames yards that were foremost in adopting new techniques, edging ahead of the royal dockyards of Deptford and Woolwich.

Bow Creek, at the mouth of the river Lea where it enters the Thames at Blackwall, had been the site of shipbuilding since the Danish invasion. The name is derived from the bridge built up river in the shape of a bow by Queen Maud in the 11th century – tradition being that floods held up her hunting parties.[17] In about 1840 the Orchard Shipyard on the west bank was acquired by Ditchburn and Mare. When the former left in 1846 Charles Mare brought in James Ash as naval architect; the company expanded to the east bank and reached its peak in 1853. Two years later they ran into cash flow problems through underestimating contract costs of gunboats for the navy. Peter Rolt, Mare's father-in-law, came to the rescue, took over as chairman and renamed the company, Thames Ironworks and Shipbuilding. Born at Deptford and married to a Brocklebank, Peter Rolt had all the qualifications of a Thames shipbuilder. In a larger world he was Conservative MP for Greenwich, Deputy Lieutenant for Middlesex and, as the *Telegraph* wrote, 'a man of pleasure and a business man shrewdly and intimately commingled'.[18] Contracts followed and the business flourished to become the biggest yard on the river.

In addition to the useful experience in large iron ship construction gained during Mare's tenure, Thames Ironworks was well established with five acres of land on the Blackwall (Middlesex) site, including the main office near the eastern end of Orchard Street. On the West Ham (Essex) bank was the major portion of the works covering 30 acres, comprising upper and lower building slipways, iron foundry, a range of smithies, angle iron ship, copper foundry, iron rolling mills shop, forge, tool shop, press shed and pattern shop. A well-planned and virtually self-contained yard employing some 4,000 men, it was fed by local railways as well as those bringing coal and other materials from the rapidly developing industries of the Midlands.[19]

Today little is identifiable of what was once a great era but in 1859 there were men and resources in the Thames that had made 'river-built and Blackwall-fashion' internationally famous.

CHAPTER THREE
Building

ALTHOUGH THE SUN was still low over the Plaistow Marshes a clear blue sky promised fine weather for May 18, 1859 as thousands of men converged on the gates of Thames Ironworks. Clad in short, close-fitting jackets and patched trousers tied with string below the knee, their hobnailed boots clattered over the cobblestones of the approach roads. Cloth caps pulled down to the eyes, many carrying dinners in coloured handkerchiefs or small metal boxes, the human stream flowed into the yard to start work. Even with earnings ranging from £1 to £2 for a six-day, 54-hour week there were those able to afford an indulgence. Wiping their mouths with the back of their hands they could be seen emerging from a nearby public house after taking a penny nip of gin. Life was hard but the company paid a decent wage and there were rumours of a new ship to be laid down.

An hour or so later the Orchard Yard buildings witnessed an unusual commotion as senior employees in their best suits hurried to the assembly hall for what seemed an important occasion. It was to be the first meeting of the company with the Surveyor's department after acceptance of its tender. Arriving from London by the Blackwall Railway the visitors were escorted by a posse of directors into the yard where no time was lost in getting down to business.

At the head of the horseshoe-shaped table sat the genial chairman Peter Rolt, to his right Captain John Ford, master mariner in the merchant navy, naval architect and managing director of Thames Ironworks. Nearby sat the company's senior naval architect James

Ash, then George Mackrow, his deputy and further on Charles Jordan, an architect specially chosen for the project on the strength of having served an apprenticeship with John Scott Russell;[1] finally, John Hardy the portly superintendent of works. To Rolt's left was placed the Surveyor's team headed by Isaac Watts with Joseph Large the second assistant, William Walker the master shipwright, then the Admiralty draughtsmen James Graf and William Hinde. Beside them was the bewhiskered William Burr Bascomb, senior Admiralty inspector and overseer of the project.[2] A first class draughtsman at Woolwich dockyard, this was his first experience of a more responsible post. Various employees of the company filled the background, and in front of the assembly were several drawings. With a plum contract in his pocket Peter Rolt was in an expansive mood. Punctually at 9 o'clock he turned to his managing director to open proceedings.

Ford stood up. 'On behalf of Thames Ironworks and Shipbuilding Company I extend a warm welcome to Mr Watts and officers of the Surveyor's department of the Admiralty. May I compliment the First Assistant on the lines you see before you, uncommonly fine and clean. I am confident she will prove a fast and powerful ship. As one not unaccustomed to such labour may I also pay tribute to those responsible for the excellent drawings that have been so speedily undertaken, together with the material data and sketches in support of the plans.' *Brandishing a file of papers he continued,* 'I have in my hands the

●Thames Ironworks,
interior shot

●View of Thames Iron
Works and Shipbuilding
Company, Bow Creek

Admiralty specifications for the vessel, a document that leaves my colleagues and me in no doubt as to how this ship is to be constructed.[3] I can assure the Surveyor that our company will have little difficulty in manufacturing a very large proportion of the ironwork demanded by the hull structure in our works, noting that the deck beams are to be supplied by the Butterley Company with whom we are well acquainted. Now, sir, as to the armour plating which is to be a prominent feature of the new frigate, you will be aware of the experience gained by this company under its former name in the construction of floating batteries some years ago. Today we have no less than seven of Nasmyth's steam hammers and a plentiful supply of scrap iron so we feel confident we can meet your requirements by means of the hammered process.' *Further details were covered before he concluded,* 'the working system of Thames Ironworks is its contract between owner and shipbuilder, and contract between shipbuilder and workman. The motto of the company is *no work, no pay* and that is the motto of successful private enterprise throughout the world. In these works there is no superannuation and there are no incompetents. You have imposed on us an exacting programme but I remain confident that we shall build you the finest man o' war in the world.'[3] *Ford sat down aware that he had made his mark.*

Not given to verbosity, Watts replied briefly, 'my

lords commissioners of the Admiralty are most anxious that the ship should be built as speedily as possible and every assistance will be afforded by my department to facilitate its timely completion. Mr Bascomb will be constantly on hand not only to advise but also to ensure that proper standards are maintained.' *General discussion followed and at 2 o'clock the meeting adjourned for luncheon, after which the Admiralty men were taken on a tour of the works and slipways. When their guests had departed for London Rolt and Ford walked slowly back to their offices discussing the events of the day, and realising that they had a formidable job on their hands.*

On receiving the order work had started

immediately to prepare the 400 ft slipway for a ship that was some three times the weight of any previous vessel built at the yard. While the building blocks – on which the hull would rest – were being laid the first of the keel plates, keel beams and keelsons with their respective angle bars were fabricated. The sections were then mounted on the building blocks, aligned, marked off for the interconnecting riveting, drilled and temporarily bolted. By May 25 sufficient progress had been made to announce that the keel had been laid.

Construction started with the midships section of the hull and thence proceeded forward, aft and upwards. Thus a strong cage of ironwork was assembled upon which the stem and stern could be accurately aligned. As the centre section of the framework and longitudinals began to rise the keel and lower sections of the frames and longitudinals were extended outwards and upwards. Although progress appeared adequate it is probable that reports from Bascomb reached the Surveyor's office indicating that the ship was dropping behind schedule.

Meanwhile Pakington had fallen out with Disraeli, then Chancellor of the Exchequer, over the politics of the commander-in-chief proposed for Portsmouth. That the First Lord was in the right made Disraeli even more furious and he complained to the Prime Minister that naval members of the Board were inefficient and – referring to three-deckers – attacked the policy of 'building colossal ships which have neither speed nor power and which are immensely expensive from their enormous crews.'[4] Lord Derby supported Sir John whose stock was riding high, and he weathered the storm.

In June 1859 Lord Palmerston returned to power with a Liberal government; the Duke of Somerset was appointed First Lord and Rear Admiral Lord Clarence Edward Paget CB MP became First Secretary, an interesting combination of politician and flag officer. As was expected Sir Richard Dundas moved up to the top post. The remaining lords commissioners all changed. Despite his reputation as a big-navy man the Prime Minister was also a disciple of Sir Howard Douglas. Ironclad construction policy made little progress.

From the opposition benches Pakington now asked pointedly about the current armour plate trials and when the ordering of the second ironclad could be expected. Admiral Paget replied that there had been a delay in the manufacture of plate for tests and that the second ship would have to wait 'until the result of the experiment in the first case had been brought to conclusion'.[5] War fever continued to sweep the country and public opinion, spurred by the mood of Parliament and the press, demanded more ships. And so the Board of Admiralty required Paget – against his better judgement – to state that additional line-of-battle ships would be ordered.

Because Watts expressed concern at Blackwall's launching arrangements, particularly the breadth and depth of Bow Creek, the Surveyor sent his second assistant and a representative from Deptford to attend the launching early in June of *Seine*, a screw steam mail packet. Joseph Large and Assistant Master Shipwright Thornton reported that the slipway was suitable, that launching had been successful but recommended the creek be deepened by dredging.[6]

The importance of finding a suitable name for Britain's response to *Gloire* had not been overlooked. In tune with the country's nationalistic fervour the Admiralty had in mind a third-rate ship of the line recently broken up after many years of distinguished service in the Royal Navy, the *Warrior*. As a symbol of valour and strength in battle their lordships could hardly have chosen better, the name appealing as much to patriotic traditionalists in the service as it did to the general public. At Blackwall the news spread quickly, filling the workforce with renewed vigour. An announcement was made on October 5.

Although seldom recorded, members of the Surveyor's department must have visited the Thames Ironworks frequently during construction. Bascomb's reports of slow progress would almost certainly have prompted Walker to send his first assistant to investigate before taking action. And so either in late September or early October Watts arrived at Orchard Yard to present his compliments to the chairman before touring the yard with Bascomb. Subsequently the Surveyor despatched on October 7 the first of many letters to Thames Ironworks in which he drew the company's attention to the ship's backward state.[7]

Yet Watts must have felt a sense of pride tinged with excitement as he viewed his creation rising on the shipway. Here was the backbone of a ship with its iron keel and frame whose length exceeded that of the *Mersey* by 80 ft and the largest line-of-battle ship by 120 ft. As Admiral Ballard, the distinguished historian of the era, remarked, 'thus the *Warrior* introduced four great departures simultaneously from all traditions and customs in Admiralty shipbuilding; . . . armour protection, a length equivalent to six and a half beams, an iron structure in frame and shell and a new safeguard in flotation.' He continued, 'such a wholesale abandonment of long established practice, in a service ruled by uncompromising veneration and adherence to precedent was quite unheard of.'[8] Full credit to Watts and his project team who worked with conspicuous success to draw up the lines and prepare the specifications for *Warrior*; but it must never be forgotten that the man really responsible for her inception was Walker.

At the end of 1859 the Surveyor's title was changed to Controller, scant recognition of Walker's significant contribution to the navy. In his responsibility for ships and weapons he alone provided the essential continuity through seven successive Admiralty administrations, built up the steam battle fleet, applied lessons from the Russian war, increased frigate size and through the critical months of 1858 and 1859 maintained advocacy of evolution rather than revolution in determining the shape and size of ironclads. In Pakington he found an ideal First Lord with whom to work but the strains of office were beginning to tell and he found it hard to fit in with the new administration.

In Whitehall the whig Board of Admiralty were making heavy weather of the ironclad pro-gramme. When an attempt by Clarence Paget to substitute three ironclads for three wooden battleships was thwarted by the naval lords he submitted his resignation. Palmerston dissuaded him from leaving office but sided with the Board's policy, despite the protection value of iron plating being proven by further trials at Shoeburyness. However, a decision on the already announced second ironclad could not be postponed much longer and in September the Board, acutely conscious of the great size and proportionate cost involved, asked Walker to submit a smaller, cheaper design. By reducing the armament to 22 guns and the speed to 12 knots the Surveyor pointed out that such an ironclad would no longer be able to choose its range as well as suffering the 'serious consequences from the effect of concentrated broadsides from screw battleships from which it was unable to withdraw'. The Board paused and gave way. Tenders were called for and the contract for *Warrior*'s twin awarded to Robert Napier and Sons of Glasgow, delivery to be in one year at £37 5s per ton. The name *Invincible* was chosen but, finding the second French ironclad building at Toulon had forestalled the Admiralty choice, it was changed to *Black Prince*. She was laid down in October, 1859.

Yet the idea of smaller, slower ironclads persisted, partly due to lack of docks for *Warrior*-size vessels, partly because speed was considered of lesser importance for ships withdrawing from battle since four and a half inch plates were proven against the latest guns. Expense being the governing factor Walker, as Controller, reluctantly accepted the Board's wishes and called for a programme of six to make up numbers desperately needed to counter the four French ironclads. But in December only two were authorised, *Defence* to be built by Palmer on the Tyne and *Resistance* at Westwood Baillie of Millwall.[9] In the opinion of Nathaniel Barnaby, later to become Director of Naval Construction, their fighting ability compared with *Warrior* was in the ratio of one to four.

Following Walker's letter Rolt received another (October 8) from the Admiralty 'requesting the company to cause greater exertion to be used in proceeding with the work' to which the contractors replied that 'in consequence of her novel construction they have not been enabled to progress so rapidly as they could have wished, but hence forward they will cause the work to progress to their lordships' satisfaction'. In late October John Pembroke, Thames Ironworks company secretary, wrote to the Surveyor complaining that they had 'repeatedly applied to the Butterley Company for the delivery of welded beams without seeing any satisfactory reply and that inevitable delay will arise . . .' A prompt riposte from Butterley sparked off a mass of correspondence between the two companies and the Surveyor, culminating with a flat statement

● Warrior's hull in an
advanced state of
construction (below)

from Captain Ford blaming *Warrior*'s delay on the quality and delivery rate of the Butterley beams. At the end of November the Admiralty overseer reported that 'the *Warrior* will not be completed before September 1860 but the Superintendent of Works thinks that with the aid of additional machinery now erecting they can finish her in August next'.[7] By December the ship had been under construction for seven months.

January 1, 1860 cannot have been a happy new year's day for Captain Ford. The weather was awful, the ship behind programme, argument with the Butterley Company rumbled on and only half the first instalment on the ship had been paid by the Accountant General. To accelerate the work rate he would have to take on more labour or work time and a half. Money was getting tight. *Warrior* was proving a tougher proposition than even he had foreseen and the situation was not helped by the Admiralty inspectors' exacting scrutiny. However, on February 10 a more sympathetic letter arrived from the Admiralty authorising payment of the second half of the first instalment. In thanking them for their indulgence

Ford expressed a hope that the ship would be plated up, except for small portions round the stem and stern posts, by the end of March.[7]

A month later the Controller complained that the ship was behind because of insufficient labour force, to which Ford replied that they were doing their best, and with the hull three-quarters plated could they please be paid the second instalment. The Admiralty authorised payment, asking Thames Ironworks for the launch date. Ford confirmed that *Warrior* could not be launched before the end of September.[7]

Despite Ford's misgivings a casual visitor could hardly fail to be impressed by the scene on *Warrior*'s slipway. Surrounded by a forest of wooden scaffolding and with more than 900 men at work all was movement and noise amidst the smoky haze rising in the still cold air. Ensuring each man could fulfil his workload without obstructing others demanded a high degree of job coordination. Amidships the framework had reached maindeck level and a start made with fixing the outer skin plating, starting with the garboard strake nearest the keel. In the forge scrap pilers and furnacemen tended the fires supplying molten metal to the steam hammerers who manipulated the giant Nasmyth machines with uncanny skill. The massive stern post – 43 ft high, eight inches thick and weighing 43 tons – which had to be built up from small bars welded together under the forge hammer, was taking longer than expected. At least Ford was familiar with this problem and could handle it. Uncertainties surrounding the gun armament and armour plating caused him more anxiety.

Although marginally longer than *Victory's* 32 pdrs, the 68 pdr destined for *Warrior* was a much bigger gun. Weighing nearly five tons with a bore diameter just over eight inches it was mounted on a wooden rear chock carriage that dispensed with the rear trucks (wheels). The performance of loading, firing and absorbing the recoil with hemp roping secured to the ship's side had hardly changed in more than a century. To operate the broadside armament at best advantage the position and size of gun ports were critical: they were spaced 15 feet apart to allow the crews sufficient working room and wide enough to allow maximum training, a legacy of sailing ship engagements. Admiralty plans for *Warrior* included 19 each side, 13 being inside the citadel. The lower sill of the gunport determined the maximum depression of the muzzle when firing on the downward roll. Similarly the upper sill decided the maximum elevation. Finally when the ports were closed and the guns secured for sea it was customary to lash the muzzles above the ports. Consistent with stability the higher the gunports above the waterline the better could the guns compete with heavy weather rolling. A height of nine and a half feet was resolved as the optimum for the lower sills with ports about four

● Constructing an Armstrong gun at Woolwich Arsenal. High quality wrought iron, coiled and welded into heavy duty tubes, was the first example of a British built up gun. The breech was sealed by a copper bush mating with a ring on the vent piece

feet square. It followed that gun carriage dimensions could then be adjusted for trunnion height to allow the gun the required 12 degrees of elevation, seven degrees of depression and the housing of the gun when not in use.

In mid-1860 the Royal Carriage Department at Woolwich with the *Excellent* started to build a new gun carriage that incorporated a directing bar in its base which pivotted on a pin in the sill of the port. By this means carriage and gun could be trained over a 60 degree arc within a narrower embrasure, reducing the crew's vulnerability to enemy fire.[10] Rumours of this significant first step in making a gun mounting part of the ship's structure had reached Blackwall. More disconcerting to Thames Ironworks, however, were reports of the Armstrong gun that would 'revolutionise naval

warfare'. As long ago as June 1859 the *Times* had asserted that *Warrior* would carry a complete outfit of these guns. What was this new weapon?

One result of the Crimean war was the rifling of small arms from which evolved rifled ordnance wherein, once again, France secured a narrow lead. No British attempt had been successful until William Armstrong, a Tyneside hydraulic engineer, started to develop a three-pounder breech-loading rifled gun in 1855. Instead of casting the barrel in iron he built up the gun by shrinking wrought-iron coils onto an inner tube giving increased strength to the bore. Within the bore Armstrong devised the polygroove system – as it is known today – consisting of a large number of shallow grooves. These engaged into the lead coating of an elongated projectile, imparting an axial spin when fired. At the breech end the bore was made slightly larger to enable the projectile and gunpowder charge in that order to be loaded into the chamber. The breech was closed by a vent piece dropped into place from above and pressed against the chamber by the breech screw: in theory a promising weapon. (Illustrated page 89).

Initial trials demonstrated its superior accuracy and range over smooth bores; with a time or percussion fuse its shell burst with devastating effect. Faced with the threat of rifled guns in French ironclads Armstrong's invention was hailed as the wonder gun, Captain Hewlett of the *Excellent* recommending that the navy should adopt the Armstrong gun not only for boat service but for the larger calibres. In January 1859 an experimental Armstrong gun firing solid shot with a six-pound charge was tried against the four-inch armour of the floating battery *Trusty*. Far from penetrating the plate even at 50 yards the projectiles 'had no serious effect'.[11] Amazingly the Ordnance Select Committee discounted the failure, ordered the shot to be increased to 40 pounds and the charge reduced to five pounds. In September the 40 pdr Armstrong gun was accepted into service without further trial. A month later the inventor was knighted and appointed Engineer to the War Department for rifled ordnance. As well as starting his own works at Elswick he had control of the Royal Gun Factory at Woolwich. With orders coming in from the army and navy his position was unassailable.

A cardinal weakness in the Armstrong design was the need for a relatively small gunpowder propellant charge lest the gun burst. For example, a 12 lb charge produced a muzzle velocity of 1100 feet per second whereas the 68 pdrs' charge of 16 lbs packed a much bigger punch at close range. In October 1859 a further stage in the Armstrong saga was reached when a 'special gun of large calibre' – it was an 80 pdr – fired solid armour piercing projectiles against *Trusty's* four inch armour. Again it was unsuccessful; in contrast the 68 pdrs did rather better. It is astounding therefore to record that the War Office and Admiralty accepted an increase to 100 lbs calibre whereupon the gun went into production. Reporting in 1863 the Ordnance Select Committee excused themselves by stating, 'the political necessities of the day appear to have been so urgent as not to allow time for maturing the design previous to its manufacture.'[12] In 1860 on advice from the *Excellent* the navy accepted a proportion of Armstrong guns in the fleet, provided they could retain muzzle-loaders for armour penetration and employ the new weapon at longer ranges against wooden ship targets and for bombardment. In fact the fleet were committed to mounting a variety of Armstrong calibres, ranging from 100 pounders down to six pounders, at a staggering cost of £2½ million. It may be argued that Sir William was a good salesman but the Admiralty and the *Excellent* can be criticized for accepting a weapon without undergoing sea trials where conditions and crews were very different from those at Shoeburyness.

The outcome of all this was that at Ford's suggestion Bascomb wrote to the Controller early in May, '*Warrior* is sufficiently advanced to admit ports being framed and I most respectfully request that you will furnish me with particulars relative to the armament this ship is to carry that I may give proper directions to the contractors.'[13] Admiralty's reply was evasive – the decision to reduce the width of the gun ports to four feet by two feet was not given until November and there was no news about Armstrong guns. So Ford turned his mind to armour plating.

As *Warrior* was the first really large iron hull to be armoured Watts and his team consulted the Special Committee on Iron Plates and Guns, instigators of all armour trials. Thus they were able to define the dimensions of armour plating, its wooden backing and how it would be fastened in the ship. Three years later, when a paper on the *Manufacture of Armour Plates* was read to the Institute of Naval Architects, Captain John Ford inferred that in 1859 there was little knowledge of the construction of plates on which to write a specification.[14] Based on the technique used in the floating batteries the Admiralty decided in mid-1860 that all plates had to be tongued and grooved to give mutual support, a degree of

● This drawing gives
some idea of the vast size
of Warrior under
construction

perfection that may have created great strength
but prohibited repair of a single plate except by
removal of adjacent sections.

Weighing about four tons each plate measured
15 ft by three ft being made up from quantities of
good London scrap and puddled iron, heated in a
furnace, incorporated piece by piece and forged
by a steam hammer. After the plates had been
reheated and bent to their correct curvature the
bolt holes were marked off, edges and butts
tongued and grooved by planing and the bolt
holes drilled and counter-sunk. During manufacture strict quality control was applied by
Bascomb and his inspectors, samples being sent
for test firings by the *Excellent*. Of some 200 plates
weighing 905 tons only five were rejected, an
outstanding record.[7] Tonguing and grooving
proved an elaborate and, with hindsight, an
unnecessary process that was not repeated in later
ships. Admiralty agreed to extra expense but even
with assistance from Messrs Jackson Watkins
further back-up had to be sought from Woolwich,
Sheerness and Chatham yards to make up the
plates needed.

Contractors for HM Ships had the choice of the
best timber, almost all of which was imported.
Near the slipway stood piles of wood, cut to size in
the pits by circular saws then neatly stacked and
ready for use. By far the biggest task for
shipwrights and joiners was installing the deck
planking – four inch Dantzic deals for the upper

and lower decks and four and a half inch Dantzic oak for the main deck. No less important were the thick grains of East India teak, the hardest and toughest wood obtainable, to be fastened behind the armour plate on the ship's side and on the transverse bulkheads at each end of the citadel. On the sides ten inch baulks would be placed longitudinally and eight inch baulks vertically: when the plates were in position the whole protective layer of iron and wood would be bolted together. On each side of the upper deck the design called for oak-timbered, iron-framed bulwarks with ports cut for guns and gangways. On top of the bulwarks were iron brackets to hold the netting in which to stow 650 hammocks. Having to board or repel boarders were recognised operations in naval engagements until the turn of the century and closely-stowed hammocks afforded protection against small arms fire. This brought the total height of the bulwarks to seven feet. Finally there were quantities of oak, pine, teak and mahogany waiting for the fitting-out stage when they would be used on the upper deck and to furnish accommodation areas, storerooms, magazines and flats below decks.

The shape of Warrior's bow involved a clash of interests. A ram at the bottom of the stem, as fitted in Greek galleys 500 BC, had long been discarded but the idea revived with the coming of steam when it seemed that armour might defeat the gun. As a second line of attack the introduction of the ram in iron-hulled warships was influenced by a group headed by Vice Admiral Sir George Rose Sartorious who was obsessed with this weapon. Included in Warrior's design requirements was 'strength in running down or ramming' to be provided by a solid forged stem post well supported by bulkheads and frames. But there was an equally strong lobby that wanted a typical frigate clipper bow leaving Watts with the unenviable task of satisfying both parties. The resultant design nullified the ramming effect of the stem with a heavy overhanging bow knee, answered no useful purpose and added 40 tons of weight in a position it could least afford. However, Captain Ford, in a letter to the *Times*, pointed out that *Warrior*'s 'ram is so constructed that, at the cost of a few hundred pounds, she may be converted into an irresistible ram . . . it is only necessary to take away the overhanging cut-water, figurehead etc when a stem of gigantic proportions and enormous strength forged and fitted with this object will make its appearance to which the bow plates can be easily connected.'[15]

The value of the ram as a weapon was overstated. The near impossibility of an ungainly ironclad being able to strike an enemy added to the probable damage to the ramming ship were disregarded by its protagonists. Ramming proved more disastrous in peace than war. Curiously the fatal collision between *Camperdown* and *Victoria* in 1893 seems to have upheld the efficiency of a ram

• Midshipman Prince Alfred, later Duke of Edinburgh, second son of Queen Victoria (below)

• The stern, (right) ready for rudder and propeller to be fitted

• Main deck port side looking forward (far right)

because it continued as an integral part of a battleship's construction.

Warrior and *Black Prince* were just about the last British capital ships to be built with figureheads. Having salvaged the previous *Warrior's* figurehead an Admiralty draughtsman designed an even more formidable figure. The job of carving was entrusted to James Hellyer of Portsmouth whose family had been figurehead carvers to the Royal Navy for many years. Including the stars on the catheads and the drops (carving) on the base, the work cost about £60. Twelve feet high and weighing a ton, the pine-wood figurehead was painted white, picked out in gold and fitted while the ship was still on the stocks. The figurehead over the clipper bow symmetrically balanced by a wooden stern gallery must have been the source of great pride to the ship's companies as sailors are strangely particular about the aesthetic appearance of their ships in which they have to spend long periods. As well as being an ornamental appendage the main purpose of the stern gallery was to provide the captain with water closets port and starboard.

Warrior was exciting curiosity nationwide. Ballard records, 'never before or since have such crowds of visitors come to stare and speculate on the rising framework of a floating war machine; of whom some of the old school declared that the Admiralty had gone mad, though the general majority expressed the opinion that the Board was

showing unusual signs of understanding its business. One parliamentary wit asserted that when he went down to Blackwall he found that the deafening clangour of shipwrights and rivetters was drowned in the uproar of controversy among the onlookers round the scaffoldings.' Rich and poor, young and old, professional men and passers-by were all anxious to see how Britain's answer to the French ironclads was shaping.

The longitudinal system of construction was apparently a great talking point, as was the nature of government supervision of a private contract. Writing many years later in the *Thames Ironworks Gazette* George Mackrow remembered, 'the keen interest felt by all nations in her building brought more notables to these works than ever visited a private dockyard before . . . to wit the Grand Duke Constantine, Prince Frederick Wilhelm, the Duke of Cambridge, Lords of the Admiralty as well as Ambassadors and Naval Attachés from the courts of many countries.' Peter Rolt made sure they were well looked after and in due course the company received orders from Spain, Portugal, Russia, Greece, Turkey and Germany.

Mackrow continues, 'amongst others who came . . . was Prince Alfred, the Sailor Prince, then a youth of 15 . . . and one question he mildly asked was, "what is the difference between the specific gravity of an iron vessel and a wooden one?" I don't think that his tutor caught the remark or he

might have blushed for his pupil – and to seek to instruct a live Prince was more than I dared venture upon.' The second son of Queen Victoria, Prince Alfred was later to become Duke of Edinburgh.[16]

The sight of the great ship ascending out of Bow Creek mud also drew the press, none more enthusiastic than the man from the magazine *Temple Bar*. Writing under the pseudonym 'R' he relates his visit one summer's day in 1860. Arriving at Orchard Yard his first impression was one of tremendous activity. Waiting to be ferried across the creek 'the *Warrior* was before us, lying in a sidecut on the opposite bank. Her huge hull of iron, painted red and covered in scaffoldings, rose up as a five or six storied house

. . . workmen are seen clinging on to her in almost every spot; some are carpenters . . . but most are iron workers and the din of hammers is so loud that we are obliged to shout as if in a gale of wind. We creep along the scaffolding . . . scared by the shout, "Below there" when down comes a rivet or a bit of plate. But the men go on quite unconcerned, many of them seated all day on a wet plank close to the mud, pulling at the handle of a drill with the same kind of action that a rower uses: in this way the iron is pierced for the bolts . . .' Standing under the stern of the ship 'R' finds himself, 'looking upwards at this stupendous piece of forge work, the stern post, which goes right away to the upper deck . . . it took 13 months of ceaseless forging to get this gigantic limb of the *Warrior* into shape.'

The zenith of descriptive prose is reached when the writer enters the main deck through 'a gun port without stooping . . . Heavy blows resound on every side and it requires rather a sharp look out to avoid getting hit as you pass by some stalwart hammerer . . . hoarse cries and angry shouts from the men are answered by shrill cries from the boys who, armed with long pincers, rush madly by with red-hot bolts and take flying leaps . . . like so many young imps. Now the ship appears to be on fire in 50 places and this gives the whole scene a strange character of wild and imposing fierceness and power. . . nothing short of the terrible experiences of war could call up such tremendous effort.' Strong stuff.

At a time when *Warrior's* overdue completion was under fire it was particularly galling to learn that *Gloire* was coming along noticeably well at Toulon. Launched in November 1859 the first French ironclad frigate – frégate blindée – was ready for sea trials by August 1860. Under full steam official French sources announced a speed of 13.1 knots and an average speed of 12 knots for ten hours. Even in a gale her performance was apparently promising, while the ship's coal supply of 675 tons was advertised as sufficient for 27 days at eight knots or seven days at full speed.

Such claims contrasted with a letter from Captain Ford to the Controller on September 28, 'I write to acquaint you with some important particulars which I learned yesterday from an intelligent Russian naval officer, who it appears has been especially engaged by France for some time in learning all he could about this ship. He assures me that the *utmost* speed which has been attained by *Gloire* is 11¾ knots; but with the high pressure of steam required to get this speed the vibration at the stern was so great that the authorities deemed it necessary to reduce her speed to about 11 knots. I have great confidence in the correctness of this information and if true I feel assured that the *Warrior* and others of her class will have an advantage of at least two knots . . . be comparatively free from vibration.'[17]

Whether this Russian was a double agent is unknown but there may have been substance in his remarks which appear to match an earlier report, the result of an intelligence coup by none other than the Secretary of the Admiralty. Apparently the Board had been unconvinced of *Gloire's* true potential and were anxious to confirm the height of her main deck battery above the waterline and determine the significance of the tower on upper deck. It so happened that Lord and Lady Paget were about to holiday in Italy when the Secretary was asked to 'look in at Toulon' and undertake what he termed 'a delicate operation' in the face of strict French security. The Foreign Office offered no help so the Pagets arrived at Toulon, hired a shore boat, bribed the boatman and got alongside the ship amongst a crowd of bumboats. Having 'carefully measured my umbrella' Paget climbed the ladder sizing up the gun ports en route – and reaching the upper deck was accosted by the officer of the watch. Before departure his naval training enabled him to assess the rifle tower and before leaving Toulon he visited one of *Gloire's* sister ships where he narrowly avoided being arrested. His report to the Board was carefully studied.[18]

Gloire was squat and utilitarian with a straight stem and curved cut-away stern. Her broadside armament of rifled muzzle loaders were spaced 11ft apart and her gun deck barely six feet from the waterline. Originally intended as a three-masted barquentine, *Gloire* was given a full ship rig with reduced canvas. This did little to improve her sailing role that was in any case subordinate to steam power and served to confirm France's original intentions to confine ironclads to coastal attack and defence. In doing so her high command ignored one of the basic principles of maritime strategy, namely command of the sea, so aptly demonstrated by the allied fleets in the Russian war. Britain followed this principle and pinned her faith on heavily armed screw line-of-battle ships. Without appreciating that his naval policy would prove a ruinous strain on the country's resources Napoleon was determined not only to challenge the Royal Navy with a new class of warship but also to gain international prestige for France. In this he succeeded and

● Gloire at Toulon, 1860.
She was disarmed eleven
years later and broken up
in 1879

despite exaggerated claims for her performance *Gloire* stole the limelight to become the world's first truly sea going ironclad. Britain's response to the challenge had yet to be launched.

Admiralty were now under great pressure to get *Warrior* in the water: delay could become a public issue. In September renewed correspondence between the Board and Thames Ironworks had a familiar ring. The company was reminded of the April launch date, accused of employing insufficient men and organizing the workforce inefficiently. Ford replied that 'the iron hull is nearly finished . . . three fourths of the wood backing is fitted to the sides . . . we have commenced planking of the spar (upper) deck.' He followed this up by seeking an advance of £15,000 'for additional work done on the *Warrior*' arguing that outlay on the ship exceeded payments by £68,000. Admiralty at first refused to consider an advance but relented with a payment of £10,000, conditional on employing maximum numbers on the job. Pressed to give a launch date Ford stated that although they would be ready by December 15 there were better tides on December 29, the preferred date.[7]

This news was leaked in mid-October to the *Army and Navy Gazette* which reported, 'the completion of *Warrior* is being pushed forward with as much activity as possible . . . With the exception of a small portion of the stern the whole of the ship is completed.' Some 80% of the decks

had been laid, engine and boiler foundations were ready and a start would be made in fastening the first line of armour plates 'within a few days'. A later report stated that in Portsmouth dockyard Messrs George Smith of Pimlico were preparing for *Warrior*'s arrival by joining numbers 7 and 10 docks together to make a total length of 615 ft 'to be completed by March 1 next'.[19]

Blackwood's magazine of December 1860 carried an illuminating article on *Ironclad Ships of War*, following a visit by the author and some friends to Blackwall. Anxious to 'avoid the terrible noise of all those thousand hammers playing away upon as many rivet heads' the party timed their visit to arrive at dinner time. The indefatigable Bascomb escorted them round starting underneath the hull. ' "What a glorious bow" exclaims a visitor as he pats the sharp forefoot in love and goodwill.' Climbing the scaffolding they meet a foreman. ' "Pray" we remark, "why was the first attempt to build an ironclad sea-going vessel carried out on so ponderous a scale?" "Because" replied he "this vessel was simply constructed to beat the *Gloire*." '

As soon as the last stern plates were fixed the hull was ready first for caulking and then painting. Below, the engineering contractors had bored out the stern frame to take the propeller shaft and positioned the tail end shaft. A careful check was then made of sea connections and underwater fittings. An ordinary, as opposed to a balanced, rudder was fitted which rotated about

its axis near the leading edge. Hoisted through the counter to hang on the stern post the rudder head projected right aft on the main deck. The steering yokes were then fitted ready for connection to the steering apparatus. All seemed to be going well, especially when an 'admirer of ironclads' wrote to the *Army and Navy Gazette*, 'I will take a heavy bet that *Warrior* will prove a faster vessel than *Gloire* by two knots and that she will be in all respects a better sea boat.'

Taking advantage of the last spring tide of 1860 a launch was planned for 2.30pm on December 29. Ford gave instructions to complete the launch cradles, temporary wooden frameworks built around the bottom of the hull to support the ship down the bilgeways on launching. On taking the water the cradles float upwards before being hauled ashore.

As launch date approached tension grew, not only in the shipyard but also among the Board of Admiralty, following a visit to Blackwall at the end of October, when they expressed amazement at the size and cost of the ship they had ordered. Their lordships had cold feet and in the *Illustrated London News* of December 8 it was reported that 'after £250,000 had been spent on her . . . the Admiralty discovered that she is not the description of the vessel that will combine stability with invulnerability.' Work stopped for two days while their lordships deliberated. Then they decided, according to the article, 'that she is not

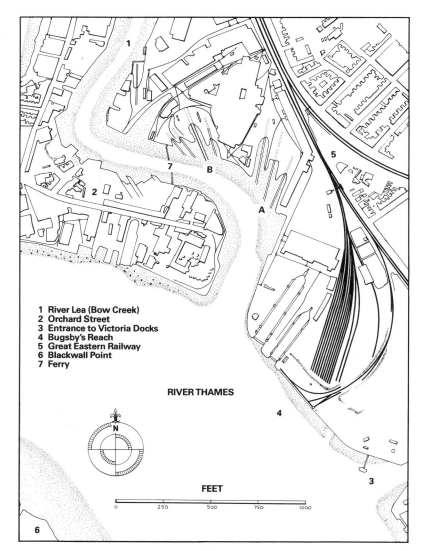

● Thames Ironworks and
Shipbuilding, Blackwall.
It is probable that
Warrior was built and
launched from slipway A

the vessel we would wish for but after laying out so much money upon her, we might as well see what we can make of her.'

With the debacle of the *Great Eastern*'s launch in mind – she stuck on the slipways at Millwall for six months – Ford was taking no chances. Starting in November the *Army and Navy Gazette* reported that 'some 10,000 tons of mud and rubbish' were dredged from Bow Creek by Shelbourne and Co 'to give sufficient depth for a vessel with an estimate launch weight of 4500 tons.' Extra shifts of workmen worked day and night below decks to finish jobs under severe weather conditions that set in a week before Christmas. There were heavy falls of snow in the south and London recorded 45 degrees of frost. Roads were blocked, canals frozen and 'great masses of ice or frozen snow floated on the bosom of the Thames in long lines, causing a loud roaring noise as they ground together.'[20] It was the coldest winter for 50 years.

After some deliberation it was decided to ask Sir John Pakington to launch *Warrior*, the invitation from the First Secretary to the Board to christen the ship arriving on December 19.[21] As First Lord, Pakington had won for himself the goodwill and good opinion of the navy; indeed there were many who would welcome the choice and opportunity to see Sir John's small dandified figure, with his long nose and slight air of pomposity, perform the honours normally undertaken by royalty.[22]

1 River Lea (Bow Creek)
2 Orchard Street
3 Entrance to Victoria Docks
4 Bugsby's Reach
5 Great Eastern Railway
6 Blackwall Point
7 Ferry

RIVER THAMES

N

FEET

0   250   500   750   1000

On Christmas Eve a start was made driving in wedges to raise the ship off the building blocks; two days later shores and blocks were removed one by one. The whole weight of the ship now rested on the two bilge ways via the cradles. At the lower end of the cradles dog shores held the ship in position ready to be released by the triggers at the moment of launch.

For weeks John Ford had driven himself, hardly leaving the yard to go to his Hampstead home. So exhausted did he look that Rolt ordered him to rest for a few days over Christmas. In a letter to Baldwin Walker on December 27 Captain Ford wrote, 'I have been so unwell the last three days as to prevent me from leaving home and to wait upon you. I am glad to say that everything is perfectly ready for the launch on Saturday and I have no apprehension whatever that the event will go off as well as you could wish. [23] His only concern was that no order had been given for another ship to occupy *Warrior*'s berth. In his view Thames Ironworks had marked advantages over Chatham dockyard. Ford need not have worried. As well as securing the tender for the ironclad *Minotaur* a number of profitable foreign warship contracts came to Orchard Yard.

Anticipating that a hard frost would reduce the effect of tallow and soft soap on the slipways, hundreds of bogey fires were placed the whole length of the ship on the night of December 28. Preparations were now complete and in case the ship did not fetch up in time in the narrow creek a large fender of floating pine logs was lashed to the Blackwall bank. Extra tugs were ordered, hawsers rove, anchors placed and drag chains ranged to check her speed as she entered the water stern first. The yard lay under a thick mantle of snow.

Saturday, December 29 1860 dawned fair but there was a 'cold and cutting wind' as spectators began to assemble. Some chanced a ferry across the river from Blackwall Point adjacent to the residential suburb of Greenwich. Aboard the ship three temporary masts flew large sizes of the admiralty flag, the royal standard and the union flag, with gaily coloured bunting along the bulwarks to set off the ship's lines. By nine o'clock everything of importance on the slipway had been removed to the high water mark and the hydraulic presses checked in position should they be needed. Under the bows a launching stage, decorated with flags and banners, had been erected. On the upper deck labourers, who were to remain for the launch, swept the snow from the bulwarks.

By noon the crowds had swollen to 'several thousands including a considerable number of the fair sex'. Booths selling hot pies and chestnuts did a roaring trade. A local militia band struck up patriotic airs as people took up vantage points or clustered round coke braziers. All was bustle and excitement. The tall hats of the constabulary were much in evidence as they strove to keep the populace behind barriers; a burly sergeant could be seen remonstrating with two gangs of urchins

engaged in a snowball fight. Thames Ironworks had stopped all other work for the day.

Some came by train to Blackwall but most official guests made the journey from London by coach through the City, along Whitechapel and down the Barking Road before crossing the iron drawbridge over Bow Creek. 'What's up, Bill?' said the driver of a hansom cab to a bus conductor. 'Oh, a launch of some sort or another' was the answer as the procession slowly wended its way past piles of dirty snow. Greeting each person individually Chairman Peter Rolt was the perfect host. Soon the large room filled with people drinking coffee, cordial and – for the men – hot rum and butter. Peers of the realm and members from both sides of the House mingled with ambassadors, attachés and senior officers of the army and navy. Wearing his full-dress uniform was the First Sea Lord, Vice Admiral Sir Richard Dundas, attended by Captain Charles Frederick. In discussion with Sir Baldwin Walker, the Duke of Somerset and Samuel Whitbread was the Persian ambassador dressed in silk finery. Sir William Armstrong conversed with John Scott Russell and Isaac Watts. Many had brought their wives for the occasion. The Pakingtons were among the last to arrive.

Shortly after 2pm Captain Ford walked up from the slipway to report to Peter Rolt that the ship was ready for launching. 'Everything all right?' asked the chairman. 'All is well, sir' replied Ford, 'but she may need a push to get moving. The slipway is frozen hard.' 'Very good, Ford. I'll bring them along in ten minutes.' The guests donned hats, coats, scarves,

muffs and gloves in the best of humour. Led by their host and Sir John Pakington the party was soon on the wooden platform within a few feet of the ship's stem, admiring the imposing figurehead poised above.

No religious service preceded the ceremony as there is today so when Ford made his final report, Rolt nodded to Sir John at precisely 2.30pm. The crowd fell silent, all eyes on the group assembled at the bow. Sir John stepped forward to exclaim loudly, 'I name this ship Warrior. May God bless her and all who sail in her.' The triggers were removed. The dog shores fell away. But nothing happened. In the words of the Engineer, 'the ship showed no disposition to move'. Sir John turned to Rolt who assured him the matter was in hand by which time Ford had already signalled for remedial action. Immediately the hydraulic rams began to press against the bilgeways, sledgehammers could be heard striking blocks and cradles, heavy tackles were manned on the slipway and on the upper decks hundreds of men moved from side to side in concerted movement. Whether a gun was fired to shatter the frosty air is not known because there was so much noise. After 20 minutes or so she began to move, so slowly that her motion was scarcely perceptible. Someone cried, 'she's off' and from that moment she never wholly stopped. By now two additional tugs had been ordered to take the strain aft, paddles churning at full speed. As the movement accelerated Peter Rolt turned to Sir John who dashed a bottle of wine on her bow and shouted, 'God speed the Warrior'. The spectators cheered, the band played Rule Britannia and John Ford quietly wept with

emotion and relief. Hats were thrown in the air, arrester chains clanked, tugs blew their whistles and the stern took the water 'as gracefully as any yacht'.[24] The tugs saw to it that she swung gently towards the river as the bows left the ways. The rest was anticlimax.

Despite the restraining gear the ship swung across the angle of the creek striking the logs on which scores of curious folk had ranged themselves. To the consternation of the onlookers the logs were sent rolling up the bank but no one received worse than a ducking which 'considering the weather was not over enjoyable'. Captain Andrew Sheewan, commanding a teaclipper moored up river, had walked across the marshes to the river wall on the Blackwall side and was cheering vociferously when 'a great wave raised by the ship swept towards us . . . we suffered no more than a wild stampede'.[25] Thirty minutes late she only just made the tide; once the tugs were able to bring her round she was moored head and stern off East India docks for the night.

Her Majesty's Ship Warrior was now afloat.

CHAPTER FOUR
Fitting out

NEXT MORNING *Warrior*'s empty hull, painted overall with red lead and floating high in the water, attracted curious eyes from both river banks. The bells of All Saints Church at the end of East India Road announced Sunday's first communion service as a launch put men on board to secure paddle tugs to the warship's bow and stern. Bridle shackles were knocked off and *Warrior* moved slowly past the mouth of Bow Creek, across Bugsby Reach and towards the narrow entrance of Victoria Docks. With tide slack and nearing high water the 500 yard passage was accomplished without incident as Henry Jones, the senior Thames pilot, directed the tugs by arm signals and shrill blasts on a whistle. On the upper deck a score or so riggers from the contractor's party took the hawsers passed up from attendant boats as *Warrior* neared the dockside.

On the pier a small group of people watched as Warrior *was manoeuvred into position. 'Well, Mr Birt, d'you think she will get through?' asked Captain John Gordon, Chairman of the Docks Board, stamping his feet to keep warm. 'Without doubt, sir' replied the Docks Superintendent, 'there's abundant room on either side and no cross wind.' 'Positively the biggest iron warship I've ever seen,' remarked Charles Capper, the Docks Manager, 'let us pray that the country will build more of them.' Turning to address the fourth person standing apart from the others, hands deep in the pockets of his tarpaulin jacket, the Chairman asked in unmistakably patronising tones, 'well, Mr Buchan, what do you think*

of your new ship?' The Chief Engineer paused for a moment, then with a broad Scottish accent, 'A'well. She'll do.' But his eyes shone with excitement as the vessel slowly made its approach.'[1]

Victoria (London) Docks had been built by private enterprise in 1855 to provide better loading facilities for more and bigger merchant ships. Laid out over 94 acres the docks possessed both excellent rail connections and the latest equipment to ensure a quick turn round. Hydraulic power was on hand to pump the docks, work the lock gates, turn the capstans and operate some 150 cranes as well as a coal conveyor, just the facilities for fitting out a large warship.

Under tow of two tugs ahead and another astern *Warrior* slipped through the entrance, past the swing bridge where a crowd of onlookers had gathered and into the basin. With hawsers taken to powerful capstans the ship was nudged into her berth at the northern end, alongside cranes and sheds where much of her equipment was assembled. Drawing 17ft aft *Warrior* was now ready to take aboard her engines and boilers, followed by masts and sails. A vast backlog of work remained to be done on the hull, in particular fitting the balance of armour plating.

At Woolwich the Royal Carriage Department had started production of the 68pdr carriage embodying *Excellent*'s modifications but the Admiralty found it difficult to decide *Warrior*'s armament until availability and trial results of

● Launch of HMS Warrior
at 3pm on Saturday,
December 29, 1860

● Impressionist view of
lifting pontoons at work
on a ship in Victoria
Docks, 1861

Armstrong guns had been established. Notwith-standing the *Engineer's* announcement (Feb 22, 1861) that 'it has been finally decided that armaments of *Black Prince* and *Warrior* shall consist of Armstrong guns only, 100pdrs on the main deck and 70pdrs on the upper deck,' the Admiralty were less sure of the new weapon. In addition to four 40pdr Armstrongs on the upper deck they agreed to replace the 68pdrs at bow and stern with 100pdrs and provide Armstrong 25- and 12pdrs as boat guns. Suggestions to increase the number and calibre of Armstrong guns on the upper deck for long range action were rejected by the Controller because of probable effects on stability; for the time being the main broadside would be 68pdrs.[2] Because shell rooms and shot racks had to be altered for Armstrong ammunition such vacillations were no help to Thames Ironworks.

Warrior was now in the final stage of construction for which a sizeable work force would be needed. After the celebrations of Christmas, followed by launching and finally the New Year, some would report for work on January 1, 1861 feeling the worse for wear but thankful for the opportunity to keep their jobs – for another seven months as it happened. Much to the chagrin of John Ford the weather remained bitterly cold during the first two weeks of January and little progress could be made outside the hull.

When in May 1859 the specifications had been sent to potential builders the Engineer-in-Chief of the Navy had given equal attention to selecting the best steam machinery. With his assistant, Robert Hughes and Inspector Afloat John Dinnen, Thomas Lloyd had laid down rigid conditions for the contractors. These included optimum reliability, simple maintenance, strict weight limitation and insistence that machinery and boilers be situated below the waterline for maximum protection. The earliest screw-driven warships, including *Rattler*, were fitted with engines similar to those of paddle vessels, an overhead crank-shaft driving a propeller shaft through step-up gearing giving four revolutions of shaft to one of engine. By the 1850s this arrangement had been replaced by direct-acting horizontal engines producing faster rotation; similarly the need for greater horsepower demanded increased engine size and weight.

At that time contracts for marine engineers were placed with less than ten companies, all bar Boulton and Watt (Birmingham) and Robert Napier (Glasgow) situated on the Thames. The manufacture and machining of massive castings and scrupulous compliance with specifications meant there were few firms able to tender for large engines. Fortunately, Lloyd, when Inspector of Steam Machinery at Woolwich Dockyard in the 1840s, had acquired an intimate knowledge of Thameside engineers and the final choice lay between the trunk cylinder engines of John Penn and the return connecting rod engines of

● John Penn, marine engineer and engine builder

Maudslay Sons and Field. In his letter to the Board on May 10, 1859 the Surveyor submitted that only these two companies should tender.[3] Both had good records, both had their yards near Greenwich but Lloyd favoured the trunk engine as marginally better so the contract went to Penn. Formalities were completed at the end of May, the Admiralty stipulating that the steam plant had to be ready in 11 months – the same period given to Thames Ironworks – with a further three months for installation after launch. Five months later Penn gained an identical contract for *Black Prince*.

Originally a builder of windmills, water-wheels and tread mills for gaols John Penn turned to

marine engines in 1825. When son John succeeded father at the helm ten years later the company prospered and by 1860 there were Penn installations in 24 warships, a royal yacht and four merchant ships. In the horizontal trunk engine the connecting rod was directly attached to the piston thus dispensing with the need for a piston rod and so reducing overall length. To achieve this the skirt of the piston was extended in the form of a hollow trunk, hence its name.

The main engine works with 1,200 employees covered seven acres on Blackheath Hill while a smaller boiler works was located at Deptford. The two were linked by traction engines at night and horse-drawn wagons by day. As well as recruiting top staff Penn insisted on getting the best horses, 'It is easier to arrive at a satisfactory conclusion on . . . the qualities of horse than a man'. He exacted and achieved the highest standards of workmanship; it was, he averred, the only way to build faultless engines.[4]

The engine assembly shop was extensive: Nasmyth steam hammers in the smithery, 50-ton cranes in the foundry, the range of shops and stores fed by horse tramways with turntables at intersections. Dominating the organisation was the forceful, typically Victorian John Penn. He alone supplied the business direction, the technical leadership and the company image. Nothing would have pleased him more than the news that his tender for the *Warrior* had been

accepted. It was worth £74,409.

Early in June 1859 drawings and documents arrived at Blackheath, to be followed by visits from Chief Engineer Charles Atherton and his assistant, David Partridge, both of the Woolwich Steam Factory, who acted as Admiralty inspectors. To confer with them were two Penn directors Mathews and Halliday. The firm then started to build the most powerful machinery plant ever to be installed in a warship. Officially described as a two-cylinder, double-acting, jet-condensing trunk engine the machinery was built piece by piece in the main shed, each unit being tested to function separately until the whole engine had been assembled. Despite strenuous efforts the process took longer than expected and John Penn not unnaturally was grateful for the breathing space afforded by delays in the ship's construction. There were visits from Thomas Lloyd himself and very soon the enormous cylinders – exceeding nine feet in diameter – drew marine engineers from all over the country. Although the Admiralty were criticized at the time for not accepting a lower tender they were quick to point out the exceptional performance of Penn's products in the Crimean war.[5] Subsequent experience justified their choice. *Warrior*'s engines gave continuously reliable service for more than 30 years: before then higher steam pressures and steam compounding made trunk engines obsolete.

If engines proved a good investment the same

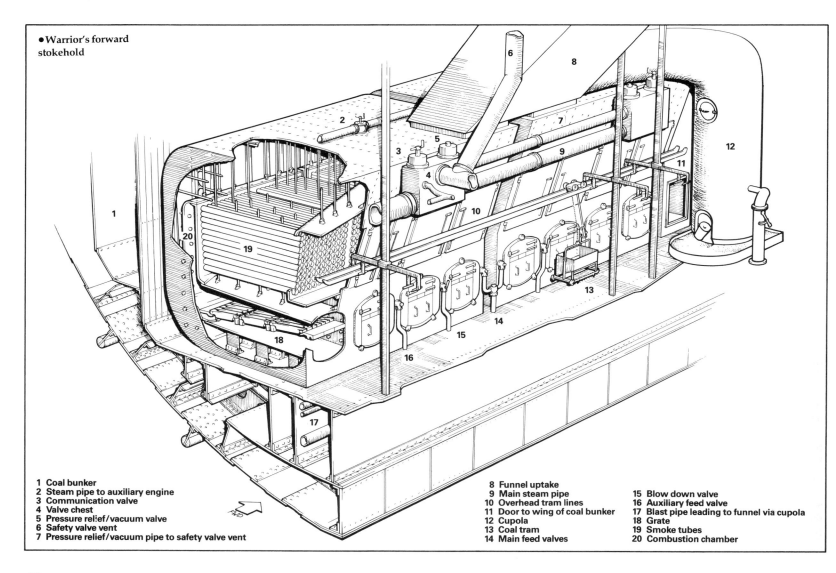

●Warrior's forward stokehold

1 Coal bunker
2 Steam pipe to auxiliary engine
3 Communication valve
4 Valve chest
5 Pressure relief/vacuum valve
6 Safety valve vent
7 Pressure relief/vacuum pipe to safety valve vent

8 Funnel uptake
9 Main steam pipe
10 Overhead tram lines
11 Door to wing of coal bunker
12 Cupola
13 Coal tram
14 Main feed valves

15 Blow down valve
16 Auxiliary feed valve
17 Blast pipe leading to funnel via cupola
18 Grate
19 Smoke tubes
20 Combustion chamber

could not be expected of the ten boilers installed in the fore and after stokeholds. Admiralty specifications called for the standard units of that day which were little more than rectangular iron boxes fed with sea water and equipped with an array of fire tubes. Within each boiler were four furnaces feeding two smoke boxes from which the return smoke tubes passed through the water to a further smoke box at the front of the boiler. The resultant steam was collected in two steam mains leading to the engine room. When under way every few hours a portion of boiler water, which had become concentrated brine, had to be blown from the boiler into the sea and replaced by water from the condenser. Smoke from the tubes was led into either the forward or after boiler flues thence into either of the telescopic funnels, each 7½ ft in diameter and projecting 25 ft above the upper deck when fully extended.

Although built to the latest design the boilers did not represent the best commercial practice, according to the *Engineer* (October 25, 1861) which estimated a 20% saving in fuel consumption if superheaters had been fitted resulting in higher boiler pressures. Another critic condemned 'the crude design as wasteful and extravagant in fuel'.[6] As it was the deadweight safety valves on the boilers were loaded to 22 lbs to the square inch – rather less than a modern car's tyre pressure. The main handicap, however, was corrosion, so rapid that the life of many boilers seldom exceeded five years although *Warrior*'s lasted ten.

An interesting innovation was the use of coal bunkers to help protect vital spaces below the waterline from the effect of projectiles. There were six main bunkers or 'boxes' on the outboard side of each stokehold and the auxiliary machinery space, smaller boxes located against the forward bulkhead of the engine room. Coal, brought in bags through gun ports, was emptied down 20 vertical chutes from the main deck through the lower deck into the bunkers where the total capacity was 853 tons, small in comparison with later ironclads but a record for 1861. An ingenious system of trams (skips) running on lines brought fuel to the boilers. Stokers filled the tram with coal, pushed it via a turntable to the boiler space where it was transferred to overhead rails, pushed to the required furnace and tipped onto the firing aisle so more stokers could fuel the hungry fires. Even so they had to struggle to maintain steam pressure at higher speeds.

As soon as main machinery had been installed the next stage was to couple the 17 inch diameter propeller shaft to the engines and test out the gear for turning engine and shaft by hand. More than 100 ft long the propeller shaft was supported by four plummer blocks, its forward end in the thrust block, its after end projecting through the stern gland ready for the propeller. Early stern bearings of brass led to abnormal wear; history records the case of a line-of-battle ship that had to be run ashore to prevent the ship sinking due to leakage through the stern tube. Thanks to John Penn the lignum vitae stern bearing was introduced in 1856 which type was fitted in the *Warrior*, an invention that lasted into the 20th century.

As with other aspects of marine engineering the screw propeller was experimental. Single screws first fitted to ships had two long, thin blades closely resembling the propellers of early aircraft. From among the many designs on the market Lloyd chose the latest model from Robert Griffiths who made a special study of propeller pitch as well as vibration and cavitation problems. Made of bronze it had a diameter of 24½ft, weighed 26 tons and when going ahead revolved left-handed to reduce wear on the engine bearing surfaces. To reduce drag on the ship when under sail the propeller could be lifted out of the water through an elliptical well in the stern. When ready the propeller was brought to the dockside, fitted into a 'banjo' lifting frame, hoisted by crane and lowered into the screw well so that the tongue in the foremost journal of the propeller fitted into the corresponding slot in the aftermost flange of the propeller shaft known as a 'cheesehead'.

As soon as *Warrior* was committed to pure sailing two evolutions had to be carried out simultaneously. To hoist the propeller a pair of sheerlegs was rigged to straddle the well and two double hemp pendants were shackled, one end to the lifting frame, the other leading to the head of the sheerlegs and down to the upper deck on to a fourfold purchase, its hauling part taken forward on either side. The ship was then hove to, propeller shaft turned by hand until the propeller was exactly vertical to enable the 'cheese coupling' to disengage. Lower deck was cleared so that 300 men could man the falls either side and at 'hoist away' up came the 'ruddy old twiddler'. As the lifting frame rose clear of the water its pawls engaged in vertical racks within the well until the propeller was right up, when a hand was sent down the ladder inside the well to secure the plate locking the propeller in position. To prevent the funnels from interfering with wind pressure on the lower sails the complementary evolution was to lower the funnels to just above upper deck level. A system of chain hoists driven through manually operated worm and worm-wheel gearing was invented by a Mr Taplin. 'Up funnel – down screw' was carried out in reverse order. *Warrior*, incidentally, carried a spare blade which could be fitted in event of propeller damage; propeller pitch also could be adjusted.

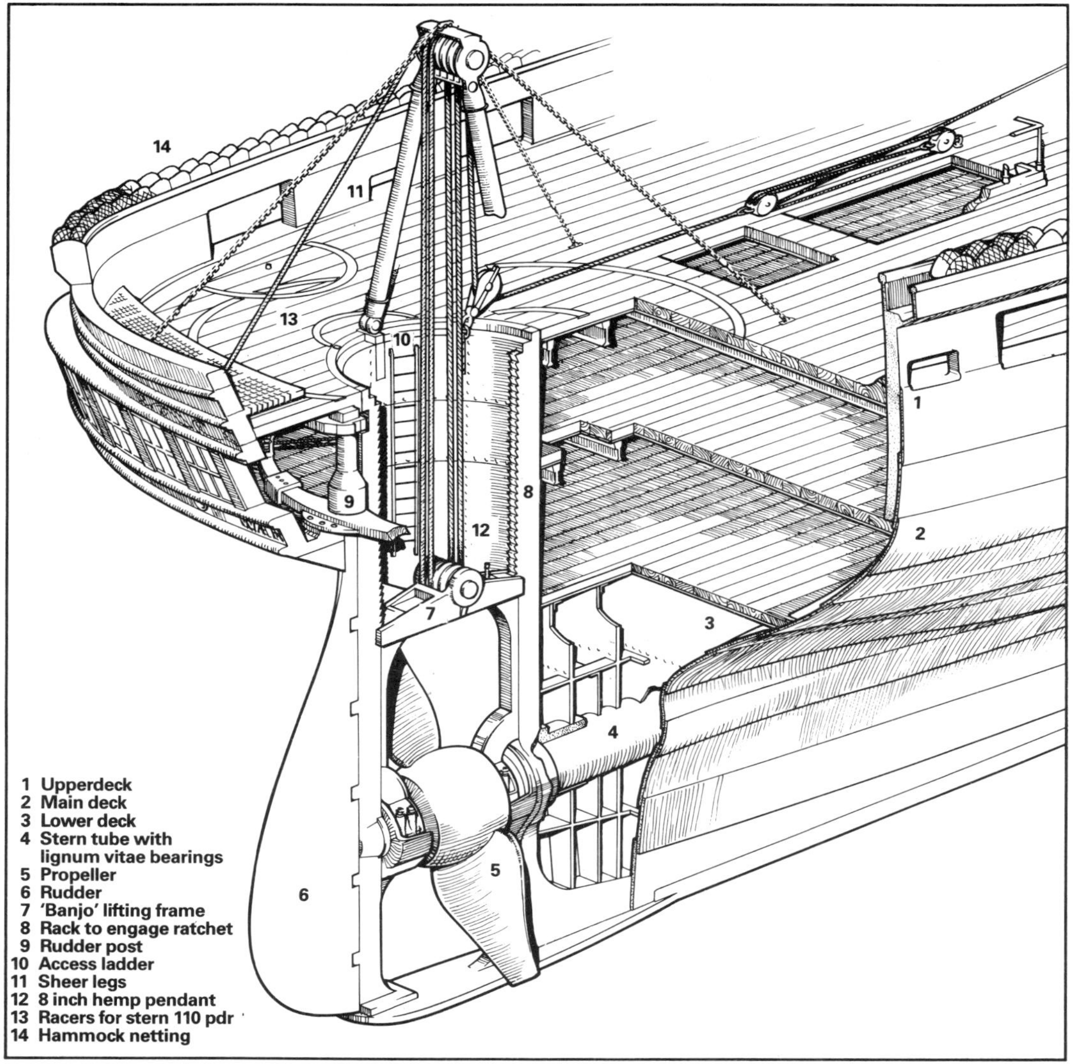

Only one main steam auxiliary was fitted, a single cylinder direct action donkey engine in the space between engine room and after stokehold, to pump the bilges or provide sea-water for the firemain. By belts it also drove the fans drawing fresh air through cowled ventilators on the upper deck which was trunked to the coal bunkers,

1 **Upperdeck**
2 **Main deck**
3 **Lower deck**
4 **Stern tube with lignum vitae bearings**
5 **Propeller**
6 **Rudder**
7 **'Banjo' lifting frame**
8 **Rack to engage ratchet**
9 **Rudder post**
10 **Access ladder**
11 **Sheer legs**
12 **8 inch hemp pendant**
13 **Racers for stern 110 pdr**
14 **Hammock netting**

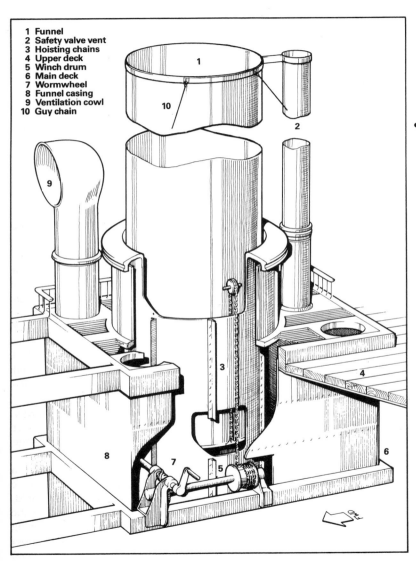

1 Funnel
2 Safety valve vent
3 Hoisting chains
4 Upper deck
5 Winch drum
6 Main deck
7 Wormwheel
8 Funnel casing
9 Ventilation cowl
10 Guy chain

● Funnel hoisting gear

main and lower deck accommodation and main gun battery. The engine could also hoist buckets of furnace ash from the stokeholds to the upper deck where it was dumped overboard. Evidently this donkey engine could operate only in one mode at a time. One other auxiliary was a small steam-driven winch or crab engine, installed on the lower deck flat immediately above the auxiliary machinery space, and used solely to work cables from the lockers below. Auxiliary machinery required main steam and it is interesting to note that *Black Prince* was fitted with a small auxiliary boiler and that her Brown's capstan was steam-operated.

With unlimited manpower available all other machinery was operated manually, the most powerful being the two capstans on the main and upper decks keyed to a common shaft and, further forward, Brown's patent capstan. On the main and lower decks were eleven Downton fire and bilge pumps while both magazines had hand-operated ventilation fans. It was man's muscle that hoisted boats, weighed anchors, made sail, braced the yards, raised the propeller and the other numberless activities to move and control a ship.

In modern naval practice it is usual for the marine engineer officer and other technical specialists to be appointed to a warship under construction before launching. The first officer to join was Chief Engineer William Buchan, appoin-

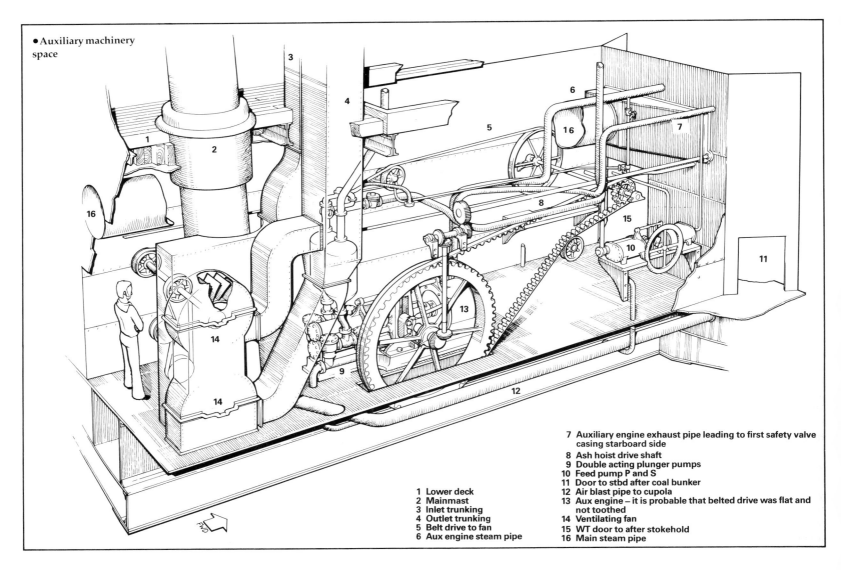

• Auxiliary machinery space

1 Lower deck
2 Mainmast
3 Inlet trunking
4 Outlet trunking
5 Belt drive to fan
6 Aux engine steam pipe
7 Auxiliary engine exhaust pipe leading to first safety valve casing starboard side
8 Ash hoist drive shaft
9 Double acting plunger pumps
10 Feed pump P and S
11 Door to stbd after coal bunker
12 Air blast pipe to cupola
13 Aux engine – it is probable that belted drive was flat and not toothed
14 Ventilating fan
15 WT door to after stokehold
16 Main steam pipe

FWD

ted on January 4, 1861, according to the *Naval Chronicle* 'to superintend the fitting of the colossal engines now constructing by Penn and Son'. As with later arrivals Buchan was accommodated in the old sailing frigate *Fisgard* lying off Woolwich dockyard to cross daily to Victoria Docks by the Woolwich ferry, a service that exists today.

Although the fleet was prepared to accept steam propulsion it was reluctant to admit a status for engineer officers. Stokers and trimmers fell easily into the hierarchy of a ship's company – as long as they did not appear on the upper deck in daylight wearing dirty clothes – but officers were a different matter. The navy did not know how to treat them.

When engines were first fitted in HM Ships engineers came with their installation in the form of a package deal. Possessing little education, somewhat rough and ready in approach and under no obligation to authority it was hardly surprising that a poor view was taken of them. When the Admiralty realised their indispensability they were properly signed on and graded first, second or third class engineer. However, an Order in Council (July 19, 1837) granting them warrant rank did not go far enough and there were recruitment shortages in the following years. Unfortunately there were senior officers who did not – or did not want to – understand steam machinery, regarding steamships as tugs for line-of-battle ships and insisting that engineers

had no place in the wardroom. A letter to the *Times* (Nov 24, 1846) summarised public opinion by stating that, '. . . engineers were a useful class of men but no gentlemen'. However, the problem would not go away and in February 1847 another Order in Council granted engineers commissioned rank, their names to appear in the *Navy List* with chief engineers equal in status to masters. Second and third class assistant engineers ranked with but after second class warrant officers.

The adoption of the propeller and better pay enhanced the prospects of engineers who realised that the Royal Navy offered them a future. This was William Buchan's background who was born in 1814 at Leith, served for seven years in the merchant service, then joined the Royal Navy in 1848 as a first class assistant engineer-in-charge with exceptional qualifications. His second ship had been the screw-driven sloop *Malacca* whose inclined trunk engines of 200 hp introduced him to John Penn's machinery. Prior to joining *Warrior* Buchan was Chief Engineer in *Orlando,* latest of the large wooden frigates. On her steam trials on August 22, 1860 the *Times* reported, 'the *Orlando* shook and twisted considerably especially in the extremities and her top gallant masts and bowsprit were vibrating constantly'. There was difficulty in steering, men could not get out along the yards and it was evident her 1000 hp engines were too much for her hull. Conditions in the engineroom must have been exacting, all of which

gave Buchan first class experience. Late in October *Orlando* was due to refit and Lloyd seized the opportunity to transfer Buchan to the *Warrior*. At the same time he increased the complement to include an assistant chief engineer. So enthusiastic was Buchan to join that he travelled south to see the ship into Victoria Docks and early in the New Year, on Lloyd's advice, called personally on John Penn. He made a favourable impression and in no time Penn's engineers and artificers readily accepted the dour Scot who spoke little but knew as much about engines as they did. In the middle of January he was present when, according to the *Engineer* (Jan 18, 1861), 'one of the cylinders (cylinder blocks) weighing upwards of 28 tons was conveyed from the establishment of John Penn and Son to their Wharf at Deptford. Two of Bray's traction engines were in attendance . . . the removal accomplished with signal success' despite the severe weather. Buchan took an active part in installation and testing but, notwithstanding the *Naval Chronicle's* statement, the engines and boilers were still under charge of the contractors – the moment of handover had not yet arrived.

When it came to the all-important matter of steering the ship naval convention dictated that engineering should play no part in arrangements. Early ironclads were notoriously difficult to steer under certain conditions of sailing and when steaming slowly for reasons not hard to discover.

Apart from the wind effect on hull and upper-works *Warrior*'s great length and displacement – added to a small unbalanced rudder that was both slow and restricted in operation – combined to make the ship awkward to handle. Unlike later ironclads with twin screws her single two-bladed propeller militated against tight manoeuvring.

A major handicap lay in the complicated steering gear. Right aft on the main deck the rudder stock rose through the counter; two feet further forward was the large screw well which precluded the use of a conventional tiller to apply leverage on the rudder head. Instead, two yokes were initially fitted. Shaped in a curve and restricted in length by the confines of the hull, one yoke was positioned at the top of the stock near the deckhead, the other about two feet off the deck. At the end of each were metal sheaves through which tiller ropes were rove as part of a purchase, thence the ropes were led through bulkheads and decks to the steering positions. There were two main positions, one on the upper deck before the mizzen mast, the other on the main deck inside the citadel. Directly below on the lower deck a third position was installed to be connected in the event of action damage. The upper yoke ropes went to the upper deck position, the lower to the main deck; under conditions of difficult steering it was customary to rig relieving tackles to the ends of the yokes to increase turning power on the rudder.

Each steering position consisted of two pairs of wooden steering wheels, more than six feet in diameter with 12 spokes, each pair of wheels enclosing a wooden barrel or windlass on which the tiller lines were wound with nine turns. Current practice insisted that putting the helm or rudder hard over should require exactly three revolutions of the wheel; furthermore the Surveyor's department specified tiller ropes made of hide rather than hemp, since the former's elasticity was better suited to yield to the movements of the sea. With the lower yoke restricting maximum rudder angle to 25 degrees, the friction on the tiller ropes and the not inconsiderable backlash in the whole intricate system, it is surprising that accurate and responsible steering was ever achieved. Helm orders from the captain or officer of the watch were given direct to the quartermaster in charge of the helmsmen on the upper deck or through voice pipes to the main deck. On being ordered to steer a course the quartermaster or helmsman on the wheel referred to his port or starboard compass.[7]

As soon as *Warrior* berthed in the dock basin Penn's sheer hulk was towed over from Deptford with the first load of machinery. Sheerlegs and cranes plumbed the openings left in the three decks to allow first the engines and then the boilers to be assembled. After everything was in position the casing to the boiler uptakes was fitted and the funnels erected. The work of installation and connecting up – culminating with the propeller – took seven weeks. At the end of February the ship was moved to the east end of the basin to raise steam. Because only one boiler was operating it could not constitute a proper basin trial, but it was successful so far as it went and by March 5 the ship was back in her original berth.[8]

After the euphoria of *Warrior*'s launch had subsided the Admiralty began to prod Thames Ironworks to complete. On March 18, 1861 their lordships 'expressed extreme dissatisfaction at the report . . . received of progress in putting on the remaining armour plates.' The letter went on to remind the builders that making every allowance for difficulties encountered 'which my lordships have done all in their power to diminish by making advances of money', the Admiralty were far from satisfied with Thames' efforts.

John Ford reacted immediately, expressing 'surprise that their lordships were not satisfied', and pointing out that they had already explained circumstances in various letters. While admitting that the company had been over optimistic in time factors, he blamed the Admiralty for extra work caused by alterations in design and the incorporation 'of great and many improvements'. As regards the armour plating the company would mention the severity of the January weather, the overriding requirements of Penn 'to fix the machinery on board and the problems of tonguing and grooving iron plate. As far as

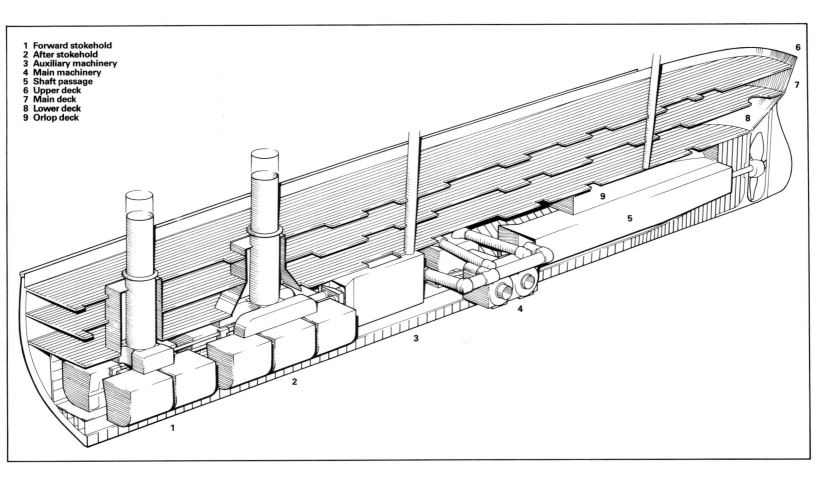

● Layout of boilers and engines

1 Forward stokehold
2 After stokehold
3 Auxiliary machinery
4 Main machinery
5 Shaft passage
6 Upper deck
7 Main deck
8 Lower deck
9 Orlop deck

payment was concerned . . .'[8]

The age-old controversies between builder and Admiralty over delays to contract-built ships were no different from those of modern times, except that there were no union disputes to lengthen delivery times. Already *Warrior*'s name had appeared in the *Navy List* under 'list of effective ships' since March 1860, but now she appeared in March 1861 classified as 'screw steam ship. 1250 horsepower' with her number – 532 – that she retained for easy reference throughout her career.

After Buchan, the second officer to be appointed from *Fisgard* for service in *Warrior* was the master, George Henry Blakey. What role did he play in fitting out? In the days when merchant ships were commandeered by the Crown to become men o' war the skipper or master was retained to navigate and manoeuvre the ship into battle, handling its masts and sails. In 1843 the master was granted a commission but unless senior enough to equate with a commander he ranked with, but after, lieutenants in the grading of 'military' as opposed to 'civil' officers in the fleet. By the 1850s masters composed the navigating branch of the Royal Navy, with second masters serving 'additional' in larger ships. Further back-up was supplied by masters' mates, later to be called masters' assistants.

Blakey joined the navy in 1844 as an 18-year-old to serve at sea for an almost unbroken period of 15 years. An acting master in the four-gun

paddle ship *Stromboli* operating in the Particular Service squadron, he had spent three years in the West Indies. In the Russian war he served in the 60 gun *Edinburgh;* when Captain Hewlett left her to command *Cambridge,* the gunnery training ship at Devonport, he took his master with him. During this period Blakey invented the stadiometer, a simple telescope-like rangefinding device to measure distances between ships in company. Because the instrument promised to improve tactical manoeuvring under steam it gained the navy's full support and a number were manufactured through W Heath of Devonport for fleet use. Blakey was serving in the Channel squadron in 1860 when he was selected for *Warrior*.

In his *Naval Officer's Manual* Captain Glascock stated, 'the qualifications of the master are by no means few, and, indeed are seldom possessed by one individual . . . He should be a thorough seaman, a practical rigger, accustomed to stow and distribute ballast . . . be proficient in every branch of navigation . . . and to these attainments he should add a character of nerve and decision.' *Queen's Regulations and Admiralty Instructions (1861)* further charged him with the stowage of stores, watertanks and firewood, the keys of the spirit room, the setting up of the rigging, keeping anchors and cables clear for running and for writing up the ship's log. The appointment of an experienced and resourceful master at this stage was not a moment too soon.

Wearing his undress frock coat uniform and sword, Blakey went aboard early on March 8, 1861 to be greeted by the Chief Engineer. 'Welcome to the *Warrior*, Mr Blakey, I'm verra pleased to make your acquaintance'. For the next two days they made their way over the ship, studied the plans, looked at the cable lockers and noted that *Warrior* was to carry 92 tons of fresh water stowed in 84 iron tanks, equally distributed between compartments immediately above the fore and after magazines. Blakey's principal interest was in navigation and he observed that there were to be fore and after standard compasses on the conning bridges and another at the top of the mizzen lower mast. These and the steering compasses on upper and main decks would be subject to considerable deviation from *Warrior*'s iron structure. The three chronometers would be stowed in the chronometer room on the lower deck and the barometer fitted in the half deck. Blakey wondered if the Admiralty would supply clocks, in addition to the sandglasses, to keep the ship's time. Charts and navigational publications would be kept in his cabin, together with his own sextant.

That same week three warrant officers joined to complete the team to prepare the ship for service. In order of seniority they were the Gunner, Daniel Colinburn, the Boatswain, Charles Beaton and the Carpenter, James Davidson. Named after the warrant they received from Admiralty on promotion from the lower deck, these men were not of wardroom rank and were ineligible for commissions. As descendants of the 'standing officers' who managed the ship for the 'fighting men' they had been relegated to humbler positions than their ability deserved, thus feelings of frustration and discontent had grown up within their ranks as they witnessed masters, surgeons, chaplains, paymasters and – as a last straw – engineers pass through warrant to commissioned grade. Although minor improvements in pay and conditions were implemented in 1860 it was a long time before their status was recognised. However, the morale of the branch must have been boosted in 1856 when six of their brother officers were decorated with the Victoria Cross for gallantry during the Crimean war.

Approaching 45 and wearing side whiskers, Dan Colinburn was the oldest of the three, having qualified Seaman Gunner, then Gunner's Mate and finally Gunner. Though set in his ways he was a conscientious man, with a good seagoing record and from the *Excellent* where he returned in 1857 to gain a first class certificate. After a spell in the gunnery school in charge of ammunition instruction he had been recommended for *Warrior*. Married with a family at Portsea he was quietly proud of his new appointment.

Since his prime responsibility lay in the upkeep, stowage and safety of the ship's two powder magazines and shell rooms it would be these compartments, together with their light rooms and handing rooms, that he would first explore. Colinburn had to determine how the powder charges would be brought from the magazines through a series of scuttles up to main and upper deck guns. Next there were stowages to check for shot and shell, rifles, pistols and cutlasses as well as sidearms and various appliances in the battery. Up forward in the hold was the gunner's storeroom. Armed with the gunner's establishment of stores, drill books and manuals there was much to occupy his attention.

Charles Beaton, the Boatswain, was the truly professional seaman of the ship. A well-educated man with a cheerful personality he had passed his examination for warrant rank at the age of 30 and recently served in Devonport dockyard. His responsibilities embraced sails, rigging, anchors, cables, cordage, colours (flags), boats and canvas. When the ship commissioned he would be constantly on deck as the commander's right-hand man, assisted by a sailmaker and ropemaker. On commissioning the Chief Boatswain's Mate and seven boatswain's mates would play an indispensable part in running the routine of the ship.

The last of the trio, James Davidson, the Carpenter, was in reality a shipwright who knew how ships were built and how to maintain their structure. After an apprenticeship to a dockyard shipwright he served afloat as a caulker's mate for three years when his ability was quickly recognised. His duties covered the maintenance of pumps, masts and yards, boats, ladders, gratings and especially the repair of damage in action with shot plugs and fearnought. For that reason he would be responsible for keeping the wing passages clear on either side of the lower deck and at orlop deck level. When the ship was stored his share would include timber, tools, oil, paint, cooking utensils, nails and innumerable fittings. As chief artisan of the ship he would supervise the work of the carpenter's crew, blacksmith, plumber, caulkers, cooper, painter, tinsmith and lamptrimmer, all of whom would have to be found a place to work. He was pleased to note that *Warrior* would have a blacksmith's forge and a cupola – a small blast furnace for melting iron.

By tradition warrant officers were accommodated forward on the lower deck within easy reach of their stores and, having no mess, were served their meals in the solitude of their cabins attended by a servant and a cook. In another part of the flat was the engineer officers' mess for nine assistant engineers, their lockers and some hammocks. Further aft was the flat containing the engineers' chests and sleeping berths.

Once engines were installed the next step was to rig the ship. Combining sail and steam in a ship the size of *Warrior* confronted Isaac Watts with a problem. First the vessel had to be sufficiently 'stiff' to carry full canvas and yet be a good all-round sailer. Secondly, it was vital to maintain a stable gun platform when under steam and without the steadying effect of canvas. To improve seakeeping *Warrior* was among the first ships to be given bilge keels, two each side. Subsequent records indicate that she rolled less than wooden steam liners but a little more than her successors. As usual the architect had to compromise in designing the hull and distributing weights within the ship to produce an acceptable metacentric height. When it came to the test Watts' calculations proved just about right.[9]

Argument had arisen over the number of masts to be carried. From experience with the big frigates of the 1857/59 programme Baldwin Walker questioned whether three masts were sufficient for such a long hull and was anxious to give *Warrior* four or five.[10] Watts disagreed, pointing out that three masts would be advantageous for tacking under sail, to keep canvas clear of the funnels and for stepping masts within the ship; he saw no objection to giving *Warrior* wooden masts. Spencer Robinson, the new Controller, supported Watts.[11] Having settled that point would *Warrior* and *Black Prince* be rigged as barques – with square sails on fore and main and fore and aft sails on the mizzen – or would they be rigged with square sails on all three masts? In the event the latter rig found favour. But it was not until December 1860 that the Chatham yard was asked to prepare the ship's masts, rigging and sails.

Commander Charles Pope, Master Attendant at Chatham, eventually received the Admiralty documents which included a sketch of the sails and a rigging warrant that specified every item of standing and running rigging to be fitted. In conjunction with the Master Shipwright and Master Rigger they went over the dimensions of every spar, block, fitting and cordage that was appropriate to an 80 gun ship to which standard *Warrior* would be rigged.

For more than half a century everything aloft had conformed to rules that remained unaltered except in minor detail. Following the standardization introduced by Symonds in the 1830s royal dockyards held comprehensive stocks of gear while shipwrights and riggers grew proficient in uniform construction and repair. Seamanship manuals and ships' orders laid down drills common to all ships which the fleet performed constantly at sea and often in harbour. Ballard remarks, 'every item of running rigging from the main tacks to the royal halliards, from the spanker brails to the jib downhaul followed precisely the same lead . . . and in every vessel whatever her rig the spars on the fore and main were of equal dimensions, that one spare set did for both.' [12]

'Have you any comments?' asked Commander Pope of the assembled company. Master Shipwright Oliver Lang spoke up first, 'I note that the lower masts are to be made of wood not iron as has been rumoured. I am glad as the yard has plenty of timber masts. Secondly, are we to take account of Warrior's *iron hull in fastening, for example, the shrouds and chain plates on her side, or do we rig her as for a wooden ship?' The outcome of the first comment was that in view of timber stocks the Admiralty decided that* Warrior *and* Black Prince *would initially be given all wooden masts and spars. Lower shrouds, however, would be of iron wire – to be supplied by A J Hutchings of Millwall – and there were many iron fittings such as chain slings for the lower yards. On the second point the decision was to conform to the rules and rig her as for a wooden hull, an unnecessary measure as it turned out.*

In March 1861 the Chatham sheer-hulk was towed to Victoria docks carrying the first load of gear including the bowsprit. Floating astern of the hulk were the three lower masts, the biggest being the main, more than 120ft long and 40ins in diameter. The hulk, heavily ballasted, had a tall single mast supported by stays and two long stout spars known as sheers. When she was secured alongside *Warrior* sheers were rigged until they were nearly vertical, their heels resting on each side of the hulk, their heads lashed together to form a derrick. The top was supported by a jib from the mast and controlled by guys so that the sheers could plumb the centre line of the ship. Heavy tackles and two capstans completed the deck equipment.

The first job was probably to secure the 49ft bowsprit in position. Then the hulk was moved so that each of the three masts could be lifted over

● HM Dockyard,
Chatham, showing the
sheer hulk used to step
Warrior's masts

CHATHAM DOCKYARD

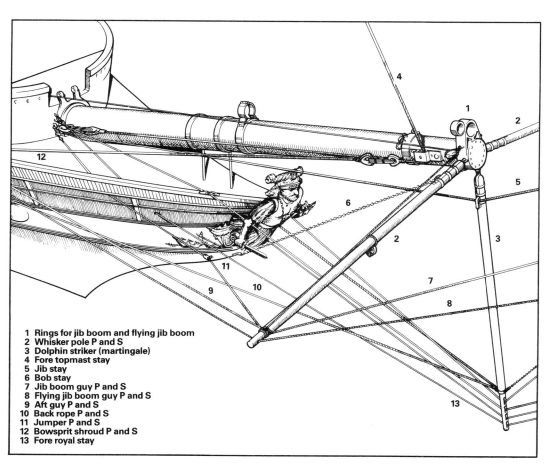

1 Rings for jib boom and flying jib boom
2 Whisker pole P and S
3 Dolphin striker (martingale)
4 Fore topmast stay
5 Jib stay
6 Bob stay
7 Jib boom guy P and S
8 Flying jib boom guy P and S
9 Aft guy P and S
10 Back rope P and S
11 Jumper P and S
12 Bowsprit shroud P and S
13 Fore royal stay

Warrior's upper deck, canted vertically and lowered into its housing. The mizzen stepped on the lower deck in the wardroom while the fore and main went right down to the floors of the foremost hold and auxiliary machinery space respectively. As soon as lower masts were in position masthead pendants, shrouds and stays were sent aloft followed by the tops. Top masts were then hoisted and so on with each stage of standing rigging working upwards, shrouds providing the athwartships support and stays the longitudinal support. Then came the yards – the main lower yard was 105ft long, three feet in diameter in the middle and strong enough for hoisting heavy weights on board. Finally the running rigging which would be used to sail the ship. Despite high winds and driving rain the team of Chatham riggers demonstrated consummate skill in moving or hoisting awkward loads in any direction. All this took time.

On April 20 *Chatham News* reported that the lower masts had been fitted and that the remainder of masts, spars and gear were on their way by lighter. May saw the topmasts and jib-boom in position and the top gallant masts tried before returning them to the deck. With funnels, masts and both standing and running rigging in place *Warrior* not only looked but smelt like a real ship, the atmosphere redolent with tarred hemp.

Warrior's canvas plan comprised 11 so-called square sails, bent and sheeted home at head and

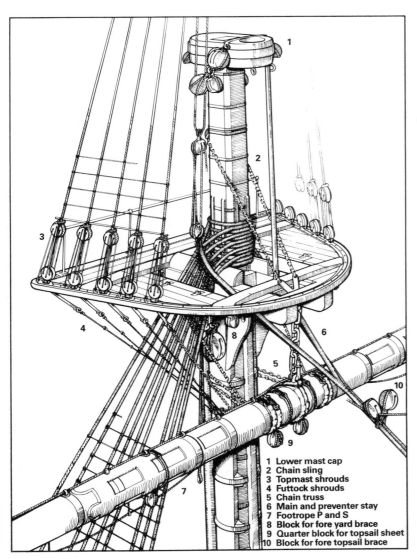

● Maintop and yard

1 Lower mast cap
2 Chain sling
3 Topmast shrouds
4 Futtock shrouds
5 Chain truss
6 Main and preventer stay
7 Footrope P and S
8 Block for fore yard brace
9 Quarter block for topsail sheet
10 Block for fore topsail brace

foot to yards crossed, hoisted and pivoted on their centres athwart the ship's fore and aft line. They combined essentially with the three head sails forward and the spanker on the mizzen. These 15 sails formed the working canvas or plain sail of square rig. Additionally the outfit included studding sails or stun'sails – outward extensions of square canvas – as well as gaff headed trysails, similar to the fore and aft sails and particularly suitable to steam power. With all plain sails set *Warrior* could carry 37,000 square feet of canvas; with stun'sails and trysails a further 18,000 square feet. A spare suit of sails would be stowed in the sailroom situated in the cell flat, while spars not required aloft were stacked in the booms amidships abaft the funnels.

Among the boatswain's stores were the colours – flags and pendants to be displayed or hoisted by halyards to the fore, main and mizzen mastheads for ship-to-ship and ship-to-shore communication. By day *Warrior* would wear a union flag at the jack-staff if in harbour and a red, white or blue ensign aft because ships were still required to fly ensigns of the colour appropriate to the rank of the flag officer commanding their squadron. For more than two hundred years the navy had been divided into three squadrons distinguished by their respective ensigns, a system that puzzled foreigners, inconvenienced ships by having to carry three sets of colours and annoyed peaceful merchantmen wearing the same ensign as the red squadron; from August 1864 all warships wore a white ensign.[13] For everyday usage lockers amidships held the colours, including an interesting set of foreign ensigns. These were in the custody of the Yeoman-of-the-Signals assisted by two signalmen.

The building of *Warrior* had not escaped the notice of marine painters. First off the mark was Thomas Goldsmith Dutton. Described as one of the finest 19th-century lithographers and happily most prolific, his originals appear to have been watercolours. At any rate he started preliminary sketches while the ship was in Victoria Docks and rigging in progress. The result was published by Day and Son, lithographers to HM the Queen, on May 27 when the *Naval Chronicle* described it as 'an accurate portrait of the noble craft as she will shortly appear when rushing forward under the combined impulsion of canvas and steam to breast, as the case may be, either the "battle" or the "breeze", has just been issued . . . and realised with admirable fidelity the spirited delineation of that eminent marine artist Mr T G Dutton'. Although the ship may not have been accurately portrayed the picture was considered one of the most striking.

To settle problems calling for ship's officers' advice Blakey, Ship's Overseer Bascomb and Superintendent Hardy toured the ship weekly, usually accompanied by de Vries, Buchan and the warrant officers. Assembling aft on the quarter-

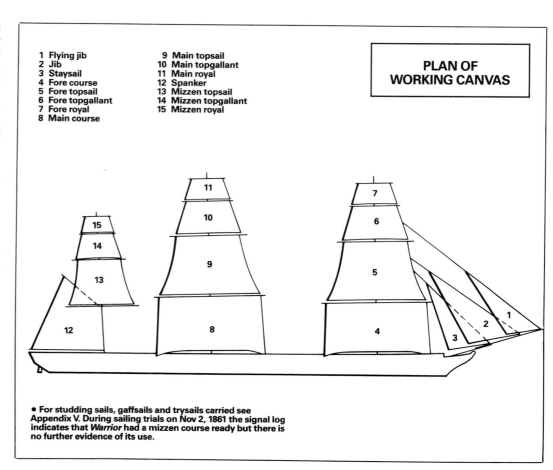

1 Flying jib
2 Jib
3 Staysail
4 Fore course
5 Fore topsail
6 Fore topgallant
7 Fore royal
8 Main course

9 Main topsail
10 Main topgallant
11 Main royal
12 Spanker
13 Mizzen topsail
14 Mizzen topgallant
15 Mizzen royal

PLAN OF WORKING CANVAS

• For studding sails, gaffsails and trysails carried see Appendix V. During sailing trials on Nov 2, 1861 the signal log indicates that *Warrior* had a mizzen course ready but there is no further evidence of its use.

deck a typical programme started by examining the steering wheels where the tiller ropes had recently been rove, then up to the after conning bridge to check the engine telegraphs and voice pipes before discussing the boat stowage in the booms either side of the funnels. At this stage the Chief Engineer joined them to settle the route for the ash buckets from the top of the chute to the ship's side.

'Now, sir,' said the Carpenter to Blakey, 'for such a large ship's company we don't appear to have enough seats in the heads.' The party looked over the bows where shipwrights were constructing long wooden platforms either side and below the bowsprit. Blakey glanced at his copy of the specifications covering the forepart of the ship. 'The head of the ship to be . . . completed with all necessary Rails, Timbers, Cheeks, Bolsters, Carlings, Straps for Gammoning and Bobstays, Berthing, Seats of Ease, Urine Dales (urinals), Boomkins, Head Pump and all other necessary and usual fittings, in accordance with the direction of the Overseer.' Standard directions but they did not specify the number of 'seats of ease', a euphemistic description of the holes in the wooden plank fitted over a narrow trough on each side of the bowsprit. Protected from outboard by a canvas screen with no other privacy the heads were exposed to wind, rain and frequently the sea; primitive conditions accepted by generations of seamen as normal. A bucket of salt water was handy for ablutions and the head chutes were cleared, if necessary, by dropping down 32 pdr shot. Officers' heads forward and aft on the maindeck fared little better. 'Yes, Mr Blakey' said Bascomb, 'six seats for 640 men does seem a trifle few. I am sure I can contrive additional.' And so two more seats each side were added. Bascomb thanked his lucky stars he did not earn his living at sea while Blakey wondered how heavy the swell would have to be before the heads became unusable.

The party descended the ladder to the main deck and checked the arrangements for bringing the cable through the hawsepipes before walking aft through the heavy armoured doors that had just been fitted either side of the athwartships bulkhead. In the messdeck approval had to be given to the contractor's design of mess shelf to take the bowls, plates and cutlery for each of the messes; then the recently installed ship's galley was inspected by de Vries who opened the grates, examined the boilers and checked the coal box while Buchan looked at the funnel that would project well above the upper deck. That job done where was the best position to stow the capstan bars and what should be the height of the ship's bell? Around the mainmast would be fitted wooden furniture to take the quartermaster's gear, deck log and notice boards from where the ship's harbour routine would be run.

Walking aft into the half deck they glanced into the commander's and master's cabins, where joiners were busy completing chest storage and bookshelves, before entering the captain's quarters. His day or fore cabin, with space for a large dining table, heating stove, deck and perhaps two or three easy chairs, together with his sleeping cabin – where he would sling his cot – extended the beam of the ship. Separated by a movable partition was the space either side of the screw well, optimistically called his after cabin.

On the lower deck they scrutinized joinery work in the officers' cabins, wardroom and gunroom; up and down again to look at the two library cupboards and band instrument room. In the bathroom flat over the fore stokehold Carpenter Davidson found fault with the methods proposed for draining water from the stokers' baths. Gunner Colinburn wanted alterations in the fore magazine, Paymaster de Vries suggested a better way of hoisting rum casks from the spirit room; finally the chain lockers and storerooms were checked. At the end of the day the inspecting team emerged tired, dirty and dishevelled but satisfied that progress was being made.

Provision of lighting below decks also exercised the minds of the ship's officers. With gunport lids and upper deck skylights open *Warrior's* main deck and even parts of the lower deck received adequate daylight. But when battened down or at night the main and lower decks by modern standards were badly lit since the prodigious consumption of candles restricted permanent lamp positions to a minimum. Supervised by a lamptrimmer, a limited number of police and wing lanterns would be positioned to illuminate traffic routes, hatchways, ladders and access to storerooms. A daily ration of candles would go to officers' cabins and to the broadside messes, where they would be placed in sconce holders or stuck on tables. Oil lanterns were reserved for the captain's day cabin, wardroom, gunroom and engine room while many compartments in the hold would remain in permanent darkness except when inspected. In action fighting lanterns illuminated the breeches between each pair of guns; the powder magazines and handing rooms had specially fitted light rooms with lamps that burnt day and night. On the upper deck binnacle lamps and navigation lights were lit by oil but apart from hand lanterns there was no other lighting. Men found their way by habit and touch.[14]

Since the New Year speculation had been rife as to who would command the *Warrior*, an appointment on which the eyes of the navy would be concentrated. Writing in the *Army and Navy Gazette* in April 1861 it was suggested by a 'naval officer who is a very good authority on the subject' that *Warrior* should be sent to sea 'with a well selected committee on board whose duty it would be to report on the general qualities of the vessel'. The committee would consist of a 'captain, a shipwright, a gunnery officer and an eminent engineer' to guide the Admiralty. Needless to say that idea did not take off.

A number of captains of the right seniority and qualifications were considered but final selection during May must have occupied the closest attention of the naval lords, as well as the First Lord, the Duke of Somerset. A few days after a decision had been made Sir Richard Dundas, the First Sea Lord, died suddenly of a heart attack at the age of 59, followed a few weeks later by the death of Admiral Pelham, the Second Sea Lord.[15] In effect what was almost certainly their last important appointment was confirmed by the First Lord whose secretary, Captain John Moore, wrote to the officer concerned on May 31. 'The Duke of Somerset has desired me to inform you that it is his intention to appoint you to command the *Warrior* when she is ready for commission if it is agreeable to you. As it is desirable that whoever commands her should be present to superintend her fittings I believe you will be at once appointed additional to the *Fisgard* for that purpose, but you had better come to the Admiralty . . . as the Duke would like to see you on the subject.'[16] After accepting the appointment Cochrane wrote to his mother on June 3, 1861.

My dearest Mother
You will without doubt be very glad to
hear that I am appointed to the *Warrior*, the
finest and largest command in the British
Navy – Hoping you are well.
Believe me
your affectionate son
                      A A Cochrane.'[17]

CHAPTER FIVE
Commissioning

CAPTAIN THE HONOURABLE Arthur Auckland Leopold Pedro Cochrane was the third son of Admiral Thomas Cochrane, tenth Earl of Dundonald, considered by many – after Nelson – to be the most brilliant and daring naval commander of the 19th century. The last christian name was a reminder that at Arthur's birth in London in 1824 his father was serving Don Pedro, Emperor of Brazil, whose country was fighting Portugal for its independence. Evidently Arthur was embarrassed by his plethora of names as the last two were usually dropped soon after he joined the navy.

Scarcely 14 he left London one evening in a Red Rover stage-coach bound for Portsmouth to join the *Benbow* and within a year had tasted action when his ship helped bombard Acre. The allied squadron came under heavy fire from the batteries when Midshipman Cochrane 'gallantly distinguished himself' gaining the General Service medal (Syria) and a Turkish medal. In 1845 he served in the Pacific, first as acting mate in the paddle sloop *Salamander* and then in *Collingwood*, under Captain Robert Smart. Transferring to the brigantine *Spy* he visited Pitcairn Island early in 1847 where he met Jemima Young, granddaughter of one of the original mutineers from the *Bounty* whose family are resident there today. Jemima must have been bowled over by the handsome young Scot because two years later she was still writing fervent letters.[1]

Returning to England he took passage part of the way in the 42 gun frigate *Fisgard*, arriving to take his gunnery and navigation courses at Portsmouth. His father wrote warning him to avoid the temptations of 'coffee houses or billiard rooms' and to 'set his mind to passing examinations with distinction'. He concluded, 'I have set my heart on you . . . leaving all competitors far behind, and I am hopeful that you will not by any negligence disappoint me.' From his mother in Paris came a somewhat pathetic letter begging him to visit her.[2]

Few were surprised at Cochrane's nomination in 1848 to become flag lieutenant to his father who had accepted command of the North America and West Indies Station. Although 70, the admiral was still a spry, active-minded figure who took exceptional interest in the West Indian islands and expected his staff to do likewise. When father hauled down his flag Arthur was among those recommended for promotion, an act of nepotism by no means unusual then. He was 27.

First command is a memorable step in any naval officer's career and Commander Cochrane must have been gratified with the prospect of a commission in the little sloop *Sappho*, even if it meant returning to the West Indies. Back in England two years later he obtained permission to study steam for several months at Woolwich, where his ideas of building a water tube boiler may have originated. At the outbreak of the Russian war he was given command of the six gun

paddle sloop *Driver* for operations in the Baltic where, following the bombardment and capture of the fortress at Bomarsund, the 30-year-old Arthur Cochrane, was promoted captain.

Within a year trouble in China came to a head and Captain Cochrane found himself commanding the screw sloop *Niger*. Arriving off Canton late in 1856 he took part in a boat action that seized the Dutch Folly Fort. *Niger* then joined Admiral Sir Michael Seymour's squadron engaged in punishing Chinese pirates for capturing a British ship. Hundreds of heavily armed junks were located in the shallows of Fatshan Creek, an inlet off the Pearl River; the only way to flush them out was by ship's boats. In the cutting-out expedition, com-

●**Captain Arthur Cochrane. On advice of the late Earl of Dundonald the right hand photograph dated** 1854 and the centre dated 1863 are authentic while the left hand is probably Arthur then aged six

manded by the impetuous Commodore Keppel, Cochrane was in the vanguard of the flotilla in his gig rowing some seven miles against daunting opposition. Receiving a grape shot contusion of the arm he was highly commended for his part in the desperate action that won the day. He was again wounded during a minor action against a junk and in December 1857 led the third division of Elliot's naval brigade in the final assault on Canton. Cochrane had acquitted himself well and on returning home the following year was awarded Companionship of the Bath and later the China medal with Canton and Fatshan clasps.

Anticipating a well-earned rest on half pay, Arthur found himself entangled in family

disputes, his mother still estranged from his father who was now past 80 and failing slowly. Fortunately an appointment to a committee convened to investigate and report on the defence of the country's ports and arsenals gave him breathing space to deal with personal affairs.[3] At the end of October 1860 Lord Dundonald died and England was the sadder for it, the *Times* recording, 'history can produce few examples of such a man or of such achievements'. In his father's will Arthur received his maritime patents but little else.

When the naval lords contemplated the list of captains suitable to command *Warrior* Arthur Cochrane now aged 37 was among the chief contenders. In addition to being a good seaman and natural leader he had inherited his father's resource and a large measure of his technical genius. As such he was a rare creature in the ranks of senior officers and ahead of the opposition.

Receiving the First Lord's letter Cochrane made an immediate appointment to wait on the Duke of Somerset who underlined the significance of his command and arranged for him to join *Fisgard* at Woolwich. Next call was on Rear Admiral Spencer Robinson, the Controller, who told him of *Warrior's* progress, about relations with Thames Ironworks, of the decision to install a proportion of Armstrong guns and of the great urgency for the ship to be commissioned to strengthen the Channel squadron. At lunch next day in the Junior United Service Club his appointment was received with much acclaim and not a little envy by his brother officers.

With so much at stake in a new, untried ship the most important step was to find a commander, the man who would not only be his deputy but also direct and administer the ship's company. Cochrane did not have far to look because by the odd quirk of fate that has so often characterised officers' appointments he found the name of George Tryon on the short list. No one could have suited better.

Born in 1832 George Tryon was half way through his schooling at Eton College when he told his father he wanted to join the navy. Aged 16 Midshipman Tryon was appointed to the *Wellesley*, then fitting out as flagship to the Earl of Dundonald whose flag lieutenant, as we know, was Arthur Cochrane. On passage to the Caribbean Tryon impressed his seniors, which stood him in good stead because on arrival in Port Royal he was due to be discharged to a receiving hulk, heavily infected with yellow fever, to await another ship. Largely through intercessions to the admiral he was allowed to remain in *Wellesley*. In those days it was not unusual for a lieutenant to take a promising midshipman under his wing, allowing him the use of his cabin for study and generally acting as his nurse. In this manner Cochrane got to know Tryon pretty well, realising that he had uncommon potential. Three years later Tryon was appointed as senior midshipman in *Vengeance,* one of the squadron that visited Sinope, scene of the massacre of the Turkish ships by the Russians in 1853. When Britain and her allies declared war *Vengeance* moved in support of the army into the Black Sea where, writing to his mother, Tryon described the battle of Alma as seen from the maintop as signal midshipman.

Promoted lieutenant he served in *Royal Albert;* his record as 'a most resourceful officer' earned him a recommendation for the royal yacht and in 1858 Her Majesty approved his nomination to *Victoria and Albert.* The job was a sinecure but useful for contacts in high places and subsequent promotion, which he received in October 1860.

Aged 29 and on half pay awaiting appointment Commander Tryon was delighted to receive news of joining *Warrior.* There was much to discuss with his former patron: one topic needing clarification was the number and qualifications of the officers and men who were to man the ship. Here

Cochrane found it difficult to follow Admiralty reasoning. Because of her single gun deck *Warrior* was classified as a frigate but by the existing rules the actual rate was fixed by the number of guns which, if applied to *Warrior*, would have graded the largest, most powerful warship in the world as a fifth rate, with a complement of 400. This was absurd so the Admiralty agreed that the number and specialities of men required to fight the guns, as stated by the quarter bill, was a better criterion. Including marines, artisans etc the Admiralty calculated the figure as 740 which did not tally with any of the standard complements but was not far off the 705 of a third-rate ship of the line. And *Warrior* was so graded despite being more than a match for all the first-rates. She set a precedent in that irrespective of armament later ironclads were also given a complement of 705, although in practice the rules were flouted because the Admiralty permitted supernumeraries to be carried.[4]

From accommodation provided in *Fisgard* Cochrane and Tryon were able to visit *Warrior* daily to get to grips with the ship and plan the future programme. On commissioning *Warrior* was entitled to five lieutenants who, with the captain, commander, master, warrant and subordinate officers, made up the executive element or military branch of officers. Cochrane was allowed to take his pick; the most senior was Henry Phillimore who had qualified after a six-months

course in the *Excellent* before serving as Gunnery Lieutenant in *Malacca*, with the same William Buchan as Chief Engineer. More recently Phillimore had come home from three years in *Ganges*, flagship of the Pacific station, with a fellow watchkeeper, George Parker, also destined for *Warrior*. Joseph Wilson was the second senior lieutenant having just paid off *Marlborough*, the Mediterranean flagship. Finally Henry Perceval, recently on the China station, was the last to join *Fisgard*. The fifth lieutenant was Noel Digby who joined in October.

Besides the assistant chief engineer, Glasspole, the only other senior civil branch officer to appear on board shortly before the official commissioning date of August 1 was the 37-year-old Paymaster John Nicolay de Vries. Origin of his rank lay in the captain's clerks and pursers who as commissioned officers were formed into the paymaster branch in 1852. From that date greatly improved pay and conditions compensated for the often abused system of remunerations that had previously made up their salary. Admiralty now stipulated that in future officers receiving 'any commission or purchases, poundage, fees or emoluments will be visited with their Lordships severest displeasure'.[5] As the ship's accountant officer, with assistant paymasters to help him, de Vries would pay the ship's company monthly, be in charge of victualling and responsible for 'disbursements required for public service'. He

had proved a capable paymaster in *Illustrious* at Portsmouth and had recently served in *Ajax* on coastguard service in Queenstown.

On receiving Lord Paget's report of the armoured tower fitted in *Gloire* their lordships had been sufficiently impressed to direct the Controller to design and install a similar structure on *Warrior*'s upper deck. Early in July 1861 Woolwich dockyard shipwrights were busy preparing timbers and iron for erection between the main and mizzen masts. Described in the *Army and Navy Gazette* as 'an oval kind of gallery 7ft high, 10ft long and 9ft wide' it was open at the top with '12 loopholes for rifle firing and of larger circumference at each angle for swivel guns'. Protected by 12in baulks of teak behind three inches of iron it looked a formidable sort of blockhouse, but nobody had much idea how it would be used and its appearance attracted adverse criticism.[6]

By mid-July the same journal reported that *Warrior* was 'rapidly approaching completion' and that 'screw machinery had been tested with most satisfactory results'. The paper also reported that dockyard engineers and artificers had built the 30hp donkey auxiliary engine, illustrating the increasing naval support to finish *Warrior*. Thames Ironworks had already started to work night shifts.

As is usual with a new ship committed to a tight schedule activity aboard was intense as shipwrights, carpenters, painters and cleaners

put finishing touches above and below decks. Throughout the main deck men were fitting some 34 wooden mess tables, one end on the ship's side and the other slung on an iron crank from the deckhead, with their stools and mess shelves. Hatchways were jammed with furniture on its way to the lower deck obstructing labourers bringing up rubbish for the dockside. All was bustle, noise and wet paint. Anyone who has stood by a warship under construction will remember the strained atmosphere between ship's officers and the contractor's employees that usually accompanies the last few weeks of work. However, Cochrane had discouraged visitors from London, the weather was kind and both Commander Tryon and Superintendent Hardy kept cool heads.

From late June onwards chief petty officers, a sergeant of marines and key ratings for *Warrior* trickled in to *Fisgard* where they found Commander Tryon had set up office to receive them and arrange their accommodation in *Hebe*, the Woolwich receiving hulk. Assisting Pay-master de Vries to prepare the storerooms were William Cheeseman, the Ship's Steward, and George Gladman, Captain of the Hold, while the executive element, led by Master-at-Arms George Hendlay, included Chief Boatswain's Mate William Rutter, Chief Quartermaster James Adnams, Sailmaker Joseph Roper and Chief Captain of Forecastle William Percival. This

experience helped Tryon and Phillimore prepare the organisations necessary to move, fight and safeguard the ship. These had to be matched to the scheme of complement showing details, but not names, of the 50 officers and 655 men who made up the *Warrior*'s crew.

Making out the watch bill entailed dividing the ship's company into port and starboard watches whereby each man on the bill would be allocated a number, odd numbers starboard watch, even numbers port watch. Next came the station bill when each number was allocated a specific duty in a part of ship – forecastle, foretop, maintop, mizzentop, afterguard and gunners to cover work aloft, on deck and cleaning. Sailing the ship would often claim the support of marines, stokers and idlers. Idlers were anything but idle but being daymen did not keep a watch and had their nights in, although they turned out at four in the morning. Ranging from artisans to sick berth attendants they were divided into 'working idlers' or 'excused idlers'. Working idlers were older, reliable men such as the sailmaker who would be called out occasionally to reef sails or wear ship but excused idlers, such as the ship's cook or captain's steward, were used only in emergency.

At sea, seamen and marines worked in two watches – four hours on, four hours off – though at night those not actually on trick as lookouts or helmsmen were allowed to snooze. Under steam stokers worked in three watches but when sailing

reverted to two for maintenance and cleaning. Except for watchkeeping lieutenants and mid-shipmen all officers were designated daymen, although the executive element could be – and were – called on deck at any time.

Wearing his gunnery hat and advised by Colinburn and Chief Gunner's Mate Pearce, Lieutenant Phillimore compiled the quarter bill based on the *Excellent*'s guide. Detailing officers, gun's crews (18 men for a 68pdr), magazine and handing room crews, he also had to find men at general quarters to man the helm positions, act as marksmen in the tops, stand by in the wing passages for damage control and attend the surgeons either in the sick berth or the wardroom rigged as a first aid position. Lastly, the fire bill – as the organisation of a 12-strong fire brigade was called – needed stokers and carpenters on the basis that 'so many destructive projectiles . . . rendering it probable that the ship would be set on fire soon after commencing action'.

All that was left now were the messing organisation and sleeping billets. It was logical that men should eat their meals as close as possible to their gun quarters and parts of the ship in which they worked. In each of the 34 messes of approximately 18 men half would belong to the starboard watch and half to the port, which meant that each man had an opposite number who performed the duty of the other when only one was on watch. It also ensured that when one watch was on deck the weight of men below was equally distributed. The same principle, which originated from sailing ships, applied to slinging hammocks so that port and starboard watches berthed alternately athwartships to balance the number of men in and out of their hammocks. Special duty men, such as boatswain's mates, slung their hammocks near hatchways. Marines and stokers messed separately as did chief petty officers, certain petty officers and boys. By convention each mess and each gun was numbered from forward to aft.

So many different organisations to operate *Warrior* may appear complicated but they were standard practice and readily understood by a partly illiterate ship's company. Traditionally watch bill numbers would be stencilled on the black painted bottom of each man's canvas bag containing clothes, as well as on hammocks, one of which had a white and the other a black patch. Distinctive watch stripes in the form of tapes would also be issued to seamen to sew on the arms of their frocks – starboard watch on the right arms, port watch on the left arms. With so much dependent on team work the Royal Navy prided itself on man management down to the ultimate detail; the system had a further advantage in that if a man dropped out through sickness or absence over leave his station could be covered readily.[7]

Shortly before commissioning John Ford brought his directors and managers to Victoria Docks to discuss final arrangements for handing over *Warrior* to the Royal Navy. Isaac Watts and Thomas Lloyd represented the Controller, John Penn was there in person, as was Commander John MacDonald from Woolwich and Captain Cochrane with some of his officers. After a long day it was agreed that the ship was now ready to take her complement, that most oustanding work would be finished by the date of acceptance, August 8, that John Penn's engineers would remain on board to service the engines until after full power trials and that Woolwich yard would install the donkey engine. Isaac Watts made a brief speech thanking Thames Ironworks and the meeting broke up with handshakes and smiles.[8]

Punctually at nine o'clock on Thursday, August 1, one of *Fisgard*'s boats left Woolwich for Victoria Docks with Captain Cochrane in full dress uniform – cocked hat, epaulettes and sword. Landing at a jetty he was escorted to the quarterdeck where the commander, first lieutenant and master were drawn up to receive him. The boatswain and chief boatswain's mate piped the side and all present removed their hats as the captain officially stepped aboard his ship for the first time. Drawing a paper from an inner pocket Cochrane cleared his throat and read, 'To Arthur Auckland Cochrane, Companion of the Bath . . . by virtue of the power and authority to us given . . . We do hereby constitute and appoint you Captain of Her Majesty's frigate the *Warrior* . . . Willing and requiring you forthwith to go aboard and take upon you the Charge and Command of Captain in her accordingly . . . Strictly Charging and Commanding all the Officers and Company of the said frigate to behave themselves jointly and severally in their respective employments with all the due Respect and Obedience unto you their said Captain . . . you likewise to observe and execute as the General Printed Instructions and such Orders and Directions as you shall from time to time receive from us or any other your Superior Officers for Her Majesty's Service . . . Hereof nor you, nor any of you, may fail us as you will answer to the Contrary at your Peril. And for so doing this shall be your commission. Given under our hands

● First Lieutenant of
Marine Artillery,
F Hastings Owen

and the Seal of the Office of the Admiralty . . . By Command of their Lordships . . . signed William Govett Romaine; Secretary.'

As soon as hats were replaced Cochrane ordered, 'hoist the pendant'. Having anticipated this order Yeoman-of-the-Signals Beaver sprang to the halyards at the mainmast, gave a sharp tug and a strip of bunting broke out to flutter in the breeze. At least 20ft long and narrow with a red St George's cross on a white field the long pendant had been worn traditionally night and day by ships to indicate that they were in commission. Since the ship's company had yet to join there was no ceremony as there is today, nevertheless the occasion was significant. *Warrior* was now in active commission. Supervised by the master the ship's log was started, bells were struck and Cochrane went below to write his standing orders. The officers were particularly pleased – they were now entitled to full pay.

True to custom the first arrivals on Saturday morning were the Royal Marines. Designated a light corps in 1855, with a marine artillery division established in 1859, the 'Royals' had come a long way since their inception in the 17th century. In contrast to seamen and stokers, marine recruitment found little difficulty in maintaining an official strength of 18,000 men and because volunteers were drawn right across the country the corps contained a higher proportion of robust, solidly built agricultural workers. Unlike the

seamen they were sworn in to undergo arduous barracks training before going to sea where their high standard of discipline and steady performance earned them respect, spiced with many a leg pull on the lower deck. In common with their naval contemporaries marine officers found progress up the promotion ladder sluggish but, as today, family traditions counted.

Under the command of Captain Henry Way Mawbey *Warrior*'s detachment was unique in that it consisted entirely of Royal Marines Artillery. They included First Lieutenants Herbert Everitt and Hastings Owen, three sergeants, three 'corporals and bombardiers', two 'drummer and buglers' and 114 gunners. There were no red-coated infantrymen, *Warrior* being the first and only ship to have an all-gunner contingent as an experiment in manning.[9] As early as March 1860 the *Army and Navy Gazette* reported that 'an Armstrong gun manned by Royal Marines Artillery fired . . . five rounds in two minutes, at a range of 3000 yards, hitting the target every time' at Fort Cumberland, Southsea.

The marines looked impressive as they came across from Woolwich in two launches to form up on the dockside abreast the ship. Dressed in short blue jackets, white duck trousers and pill box hats with badges of crossed guns and a bursting grenade, each man carried his Enfield muzzle-loading rifle and musketry order that included a bayonet. While the younger men were clean-

shaven the older sported moustaches or side whiskers and many wore General Service medals. As soon as they were assembled in two ranks, Captain Mawbey called them to attention and went aboard to report to Commander Tryon; ten minutes later they were on their way to their messes in the after end of the battery. Traditionally the marines always messed between officers and seamen; in *Warrior* they would man the after section of 100 pdr and 68 pdr guns.

As the marines went below the first drafts started to arrive at Victoria Docks to join ship. Some came from *St Vincent*, the reserve depot ship at Portsmouth, others from *Cumberland* at Sheerness, 30 seamen gunners from the Devonport gunnery training ship *Cambridge*, a few from *Royal Adelaide* and more than 70 from *Fisgard*. In contrast to the smart turn out of the marines the seamen were irregularly but not untidily dressed; as it was summer the majority wore white frocks and trousers, a few with blue jackets and either blue caps or sennet hats. Shepherded by the ship's corporals each man shouldered his bulky canvas bag to file up the gangway. First came petty officers with badges of rank and good conduct on the left arm, gunnery badges on the right, veterans of 35 and 40 with years of service behind them, staunch, dependable, married men with weathered, bewhiskered faces and huge hands. Several were artisans carrying heavy tool chests, their personal possessions carried in ditty

boxes. After them came leading, able and ordinary seamen, stokers and trimmers, shipwrights and shoemakers, cooks and stewards, mainly younger men on either side of 20, a few joining a ship for the first time. Short of stature – average height barely five feet four inches – bred in dockyard ports, mostly unmarried, one or two scarred with smallpox, they looked a rough and ready lot.[10]

The first drafts arrived on *Warrior*'s upper deck – documents ready to hand – to be assigned their duties. As each man stepped forward his name was written on a card containing watch and station particulars. This he took first to the gunner who filled in his gunnery station, thence to the ship's clerk to get his ship's book number and lastly to the master-at-arms who allocated his mess. Each seaman was briefly interrogated and scrutinized before allocation to a part of the ship.

The forecastlemen were chosen from the strongest and most experienced seamen who wore their hats a little differently from the others. Those on the fore course would be known as lower yardmen and those on the headsails as headsail loosers or headsail furlers. Forecastlemen also had stations for working anchors and cables. The three categories of topmen were divided into topsail yardmen and upper yardmen – chosen from the smartest and most active men in the ship – who were further divided into royal and topgallant yardmen. Mizzentopmen also worked the spanker, while the afterguard and gunners would look after the main course and sometimes assist with the mizzen topsail. Gunners were selected from older men, not very quick aloft, while in the afterguard would be the inexperienced, less reliable youngsters placed under the eye of the commander. Similarly the chief engineer chose men for working in the stokeholds or engine room. Before going below each man collected two hammocks, clews and lashing from the boatswain.[10]

When the last man had gone below the lieutenants made out their own pocket watchbills and compiled divisional lists. It was Cochrane's wish that *Warrior's* officers should look to the well-being of those under them, a principle that applied to all departments. In the case of seamen each lieutenant was allocated a division of about 50 men to administer and inspect whenever divisions were paraded on deck. As first lieutenant Phillimore was also responsible for the mess decks.

Seated in what appeared capacious mess decks unencumbered by guns, their hats and bundles discarded and a chance to remove their shoes to feel the deck under their feet, the older men contemplated their surroundings. Those nearest would be their messmates and their mess would be their home for the next three and a half years, their life in it regulated by an unwritten but inviolate code of conduct. First impression of food was good because Ship's Cook Charles Holding had prepared a welcome hot meal of roast beef, potatoes and cabbage. But dinner was not piped by the boatswain's mates until grog had been issued to the senior ratings or 'captains' of messes. The rest of the day was spent in drawing mess utensils, bedding, victuals and all that men needed to live, eat, sleep and work on board a warship. Bags were taken down to be stowed in numbered racks in lower deck flats – stokers forward, seamen and boys amidships, marines aft. Then hammocks were made up for slinging on their first night aboard; above all, men found their way around the ship, remarking on the exceptional headroom and large spaces below decks. First impressions were favourable.

Insufficent depth of water in the basin prevented *Warrior* from being fully laden and waiting to be embarked down river were 375 tons of guns and ammunition, 500 tons of coal, a quantity of stores and the balance of anchors, cables and boats. So Sunday, August 4, was a work day and on Monday and Tuesday all hands prepared a move to Greenhithe by which time Engineer Walter Fry, Assistant Engineers William Milln, Peter Baldwin and George Hosteys, together with Assistant Paymaster Nicholas Aaron had joined the ship. The remaining 40% of the ship's company would join when the manning situated permitted.

Promptly at six thirty on the morning of Thursday, August 8, 1861, fires were lit in all boilers and soon volumes of black smoke poured from the funnels. Within two hours steam was raised and throughout the forenoon there was feverish activity on board as employees of Thames Ironworks finished their jobs, collected their tools and hurried off. On the dockside men singled up the hawsers that secured the ship, cranes positioned their purchases to hoist out the gangways and a cable party of seamen under the first lieutenant and boatswain prepared anchors and cables for letting go. Quartermasters and helmsmen went to wheel positions, leadsmen to the chains while seamen rigged cutters as seaboats, placed lifebuoys, closed gunports and made the ship ready for her move down stream.

Predictably approached by a number of senior officers eager to take passage, the captain decided that the principal guest would be none other than his old friend from Fatshan Creek days, the redoubtable Henry Keppel, now a rear admiral of the white. Accompanied by Rear Admiral Charles Eden, a junior lord, the 'little admiral' – as he was later known – arrived on board. They were joined by Commodore Sir Frederick Nicholson from *Fisgard*, Superintendent Evans of the Admiralty Compass department and according to a newspaper report, 'numerous naval and marine officers' who managed to secure invitations. The report continued, 'the banks of the river at every available spot were crowded with spectators' but another recorded that 'there was an almost total absence of curiosity to witness her departure from the docks'.[11]

While the visitors assembled on the quarterdeck the captain joined the master, officer of the watch and the pilot Barnes on the after conning bridge. Just before high water a regular team of paddle tugs from John Watkins – including *Punch* – made fast to *Warrior*'s stern and 'the gates being opened, went blustering and splashing out into the Thames towing the massive, black and ominous-looking ship stern foremost after them'. As she cleared the dock gates the band struck up *Rule Britannia* but 'no cheering was attempted for there was plenty to be done at once, as the force of the tide and wind came on her full broadside and in spite of the sturdy efforts of the tugs began to drift her up stream'. Clearly the stiff breeze added to the last of the flood tide was too much for the tugs and *Warrior* was in trouble. Fortunately the pilot kept his nerve, ordered engines to slow ahead and the helm hard over to bring her round. 'As it was, a few turns of her gigantic screw, which seemed to stir up the very bottom of the Thames, soon checked her progress and sent her into the middle of the river, facing fair down stream'. Exchanging meaningful glances, Cochrane and Blakey breathed sighs of relief, sensing the problems that might arise on future occasions.

No further crisis occurred as *Warrior* proceeded down Woolwich Reach under tow, into Gallions Reach and past Barking Creek where 'in the sharp turns it was necessary to use considerable care and to screw astern till she was sometimes brought almost to a standstill'. The *Engineer* went to some pains to contradict the *Army and Navy Gazette*'s assertion that 'she answered her helm like a yacht' by stating that 'she did nothing of the kind', and stressed the shortcomings of her steering gear that needed maximum hands on the wheels and relieving tackles. After successfully negotiating the Erith bend and entering Long Reach, engines were stopped and tugs brought her slowly to berth about 300 yards off the Kent bank opposite Greenhithe, where the river was half a mile wide. Letting go anchors she lay in six fathoms of water. The log recorded that during her 15-mile passage down river her steam machinery consumed 50 tons of coal, 22 gallons of lubricating oil, 160lbs of tallow and 6lbs of oakum. But the engine performance had been excellent and in the words of the *Naval and Military Gazette*, 'she fouled nothing, never touched the ground and was at her mooring less than two hours after she started'. After anchoring, the operation of getting out boats, booms and ladders took much longer than expected and by the time *Hebe* had been secured port side – she had followed *Warrior* down river – everyone was a bit frayed and thankful things had gone without mishap.

When the visitors had gone ashore and the commander reported that all was secure for the night, the captain approved an extra tot of rum all round, a gesture that found universal favour. In the wardroom the officers sat down to formal dinner concluding with a toast to the ship. Later when the ship's company had piped down the captain sent for the commander and chief engineer to discuss the events of the day over a nightcap. 'Well, Mr Buchan, and how did your department perform?' The chief engineer responded immediately, 'Verra guid, sir. Ay and ye'll find none better in ma stokehold. Yer Mister Glasspole – a verra capable mon.' William Glasspole had but recently joined as assistant chief engineer. Cochrane turned to Tryon, 'and how are the men shaping?' The commander paused. 'It's too early to venture an opinion, sir. May I say . . . so far I'm not disappointed.' Cochrane nodded, 'I'm bound to say I was encouraged by what I saw today. But we still have a long way to go.'

The next few days were spent settling down to harbour routine, removing the traces of dockyard dirt and establishing communications with Greenhithe. Little warning was given of the arrival of the Grand Duke Maximilian of Austria and his entourage to pay an official visit, the first of many that the ship had to endure. Each celebrity demanded a display of ceremonial that was part and parcel of the Victorian scene afloat whose punctilious observance was as dear to the bestowers as the recipients. As a brand new warship with singular appeal, *Warrior* came in for more than her fair share of such visits but, before long, was able to take them all in her stride. With the need to extend hospitality after a tour of the ship the captain came off worst since the bulk of entertaining sprang from his own pocket. Cochrane was not rich but kept a good table.

'I find my cabin a capital size' exclaimed Lieutenant Wilson to the captain of marines, 'far more commodious than my last ship.' With deck

head space of more than seven feet the officers' cabins were indeed spacious though sparsely fitted: a bunk over a chest of drawers, a hinged flap that served as a desk, bookshelf and corner wash-stand was all. Everything else the officer provided – mirror, bedding, blankets, linen, tin bath, water can, curtains and carpet. Little light penetrated the scuttle glass making candles obligatory but despite the gloom most officers contrived their cabins as a snug retreat with family knick-knacks, books and sporting equipment. Better illuminated, the wardroom occupied the space amidships between cabins on either side having a table and chairs centrally positioned, a buffet and cupboards on either side of the mizzen mast, a pantry in the after cabin flat and room for precious little else. Compared to a three-decker it was not a comfortable wardroom.

Probably the first serious accident in the ship occurred when Second Captain of the Hold Toomey injured himself, his discharge to hospital coinciding with the arrival on board of Surgeon Samuel Sloane Dalzell Wells in the last week of July. In view of a recent directive that surgeons should combine the functions of 'ordinary professional attendant with sanitary officer', to promote hygiene and prevent diseases afloat, it is probable that Cochrane sent him off to Haslar hospital for instruction.

In common with the purser and chaplain, the surgeon had emerged from warrant to commis-sioned status, receiving his training in a civilian hospital. Joining the navy in 1845 Assistant Surgeon Wells had been through the mill and was glad to be granted wardroom status in 1855, one of his first appointments being to a Portsmouth-based screw frigate. After promotion and prior to joining *Warrior* he had spent three years in the corvette *Racoon*. Against his name in the list of naval medical officers Director General of the Medical Department, · Sir John Liddell, had scribbled, 'a good medical officer. Writes pretty well. Has not operated on a living subject.' Ten years later when Wells was a staff surgeon on half pay – and probably earning good money in private practice – Liddell added, 'able, ill-tempered man in uncertain health'. At any rate, at the age of 39 in August 1861 Wells commissioned his sick berth and dispensary with two assistant surgeons – Josiah Austen and Edmund Coleman – two sick berth attendants and a sick berth steward. Right forward on the lower deck with scuttles on either side the sick berth included a dispensary, ten cots, an operating table and a curtained-off enclosure to interview patients. Wells was required to keep a journal and submit a daily sick list to the captain, the number being noted in the ship's log.

Sunday, August 11 was a fine day as the ship's company assembled on either side of the upper deck, not by divisions but in hundreds as entered in the ship's book or muster list. As soon as each hundred had been formed up the ship's company 'mustered by the open list'. This form of muster, originating from the days when the purser's salary was made up from nefarious practices, took place about once per month to ensure that each man was correctly paid according to his rating, good conduct badges etc. At a table amidships with the muster list stood the paymaster and his assistant, Joseph Howe, while the captain, commander, medical officer and master-at-arms were close by. Starting with chief petty officers each man advanced in single file to halt in front of the captain, remove his hat and state as follows, '218, sir – John Morgan – Leading Seaman – Seaman Gunner 1st Class – first class for conduct – one good conduct badge'. Replacing his hat he marched off. Surgeon Wells with his sick list answered for those in sick berth or hospital while the master-at-arms stated laconically, 'duty, sir' for those on watch. The ceremony was useful in that officers got acquainted with men's names and in the background lurked ship's corporals ready to pounce on anyone with particularly untidy appearance. Hardly had the ritual completed when there was a cry from the marine stationed as foc'sle sentry because attempting to cross the bows and bearing down fast were the mast and sails of a coastal vessel. It was the *Rover of Whitby*, possibly a collier, whose skipper had misjudged the strength of the tide which swept his ship down the starboard side of *Warrior*, his bowsprit carrying away one of the cutter's davits and an awning stanchion. The first lieutenant delivered a verbal broadside – to the delight of his audience – the incident was duly recorded in the deck log, the carpenter came on deck with his mates to assess the damage and the ship settled down to its first afternoon's rest for ten days.

Throughout the next five weeks without break all hands worked six days out of seven to prepare *Warrior* for sea. Aloft, the topgallant masts were hoisted, backstays set up, running rigging rove through blocks, standing rigging tensioned and blacked down, masts and yards scraped clean and sails either bent on to the yards or stowed below in the sail locker. After hoisting out the jib-boom, the fore topgallant and fore royal stays were set up, but on Sunday, August 28 the *Jesse of London*, while tacking across *Warrior*'s bows fell across the hawse and carried away the dolphin striker, not serious but annoying. The hulk *Hebe* was useful in that it provided accommodation not only for Penn's artificers but also for caulkers to complete sealing the decks and what the log describes as 'contract people' to assist cleaning the ship. A succession of lighters and hoys came down river to make fast to the starboard side, disembarking provisions and stores, some 2,000 rounds of 68 pdr shot and shell and additions to complement in the shape of petty officers, seamen and stokers. Among the subordinate officers who joined was Midshipman Henry Arthur Keith Murray. Finally came a visit from HRH the Duke of Oporto pro-

viding a rehearsal for a more important inspection a week later when the First Lord, the Duke of Somerset, accompanied by the First Sea Lord, Admiral Sir Frederick Grey, were to arrive.

For years the captain of a warship had been an aloof and somewhat remote figure with a status just a little below that of God. As he came up onto the quarterdeck – which in *Warrior* stretched from the stern to the after conning bridge – everyone on deck would move forward or vanish quietly. In his immediate presence hats were removed and nobody, not even the second-in-command, could speak to him except on service matters. The captain kept his distance and made sure others kept theirs, not from snobbery or arrogance, but because tradition demanded that there should be a gulf; moreover the ship's company liked it that way. In a new ship officers and men were invariably curious to assess the character of their commanding officer and the first opportunity would come when he addressed the ship's company, to tell them about the programme and what he expected from them. One captain delivered a commissioning speech that must have held the record for brevity. After assembling his men he ordered, 'sit down! . . . now stand up, you buggers. That's the last bloody sit you'll get this commission.'[12]

Arthur Cochrane was not of that ilk. Quite apart from his name – and that counted for a lot – he had a reputation for courage. On the lower deck were old shipmates who spread the word that 'the old man was all right'. Standing over six feet his articulate delivery evinced a sense of dignity and breeding that few could fail to admire. In disciplining defaulters over minor cases he had shown himself just and firm; the fact that he was a bachelor was further example of his total dedication to the Royal Navy. But the men had yet to hear him speak.

The opportunity came after captain's inspection of the ship above and below decks one Sunday in late August. As soon as divisions had closed either side of the upper deck abaft the mainmast, Cochrane ascended the ladder to the conning bridge to face his officers and men for the first time. He began by telling them about the ship, why and how it had been built and in what ways it was superior to Gloire. *About that vessel he added, 'and what's more at 12 knots she rattles like a brewer's dray on cobblestones' which brought a few chuckles. He told them of other ironclads being laid down and how they would strengthen the navy and in conclusion he emphasised, 'there is plenty of hard work ahead before we are fit to join the Channel Squadron. After docking at Portsmouth we shall be undergoing steam trials at Spithead and then cruising to Ireland to ascertain our sailing qualities. Everywhere we go we shall be closely watched and every admiral will want to come aboard. As well as being the most powerful ship in the navy, I can rely on you to show them that* Warrior *is also the smartest.' With that he nodded to the commander who ordered hands to dinner. As the men moved forward to*

●100 (110) pdr Armstrong
after pivot gun on
revolving carriage
and slide

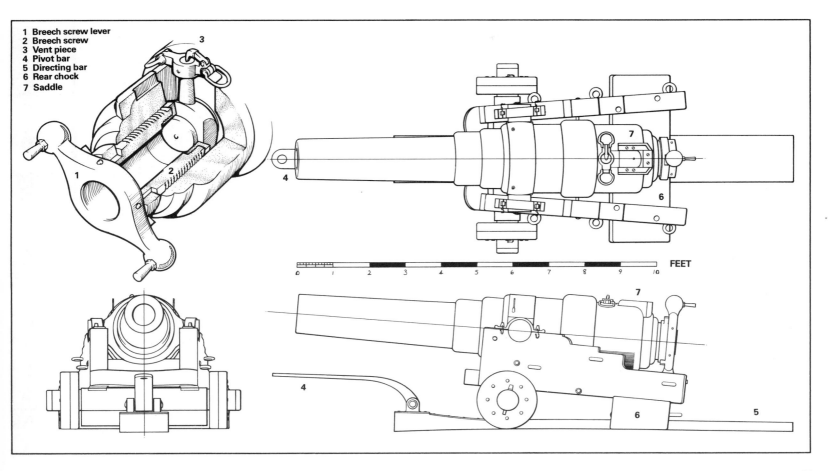

●100 (110) pdr Armstrong
on rear chock carriage

1 Breech screw lever
2 Breech screw
3 Vent piece
4 Pivot bar
5 Directing bar
6 Rear chock
7 Saddle

FEET

0   1   2   3   4   5   6   7   8   9   10

● Rev R Noble Jackson's portrait hangs in Winchcombe Parish Church, Glos

go below everyone was walking a little taller.

It had been intended that *Warrior* should receive her armament at Portsmouth but this was changed early in 1861 when orders were given to bring the ship forward for operational service 'as speedily as her progress in fitting out will admit'.[13] Instructions were given by the War Department at Portsmouth to the Royal Arsenal at Woolwich to prepare guns and carriages. The first instalment of Armstrong guns were loaded onto lighters at the Royal Arsenal pier, towed to Greenhithe and embarked at the end of August. First came the two 100 pdr pivot guns, then four 40 pdrs as secondary armament and finally the smaller 25 and 12 pdr boat guns. As all were mounted on the upper deck it did not take long to hoist them aboard by purchases rigged from the main lower yard. The first to be mounted in a major warship the guns became the centre of attraction as those seamen and marines trained in Armstrongs explained the breech mechanism to their messmates.

Early in September all 34 of the 68 pdrs were taken aboard in stages and again the main yard was used in conjunction with a heavy tackle rigged to the lower masthead, hoisting in first the carriages and then the guns themselves through a maindeck gun port amidships. Weighing nearly five tons each they were lowered carefully onto a carriage to be hauled away to their position in the battery where they were secured with breeching

rope, train and side tackles. Then captains of guns drew their equipment and side arms – rammer, sponge and worm – from the gunner's store and secured them in their allotted space. Stowage off the deck was essential since guns, which could be trained 30 degrees either side of the beam, recoiled up to six feet on firing, caused considerable concussion. Within 48 hours the deck had become crowded with the ship's armament.

In the days that followed guns' crews set to work scraping and cleaning; guns were painted black, carriages were treated with oil and the staves of side arms scoured until they were almost white. When the powder hoy came alongside flying its prominent red flag, all hands had to observe the strictest precautions against fire – no hot meals from the galley – while the metal powder charge containers were passed down with the greatest care through the gun ports to the fore and after magazines.

As *Warrior* dropped anchor off the little port of Greenhithe the locals came in their hundreds to marvel at the monster warship. Bumboats with bread, fruit and vegetables did a roaring trade during the dog watches when visitors were permitted to board. Among them was Charles Dickens, then aged 49 and living at Rochester. His impressions were recorded in *All the Year Round*[14] 'Yonder, a few hundred yards across the water, lies the *Warrior*; a black vicious ugly customer as ever I saw. Whale-like in size, and with as terrible

a row of incisor teeth as ever closed on a French frigate.' Clambering aboard by the ship's side ladder he meets up with what he calls the 'master gunner' – probably David Colinburn – who gave him a guided tour. After being told her vital statistics, Dickens is shown the armour on the gundeck and informed with great pride that 'the new vessels are to be an inch or two inches thicker and it is not improbable that in these vessels the woodwork will be altogether done away with. There are talks too of having four iron masts and rigging worked by machinery.' On the upper deck the author is shown the armoured tower describing it as 'a huge cauldron of some eight feet high pierced with loopholes for riflemen. It has been proposed to cut square ports at the base out of which would be run carronades to sweep the

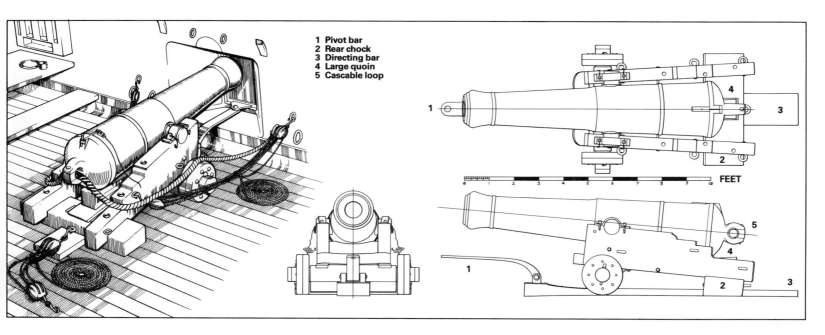

1 Pivot bar
2 Rear chock
3 Directing bar
4 Large quoin
5 Cascable loop

FEET

decks with canister shot if boarders once got a footing.' He also noted that 'sailors are working up and down stairs, mechanics were fitting up tables in the officers' cabins, marines were tugging at gun carriages, everyone was busy for the vessel was soon to be off to Portsmouth and thence to start in search of a storm, in order to test her sea-going powers. Going to look for a

tempest! What a young Titan it must be . . .'

His article concluded, 'the moral of all this is, that shipbuilding like all other human things – except Toryism – has changed, is changing and will continue to change . . . our ships . . . are now great machines – no longer the slow ships of Nelson's time. They require new fitting, new manoeuvres, new handling. Admirals and

captains will no longer be the men they once were. Mere dogged bravery and reckless bulldog courage will not do now; we shall want science and more comprehensive schemes of combination. The next war will show us that all sorts of new elements are introduced into fight by the use of iron steamships; and woe to those who are slowest to learn the new lessons . . .' Dickens was

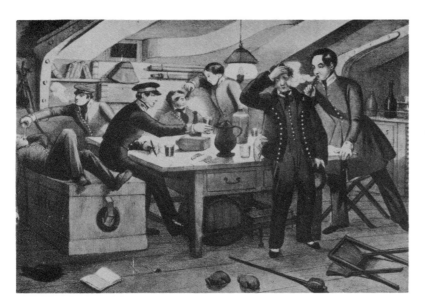

well ahead of current naval thought.

After divisions and captain's inspection on Sunday, September 8 hands were piped to 'rig church on the main deck'. Amidships either side were placed mess stools for the ship's company and chairs for the officers. The band arranged themselves in a convenient position. As Quartermaster Richard Smith tolled the bell for *Warrior*'s first divine service the Reverend Robert Noble Jackson MA felt mildly apprehensive. Born and bred in Leicester, Jackson went to Sydney Sussex, Cambridge, entered Holy Orders and joined the Royal Navy in 1855. To add to his emoluments he acquired the additional rank of naval instructor and on return from active service in the Pacific had married before joining *Warrior*. He was quite a character.[15]

Attendance at divine service in ships carrying chaplains was not only compulsory for members of the Church of England but accepted as an integral part of Sunday routine in the Royal Navy until after World War II. Since singing was popular both on the lower deck and in the officers' messes, Jackson had the sense to choose well-known hymns. The result was deafening. The captain and commander read the lessons; the padre's sermon held the congregation's attention for all of 15 minutes. The fact that the captain gave him a nod as they dispersed indicated that he was over his first hurdle. He was less successful when instructing the midshipmen in mathematics.

The gunroom flat was just forward of the wardroom, the midshipmen's mess or gunroom being on the port side with cabins and pantry to

starboard. Only a square table surrounded by lockers for seats furnished the mess; here some 20 to 25 'young gentlemen' – sub-lieutenants, midshipmen, cadets, assistant paymasters and clerks – lived, ate, drank, received instruction and took what leisure was left to them. They slept in hammocks slung wherever they could find a billet but mainly in the chestroom in the hold, which also contained water-tanks and an 18½in hawser. A cheerful, rumbustious crowd, the majority underwent a vigorous programme of training, were required to go aloft daily to the tops and had to keep a log of events. Always hungry, forbidden to drink spirits until 18, they were kept firmly in their place by Sub-Lieutenant Kelso.

For their future seamanship examination midshipmen were required to have a good knowledge of anchors and cables; in *Warrior* they would have found the heaviest in maritime history to be worked manually. Unlike today when warships berth alongside a jetty in harbour and have powerful engines at immediate call Victorian men o'war almost always anchored or moored in open water. Steam took a matter of hours to raise so plenty of anchors were needed to keep them out of trouble – *Warrior* had nine. Weighing five and a half tons the best bower (starboard) and small bower (port) were of equal dimensions and used for normal anchoring. Letting go first one and then the other it was usual to join the cables at the bow with a mooring swivel

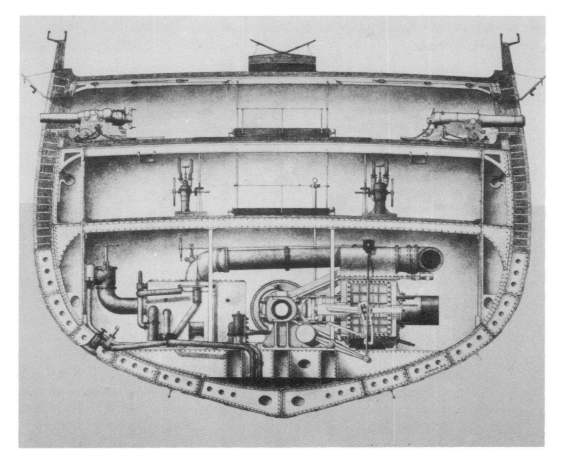

● Cross section of hull at engine room, drawn by Asst Engineer 1st class W Milln of the Warrior

to avoid getting turns in them when swinging to tide and wind. Of similar size and stowed abaft the bower anchors were the port and starboard sheet anchors – for use in emergency. Right aft were two stern anchors, a stream anchor and two of Rodger's patent kedge anchors, none weighing more than half a ton. The lead of hawsepipes brought the iron bower cables into the foc'sle at main deck level. The messenger technique for weighing anchor, similar to that used in Nelson's ships, is described in appendix VIII. There is evidence, however, that the bower cable was brought direct to Brown's patent capstan, the first to be fitted in a major warship.

The remainder of ship's boats now arrived from Woolwich. Throughout her first commission *Warrior* had ten boats – two launches, a pinnace, a gig and a galley, two cutters, a cutter gig, a jolly boat and a dinghy. Five were carried in davits aft, the remainder stowed amidship in the 'booms'. Under favourable conditions boats hoisted sails but otherwise the crews thought nothing of rowing inshore for hours or more at a stretch. By custom the 30ft gig, known as the galley, was the captain's boat and taken in hand by his coxswain, Petty Officer Peter Kinsley. The galley's crew of six seamen also looked after his quarters. At sea the two cutters were rigged as seaboats, ready to be lowered in event of a man overboard; on arrival in an anchor berth it was usual for various boats to be lowered to transport officers, men, victuals,

stores, ammunition and water to and from the shore. By day, when not in use, they were secured astern or to one of the 50ft lower (stunsail) booms fitted to the ship's side. At sunset it was customary to hoist all but the duty boats.

Of all the letters written to Cochrane on achieving command of the *Warrior* that from his old friend and gunnery officer Captain Arthur Hood was most valued. 'I must congratulate you . . . and say without any flattering that I don't think the Admiralty could have chosen a better man. I was very glad to see that you had selected Tryon . . . and think him peculiarly fitted for a commander of a large ship . . . his ideas of discipline and management of men are I think as good as any officer I have ever met. I . . . spent a couple of hours on board the *Warrior*; she certainly is a magnificent ship, handsome and I shall say must have great speed. I thought her bulwarks rather low and stokeholds rather confined and don't envy the poor devils as stokers. The quarter galleries I thought extra heavy. I heard that she was to have 68 pdrs on the main deck, from the ports having been so much narrowed. I think you will find difficulty in quick-firing with much elevation with them, which would not have been the case with Armstrongs. The iron lining of the upper deck seemed to be so very thin as to be of little real service, as any plunging shot which would penetrate a wooden deck will most certainly come through both . . . I hope you intend

(taking) the cable to the capstan which was – I saw – fitted for a messenger. It saves time and men so very much in weighing . . . You might get a good ship's company now with so many old men of wars being lately paid off and I wish you every success . . .'[16]

By the second week in September preparations for sea, aloft and in the engine room, were well ahead. During the first slow time evolution of 'up screw down funnels' the latter functioned correctly but after the screw-hoisting purchase had been tried efforts to raise the propeller had to be abandoned thanks to a bent pinion on the sheerlegs. To obtain the deviation error in the compasses on Monday, September 16 the ship was swung in circles on given bearings by a paddle tug towing the stern. Two days later the cable party removed the mooring swivel, gangways were hoisted and gun ports closed. *Warrior* was ready for her first sea passage.

CHAPTER SIX
Trials

EARLY ON THURSDAY, SEPTEMBER 19, 1861 the ship was unmoored to lie at a single anchor and precisely at eight o'clock the chief engineer reported that he was ready. Taking passage to Portsmouth – according to the *Times* – were Peter Rolt, Captain Ford and John Penn while ship's victualling records show that the party included Isaac Watts, William Bascomb and, representing Woolwich yard, Assistant Master Shipwright Philip Thornton with Chief Engineer's Assistant David Partridge. One wonders how cabin space was found and where cots were slung because arriving later in the forenoon and destined for the captain's suite was the First Sea Lord, Vice Admiral Sir Frederick Grey accompanied by Rear Admiral Charles Elliot, Cochrane's old friend from naval brigade days at Canton. A marine guard of honour was drawn up on the quarter-deck, but little time was wasted before Cochrane led the admirals to the conning bridge where the master and Mr Barnes, the pilot, waited. With permission to proceed, the captain ordered 'up anchor', the band struck up *Heart of Oak*, the first lieutenant bellowed 'heave round', and 200 men stepped it out round the capstans to bring the riding cable rattling through the hawsepipe. Shortly after 12.30 the report 'anchor's aweigh' was followed minutes later by 'clear anchor' as the best bower broke surface. The log recorded that the anchor buoy and 50 fathoms of rope had been lost, recovered later no doubt by some observant

waterman delighted with his good fortune.

Warrior's departure was unannounced, the *Times* remarking, 'there was no stir, no public excitement, no boats on the river to see the departure'. Ship's company lined the upper deck behind the bulwarks now raised to seven feet by the hammock nettings surmounted by a canvas 'cloth'. Conditions were perfect with little or no wind beneath puffy cumulus clouds. 'So quietly was everything managed that it was hard for those on board to know exactly when she did get under way and the first public exclamation was given by seamen riggers and work people on the hulk *Hebe*, who gave three tremendous cheers as the great vessel slowly and heavily moved down stream.' Commander Tryon reacted immediately whereupon 'the crew of the *Warrior* swarmed into the rigging and returned the compliment . . . and with this faint show of ceremonial the first voyage of the first and finest of our iron frigates was commenced'.[1]

Off Gravesend the river was so congested that speed had to be reduced to dead slow which caused a few uneasy moments. Then the channel broadened; and with less shipping about now the two tugs could be sent home, leaving the Woolwich paddle tender *Vivid* to follow astern. As *Warrior* increased speed the log recorded 'engines and boilers working very satisfactorily'.

Off Garrison Point, approaching Sheerness naval base, the sharp eyes of Yeoman-of-the-

Signals Beaver espied the tender *Wildfire* flying the flag of Vice Admiral Sir William Johnston who had come to watch *Warrior* pass. This called for the ship to hoist her pendant numbers, 42, the opening entry in the signal log, followed by the commission's first gun salute fired from the midships 68 pdrs starting with a starboard gun. The regulation five seconds between each gun was estimated by Gunner Colinburn using his own rigmarole, 'If-I-was-not-a-gunner-I-would-not-be-here-fire-two' and the port gun crashed out. Thirteen guns were fired, causing much smoke. To everyone's satisfaction the concussion effect was significantly less than in a wooden hull and little smoke penetrated the gunports. When

the salute had been returned *Warrior* headed for the open sea. At this stage the pilot 'proposed to anchor for the night as there was not water enough to take the vessel with safety over the flats'. But Cochrane was determined to press on for Portsmouth and it was agreed that the ship would take 'passage through the Swin, outside the Goodwins'. As *Warrior* gradually worked up speed to nine knots, the little *Vivid* dropped astern soon after five pm. *Warrior* promptly signalled, 'proceed at your utmost speed'.

As much to exercise seamen in handling new gear as to stretch untried canvas, the fore and aft sails were set on passing Margate Roads but handed (furled) again before turning to head the

wind off North Foreland. Dusk fell as *Warrior* passed the three bright lights of the Goodwin light vessel to starboard. By midnight, the flashes from Dungeness light, powered by the new electrical carbon arc lamps, were clearly visible. Considering the drag caused by part of the launching cradle, which was still fixed to the ship's bottom, her ten knots was more than creditable.

With the dawn of Friday, September 20 came rain squalls, low clouds and a freshening westerly wind as *Warrior* passed Beachy Head, the Owers and finally the Nab light vessel – the tower had yet to be built. Speed was reduced to embark the Admiralty pilot from *Pigmy*. Once Mr Jones was on board *Warrior* shaped course for Portsmouth.

The advent of the rifled shell gun and armoured warship had influenced not only the balance of naval strength but also the defences of dockyard ports, not least those of Portsmouth, then Britain's largest and most important naval base. Already the yard had been expanded to maintain steam vessels with machine shops, foundries and larger dry docks. In 1848 Queen Victoria had opened the Great Steam Basin, now known as Number Two Basin. Fear of a French invasion had caused the setting up of the Royal Commission of 1859 to advise on the country's defences; the committee, on which Cochrane had served, had recommended an arc of forts – six along the crest of Portsdown hill with five smaller ones guarding the approaches to Gosport – to protect Portsmouth from a possible landing by the French. To defend the dockyard from seaward four forts were to be built on Spithead shoals – Spit Bank, Horse Sand, No Man's Land and St Helen's off Bembridge. So expensive were they that Mr Gladstone, then Chancellor of the Exchequer, threatened to resign; but Lord Palmerston, the Prime Minister, was determined to have them and is reputed to have told Queen Victoria that he would rather lose Gladstone than Portsmouth. Years later the forts were referred to as 'Palmerston's follies', but still today they stand as solid examples of Victorian defensive strategy and military engineering.

Sails were furled before *Warrior* passed the Warner light vessel when Grey and Elliot joined Captain Cochrane on the bridge. With permission to anchor the ship circled the man o'war anchorage, saluted Vice Admiral Sir Henry Bruce's flag flying in *Victory* and 'came to' before nine in the morning in ten fathoms of water. Shortly before high water the anchor was weighed and Jones conned the ship into harbour, the entrance between Blockhouse Fort and Portsmouth Point having been cleared of shipping. The *Hampshire Telegraph* recorded, 'a number of persons assembled on the beach, the piers and ramparts to watch this splendid vessel which, when lying in Spithead near the *Emerald*, threw that frigate . . . into comparative insignificance . . . At about one o'clock she came into harbour . . . her length appeared enormous as she steadily passed along and eventually brought up alongside the (Masting) Sheers Jetty in the dockyard.'

First ashore when the ship was secured to the wall was an elated First Sea Lord. Both watches of seamen then cleared *Warrior*'s powder magazines into hoys that were towed across the harbour for temporary safekeeping in the Great Magazine at Priddy's Hard. To minimise the risk of sparks, no iron had been used in the magazine's construction. Doors, windows and shutters were sheathed in copper while double-skin brick walls ensured a cool, even temperature inside. Today it houses the Naval Ordnance Museum, a superb collection of weapons and ammunition.

Next day, Saturday, September 21, the ship's company 'turned over' to *Bellerophon*, the hulk used to accommodate personnel from ships refitting. The local paper then reported that 'the ship was successfully placed in dock number ten (which had been especially lengthened) . . . the operation being carried out with as much ease and regularity as attends the docking of an ordinary frigate. At noon the ship's head was brought to the entrance of the dock and at half past 12 she had been warped into the desired position over her blocks, with 15 inches to spare under the keel in the shallowest part of her block line. The water was afterwards pumped out of the dock to the ship's 10 ft water mark aft.' Men from Thames Ironworks then recovered 'the launching cleats from her bows and quarters' which had not fallen away after launching.[2] The remainder of water was pumped out of the dock and for the next two weeks the ship was in the hands of Portsmouth yard commanded by the Rear Admiral Superintendent George Grey.

We learn that 'workmen were employed in scrubbing her bottom which, contrary to expectation, was not found to be very foul' and that 'Hay's composition will be used to prevent dirt and weeds accumulating in future.' W J Hay was the Admiralty chemist and lecturer at the Central School of Mathematics and Naval Construction at Portsmouth and a pioneer in antifouling paints. His composition included protoxide of copper mixed with boiled linseed oil.

Penn's artificers examined the propulsion machinery while seamen rigged sheers to raise the propeller, successfully this time. New wheel ropes were obtained from the ropery presumably with advice from George Lane, the yard boatswain, while seamen transported the mizzen topmast to the mast house to have iron fittings replaced by copper, thus reducing deviation in the mizzen masthead compass. Dockyard workmen were working overtime to complete the ship said the *Hampshire Telegraph,* leaving an impression of haste in quitting Greenhithe. At that time the dockyards were responsible for completing much of the work on ships built in private yards.

Particularly pleased to be in Portsmouth was Reverend Jackson whose wife had given birth to a daughter at Ryde on the night of the passage from Greenhithe.[3] Assured that the dockyard chaplain would stand in for him he plucked up courage to seek leave from the captain. There was little rest for Cochrane himself because apart from the usual mass of callers he found himself a member of a court martial in *Victory* to try a marine private accused of stealing. Among the large number of visitors to *Warrior* was a detachment of Kingston Rifle Volunteers, complete with band, whose commanding officer, Major Cochrane, was distantly related to *Warrior*'s captain.[4] Despite the 'semi darkness which prevailed between decks'

said one Volunteer, they were amazed by 'her gigantic proportions', the impression of countless others, most compelled to gape from the dockside. In October Lord Palmerston called, followed by the Duke of Cambridge, the Bishop of Winchester, the Grand Duke Constantine and the Mayor of Portsmouth, starting an association between *Warrior* and the premier naval port that has never flagged. From trade came officers' tailor James Gieve and a representative of Stokes & Co who supplied wines and spirits to *Warrior*'s wardroom for the next two decades.[5] Examination of the wooden blocks under *Warrior*'s keel in dry dock revealed that they had been pressed down by three inches and as the *Army and Navy Gazette* reported subsequently 'sprang back to their original height from the floor' with no damage to the stone. As number ten was the only naval dock in England to take ironclads the Admiral Superintendent must have been duly relieved.

On Saturday, October 3 the dock was flooded, the caisson removed and the ship hauled out to a berth on Sheers Jetty. First task was to coal ship from lighters. Bags of coal came through gun ports and were emptied down chutes into the bunkers, an evolution which covered everyone and the entire mess deck with a fine coating of coal dust. Coaling rig was issued to the ship's company only at a later date.

Since leaving London's Victoria Docks there had been little chance to attain the spruce

appearance associated with the Channel squadron. So wooden stages were slung for hands to apply two coats of black paint from bulwarks to waterline. In contrast, a white line was painted on top of the bulwarks; davit boats, figurehead and conning bridges were also white. Funnels and rigging were painted black while masts, yards and tops were given a yellow buff colour. *Warrior*'s black hull set the tone for what was later to be called the Black Battlefleet and so distinctive that the Emperor of France was alleged to refer to *Warrior* as the 'black snake amongst rabbits'.

Painting completed, the ship moved alongside *Bellerophon,* transferred crew and baggage, sent up topgallant masts, bent on sails and prepared for sea. As the Admiralty's representative Rear Admiral Eden came aboard to observe sea trials. Leaving harbour on October 10 *Warrior* passed so close to a 131 gun warship moored midstream that the log recorded 'carried away port whisker (by the bowsprit) by fouling *Duke of Wellington*', an anxious moment for Captain Cochrane but nothing worse. The *Hampshire Telegraph* reported that, 'several hundred persons were assembled on the fortifications and on Southsea beach in order to see her pass to Spithead. The effect of improvements on her bestowed by painting etc was manifest and she presented a neater appearance than she did prior to entering her dock.'

After anchoring in Spithead a gale blew up that night and the duty watch were called to veer more

cable. When the wind eased powder hoys came alongside to fill *Warrior*'s magazines and shell room with her operational outfit. Now came the most important stage in *Warrior*'s extensive trials – proving her speed. Apart from *Gloire*'s claim to 13 knots – about which many were sceptical – the best speed on trial was attributed to *Mersey*, with 13.29 knots. Failure to better this would be disastrous for the navy's reputation and those responsible for the expensive, new ironclad. And the press were out in force!

On Monday, October 14 the weather set fair as *Warrior* with 800 victualled aboard left Spithead via the Nab for her trials. Besides the Controller there were four admirals and the private secretary to the First Lord, together with Captain Broadhead of the Steam Reserve, three other captains including Hewlett of the *Excellent*, Messrs Murray and Miller of the dockyard's engineering department and two of Penn's directors.

After clearing the Isle of Wight a channel swell began to be felt. By noon engine revolutions per minute had worked up to 52 but vibration was slight at bow and stern and none was felt aloft. By patent log over eight miles the speed was 12½ knots, sufficient to start turning trials. A complete circle to port took 11 minutes, nine minutes to starboard, each turning circle diameter being about 900 yards. Then 'from dead stop . . . the engines were started ahead to full speed in 11 seconds and from full speed were stopped dead in

31 seconds. From full ahead they were stopped and put on at full astern in 49 seconds,' no mean achievement.[6] The engines were then stopped so the ship could roll in the swell up to 15 degrees, no more than any other ship in the circumstances. Finally with wind and sea from astern she recorded 13 knots, a good augury.

On October 15 and 16 the ship was again swung to adjust compasses; bunkers were topped with fuel, boiler tubes swept, and the ship trimmed 12 ins by the stern. The arrival of a Russian corvette may have been coincidental but the Admiralty were taking no risks and signalled, 'no strangers are to be allowed on board *Warrior'*. Since Monday funnels had been lengthened by six feet to improve furnace draught; moreover engine room and stokeholds reaped the benefit of increased ventilation through the rigging of wind chutes as suggested by Captain Cochrane. Temperatures dropped dramatically thereby.

The morning of Thursday, October 17 saw a gentle south-easterly breeze and by nine am the commander-in-chief's steam yacht *Fire Queen*, the gunboat *Traveller* and the *Pigmy* had brought fresh visitors, more numerous and important than Monday's. Sir John Pakington was accompanied by Isaac Watts, Thomas Lloyd, Peter Rolt, Captain Ford, Mr Cradock of Portsmouth dockyard and others who had managed to be invited. Nominally in charge of the programme was Captain Broadhead; William Jones, the Admiralty

pilot, was to take the ship over the measured nautical mile. Situated between two pairs of beacons in transit, one pair at what is now Gilkicker Point and the other further west and inland from Stokes Bay, the measured mile was the accepted distance over which warships, including many from foreign navies, were steamed to determine best speed. Depth of water was just adequate for *Warrior's* size and speed.

Once underway *Warrior* headed for the Nab increasing to full power before turning to run in. Approaching Stokes Bay the engines had to be slowed to allow boilers to blow down but after that there was no stopping her as she carried out six runs averaging 53.8 revolutions per minute, three to the westward with the tide and three to the eastward against it. Eager for news the ship's company lined the upper deck while the officers packed both bridges to watch the seconds tick by on their half hunters. The captain even had to intervene to prevent the over-eager from obscuring the master's line of vision as he timed the four-minute runs between marks. After each run the ship made a 180° turn which took up considerable sea room. On one such turn from below the wardroom skylight came the sound of breaking crockery when breaking records was all that mattered. After the sixth run engines were eased; half an hour later Captain Broadhead announced results to a hushed company on the upper deck, 'subject to confirmation the average

speed was 14..4 knots,' which brought a spontaneous cheer followed by another when Chief Engineer Buchan came on deck to receive Cochrane's congratulations. Granted sea conditions were suitable, the ship had the right trim and the furnace coal from Aberdare reputedly possessed '20 per cent greater power than ordinary Welsh coals'.[7] *Warrior* was now the fastest warship in the world, a record unsurpassed for eight years and then only by half a knot. Even more gratifying, as the *Annual Register* later pointed out, 'the tremendous action of the engines and screw necessary to force the ship to the great speed, did not cause the slightest vibration – it is this perpetual shaking which speedily destroys the strongest built of the wooden men-o-war and suggests whether any nation can bear the expense of the perpetual renovation. Such however is the massive construction of the *Warrior*, that, so far as this action is concerned she is likely to last for ever.' Prophetic words.

Luncheon in the captain's cabin at Spithead was a festive affair with Sir John Pakington, Isaac Watts, Peter Rolt, John Ford and Mr Mathews (representing John Penn) among the guests. After the loyal toast Cochrane proposed the health of 'Sir John Pakington and success to the *Warrior*.' Sir John is alleged to have remarked to the chairman of Thames Ironworks, 'I often wonder, Mr Rolt, how I mustered sufficient courage to order the

●Rear Admiral of the
White Robert Smart

construction of such a novel vessel', to which Rolt replied, 'I often wonder, Sir John, how I mustered sufficient courage to undertake its construction.' It had been a memorable day not least for Isaac Watts whose award of Companionship of the Bath was announced shortly afterwards.[8]

For a week *Warrior* lay at Spithead, the first three days with Tryon in command while Cochrane was reporting progress to the Admiralty and discussing the future programme. On board the engines were inspected, the propeller raised and lowered for examination and some evolutions performed aloft. Meanwhile at the Shoeburyness artillery range on the Essex coast naval officers, led by the First Lord, watched the trials of 100 pdr Armstrong and 68 pdr guns firing at an exact replica of *Warrior*'s armoured belt measuring 20 ft by 10 ft. No projectiles penetrated the target; according to the *Army and Navy Gazette* the results proved 'of so satisfactory a character, as far as the old smashing 68 pounder is concerned, that for the present all intention of landing that portion of the *Warrior*'s armament which is made up of guns of this calibre has been abandoned.' This, added to the *Trusty* trials in September when the 68 pdr was found to be superior to the 100 pdr Armstrong for armour-piercing, led to the decision that only a small proportion of the latter would be mounted in *Warrior*'s broadside.[9]

For her next trial *Warrior* ran the measured mile on October 25 under reduced boiler power to determine fuel consumption. After runs with six out of ten boilers alight the average speed was 12.2 knots; with four boilers slightly more than 11 knots.[10] Fuel consumption disturbed the Admiralty to the extent that ships' logs were required to record the raising of steam by underlining the entry in red; unless curbed the new ironclads were going to devour coal. Meanwhile *Black Prince* joined the ships at Spithead and did a preliminary trial over the measured mile before going into harbour to be rigged. Results were inconclusive.

On October 28 *Warrior* sailed under steam and with reefed canvas, to anchor in Portland Roads that evening ready to start open sea trials or the 'first experimental cruise'. After embarking Lord Clarence Paget and Captain Drummond the ship sailed to meet and salute *Revenge* flying the flag of Rear Admiral Smart commanding the Channel squadron. Built in 1855 *Revenge* was a 90 gun liner but with an auxiliary engine and reputedly a good sailer. Next day Admiral Smart inspected *Warrior*'s company mustered at general quarters. Since Cochrane had served under Smart in the Pacific as a midshipman the admiral greeted him warmly. Three days later the two ships sailed in company for Queenstown (Cobh).

Almost immediately they ran into a westerly gale, ideal conditions for *Warrior*'s shake down and for comparing performance of vastly differing designs. Under steam *Warrior* had no trouble in maintaining ten knots with six boilers while *Revenge* not only struggled to keep up but consumed relatively more coal. When screws were raised, however, *Revenge* forged ahead both on and off the wind and was much quicker to turn. Finally on November 4 *Warrior* accomplished a 24-hour full-power trial under steam and sail, off the wind exceeding 16 knots and 'against a head wind and sea 9.8 knots'. Smart reported 'the performances of *Warrior* under steam have been most satisfactory.'[11]

Experiencing her first taste of moderately heavy weather it was hardly surprising that some of *Warrior*'s sails carried away; seamen had to be sent below to help stoke the boilers; the ash chute was lost overboard; water penetrated gun port lids and hatches and most of the younger ratings were seasick, a malady that the navy completely ignored. At general quarters guns were fired successfully; nevertheless the ship's company, learning all the time, were more than glad to anchor in the sheltered waters of Cork harbour on the evening of November 5 when a local paper hinted, 'on entering harbour *Warrior* was by no means obedient to the helm'.[12] Queenstown, commanded by Rear Admiral Talbot, had been a naval base, recruiting centre and coast-guard headquarters for some years.

After a short break the two ships sailed for Plymouth. As well as firing guns at extreme elevation and training, two different systems of night signals were tried out, one devised by Mr W H Ward and the other, more successfully, by Lieutenant Colomb, who took passage in *Revenge*.

Late on November 23 *Warrior* moored in Plymouth Sound, the focus of attention of naval and dockyard personnel alike. For a week she settled herself into fleet routine, cleaning and painting ship. For the next trial Spencer Robinson, the Controller of the navy, came aboard just before *Warrior* sailed for Portsmouth on November 23, when she worked up to full power with sails set.

Soon after departure Robinson expressed a wish to visit the engine room, so Cochrane had the chief engineer fetched to the bridge. 'A pleasure to escort you, sir,' exclaimed Buchan, 'but it can be terrible hot.' On the lower deck moving machinery could be seen from the engine room hatchway and as they went down further to the upper platform Robinson sensed a warm oil-saturated atmosphere in a space so dimly lit that he had to pause to get his bearings. Ahead he could make out one of the massive cylinders while below the huge crankshaft, connecting rods, trunk ends and pump rods moved in perfect synchronization. Buchan thrust a piece of cotton waste into his hand and beckoned him below. On the engine room floor a door was opened to allow him to see down the shaft tunnel and hear the distant rumble of the propeller. Then, with a wary eye on the rotating worm wheel of the engine-turning gear, he regained the platform on which stood the two engineers, one between the link motion control wheels watching the engine room

telegraph, while John Heffernan (later Admiral Sir John) – the senior engineer of the watch – logged readings of condenser vacuum and steam pressure. Speaking briefly to each officer Robinson noticed a leading stoker coming to report the amount of tallow used as two stokers lubricated moving parts with their oil cans. At 50 shaft revolutions to the minute the noise level was not high, just a ponderous humph - humph - grind, accompanied by the sharp hiss of steam from the trunk glands as the pistons reached the end of their stroke.

'D'ye want to see the boilers, sir?' asked Buchan. No turning back now, thought Robinson. Putting on a brave face he followed Buchan down to the auxiliary machinery space, groping round the foot of the mainmast. Avoiding the large rotating flywheel of the donkey engine the Controller was suddenly conscious of the gangway narrowness. Ahead was a door to the after stokehold.

After the ordered regularity of the engine room the activity in the 10ft wide passage between boiler fronts was Dantésque. Through the dust-laden gloom stabbed by the fierce light of furnace fires a few figures could be seen as the contents of a coal tram were tipped on the floor. Athwartships a muscular stoker in a sweat-soaked flannel shirt and fearnought trousers fed coal into an open furnace door. Methodically after each movement his shovel rebounded on the deck plate – a mysterious but apparently necessary stokehold custom. At the adjoining boiler another stoker armed with a slice or poker some nine feet in length, repeatedly lunged into the fire,

*shaking and breaking a mass of clinker while his mate
held a shovel in front of the furnace door to protect the
man's face from the fierce heat. As clinker came free the
slice, now red hot, was withdrawn and flung smartly
into a rack overhead. With a huge rake the stoker pulled
a cascade of white hot clinker onto the plates to be cooled
by a jet of water from a leather hose. Fumes and steam
rose as the water hissed into the bilges leaving a pile of
ashes to be hoisted up the vertical chute and dumped
overboard when time allowed.*

*Picking his way forward through the stokehold crew,
the harsh clangour of iron instruments ringing in his
ears, the Controller was thankful to reach the sanctuary
of the forward ladder. Half way up to the lower deck he
still found the heat so intense (120°) that it seemed to
scorch the very membranes of his nostrils. Back on the
bridge, his clothes soaked with perspiration, he gulped
fresh air – thanking God he wasn't an engineer.*

Ten hours after departure *Warrior* anchored in
Portsmouth having 'made a splendid run . . . nine
hours at full speed . . . the tide unfavourable
nearly the whole time'. The *Hampshire Telegraph*
continued, 'the maximum speed during the day
was 17½ knots under steam and plain sail to
royals; with the wind on the port quarter'. By any
standard it was good going.

*As soon as the ship had anchored Robinson and
Cochrane discussed the day's events, the Controller
clearly delighted with the ship's performance. Cochrane
was less happy. 'You will remember my concern, sir,
over the steering gear when I reported to the Board after*

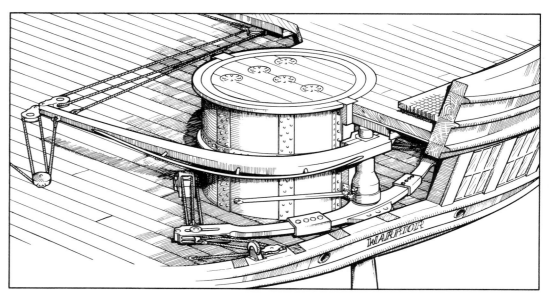

●Steering gear, as fitted
with new tiller (upper
yoke), 1862

the measured mile. New wheel ropes have been fitted and
all the slack taken up, but they function no better and if
anything they're worse. The yoke on the rudder is too
short and the distance to the steering wheels too great.
Under steam at slow speed the rudder loses its power due
to the escape of water through the screw aperture. She
won't answer her helm; in confined waters Warrior is a
danger to herself and to shipping.' The Controller
thought for a moment, 'so what do you propose?'
Cochrane handed over a drawing, 'after consulting the
Chief Constructor I intend replacing the upper yoke with
a curved tiller about 20ft long to improve the leverage, to
be fitted when we go into the dockyard. However, I've
something better in mind – a hydraulic steering
apparatus invented by Mr Renton. This does not require
the screw trunk to be reduced or any notable alterations
made to the rudder. What's more, the apparatus can be
plated with iron and the lower yoke, which restricts the
rudder to a movement of 26 degrees, can be removed. We
can then retain the upper yoke which is capable of being
put over to 35 degrees.' Spencer Robinson scrutinised
the sketch. 'It's worth a trial. Send me a letter about it
through the commander-in-chief and I'll see it gets a fair
wind.[13] The steering of other ironclads is also causing
concern and I'll be writing to you when I've spoken to
Mr Watts.'

Having despatched 'a list of some alterations
and defects desirable to be made good',[14] the ship
discharged powder and shell prior to going up
harbour on December 2. Warrior's steering again
proved ineffective and the best bower had to be let

go hurriedly to avoid hitting the 99 gun Duncan
moored in the stream; once Warrior was safely
alongside Sheers Jetty, the ship's company
moved over to Bellerophon leaving the ship largely
in the hands of the yard until new year's eve.

Although intended for Channel squadron
service rumours circulated about employing
Warrior on the North American station. Because of
outrages against foreigners in the Mexican civil
war the Prince Consort had suggested that Warrior
might be included in the Franco-British-Spanish
expedition to Mexico. Prime Minister Palmerston
contended that it would be imprudent 'to show
the French our hand before we have to play it out
against them. If we hasten to let them find out the
good qualities and faults of the Warrior we help
them to copy the merits and to avoid the defects'.

The Prince could but agree.[15] In the American
civil war Britain remained neutral although circumstances necessitated a show of British naval
strength; the possibility of war against the North
was openly discussed. There is apparently no
evidence that Warrior was seriously considered for
this role but not unnaturally their lordships had
no wish to be caught unprepared. Sadly Prince
Albert never lived to visit Britain's first ironclad,
there would have been much to challenge his
fertile brain.

All in all there was every reason to get Warrior
ready for service again as quickly as possible and
with Black Prince also on their hands Portsmouth
yard was hard pushed. The ship was moved until
first the screw with banjo frame and then the spare
blade could be lifted out when Penn's artificers,

according to the log, would 'repair and fit the spare blade'. Eight 68 pdrs were exchanged for eight 100 pdrs – now called 110 pdrs – and positioned at each end of the battery. Although the four 40 pdrs were due to be exchanged for 70 pdrs this never materialised. In her role as experimental ship main deck gun port lids were removed to try 'vulcanized india-rubber linings on their inner edges to render them watertight'; on Cochrane's suggestion the rifle tower was modified to make it an armoured conning position from which to fight the ship in battle. An access hatch was cut in the floor above the half-deck and engine room telegraphs led in together with voice tubes to magazines and battery. Despite Cochrane's enthusiasm the idea did not take off in later ironclads, even when a steering wheel was introduced with Renton's hydraulic gear. Ballard condemned them as impractical.[16] Another dockyard job was to install the new two-and-a-quarter ton tiller which must have played havoc with the captain's quarters.

Judging by the correspondence in the captain's letter book there was a great deal going on, much arising from Cochrane's initiative. A request was made for an additional 110 pdr gun on the upper deck – without addition to complement – and other letters sought the supply of a diving dress, a stove to heat the sickbay, scaling ladders for the use of boarders, a magazine ventilating fan with 80 ft of flexible hose and an aero-hydrogen blow

pipe 'for the heavy soldering' of ship's piping. Finally he asked for an additional blacksmith to tackle action damage, a lamp trimmer, three boatswain's mates to pass the word more efficiently through 'the great length of the ship' and an extra marines' gun grew.[17] Several officers took four days' leave for which privilege permission had to be granted by the commander-in-chief. Christmas day fell on a Wednesday and after divisions and church the captain and commander made the traditional rounds of the decorated messdecks.

From London the Controller wrote to Cochrane that Admiral Eden wanted to 'muster the Warrior at quarters on Monday (December 28) as he could not give another day to it'. In view of the critical situation in North America he concluded 'any moment may bring us news of peace or war'.[18] The day after the inspection Warrior cast off from Bellerophon and proceeded gingerly out of harbour, wondering if the new tiller would work. When the ship was anchored in Spithead an irate signal from the commander-in-chief demanded to know why the accommodation hulk Bellerophon had been left in such a deplorable state. Cochrane's reply was a masterly exercise in excuses that did not stop an officer and several men being sent to tidy up.

On January 4, 1862 berth was shifted to Cowes Roads where both funnels were yellow-washed prior to visits from the Prince of Wales, the Prince of Hesse and others eager to look round the ship.

When unmooring to return to Spithead the port cable parted at the anchor shackle. Within two days the anchor had been recovered by Lieutenant Digby and 80 men in a lump, (a heavy dockyard anchor lighter) and restored to the ship before she sailed to Plymouth, a feat of seamanship that earned young Digby Tryon's benison.

Before sailing on January 18 for the second experimental cruise, Cochrane received another letter from the Controller answering his recommendation that larger rudders should be fitted to ironclads.[19] The Controller doubted their efficiency, pointing out that the ship would steer better with the screw blades stopped athwart the stern and that to ensure the helm was properly put over an officer should be stationed right aft. Not a helpful letter.

The passage west was made at ten knots without sail on a fuel consumption trial. After anchoring inside the Plymouth breakwater on Sunday, January 20 the port watch was given overnight leave. Next morning nine returning libertymen took a waterman's boat which hoisted sail and set course for Warrior. When clear of the land the overloaded boat was struck by a squall and capsized. Four seamen, a marine and the waterman were rescued by Revenge's gig that happened to be passing but the waterman never recovered. He had previously lost both legs 'and used wooden ones which kept him afloat but reversed his body so much that his head was

almost continually under water'.[20] Two able seamen, a cook's mate, a carpenter's crew and a gunner marine also drowned. Shock and sadness was felt throughout the ship.

With 67 Gibraltar-bound supernumeraries on board *Warrior* sailed for Lisbon on January 21, 1862 under steam and with double reefed topsails. According to Cochrane's letter of proceedings, 'the wind was fair for a short time after leaving port when we encountered a series of heavy gales from south to south west until our arrival in Lisbon. I may mention that in the *Times* newspaper Admiral Fitzroy had stated that a SW gale was due the day of our departure from Plymouth. We were also exposed to the heaviest beam swell or rollers from the westward that I ever saw.'

On the first night out in pitch darkness and with the ship rolling heavily the watch on deck had to put in a third reef in the topsails, furl the mainsail, send down the topgallant yards and house the topgallant masts. Losing sight of the Lizard on January 22 the ship encountered a confused cross swell, the carpenter's crew were engaged securing bag racks that had carried away and the sick list went up to 75. For three more days the wind blew steadily fresh to strong gale reaching force 11 (storm) on the Beaufort scale. Altering course to south south east for two days *Warrior* snouted into the Atlantic, engines turning at 14 revolutions to make good 110 miles in 24 hours. Because seas continuously broke over the forward bulwarks, lifelines had to be rigged on both sides of the upper deck. Here the experience

of petty officers and older hands told. The barometer logged what today would be called a small intense depression that brought cold leaden skies with scudding clouds and frequent showers.

With minimum sail, and that heavily reefed, all eyes were aloft to watch the movement of spars. It was probably the boatswain who first noticed that the main yard had sprung. When the wind moderated under the lee of Cape Finisterre the cracked spar with its sail and gear was lowered to the deck to be fished (stiffened) by binding it with two specially shaped pieces of wood before rehoisting. Two booms were washed over the side, sails were split, stays parted, one of the jolly boat's davits on the stern carried away and the boat nearly lost. With engines stopped the jib-boom was brought in to avoid damage, a dangerous operation personally conducted by the commander and boatswain. Below decks conditions were less than comfortable, 68 pdr shot broke loose, there were many breakages and, despite recent dockyard work, water found its way down to the engine room. Alongside the eight helmsmen wrestling with the steering an exhilarated Cochrane felt confident of *Warrior's* ability to weather any storm. In his words she 'did not strain nor did any of the armour loosen in any way . . . the ship and engines arrived in Lisbon in thorough working order, if a slight spring in the main yard which was . . . thoroughly well fished and the clews of the fore and fore topmast staysail being torn out by the violence of the wind be excepted . . . the passage was made without accident of any kind.'[21] The harder the blow the higher officers and men will rise to the occasion and the more cheerful they become.

If seamanship had been tested during the eight days so was engineering since the ship was under steam with six boilers or more all the time. For three days and nights the two chief engineers worked watch and watch because 'the boilers were foul, coals small and inferior and steam was kept with great difficulty'. Three gauge glasses were broken by seas washing down from the upper deck and eight seamen had to be sent below to lend a hand in the stokeholds. Daily at noon Buchan reported to Cochrane the amount of coal remaining. When they reached harbour there were just 49 tons in the bunkers – mostly slack!

On January 28 *Warrior* passed inside the Portuguese Burling Islands and hove to for a night off Cape Roca before proceeding up the Tagus early next morning to Lisbon. 'Then we joined the flag of Rear Admiral Sydney Dacres in the *Edgar*, which vessel sailed on February 1 and on the third . . . HM Yacht *Osborne* arrived and sailed. This vessel had encountered similar weather to ourselves and had put into ports twice for several days to avoid it . . . the mail packet from England was also delayed some days by the weather.' While moored in the Tagus *Warrior* took on 254 tons of Welsh coal, cleaned ship, repaired storm damage and sent down Joseph Hemming, ship's diver, to shackle on the rudder pendants. By February 3 the ship was ready and waiting for the 'whole of the Corps Diplomatique at Lisbon' which arrived en bloc to visit – or spy on – the new ironclad. On their departure gun salutes were given to the Russian, Austrian, Swedish, Spanish, Italian, Dutch, Prussian, Danish and Belgian ministers. When the smoke had cleared and the guns sponged out Daniel Colinburn uncharacteristically took the chief gunner's mate down to his cabin and in companionable silence – both now rather deaf – they swallowed a stiff tot of rum. It was not often that a total of 107 saluting rounds had been fired without delay so early in a commission.

Next day, the ship dressed overall with flags

and yards manned, a royal salute of 21 guns thundered out to the King of Portugal who 'honoured the ship with a thorough inspection'. On February 6 while unmooring ship Cochrane reported, 'the foremost (Brown's) capstan gave out and is now completely useless . . . a miracle some more serious accident did not happen. The messenger was then got up and the two after capstans used. The operation of heaving in was very slow when suddenly the connecting plate of the capstans gave way. . . . it was too dark to cross the bar and we waited to the next morning.

Cochrane continues, 'I had intended to have made a first class passage between Lisbon and Gibraltar, the same way as *Gloire's* run from Toulon to Algiers. So on leaving Lisbon we made sail and steamed with ten boilers. Rounding Cape St Vincent one of the cylinder covers was found cracked.' Steam pressure was reduced and 'the cylinder cover shored up from the side'. In spite of that setback 'we made the passage . . . to Gibraltar in 22 hours which I believe is the shortest passage on record, giving an average speed of 14 knots.'

During the ten-day spell at Gibraltar repairs were made to both cylinder covers – the other cover was found cracked on arrival – and the 'after capstan re-cast'. Stoker Phillips died of heat exhaustion, to be buried with full honours in the naval cemetery. The Governor, General Sir William Codrington, visited *Warrior* as did many of the public. After embarking 'naval and military

●Gunner, Royal Marine
Artillery, William
Mallion

invalids for England', mails – and a case of wine for the C-in-C – she sailed for Plymouth.

Cochrane reported, 'steam was used on leaving Gibraltar. On rounding Cape St Vincent the wind was scant for laying along the coast and the heavy rollers still continued; so steam was used with the greatest economy in combination with sail until northward of Oporto when we proceeded under sail across the bay.'

On February 22 general quarters were exercised and a barrel with stave and flag dropped over the side as a target. While leaning over the stern to remove the tampion from the after 110 pdr William Mallion, Gunner RMA, fell overboard. Corporal John Nye, captain of the gun, saw him disappear, shouted 'man overboard' and ran to release a lifebuoy. Lieutenant Perceval, officer of the watch, ordered 'stop engines – full astern – away lifeboat's crew'. As the crew manned the weather-side cutter a seaman was sent aloft to keep an eye on the gunner who had managed to reach the lifebuoy and was now bobbing in the ship's wake. By the time the boat was lowered to the waterline way had been taken off the ship, making it easier to slip the boat using Clifford's gear. The captain and other officers were now on deck as the boat in charge of Midshipman Cockell pulled towards the lifebuoy. Ten minutes later he was back having recovered Mallion apparently none the worse for his dip. Gunnery training resumed. The ship steamed at six knots round the

target for her first practice shoot, firing 48 rounds of 68 pdr and ten from the Armstrongs at a range of half a mile. Performance was satisfactory.

After stopping to use the deep sea lead off the Lizard, Blakey's ability as a navigator was rewarded by sighting the Eddystone dead ahead. Cochrane reported that *Warrior* then 'steamed into Plymouth where I have the honour to report my arrival and to observe that the ship and engines are ready for service.' Forwarding a list of defects that dockyard staff would have to make good during *Warrior's* forthcoming refit in the Hamoaze, the commander-in-chief assured their lordships that while it was essential to make good the deficiencies there was nothing to stop *Warrior*

proceeding on any special service, if so required.[22]

Carpenter Davidson's considerable list of defects that dockyard staff would have to put right during *Warrior's* forthcoming refit stemmed from the severe Biscay weather which included damage to the figurehead, heads, hammock nettings, bow light box, anchor stock and bowsprit wedges as well as water penetration. In his final report Cochrane stressed 'the very great danger to a bowsprit and jib-boom in steaming head to a heavy sea with any speed. The ship would be much benefited by being lightened at the bow, were it possible to dispense with the bowsprit.'

Commenting on the ship's heavy weather performance Cochrane's letter of March 15 to the commander-in-chief mentions the need to 'lay to under fore-and-aft sails *and* steam' when confronted with exceptionally severe weather. But 'the ship did not strain and indeed from her immense strength, iron decks and iron vertical bulkheads it does not seem possible she ever can'. Rolling 'was easy but deep' and the pitching was not abnormal, although it might have been if 'urged by her immense engine power in heavy weather'. The Controller would have been glad to hear that 'the new tiller gave much greater facilities for moving the helm' and, as regards armament, 'she could well carry three more guns on the upper deck'. He alluded to the problem of vibration in the compasses and again argued that the ship would benefit from a larger rudder with better configuration.

After analysing Cochrane's reports and diagrams covering every detail of weather, ship behaviour, sail settings and fuel consumption, the Admiralty must have been gratified that their gamble had paid off.[23] Although *Warrior* had passed her trials with flying colours the country and the rest of the navy would want to assess how she matched expectations.

As there was then no Official Secrets Act the press were seldom inhibited from discussing new warship construction, and *Warrior* was no exception. There had always been criticism of her design, mostly unfounded, but for such a radically new ship it was inevitable, did little harm and generated publicity. Using experience with *Mersey* to best advantage and faced with the need to build a hull strong enough to withstand adverse weather, the weight and recoil shock of large calibre guns and the effect of damage from enemy gunfire, Watts had been cautious – perhaps overly so – in his design. The result was heavy but immensely durable, a pivotal point in naval architecture. That *Warrior* has survived until today is a lasting tribute to his skill and to the vision of Admiral Sir Baldwin Walker. '*Warrior* is a grand success, wrote John Briggs, the Admiralty's chief clerk to Walker, 'Your last triumph in your capacity as Controller.'[24]

Her trials performance silenced many armchair critics, particularly those who queried her seakeeping qualities, leaving the vulnerability of her bow and stern, particularly the latter, as the flaw never to be tested in battle. More serious perhaps – due to the ship's great length – was the ship's unhandiness in steering. But shortcomings were more than outweighed by her good points and the invaluable lessons learned for subsequent construction. By the spring of 1862 *Warrior* and *Black Prince* were accepted as the most powerful warships afloat.

● Warrior moored in
Hamoaze, Plymouth
probably June 1862
(photo by Long)

CHAPTER SEVEN
First commission

ON WEDNESDAY, MARCH 5 1862 *Warrior* moored in the Hamoaze off Devonport dockyard to undergo alterations and make good defects. With no dock large enough to take her, there she remained for three months while work progressed.

Under Admiral Superintendent Sir Thomas Pasley senior yard officers were determined to outdo their Portsmouth rivals and the fact that *Warrior*'s boatswain had recently worked in the yard foreshadowed an easy relationship. Apart from repairing defects the ship had to be made less bow-heavy and weather-proofed below decks. Seven feet were cut off the jib-boom and a shorter, thinner bowsprit fitted; sheet anchors with their catheads and fish davits were moved aft to improve trim. So too were the 68 pdr guns: the two mounted in the cabins of the commander and master cannot have been popular with them! As heavy seas made the forward heads virtually unusable, Cochrane insisted upon additional heads on both sides amidships which proved a godsend although they hardly improved the ship's appearance. Water continued to enter the gunports, causing Carpenter Davidson to spend hours discussing solutions with James Peake, the yard's master shipwright. They proposed fitting the gunport lids with india rubber on the port side and fearnought to starboard to see which made the best seal. When fighting the guns it was accepted that water would be shipped through the open ports but the free water slopping around

in the bilges could not be reached by existing pumps. To raise the level of water to where it could be pumped out 70 tons of bricks and mortar were built into several compartments. Chief Engineer Buchan then turned his attention to improving his stokers' conditions. Doors were fitted between fore and after stokeholds, and to reduce heat exhaustion ventilation at furnace fronts was increased by altering funnel casings. Elsewhere hatches and skylights were made watertight, two stronger capstans and towing bollards fitted, four boats exchanged and one of the new patent Trotman anchors supplied for trial.[1] Finally a fresh carpet was provided for Cochrane's cabin to replace what was 'very much worn and discoloured . . . so often wet it has shrunk two feet'. Evidently *Warrior* was a wet ship.[2]

Throughout the refit officers and men remained on board. The hulk *Atholl* was brought alongside so that the sailmaker could lay out more readily those sails needing attention. There were many, thanks to that last gale. The midshipmen were kept busy drawing the contents of each deck of the ship for their logs, Midshipman Keith Murray's efforts being commended by the captain. In April seamen and stokers were sent for gun drill in *Foudroyant* and the gunnery training ship *Cambridge*. Even so dockyard routine disrupted discipline and there were cases of insubordination and drunkenness that would have occurred less frequently had the ship been

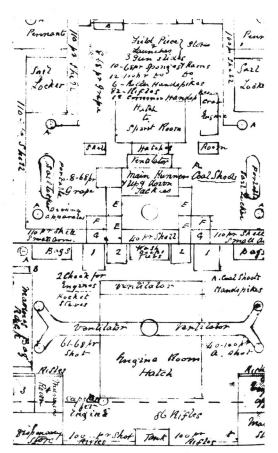

● Part of sketch in Murray's journal showing lower deck

● Midshipman Henry Keith Murray

● John Wigston recaptures the atmosphere of a typical *Warrior* messdeck

fully operational.

Each morning Master-at-Arms George Hendlay reported to the commander with the conduct book. A gaunt, iron grey-haired man, Hendlay was respected by the ship's company and feared by the rogues. Through the four ship's corporals he had established an effective intelligence system and invariably knew what was going on. Behind seven years' experience lay a deep interest in the lower deck's welfare. This morning, May 12, he was worried and showed it. 'Fifteen defaulters to see you, sir, 12 men absent without leave and there's a telegram from Portsmouth police saying they've got Boy First Class Morgan'. Commander Tryon sighed; the defaulters list was lengthening daily. 'And that's not all, sir,' continued Hendlay bluntly, 'we've thieves on board. Ordinary Seaman Todd 'as reported two sovereigns taken from his ditty box, probably by Morgan before he deserted. Bounty scum, sir, if I may say so, are behind it all. Barry is one and maybe Harries another. But I'll catch 'em, sir, that I promise.' Warrior *had certainly received her share of disreputable characters, but thieving had to be stopped.*

Three days later Harries and Morgan were charged with a variety of offences. Neither had anything to say, Harries remaining almost contemptuous, 'a troublesome and worthless character holding out no hopes of reformation'.[3] *Morgan had drifted into bad company and wanted to quit the navy. Next day warrants for their punishment were despatched to the commander-in-chief for his approval.*

At daybreak on Tuesday May 20, the morning gun daily fired by the flagship was answered in other ships by sentries' rifles and the beat of the drum sounding reveille. In Warrior *it was followed by the pipe, 'clear lower deck — hands lay aft to witness punishment'. Officers and men assembled by divisions with a Royal Marine guard paraded port side. A heavy grating had been lashed vertically on the starboard bulwarks where four boatswain's mates stood, each carrying a cat o' nine tails in a red baize bag. Hats were removed as Cochrane read out the appropriate article of war followed by charges, results of investigation and the sentence of 48 lashes. Harries was stripped to the waist and a handkerchief tied round his neck. Spread-eagled over the grating he was bound hand and foot. At the order 'carry out the sentence' the master-at-arms nodded to the senior boatswain's mate who delivered 12 lashes, each shouted out and recorded by a ship's corporal. Early strokes produced red streaks making the victim's muscles quiver visibly. By the end of the first dozen Harries' back was a dull red mess. Another boatswain's mate took over and at the 18th stroke his back was like a lump of meat. Well-built and hardened, Harries bore his punishment without a murmur — until he was unlashed and half carried to the sick bay. Barely 18-years-old and far less accustomed to pain Morgan found 36 lashes unbearable; towards the end many turned away from his cries. By 6.30 the ship's company had dispersed in silence. Unable to face breakfast Midshipman Harry Grenfell ran to the heads and was violently sick.*[4]

The 1862 naval return of crime and punishment records the flogging of more than 1,000 men

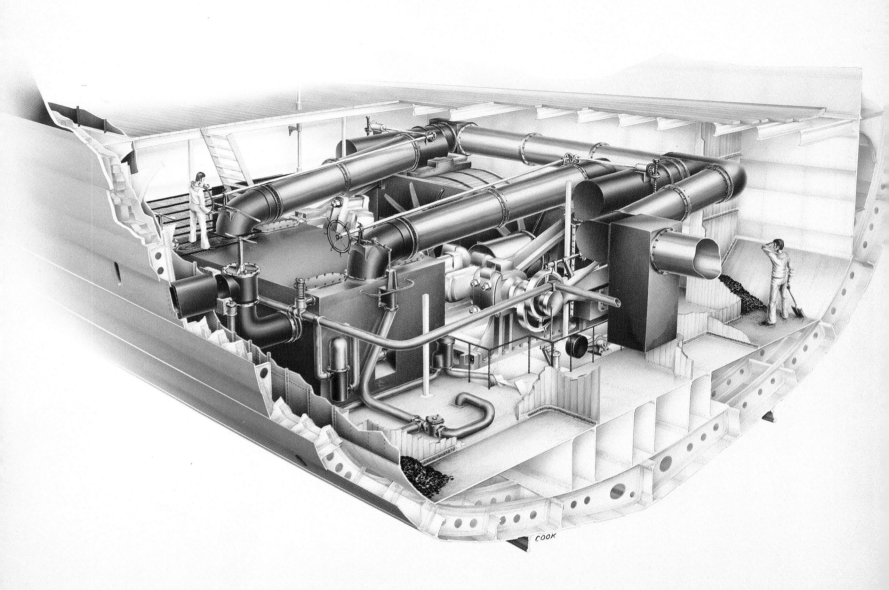

COOK

out of a total strength of 54,000, averaging 34 lashes per man. Leave-breaking accounted for 70%, drunkenness 19% and insubordination 9% of the crimes committed. In *Warrior* it had its effect once troublemakers realised Cochrane meant business. The defaulters lists shortened, thieving stopped and the lower deck were happier for it. After nine months in commission most of *Warrior's* ship's company were proud of their ship, particularly so when news was passed that approval had been given for the purchase of '500 hat ribbons with the name of the ship traced upon it in gilt letters . . . cost to be one shilling each'.[5]

Escorted by four tugs and piloted by Commander Harry Paul, assistant master attendant, *Warrior* sailed for a full power trial to the Eddystone on Friday, June 6. Aboard were Captain Astley Cooper-Key in charge of the Steam Reserve, together with Chief Engineer John Trickett from Keyham Steam Factory. A fresh southerly gale and a barnacled bottom prevented a repetition of the performance in Stokes Bay, but authorities expressed 'satisfaction with results'. All on board were glad of a good blow to remove the cobwebs before returning to the Hamoaze.

Four days later *Warrior* sailed for Queenstown to join the Channel squadron. Rounding Land's End with double-reefed topsails and topgallants, the ship ran into a heavy swell but to everyone's delight little, if any, water found its way below. Leading Seaman Pascoe, the newly appointed captain of the midships heads, reported to the first lieutenant that the new arrangements were much appreciated. In Cork harbour hands worked over the weekend to make the ship presentable for Admiral Smart's arrival in *Revenge*, accompanied by the frigate *Emerald*, the sloop *Chanticleer* and the paddle sloop *Geyser*. When the squadron sailed for Milford Haven to attend the launch of *Prince Consort*, *Warrior* carried out another full power trial, this time successfully.

Laid down in 1861 as the 90 gun *Triumph*, the *Prince Consort* was one of five wooden battleships converted to ironclad, her name changed to commemorate the sovereign's late husband. It was a festive occasion for Pembroke Dock and the signal log records that *Warrior's* Commander Tryon and Lieutenant Perceval, son of the Queen's Chaplain, were invited to dine with the admiral in the flagship to meet young Prince Alfred. Immediately after the launch the squadron sailed for Spithead where *Warrior* spent ten days receiving visits from the Prince of Wales, Prince Alfred, Prince of Hesse, the Viceroy of Egypt, the Crown Prince of Prussia and Prince Napoleon. Four days in dock were followed by efforts to lighten the bows further by transporting hemp cable, carpenter's stores, 68 pdr shot and some water tanks as far aft as possible enabling the ship to achieve her 'best sailing and steaming trim' of 25 ft forward and nearly 27 ft aft. After undocking and coaling *Warrior* returned to her Spithead berth

● Channel squadron circa
1863, showing Warrior on
right

by which time the donkey engine was able to pump water on the upper deck to ease the job of holystoning coal-caked decks. Hitherto pumping had been done by hand.

Soon after commissioning Cochrane had reported to the Admiralty that he had been approached by a Mr Williamson of High Holborn about installing a clothes-drying apparatus in *Warrior*. Since hammock gantlines strung above the upper deck during wet, winter months were clearly useless the advantages of such a 'drying closet' he considered 'would be . . . very great'.

Their lordships gave the go ahead and a compartment under the sailroom was fitted out with a special stove when the ship was in Devonport. The first drying room in the Royal Navy commissioned in ·June. Writing to his commander-in-chief Cochrane remarked that the apparatus was able to dry 120 hammocks or 320 pieces of clothing in about five hours using only 80 lbs of coal.[6] *Warrior* had scored again.

Trials and refit behind her, *Warrior*'s task now was to become proficient in sail drill, gunnery and seamanship. After another swing under the

guidance of Evans and Craigie to record compass deviation the ship sailed for Portland. Half way between Portsmouth and Plymouth, Portland was a day's steaming from either, ideally situated for training. Although a breakwater was half built the anchorage in the Roads was safe but exposed; in winter it could be bleak.

For major evolutions Tryon had three manpower options – 'all hands', 'both watches' or a 'watch'. 'Clear lower deck – all hands' would be summoned in an emergency, for making all plain sail and often for reefing sails, wearing ship or even tacking. 'Both watches', however, often sufficed particularly at the change of watches when maximum numbers would be on deck. Drills were classified as 'all hands' or 'watch' evolutions, regularly performed at sea and often in harbour, with a hands drill at evening quarters. Shifting, or changing, sail was popular because when sails split or blew away in a gale, bending fresh canvas and rehoisting had to be done at speed. Smaller topgallant and royals were bent and unbent on deck, the yards being sent down with sails on them, but the larger topsails and courses were manhandled from the sailroom to their respective yards, furled and stopped up ready for bending on.

Proficiency depended on team-work and regular practice. With no deck lighting men had to work at night by familiarity feeling the edge ropes of the sails and knowing instinctively the lead of ropes to the belaying pins. When topmen leapt into the weather rigging in the teeth of a gale to fist wet canvas flogging with the sound of gunfire each man knew exactly what to do. To the newly-joined, knowing the ropes was no figure of speech.

Most seamen took pride in literally racing up the ratlines barefooted to run out along the yards without handhold. Developing the powerful physique and balance of acrobats they acquired an unusual degree of nerve as yard was set against yard, mast against mast and ship against ship. Such was the pride in personal achievement and so keen the competition that men were tempted to take desperate and sometimes fatal risks.

Before the training programme had got very far news broke of the imminent arrival of the Admiralty Board in HM Yacht *Osborne* to run their eye over *Warrior*; for they were still at odds over the size and shape of future ironclads. *Osborne* had no sooner anchored on August 11 when Cochrane visited her to pay respects. 'They want to see us steaming with six boilers and then under sail,' he told Tryon on his return. 'We'll show 'em, sir,' retorted the commander.

Next day when the paddle yacht left harbour *Warrior* steamed past twice at 11 knots within half a cable (100 yards). The engineers had reduced funnel smoke to a mere wisp and *Warrior* looked impeccable. Then came the real test. In full view of the Board clustered around *Osborne*'s superstructure *Warrior* stopped to demonstrate the results of months of drill.

Apart from the signalmen and lookouts there was not a rating in sight above *Warrior*'s upper deck while the captain, commander and master stood next to the officer of the watch on the conning bridge, their eyes intent on the signal hoist in *Osborne*. As it came down Tryon ordered through his speaking trumpet, 'all hands make plain sail'. Before the sharp trills of the boatswain's pipes had faded away 500 men had leapt into position.

'Upper yardmen to the tops.' Captain of tops, selected midshipmen and upperyardmen raced up both sides of their masts leaving hands on deck to man sheets and halyards. 'Sail loosers stand by' was purely precautionary to allow upper yardmen their regulation two-minute breather following Admiralty alarm at the incidence of heart disease among the *corps d'élite* of seamen.

'Away aloft masthead.' In fluid movement top gallant and royal yardmen raced to their stations while the sail loosers took up positions on the topsail and lower yards. 'Trice up, lay out, hoist the jib,' came next, each sail looser casting off his gasket and supporting the sail with both hands.

'Let fall, sheet home the topsails.' Letting the topsails fall the loosers regained the cross-trees while deckhands hauled away the sheets onto blocks on the yards below. On the command, 'topsail halyards – hoist the topsails' all three topsail yards were hoisted simultaneously. Topgallants and royals followed suit. Then the flying jib was hoisted and finally, 'let run the gear of the courses'. Down came the heavy fore and main canvas to be sheeted home by every man on deck. Apart from commands the evolution had been carried out in silence.

'I made it five minutes 40 seconds,' Cochrane told Tryon. 'You have some good men there but the main topsail was let fall before the yard-arm gaskets were clear.' As he spoke there was a loud report and the sail in question split down the middle. 'Stand by to shift main topsail,' roared

• Black Prince circa 1870. Commissioned May 1862 into Channel squadron until 1866. Coastguard, Queenstown 1867 then refitted and rearmed as for Warrior. Coastguard Clyde 1868-74. Refitted and equipped with poop, steam steering and iron masts 1874-5. Channel squadron and visit to Canada 1875-8. Reserve Devonport 1878-96. Training ship Queenstown 1896-1910. Joined Impregnable for boys training at Plymouth 1910. Sold to shipbreakers February 1923

Tryon, 'look lively there Mr Beaton.' And so it went on. The two ships parted company, their lordships satisfied that the new ironclad was shaping up and *Warrior* aware they still had something to learn. Before the end of August permission was given for the ship to cruise alone to the Scillies and back to concentrate on sail drill.

Throughout September 1862 until the Channel squadron's arrival *Warrior* continued to work up while at anchor in Portland Roads. A visit from Admiral Prinz Adalbert flying his flag in the Prussian frigate *Gazelle* enabled Captain Cochrane to pay a call and speak well of Premier Lieutenant Von Blanc of the Royal Prussian Navy serving aboard *Warrior* for training. The most exciting event was the arrival of *Black Prince* having recently commissioned in Devonport under Captain James Wainwright.

Launched from Napier's Yard on the Clyde two months after *Warrior* entered the Thames, *Black Prince* was ordered to Portsmouth under jury rig for completion in the dockyard. Although the press reported that her hull had a much handsomer and lighter appearance than *Warrior*'s they were virtually identical sister ships except for speed. *Black Prince*'s full power trials were disappointing in that 'she could not better 13.6 knots'. There was rivalry between the two but it was friendly as demonstrated by *Warrior*'s manning yards and cheering her sister on anchoring. *Black Prince* responded similarly and

wardroom visits were exchanged. A fortnight later both ships were placed temporarily under the command of Rear Admiral Sydney Dacres, second in command of the Mediterranean fleet, when he arrived in *Edgar*, accompanied by the screw frigate *Liffey*, anxious to see the new ironclads. On October 1 the four ships sailed for Lisbon, each wearing a red ensign at the gaff to signify the colour of their admiral's squadron.

There was more rivalry when the two ironclads were ordered to 'try a rate of steaming' on six boilers for an hour. *Warrior* won by 1,000 yards.

Three days later the trial was repeated, this time for two hours. Again *Warrior* forged ahead. After a brief stay at Lisbon they were off to Gibraltar where a third duel is described by Tryon writing to his father. 'We raced the *Black Prince* at full speed . . . through the "gut" into the Bay of Gibraltar. It was a pretty sight, two such immense ships tugging away as hard as they could go, with the greatest excitement on board all vessels. We passed our wooden friends as though they were at anchor and starting 450 yards astern of the *Black Prince* passed her in an hour and a half. On every trial we have unmistakably beaten her . . . Some snob wrote to the *Times* – as you saw – that *Black Prince* was fully equal to us under steam and superior under sail . . . I am glad to report that . . . those in the *Black Prince* say that they regret that anything of the sort should have been published.'[7]

At Gibraltar Admiral Dacres watched *Warrior's* men at general quarters before inspecting the ship's company. Berth was shifted to coal ship, the log recording at the end of the day, 'issued ½ gill rum to 592 men who had been employed coaling', mark of a successful evolution. At the end of October came monthly payment, 48 hours leave to each watch and some riotous escapades in Main Street. After spending their last penny most returned on board drunk or shamming inebriation, for drunkenness was the fashion among youngsters anxious to prove their manliness. *Warrior's* libertymen were no exception.

In mid-November *Warrior* and *Black Prince* returned to Lisbon now to join Rear Admiral Smart in *Revenge*, his squadron augmented by *Defence* (Captain Augustus Phillimore) and *Resistance* (Captain William Chamberlain). Smart, anxious to pit the sailing qualities of his flagship against the 'hogs in armour' as the ironclads were known to the lower deck, ordered the squadron to sea. On return to the Tagus they were struck by a violent squall – 'the sea like waterspouts' – with no time for shortening sail. As well as losing gear overboard *Warrior's* 105ft 15 ton lower main yard came down with a rush and broke in two. Sails were split, braces, sheets and halyards parting like bowstrings but by midnight it was flat calm. Sailmakers worked the clock round while parties were sent to a very co-operative Portuguese dockyard to make new spars. Repairs completed *Warrior* shifted berth to carry out target practice firing with Martin's incendiary shell filled with molten iron heated in the stokehold cupola, a complex practice for the 68 pdr crews but considered more effective than explosive shell against wooden ships.

On December 20, 1862 the Admiral took his squadron to sea where ships exercised circling to port and starboard at six knots to establish data for steam tactics; with 16 men on the relieving tackles and six on the wheels *Warrior* was just able to get her helm over to 34 degrees. When raising propellers as a squadron competition *Warrior's* time

● HMY Victoria and
Albert II, 2000 tons
built 1855

of 26 minutes was the best. On Christmas day the squadron anchored in Madeira but after three days they were off again, firing at targets and practising night signalling. Throughout the programme Smart appeared to give little thought to the role of armoured ships in line-of-battle.

Before the end of February *Warrior* was back at Spithead to take on coal and then sail with *Revenge, Defence* and *Resistance* to the Downs for a ceremonial assignment. The gloom in royal circles caused by the death of Prince Albert had been broken by news of the engagement of the Prince of Wales to Princess Alexandra, daughter of the Crown Prince of Denmark, whose charm and beauty had captivated mother as well as son. The royal yacht *Victoria and Albert* – a paddle vessel – was to bring the bride across, escorted by the Channel squadron. Admiral Smart sailed his ships up the Scheldt to Antwerp to await departure. On March 5 *Warrior* took up station with the others ahead of *Victoria and Albert*. Once across the Channel the royal yacht, with Danish and English standards flying in the breeze, overtook her escort and passed through the lines in the twilight. All ships fired a royal salute, manned yards and illuminated ship with coloured lights for the shy 18-year-old princess watching with her family. After anchoring overnight in Margate Road, the ships were dressed next morning with bunting before firing two salutes, one at eight am for Alexandra and another for her

● HRH Princess of Wales
circa 1866

father, Prince Christian, who came aboard *Warrior* with his suite.

Among the officers later presented to Princess Alexandra aboard *Victoria and Albert* was Arthur Cochrane to whom she must have made complimentary remarks on the appearance of his ship. En route to the Nore *Warrior* was ordered by Smart to take station ahead as sole escort, by which time her yards were manned by 200 seamen in white suits and beribboned hats. 'Three cheers for Her Royal Highness Princess Alexandra of Denmark,' shouted Tryon as *Warrior* passed abeam.

'Well done – Princess pleased,' came a signal. That night the anchored ships could see bonfires on both shores; on the Sheerness beach the word WELCOME blazed in blue lights ten feet high.

'Are all these things for me?' the young princess asked her mother.[8]

On Saturday, March 7 *Warrior* led the royal yacht up river to anchor off Gravesend amid a mass of small craft. On letting go the small bower – Trotman's patent anchor – *Warrior*'s stern swung round touching the opposite bank of the river. The cable parted causing the other bower to be dropped smartly to avoid serious mishap. Meanwhile Captain George Seymour manoeuvred the *Victoria and Albert* alongside the quay and the Prince of Wales, struggling through the press of people, almost ran aboard to kiss his bride in full view of cheering crowds. In conversation a

few days later Seymour told Cochrane that it was the express wish of Her Royal Highness that *Warrior* should know she was *much* pleased. Back on board Cochrane sent for Tryon. 'When we get to Devonport I would like a brass plate on the quarterdeck steering wheel inscribed . . . "PRINCESS IS MUCH PLEASED".' With the indefatigable Blakey alongside Cochrane had remained calmly in control throughout the unusual and unrehearsed operation. According to Lieutenant Hastings Owen, RMA, 'the Princess was so pleased with the beauty of the ship' that she ordered a black and white lithoprint by Dutton 'to be engraved and sent to each officer in the ship'. The signal also appeared on the wardroom notepaper.[9]

Before *Warrior*'s annual refit two interesting events occurred at Spithead. The first was when the Prince and Princess of Wales in *Fairy* passed through the anchorage on their way to honeymoon at Osborne House. The second was the departure from the ship of Lieutenant Owen and 41 marine artillerymen. Presumably the experiment of a contingent made up exclusively of gunners did not suit the ship; in future *Warrior* would conform to fleet practice of two thirds artillerymen and one third infantrymen. The detachment had been both effective and popular, manning the running gear on deck and occasionally surpassing the seamen at gun drill. They provided sentries at the entry port in harbour, in

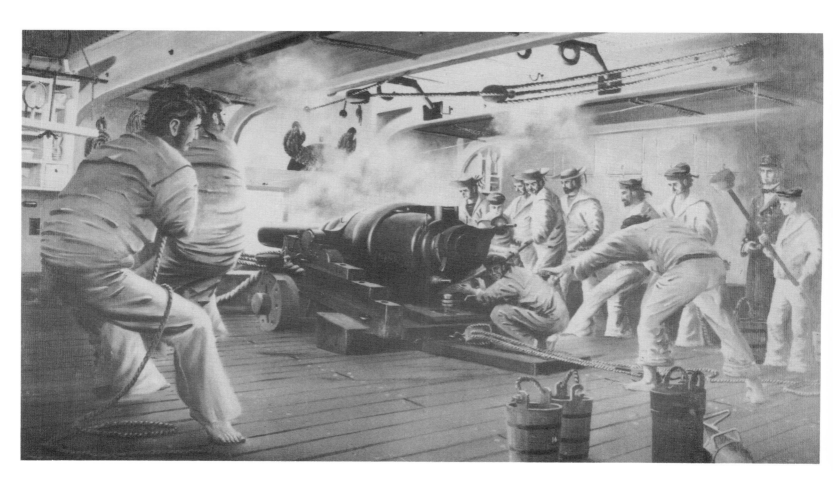

● 110 pdr gun's crew at drill, supervised by Gunner Colinburn

● John Fisher, acting Mate, 1860

the cell flat and outside the captain's cabin as well as providing the guard for the daily hoisting of colours. So Mawbey, the marine captain, had no easy task in deciding who should stay or go, although he ensured the outgoing draft included the troublemakers. On their departure officers and men lined the side and shrouds to give them three cheers. Two hours later the same boat brought off Lieutenant McCall and 41 red-coated infantrymen as replacements. As they mustered in the waist Blacksmith Watling lifted each man's foot behind him like a farrier, then wrenched off the metal heel of each boot. After months of holy-stoning *Warrior*'s upper deck planking was in immaculate condition and nobody was going to blemish it.

For the next ten weeks in Devonport yard the ship's programme was largely repetitive of the previous year there with one exception. Cochrane had been working on Renton's hydraulic steering gear ever since receiving the Controller's go-ahead late in 1861. Work involved fitting a hydraulic tiller with an actuating cylinder on top of the rudder head together with a steam pump at engine room level. As this affected the captain's quarters Cochrane went on leave to London there to appear before the Ordnance Select Committee eager to hear his views on Armstrong guns. Their range and accuracy were valuable assets he stated, but disadvantages lay in the dense smoke caused by their powder charges 'which impaired the efficiency of the whole battery', the tendency to misfire and 'the very numerous occasions the vent pieces have jammed in the bore'. Numerically the 68 pdrs and the Armstrongs were in about the right proportions, had the same rate of fire but the latter were incapable of ricochet firing. The committee appeared to be against the Armstrong breech-loading gear but in favour of

their rifled bores.[10]

While in Devonport the regulating staff took especial precautions at the gangway, the local paper reporting that Mary Ann Warren was brought before the magistrates and charged 'for bringing intoxicating spirits aboard HMS *Warrior* fined nine shillings and costs'.[11]

More important a 22-year-old gunnery lieutenant joined on April 1 to relieve Phillimore now promoted commander. The newcomer's name was John Arbuthnot Fisher. Born in Ceylon Fisher entered the navy in 1854 and as a midshipman saw action in China at Fatshan Creek (where his new captain had served). Despite winning the navigation prize in his lieutenant's examinations he preferred gunnery and 1862 saw the beginning of a long and distinguished career with the *Excellent*. When the vacancy in *Warrior* was announced Captain Hewlett knew he had the right man for the navy's first ironclad.

Fisher was delighted. In *Memories* he later wrote, 'the *Warrior* was then . . . the cynosure of all eyes. She had a famous captain and a still more famous commander . . . she had a picked crew of officers and men, so I was wonderfully fortunate to be the gunnery lieutenant and at so young an age.'[12]

Once more refit routine brought a rash of punishment warrants, including two for men convicted of selling their clothes ashore, a fairly common practice then. Leave presented its usual problems. Whereas a man in the service today who fails to return on board is treated as 'absent without leave', the Victorian navy had good reason to mark a leave-breaker in the ship's books as R (Run), a deserter, or RQ (Run Query) – possible deserter. Both markings meant immediate stoppage of pay and forfeiture of time for completion of engagement or award of pension. This led to hardship when genuine sickness or unavoidable circumstances caused a man to miss his ship. One of Cochrane's many letters to the Admiralty pleaded leniency for men sincerely intending to return from leave.

By the end of May Fisher was busy introducing the latest gunnery school drill refinements while the engine room worked overtime to activate the hydraulic steering gear which was given its first trial in Plymouth Sound. That done the ship sailed early in June for Portsmouth where the new commander-in-chief, Admiral Sir Michael Seymour, invited Cochrane to luncheon. Selected for their oarsmanship, the galley's crew thought nothing of rowing the captain to King's Stairs, a mere mile and a half against the tide.

For some months Tryon had been concerned about behaviour in the engineers' mess following complaints of rowdiness by the warrant officers who shared their flat. During the forenoon of Warrior's *arrival in Spithead Engineer Fry had appeared on deck improperly dressed and the worse for drink following a birthday celebration. He happened to meet the Commander who remonstrated*

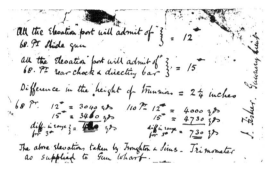

with him on his appearance. 'I don't take orders from you . . . only the chief engineer' said Fry. Tryon put him under arrest before informing Buchan, who was not best pleased about the Commander's reaction. On return to the ship Cochrane sensed that feelings were running high so called Tryon and Buchan to his cabin. His diplomacy quickly restored the situation and the incident was later recorded in the deck log after Fry 'had made a suitable apology to Commander Tryon and expressed his regrets, when he was released to duty'.

Fisher did not take long to make an impact in the wardroom where 'we were all very happy mess mates; they kindly spoilt me as if I was a baby'. He was popular, too, with his fellow watch keepers since he seldom went ashore and took their duty for them. But he got into trouble for skylarking in the mess and recalls, 'there was a dear old grey-headed paymaster (Charles Giles who had relieved de Vries), a mature old doctor (Wells) and a still more mature chaplain (Noble Jackson), quite a dear old saint. These, with other willing spirits of a younger phase, I organised into a peripatetic band. The parson used to play the coal scuttle, the doctor the tongs and shovel, the paymaster used to do the cymbals with an old tin kettle. The other instruments we made ourselves out of brown paper and we perambulated doing our best. The captain came out . . . and asked his sentry what the noise was. We were all struck dumb by his voice, the skylight being open . . .

consisting of *Black Prince, Royal Oak* (wooden battleship conversion) and *Defence.* Sailing on July 11 *Warrior* tried out her hydraulic steering gear, caught up the main body to transfer leavebreakers and took station astern of *Black Prince.* En route for Yarmouth when line of battle was exercised at six knots the Admiral found his assorted squadron somewhat unwieldy to handle.

Warrior's signal log for this period shows a notable difference in the tone of communication with ships between Smart and Dacres. Both went by the book but Dacres showed the greater sense of humour and understanding. His genial personality made him a far more popular figure than his intolerant and somewhat sour predecessor.

After a brief stop at Yarmouth the squadron reached Sunderland where crowds flocked in from Durham, Hartlepool and Newcastle. *Warrior* reported that in 12 hours, '13,000 people came aboard in 190 steamers'.

Running in to the Firth of Forth under all plain sail the squadron must have made an impressive sight, the two big ironclads keeping station with an occasional touch of the screw before anchoring off Inchkeith by the Port of Leith. Six days of Edinburgh hospitality proved too much for the bluejackets and pickets had to be sent ashore to round up stragglers. When a general signal was made asking which ship was missing a 'ship's corporal and bombardier found drunk on the jetty' *Warrior* had to own up. From Leith the

The sentry said, "it's only Mr Fisher, sir", so he shut his door. The commander wasn't so nice. He sent a message to say the Gunnery Lieutenant was "to stop that fooling". This only drove us to another kind of sport.'[12]

On June 13 the ship steamed into Portsmouth harbour for a fortnight in number ten dock – now known as the *Warrior* dock. Several new 68 pdr gun carriages were embarked which allowed the guns to be secured horizontally for sea instead of having muzzles lashed above the gun ports. All 40 pdr Armstrong guns were exchanged for a better model. Lower deck and wardroom were alive with rumours as to the future programme. When the Channel squadron arrived to anchor in Spithead Cochrane felt it was time to address the ship's company.

'Tomorrow we sail for Spithead,' he said, 'to join Admiral Dacres who has taken over command, flying his flag in Edgar. To show the people of Britain our new navy the squadron have been given a special duty. Over the next three months we shall be visiting ports on the east and west coasts of England and Scotland, culminating in Dublin. Visitors will be allowed aboard and where possible leave will be given. I need hardly warn you that leave breaking and misconduct will be treated severely.' As the hands broke up to go below there was a buzz of excited conversation.

Warrior was left behind to collect absentees from leave while the squadron sailed eastward for the Downs, the starboard division being *Edgar, Emerald, Liverpool* and *Resistance,* the port division

●HMS Defence, upper
deck starboard side circa
1862, much as Warrior
would have appeared

squadron sailed north past Aberdeen and Peterhead to anchor in Cromarty Firth off Invergordon for two days, followed by six days at Kirkwall in the Orkneys which must have surprised the few locals. There were three days in Londonderry and a whole week in the Clyde off Greenock. Some 120 years later a Victorian sketchbook was discovered in a Sussex junk shop which contained pencil drawings of places where the squadron had called. An illustration of Quartermaster Williams on the conning bridge confirms that the unknown artist took passage in *Warrior* or was one of her company.

Early on July 13 the squadron sailed for Liverpool and in line-of-battle crossed the bar to enter the Mersey for what was to prove the highlight of the cruise. The mayor and corporation prepared an elaborate programme which featured reciprocal hospitality by the squadron with luncheons and dances on board ships. Visitors came aboard by steamer at all hours of the day, the only way to stop them being to hoist the yellow quarantine flag when, for example, a local dignitary was being received.

The press contained euphoric descriptions of Britain's naval might. One reporter wrote, 'on the upper deck the scene is very imposing . . . the sun was reflected from the bright white deck of the ship. The rain of the previous night made it necessary to loose the sails to dry, which caused a constant noise of the flapping of the canvas . . .

Between the masts were hung in lines the newly washed clothes of the men . . . A lady remarked to her husband that she was more delighted with this washing feature than anything else she had seen . . . Several officers were explaining the working of the Armstrong guns . . . and along the deck, which looked like a broad street, men were seen rope-making, carpentering, making hammocks and handropes.

'Going down the ladder to the main deck the ear was greeted with the bleating of sheep and the cackle of domestic fowls . . . quantities of butcher's meat hanging up ready for cooking . . . cooks busy at work in the galley. It is not meat time yet here and there are seen some of the fine fellows leisurely (it being their watch below) despatching their "levener" – from the hour "eleven" at which it is taken – a goodly snack of fried beefsteak and onions. While a great many were eating most were reading newspapers or writing letters; some working hearth rugs by a quilting process or embroidering pictures. Many lay asleep having to go on deck at twelve o'clock; some sat wrapt in their own meditation; one man, a marine, chanted a song, a fine cultivated voice. We are all familiar with the British seamen as a daring man, and a light-hearted cheery man but here we see him as a homely man, mending his clothes or shoes or doing the barber. He is a pattern to all the world in the virtues of tidiness, cleanliness and order.'[13]

Lunching in the wardroom Fisher recalls complaints that even officers' cabins were being invaded by curious sightseers. Suddenly he noticed a party of girls at the skylight overlooking the wardroom who were 'indulging in wit of a cockney type which was intended to be funny but was, really, in vulgar taste'. Fisher stood this for some time and then in his most penetrating voice remarked across the table, 'if those young women only remembered the state of their *lingerie* they would not stand right over our heads!' The girls departed hurriedly.[14]

Financially supported by leading shipowners and Liverpool merchants a dinner in St George's

●Towards the end of
an evening meal in
Warrior's wardroom

● **2nd Lieutenant's cabin,**
starboard side
wardroom flat

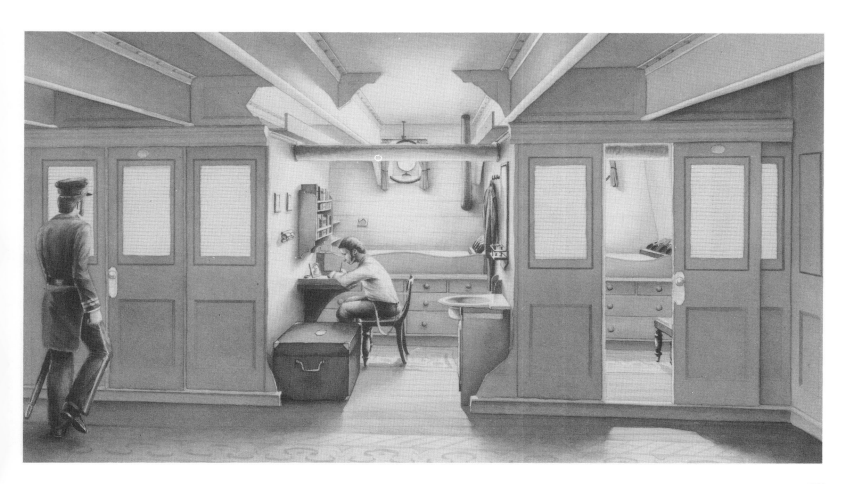

Hall was organised for 1,000 men from the squadron. Selected for good conduct nine companies of bluejackets and marines, with about eight officers from each ship 'to ensure seemly behaviour', formed up on the jetty. It was blowing hard and 'rain fell in sheets' but 'the bluejackets bore their discomfort with exemplary patience'. Led by two bands the companies moved off, each displaying a distinctive flag and decoration. *Black Prince* with a banner bearing the Prince of Wales' feathers was followed by *Warrior* with a blue flag emblazoned with the ship's crest, each man with 'a handsome bouquet of flowers on the centre of the breast'. Immense crowds lined the streets and the applause was deafening, much to the astonishment of the sailors who had no idea they were so popular.

Beef and ham followed by plum pudding laced with Crimea sauce was washed down with ale and punch. Then came the toasts and speeches. Each ship was called upon to sing a song, usually of a patriotic or deeply sentimental nature, to be marked by outbursts of cheering. When the banquet was nearly over – the Admiral had asked the mayor to restrict men to two bottles of beer – John Kiernan, captain of *Warrior*'s maintop stood on his chair. 'On behalf of my topmates I wish to thank the mayor and corporation for a jolly good dinner and best beer we have ever had.' He paused, 'Bill, 'and up that beer again.' Bill said there was none left as Kiernan knew perfectly

well. This was too much for the mayor, so in came beer by the dozen. Kiernan continued, 'here we are, British sailors, surrounded by females . . .' (frantic cheers from the gallery) whereupon Fisher told him to shut up. Finally the ship's companies, arms linked to keep steady, marched back to the jetty. It was a party to be remembered.

According to Lieutenant Percy Luxmore of *Black Prince* the officers were no less well entertained with balls and banquets. 'One old gentleman', he added, 'kept a champagne lunch on his table for the officers of the squadron from one to five pm every day. *Great Eastern* arrived one Sunday we were in the Mersey', he went on, 'and the *Warrior* and *Black Prince* looked nothing alongside her.' [15]

From Dublin the squadron sailed home to Plymouth and then split up, *Warrior* going on to Spithead and then into dock for six weeks.

Originated and planned by an enlightened First Lord (Somerset) who foresaw the publicity value of showing the fleet to the people, the Channel squadron's 12-week round-Britain cruise was astonishingly successful. As it was the first of its kind the politicians had to win over an apprehensive Admiralty Board – desertions and drunken libertymen in mind – who relented only when recruiting possibilities were appreciated. 'I cannot give sufficient praise to captains, officers and men for their behaviour,' wrote Dacres. 'In spite of having their mess places filled day after

day with strangers I never heard a word of complaint.' [16] Well over a million visited the ships during the cruise, some 80,000 people in Liverpool alone. Not surprisingly *Warrior* took the lion's share, recording about 300,000 all told.

Back in Portsmouth Cochrane found time to detail the items on trial. Trotman's anchor 'had dragged'; but gas lighting, unpopular with Portsmouth dockyard, Cochrane recommended for 'the engine room and screw alley', and finally Renton's hydraulic steering gear which, although a worthwhile experiment, was a failure. [17]

A warship's commanding officer leads a lonely monastic existence, none more so than Arthur Cochrane whose character is vividly revealed in correspondence with his devoted young brother, Commander Ernest Cochrane. Against his bachelor leanings Arthur enjoyed the recent cruise '. . . being made much of and . . . judge my amusement at an enormous dinner for 300 people . . . I was called to propose the health of the ladies of Sunderland.' He confessed to having taken up dancing again and now 'come out in deux temps and gallops'. But the ship was always next to his heart, his joy when *Warrior* did better than *Black Prince*; with an eye to his future in the navy he thought that 'as second senior captain afloat' he might overtake those employed in dockyards and coastguards and 'get into the Admiralty'. Hearing a yarn that the *Warrior* is to go to the Baltic alone '. . . it would be a great chance I might return a

• View of HM Floating
Dock Bermuda from
Warrior with *Terrible*
astern on July 26, 1869
in latitude 30° north
longitude 61°9′ west

Commodore if I wrote a good despatch . . . how I long to rise to fame and honours and wealth and if one is to marry to be able to choose a wife and not to have to humble oneself to any woman.' Such sentiments contrast with those six months earlier at Lisbon when he confessed, 'How I long to get back to the club with all its charms. I find whether at home or abroad there is no place like it. Here we have the opera and rides and drives but I have not a sliver left to enjoy anything with and the needful is the basis of all pleasure.' Lack of finance dogged his whole life but like his father he was confident that everything would be all right when he had 'ardent hopes that I may soon be in possession of a considerable fortune. I have patented a boiler and have . . . induced the Admiralty to order a first class one of 130 nominal horse power to be put on board the *Oberon.*' Although successfully fitted, it brought little reward. Like his father Arthur remained ever the optimist with ideas ahead of his time he could never implement. Ambitious and egocentric he was also a compassionate and likeable character.[18]

After a week at Spithead *Warrior* accompanied *Resistance* to Plymouth before sailing for Madeira with the squadron. Anchoring in Funchal Bay *Warrior* recorded on Christmas eve, 'fired at target with shot, shell and grape'. Following supper the ship went 'out of routine' to decorate messdecks.

On Christmas day the hands turned out an hour later than usual. Divisions on the upper deck were followed by church. At noon the band, under Chief Bandmaster Hope, played The Roast Beef of Old England *as the captain, commander and officers walked the messdecks admiring the decorations and mottoes like* Home Sweet Home, Long Live the Warrior, *and* Success to Commander Tryon. *The procession was led by the youngest boy on board, Charles Asky, dressed in the master-at-arms' uniform. Traditionally each mess offered the captain a tot of rum from the stock saved up, against all regulations. By special concession smoking was allowed on the messdecks. Fancy dress was the rig of the day and the end of rounds was marked by a spontaneous 'three cheers for Captain Cochrane and the officers'. As soon as they had left the scene degenerated. Drummer and fiddler darted from mess to mess in an atmosphere of thick smoke through which could be seen the faint glow of candles on the tables. It was the one day of the year when all restraint was lifted and judging by the way parties of bluejackets went aft to try to persuade popular officers, like Fisher and Perceval, to join them in a 'taste of grog' there was nothing much wrong with* Warrior. *By eight pm the messdecks were silent.*

Meanwhile dinner was in full swing with the captain sitting on the commander's right hand as the wardroom's honoured guest; later all three warrant officers were invited in for a singsong. On Boxing day a rigorous programme of mast evolutions soon brought the squadron back to their senses.

Training continued daily, the oft-practised drill of sending boats away with 20 pdr and 12 pdr Armstrong guns and armed men was enlivened by firing Congreve rockets from the cutters. A lieutenant wrote to his family to say that after a brief visit to Tenerife the squadron 'had to cut and run for Gibraltar. We took our time going there, every day manoeuvring or firing shot and shell at a target and all sorts of outlandish things. Directly we got to Gibraltar there was a telegram ordering us home to England on account of the Schleswig - Holstein affair. Just as we were on the point of starting out comes another telling us to go to Lisbon.'[19] Admiral Dacres had announced his intention of inspecting ships while in the Tagus and *Warrior's* turn came early in February 1864.

The first day's programme was for the admiral to inspect every compartment in the ship from top to bottom, his flag lieutenant noting comments on paper. The ship's company muster by open list induced Dacres to exclaim, 'tolerable body of men there, Cochrane,' then with a twinkle, 'but I see you have some rascals amongst them'. Turning to the group of officers at the gangway on departure he said, 'ship clean below decks. Best engine room I have seen. Ventilation bad in places. Too many men on the sick list.' So far so good.

Early next morning Chief Gunner's Mate Abraham Johnson (who had succeeded Pearce) approached Fisher and asked for a free hand when it came to magazine inspection. 'I knows the admiral's little ways!' Fisher could but agree. On Dacres' arrival the ship went to general quarters: the first gun was fired in three minutes

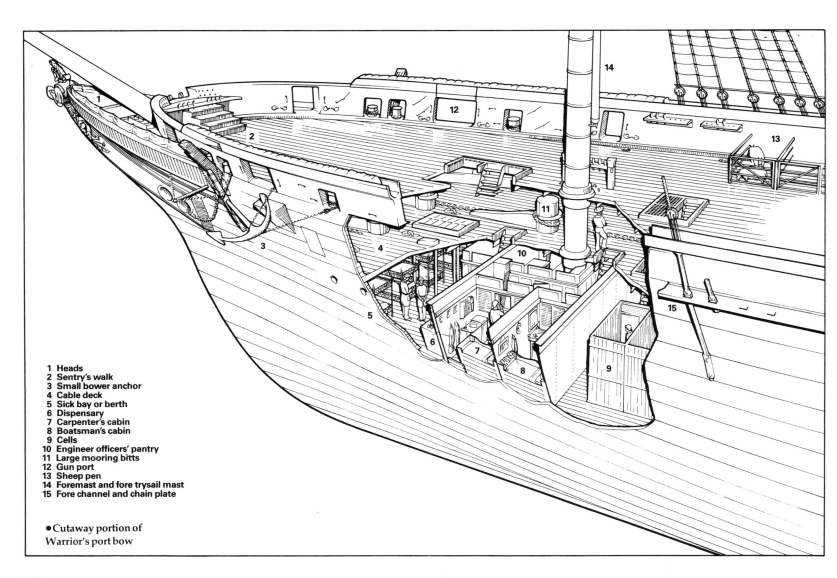

1 Heads
2 Sentry's walk
3 Small bower anchor
4 Cable deck
5 Sick bay or berth
6 Dispensary
7 Carpenter's cabin
8 Boatsman's cabin
9 Cells
10 Engineer officers' pantry
11 Large mooring bitts
12 Gun port
13 Sheep pen
14 Foremast and fore trysail mast
15 Fore channel and chain plate

●Cutaway portion of
Warrior's port bow

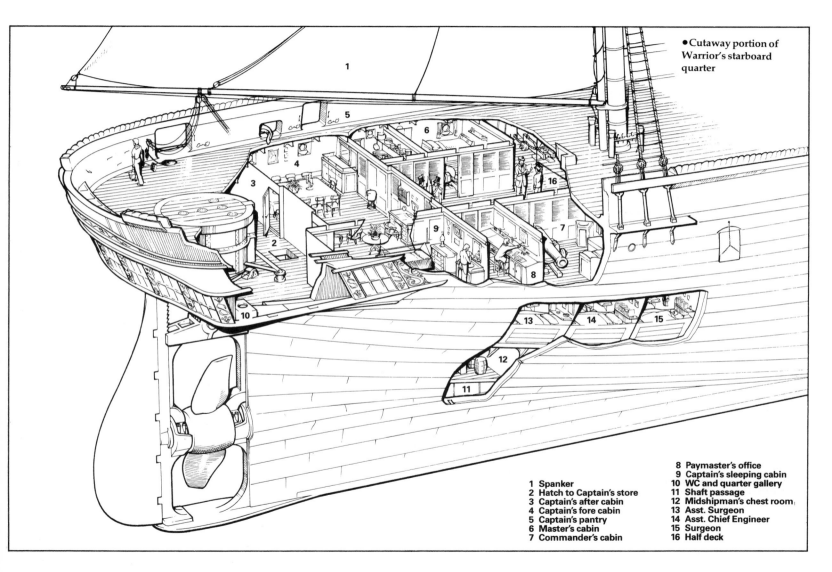

● Cutaway portion of
Warrior's starboard
quarter

1 Spanker
2 Hatch to Captain's store
3 Captain's after cabin
4 Captain's fore cabin
5 Captain's pantry
6 Master's cabin
7 Commander's cabin
8 Paymaster's office
9 Captain's sleeping cabin
10 WC and quarter gallery
11 Shaft passage
12 Midshipman's chest room
13 Asst. Surgeon
14 Asst. Chief Engineer
15 Surgeon
16 Half deck

35 seconds. Then guns were changed from one side of the battery to the other. The best time for transporting, re-mounting, loading and firing took only three and a quarter minutes. A 68 pdr was then shifted the length of the main deck from bow to stern and fired in three minutes five seconds. A spare rudder yoke was shipped in seven minutes and new tiller ropes rove in four minutes 40 seconds. The men had been well trained.

Just before the end Dacres said abruptly, 'I'll go down to the magazine,' and descended the ladder wearing his sword. From below Johnson called, 'beg pardon, sir, but you can't come down here'. 'Damn the fellow. What does he mean?' Johnson repeated his statement. 'Why not?' asked the admiral. 'Because no iron instrument is allowed in the magazine, sir.'

'Ah,' said Dacres, unbuckling his sword, 'that fellow knows his duty. This is a properly organised ship.'[20]

One novelty impressed the admiral, the use of the command 'still' to impose instant immobility on men engaged in an evolution so that mistakes could be rectified. Fisher's innovation was valuable in preventing accidents aloft or at the guns. When uttered in the gunnery lieutenant's stentorian voice its effect was electric. In his letter home Fisher wrote, 'The Admiral was awfully civil and said he had hardly ever in his life seen a ship in such splendid gunnery order and that he would bring my conduct to the notice of the Admiralty, in consequence of which when we arrived home I got a special letter of thanks from the Board.' The use of the word 'still' was inserted in gunnery drill books where it remained until after World War II.

To celebrate the ship's successful inspection *Warrior's* gunroom had a run ashore in Lisbon finishing up at a tavern run by a Mrs Amalia where they met other young squadron officers. Some of *Warrior's* midshipmen used the furniture to demonstrate aspects of gun-drill and the party got out of hand. A few days later a complaint reached the admiral. In a letter of explanation Cochrane stated that a contrite Second Master Doyle and Midshipman Neilson were willing to pay for the damage caused. Both had their leave stopped for a month.[21]

Late in February the squadron sailed for Portland where they remained until the end of April when General Garibaldi visited *Warrior*. Hero of the Risorgimento (the Italian national revival) he had arrived in this country shortly after the last of his great victories. Coming aboard with the admiral he shook hands with the lieutenants, bowed to the rest of the officers and then climbed on to the after conning bridge. Then, it was reported, 'the Commander waved his hand and every man in the ship stepped off, four deep, the band in front playing the Garibaldi hymn. It looked very well to see 700 men marching round, all good stout fellows and well dressed with white hats and gaiters, sword bayonets glistening in the sun. Garibaldi was greatly pleased and said the men marched like soldiers. He turned to the Duke of Sutherland and said he didn't wonder at the English navy beating every other when each man was so perfect in himself.

'After this we went to general quarters . . . firing away like fun. First we supposed the enemy was on one bow, then on the other; in fact the enemy was everywhere in the course of ten minutes. The men worked the guns splendidly, I never saw them move quicker.' Garibaldi commented it was the finest thing he had seen in England.[22]

Early on Saturday, April 30, 1863, *Warrior* anchored in Spithead for a few hours before rejoining the squadron in the Downs, a sad occasion for the ship because it signalled the departure of Fisher who had been appointed back to his beloved *Excellent*. In 13 months he had brought *Warrior's* gunnery performance to peak efficiency and left an indelible impression on the whole ship. Some 47 years later a member of the ship's company wrote, 'I had in mind you standing on the main hatch with a voice like a lion drilling the whole of the quarters and the landing parties. You gave us some rare rouse ups . . . it was a saying amongst the crew . . . that they had the smartest gunnery lieutenant in the service.' *Warrior* was his first rung to greatness.

After a week off Deal the squadron weighed and proceeded to Plymouth where *Warrior* moored near Keyham Point prior to entering Queen's Dock for the first time. Renton's hydraulic steering gear was hoisted out and a number of Armstrong guns exchanged, symptomatic of their failure in the fleet. From mid-June until mid-July the squadron lay at anchor at Spithead coinciding with a spell of hot weather that allowed *Warrior* to pipe, 'hands to bathe' during the dog watches. John Burke, captain of the mast, evoked a round of applause by diving from the main yardarm, a height of 80 feet.

There was another loss, this time the departure of George Tryon to command the sloop *Surprise* by special request from Smart now Commander-in-Chief, Mediterranean. A forceful personality, ambitious, shrewd and probably intolerant, Tryon possessed sufficient self-control to stand him in good stead on the many occasions when his patience was sorely tried. 'After two years intimate association with him, messing daily at the same table,' wrote the Rev Noble Jackson later, 'I never heard from his lips any word that would cause a blush.' High praise from a parson. The lower deck were sorry to see him go because he was scrupulously fair, sensitive to their welfare and outwardly never lost his temper. Most of all his departure was felt by Cochrane with whom he blended to make an unbeatable combination. At a brief ceremony in the wardroom the officers presented him with a handsome carriage clock.

No relief being immediately available the first lieutenant, Joseph Wilson, took over as executive officer until Commander William Codrington arrived in September. By now there were new faces in the wardroom. The Rev John Harrison had replaced Noble Jackson and Captain Horsey had succeeded Mawbey in charge of the marines. Gunner Colinburn, sent to Plymouth hospital for treatment, was replaced by William Dore.

During the commission's remaining five months – July to November – *Warrior* carried out short cruises, mainly in company with the Channel squadron to the west country and Irish coast. Emphasis was laid on battle tactics with a touch of realism and gunnery training for young seamen. Assistant Surgeon Hurley got into serious trouble, being arrested for debt before deserting the navy.

As well as customary reports to his admiral Cochrane wrote letters about the inefficiency of *Warrior*'s steam whistle and foghorn, improving the armoured tower with a gun-en-barbette, the adoption of his own patented vertical water tube boiler, trials with new blue serge uniforms, washing arrangements and a recommendation for Charles Beaton to be advanced to chief boatswain.[23] The programme was dull so the ship was glad to be despatched on her own to Gibraltar, to embark '100 naval and military invalids, 125 time-expired men, 57 prisoners etc' from the Mediterranean fleet. Reporting to Commander-in-Chief, Plymouth, Cochrane remarked that favourable winds had enabled him to

sail most of the way back in seven days. On anchoring in the Sound Lieutenant Digby and Clerk Doveton were commended for saving Able Seaman Endicote who had fallen overboard.

Writing to his brother Ernest in October Cochrane remarked, 'we are about to be paid off shortly and the glories of *Warrior* will have passed away like a dream leaving me many years older but at the top of the captain's list'. Simultaneously Pakington wrote congratulating him on a successful commission, 'I am so glad that the first command of England's first armour-plated ship was duly entrusted to the son of one of the bravest and most distinguished naval heroes.' Cochrane replied in similar vein, 'having now commanded the first, the fastest and the noblest ship that England ever produced . . . it is happily in my power to say she has shewn herself on all occasions worthy of the care you bestowed on her conception. No vessel has surpassed her in efficiency and speed . . . Countless scientific Englishmen and numerous foreigners of distinction have visited the ship and all testify to the surpassing merits of the *Warrior*. On our last visit to Gibraltar a French officer went well over the ship and told me that his own vessels were not comparable to her. He ended by saying, speaking of you, sir, "quelle hardiesse" you must have had, who first assumed responsibility for constructing such a vessel.'[24]

A warship's first commission sets the tone for

No. 704

THIS IS TO CERTIFY that Mr. *John Hefferman*

Dated *22 November* 18*64*

has served as *engineer* on board

Her Majesty's *Ship "Warrior"* under my command, from

the *First* day of *September* 18*61*, to the *Twenty-Second*

day of *November* 18*64*, during which period he has conducted himself * *with zeal and ability and is a very valuable officer.*

Arthur A. Cochrane

{ Captain,
{ H. M. S. *Warrior*

• Certificate of service for Engineer John Heffernan, typical of those completed for all officers prior to leaving the ship even if they spelt his name incorrectly!

the rest of her career. Although her three and a half years had been largely uneventful *Warrior* had fulfilled her purpose with conspicuous success. Thanks to exemplary leadership amongst officers and senior rates she was a notably happy and efficient ship – and a favourite with Dacres who hoisted his flag on board for her last passage with the squadron from Portland to Spithead. Then followed the final inspection by Commander-in-Chief, Portsmouth, when again the men surpassed themselves at general quarters.

Warrior reached Portsmouth on November 3, going up harbour with paying-off pendant flying from the main and the band playing 'Rolling Home'. The ship was lashed alongside Sheer Jetty and for the last time the captain ordered, 'finished with engines'. Throughout the next two weeks sails were unbent, masts and spars brought to the deck leaving only the lower masts. Stores were returned to the naval storekeeper, boats to the boathouse, guns hoisted out, anchors lowered

into lighters and the ship systematically stripped of all movable gear.

At 10.30 on Tuesday, November 22 *Warrior* was 'paid out of commission under the superintendence of Admiral Dacres'. It took more than an hour; each man came to the pay table to receive his due, Cochrane and those officers who had commissioned the ship in Victoria docks smiling to themselves as the more colourful characters appeared. Dacres presented the good service medal to William Percival, chief captain of the foc'sle, and Robert Bone, coxswain of the launch, also a pension – worth £24 a year – to John Tozer, quartermaster.[25] Bidding the captain and officers goodbye, Dacres thanked them for the loyal support and meritorious service that *Warrior* had rendered the Channel squadron. After Dacres it was Cochrane's turn. Dinner finished officers and men went over the side with their bags and belongings, some pausing to have a last look at their *Warrior* before hurrying off to find a

cab. That night would be a great homecoming, a few would paint the town red, while the west country contingent sailed in *Geyser* for Plymouth.

By four pm only the captain, commander and one lieutenant in charge of a small retard party remained on board. At sunset the ensign was lowered to the boatswain's pipe and the commissioning pendant hauled down. Just before going ashore Cochrane signed a letter to the commander-in-chief.

'Sir,
I have the honour to inform that Her Majesty's ship under my command was this day paid off.
I have the honour to be, Sir,
Your obedient servant,
Arthur A Cochrane'

The commission was over.

CHAPTER EIGHT
Second Commission

THE DAY AFTER *Warrior* paid off, the *Victoria* sailed from Spithead for Malta to become the Mediterranean fleet flagship. The latest and last wooden three-decker to go into active service, her departure was predictably criticized, the *Times* (November 16, 1864) commenting, 'if we were to have a war with France or America the admiral on board the *Victoria* would have to decide between going into port or going to the bottom'.

Although ironclads were at sea with the Channel squadron the rest of the navy, fully extended on peacetime security, would need wooden capital ships for some years to come. Even so an argument for *Victoria*, publicly stated by the Political Secretary, Lord Clarence Paget, was interesting because it concerned the health of supernumeraries required in the flagship to fill fleet vacancies, 'if you were to put them aboard an armour-plated ship the men would, from want of ventilation, speedily become utterly useless'.[1] This may explain the comparatively high numbers on the sick list recorded by *Warrior*; forced draught ventilation much superior to that installed by Thames Ironworks had yet to reach the fleet.

At the end of 1860 Baldwin Walker wrote privately to the First Sea Lord complaining that 'whilst I was in my office' Watts had been sent for to be questioned in the Board Room on ship construction, that the Duke of Somerset (First Lord) criticized the 'form of iron-cased ships' and that Lord Clarence Paget had found fault with

Warrior comparing her unfavourably with *Gloire*. He concluded by submitting his resignation. '. . . I am really weary of the constant annoyances and shall be glad to be free'. Granted a pension of £600 for his services as Controller, with a letter of appreciation from the Board he was appointed Commander-in-Chief, Cape of Good Hope.[2] At the change of Controller early in 1861 the ironclad programme did not impress the incisive brain of his more aggressive successor – Spencer Robinson; *Defence* and *Resistance* were still building, to be followed by similar coast defence ships *Hector* and *Valiant*. Work was about to start on *Achilles*, to be floated out of the new graving dock at Chatham early in 1863, the first iron ship from a royal dockyard. Intended as a repeat *Warrior* her armoured belt was extended to cover the whole waterline which meant reshaping the bow and stern. With a four-bladed non-hoisting propeller *Achilles* incorporated many improvements on *Warrior* to become, according to Ballard who served in her, 'a splendid sea boat and steady gun platform'.

At the same time alarming news came from the British attaché in Paris who reported that as well as substantial progress with the original six ironclads the Emperor had ordered a further ten of the largest class. Thus the unthinkable prospect of the Royal Navy being outnumbered two to one was fast becoming reality. The Board demanded a crash programme of ten new ironclads and the

●Battle of the Ironclads,
March 9, 1862 which
lasted four hours without
inflicting serious damage
and with only one
casualty

conversion of ten wooden ships to armour-plating. Higher authority disagreed so a compromise was reached whereby five wooden battleships, then on the stocks, were given end-to-end armour, similar guns to *Warrior* and a speed of 12½ knots. Orders were also placed for three iron-hulled ships larger than *Warrior*, the last to be designed by Isaac Watts and to carry what was then the greatest armament afloat behind the thickest armour at the highest speed. Named *Minotaur*, *Agincourt* and *Northumberland* these five-masted giants were not completed until 1867/8 and then served mainly as fleet flagships. Thus Britain sought to even the score by increasing the number of ironclads to 15. The year 1861 saw both the genesis of the gun turret and the passing of the unarmoured wooden capital ship.

Early in March 1862 civil war in North America brought about an engagement in the sheltered waters of Hampton Roads between the Union's *Monitor*, mounting two heavy guns in an armoured revolving turret, and the broadside-armed Confederate ship, *Virginia* - ex-frigate *Merrimack* cut down and iron-plated. Reports of this famous but indecisive battle of the ironclads caused a sensation in England, the *Times* asserting that the ironclad problem had now been removed 'from the region of theory to the region of fact' and that 'the British Navy had been reduced to two ships' – *Warrior* and *Black Prince*.[3] Addressing the House of Lords, the Duke of Somerset stressed

that the battle confirmed the superiority of iron over wood for ships and that Britain must possess seagoing ironclads, not vessels like *Monitor* which he described as 'a cross between a raft and a diving bell'.[4] In his view the real lesson of Hampton Roads was that if other nations were to follow America's example 'then Great Britain must be prepared to send her armoured ships to all quarters of the globe'. The battle also fuelled the controversy over the best method of mounting weapons – in a battery firing broadsides or concentrated in revolving turrets able to fire on both sides.

In 1863 Isaac Watts was succeeded as Chief Constructor by Edward James Reed, whose ability and personality appealed to the First Lord and the Controller at the moment when ironclad design needed a fresh mind. Instead of long, fine hulls pierced for broadsides but difficult to manoeuvre Reed believed in short, handy ships, cheaper to build and – with more powerful engines – just as fast. By concentrating guns in a central armoured battery and mounting protected bow and stern chasers he sought to improve all-round fire capability. The 'belt-and-battery' design incorporating a ram was used for wooden ship conversions like *Lord Warden* and *Lord Clyde*, the newly constructed *Pallas* and *Bellerophon* and finally *Hercules* and *Monarch* – the latter, however, mounted two turrets.

Leading exponent of the turret was Captain

Cowper Coles whose inventiveness and persuasive powers caused the Admiralty in April, 1862 to order first *Prince Albert*, a mastless turret-armed coast defence ship, then *Royal Sovereign*, the first British turret ship at sea. Her success encouraged Coles to mount an influential press campaign and induce the Admiralty to allow him to design an ocean-going turret ship, of necessity with masts and sails. Despite opposition from Reed and the Controller, Coles convinced their lordships that he could improve on *Monarch* and in 1866 was given approval for a ship to be built by Laird of Birkenhead. In a letter to the *Times* (April 1862) Coles boasted that his vessel would be '100 feet shorter than the *Warrior*, and in all respects equal to her with one exception, that I will undertake to disable and capture her within one hour'. The name of the ship was to be the *Captain*.

In contrast to improvements in ship construction the fleet's armament had made little progress. The Armstrongs – in lower deck jargon 'them two muzzled guns' – had been an expensive failure and before *Warrior* paid off the 110 pdrs were withdrawn from service. Controversy ensued over the relative merits of smooth and rifled bore guns in which the *Excellent* and the *Warrior* target at Shoeburyness played valuable roles. In 1865 a muzzle-loader, built on the Armstrong system with rifling to take studded projectiles, was introduced. The navy accepted it as a standard weapon suitable for a turret, armoured barbette or plain broadside. Resembling enormous soda water bottles the guns increased from seven-inch calibre, weighing six and a half tons, to the monster 35 ton 12 inch of the 1870s, with projectiles weighing up to 700 lbs and necessitating mechanical appliances for loading. At a range of 3,000 yards the rate of fire compared unfavourably with 68 pdrs, and performance was far from perfect, a handicap that had to be endured until a satisfactory breech-loader evolved. The increase in calibre was essential to penetrate iron armour now nine inches thick.

By the end of 1864 the Admiralty received reports from Admirals Smart[5] and Dacres[6] on the characteristics of each ship in the Channel squadron, little new on *Warrior* or *Black Prince* coming to light. The Controller disagreed with many of Dacres' conclusions revealing a much more cogent appreciation of warship performance. In December 1864 he classified existing ironclads, compared them with French counterparts and proposed future capital ship construction to the Board.[7]

The main feature of *Warrior*'s 30-month refit was rearming with four eight-inch and 28 seven inch guns – the greatest number of rifled barrels heavier than six inch ever carried by a British warship – all mounted on iron carriages and slides. Eight of the seven inch guns were mounted on the upper deck – bow ports modified to enable them to fire ahead – while the other 20

were positioned inside the armoured citadel on the main deck, the eight inch being amidships. Armament changes entailed alterations to the two powder magazines and shell rooms where winches and whips were rigged to hoist 180lb projectiles. On the upper deck 40 pdrs were replaced by 20 pdr Armstrong saluting guns. Photographs of the ship reveal that a mechanical semaphore was fitted right aft.

Under Chief Engineer William Buchan, in sole charge of *Warrior* during the refit, the ship was thoroughly refurbished. Engine and propeller were overhauled and the burned top sections of the funnels renewed. Abnormal humidity below decks led to 'having scupper-holes cut in her armour-plating for the discharge of water from her decks, and scuttled for ventilation. This . . . will be highly conducive of health to the crew. The iron bulkheads are also being cut and watertight doors fitted, to perfect the ventilation below.'[8] On January 7, 1866 *Warrior* was inclined 'when she had just come out of dry dock and had undergone a thorough overhaul' to check the ship's ability to right herself when deliberately heeled over.[9]

Although re-rigged, the three wooden lower masts surprisingly were not replaced by iron spars as fitted in her sister ships; while the charthouse on the forward bridge moved aft, probably confirming that this was now the primary conning position. The ship also embarked a 42ft steam launch fitted with twin propellers. Rigged with a

canvas hood forward to prevent seas swamping the fires, it proved a useful boat.[10]

At the end of her refit, the Admiralty intended *Warrior* to relieve *Black Prince* at Queenstown (Cobh) as flagship to Rear Admiral Charles Frederick commanding the coastguard. Early in 1867 plans were overtaken by arrangements for the midsummer visit of the Sultan of Turkey and Khedive of Egypt, the highlight of their programme to join the Queen in a fleet review. Since both ships were needed to swell numbers it was decided that *Black Prince* would sail for Portsmouth, transfer her ship's company to *Warrior* and embark a new complement. Although delayed in the dockyard – resulting in sharp correspondence between the Controller and the Admiral Superintendent[11] – *Warrior* managed to get away to be commissioned on July 1 by Captain Corbett and a reduced complement ex-*Black Prince*. It all happened in rather a rush.

Steaming out of Portsmouth on July 8, *Warrior* joined the Channel squadron and other vessels assembling in Spithead. The 50-strong review fleet, commanded by Admiral Sir Thomas Pasley in the liner *Victoria*, embodied an ironclad squadron with three turret ships, an unarmoured squadron of two- and three-deckers and a dozen unarmoured gunboats. The contrast between the two squadrons was conspicuous, the diversity of their gun armaments startling.

While Admiral Warden with five ironclads was

detached to escort the Sultan across the Channel, remaining ships rehearsed the review evolutions off the Nab, the *Hampshire Telegraph* (July 12) reporting, 'the famous *Warrior* became the leading vessel of the ironclad line with her sister *Black Prince* second and the smart looking *Valiant* third.' Then weather broke and on the day of the review (July 17, 1867) *Warrior*'s log entered 'strong sou' westerly gale; low clouds and squally showers'.

As soon as the *Victoria and Albert* had passed down the lines of warships, their yards manned with cheering sailors, the commander-in-chief signalled, 'prepare to engage the enemy'. Every ship opened fire with blanks in a 20-minute mock battle against the Spithead forts enveloping the whole area in dense smoke. The gunboats under the captain of *Excellent* then 'engaged' the shore defences of Portsmouth and Gosport. For a time the people ashore, stated the *Hampshire Telegraph* (July 20), 'forgot the rain and spray and drizzling mist in contemplating the scene before them'.

Some hours later the fleet dispersed. By now the Admiralty had decided that *Warrior* would join the Channel squadron instead of going to Queenstown. On July 24 Captain Corbett and his ship's company transferred to *Mersey*, now earmarked for Ireland, and the next day *Warrior* was commissioned by Captain Henry Boys before going up harbour to complete fitting out and bring her complement up to strength. Strictly speaking *Warrior* had started her third commission but

since her second was so brief and inconsequential it has been discounted for the record.

Captain Boys came of a naval family and as a 17-year-old joined the *Edinburgh* to take part in the bombardment of Acre. Commended by Captain W W Henderson for 'steadiness and ability' under fire, Boys continued to gain such good reports that he earned a specialist course in the *Excellent*. From there he was appointed gunnery lieutenant in the *Centaur*, later combining these duties with flag lieutenant to his patron, now Rear Admiral Henderson. On the Brazilian station Henry Boys commanded the brig *Express* and survived outbreaks of yellow fever; after paying off in Spithead late in 1856 he married Margaret Truscott, Admiral Henderson's niece. Settling in Kent he raised a family, was promoted captain and appointed to *Victorious*, a third-rate accommodation hulk in Portsmouth that never commissioned. After seven years on half-pay he received command of the corvette *Pelorus*, transferred to *Barrosa* and was then rewarded with the *Warrior*, 'still considered one of the finest men o' war afloat.'[12]

His executive officer was Commander Guy Twiss and his master, now called staff commander, was Frank Inglis. An additional lieutenant was allowed, bringing the watchkeepers up to six. The only survivor of the first commission, Chief Engineer William Buchan, now 53, was in poor health and had to be relieved much against his will shortly before the ship ran the measured mile at Spithead on July 21. As if mourning the loss of the man who had looked after them so lovingly for six and a half years, the engines gave less than their best. To Cochrane, now commanding the Steam Reserve at Sheerness, Boys wrote, 'doubtless you will be disappoined to see in the papers such a poor account of the speed of your ship . . . 12.003 knots . . . I trust when we get in the fleet she will repeat her former doings and keep up her good name.' Commenting that the ship was unprepared for the trial, he concluded, 'if you can give me any hints as to the ship's peculiarities at sea – for most ships, like the fair sex, have them – I shall be thankful.'[13] Sadly Cochrane's reply is unrecorded.

For five weeks the ship lay at Spithead, while the new ship's company shook down. There were minor changes on the lower deck – more first and second class working petty officers, five more leading seamen and better qualified officers' cooks and stewards.

Sailing for Ireland on September 24 *Warrior* joined the Channel squadron under Rear Admiral Frederick Warden in Queenstown, delighted to have escaped the dreary routine of coastguard flagship. Two weeks later, in company with *Minotaur, Achilles, Bellerophon, Lord Warden* and *Lord Clyde,* she sailed for Lisbon. Almost immediately the squadron ran into a severe westerly gale. The admiral commented, 'the

Warrior . . . was found repeatedly to broach to as much as eight points (90 degrees) at a time against her helm when running with a strong breeze and her screw down . . . *Warrior* appeared to roll very considerably . . .'[14] This was fair criticism because with 15 men on the wheels and more on the relieving tackles, steering was extremely difficult owing to the stern lifting out of the water.

For two months the ship conformed to the Lisbon routine of training, sending away the new steam launch for evolutions and putting to sea with the squadron for two short cruises. When ordered to 'chase to windward' under sail *Achilles* led the squadron closely followed by *Warrior* and on November 26, in a prolonged full-power trial, *Achilles* again came out the winner. Itemizing his squadron's gunnery performance, Admiral Warden considered that *Minotaur* and *Achilles* were equal first with *Lord Warden* and *Warrior* equal second.'[15]

In December the squadron returned home and shortly before Christmas *Warrior* anchored in Osborne Bay, Isle of Wight, for a special task. Throughout 1867 there had been sporadic outbreaks of Fenian activity in Britain aimed at creating revolution and overthrowing the English government in Ireland. Captain Boys received a confidential letter from the Commander-in-Chief, Portsmouth, informing officers in command of ships employed in guarding Osborne 'that the necessity of having a vigilant guard over Her

Majesty has not been suggested by vague rumours, but from positive information of intentions which will if possible be carried out by reckless and unprincipled men in whose hands even the life of the Queen might not be safe'. The consequences for a commanding officer 'should the Queen be exposed to danger' was intimated.[16]

Captain George Bowyer of the coastguard service ship *Irresistible* was the senior of the two guardships, security being augmented by four small steam tenders anchored close inshore. The duty guardship 'rowed the guard' in a cutter and a gig with an armed crew under the charge of a midshipman day and night, crews changing every four hours. Should the alarm signal be seen from the tower at Osborne – a light by night and a ball shape by day – then a party of armed seamen would be landed 'to render immediate assistance'. Nobody quite knew what they were supposed to do.

Boys was often invited to dine at Osborne, usually with the household, but once or twice at the royal table. Although not recorded in the ship's log Boys' memoirs disclosed that Queen Victoria paid *Warrior* an informal visit – perhaps to light refreshment in the captain's quarters – a great honour as she rarely went aboard any ship except the royal yachts. She is understood to have expressed her pleasure at the reception given.

When not duty guardship *Warrior* gave 48-hours leave in Portsmouth periodically and the two months passed without incident except that

Boatswain Lilly was placed under arrest 'for drunkenness and neglect of duty'. His successor was not long in joining.

Back in Portsmouth Warrior *went into dock for ten days emerging to run the measured mile on April 1. This time the ship was fully prepared for a peak performance under the supervision of Captain Chamberlain and his staff from the Steam Reserve at Portsmouth. The weather was fair and all hands eagerly awaited the announcement of results after the sixth run between the vertical black and white marks plainly visible from Stokes Bay. As the ship reduced speed turning slowly to shape course for the anchorage, Boys turned to his staff commander. 'Well, Mr Inglis, what did you make of that?' Inglis did not give opinions lightly. 'It looks good, sir, but let us wait for Captain Chamberlain.' The first captain of* Resistance *in 1862 Chamberlain was well aware that the ship had put everything into redeeming her reputation. 'Subject to confirmation, of course, I make the average speed 14.1 knots.'* Warrior *had done it again, only a quarter of a knot less than the initial trial seven years ago and nearly as fast as the later ironclads* Minotaur, Achilles *and* Bellerophon. *In fact 14 knots remained the battle fleet's maximum speed for the next 20 years. That evening Boys telegraphed the news to Cochrane at Sheerness where he commanded the Steam Reserve and by letter to Buchan who had recently taken up an appointment in Portsmouth.*

After a six hours' continuous steaming trial at full power, *Warrior* joined *Minotaur* – the flagship – *Achilles* and *Defence* en route for Holyhead when they escorted the *Victoria and Albert* with the Prince of Wales on board for an official visit to Dublin. The squadron remained off Kingstown in Dublin Bay until April 25 when the royal yacht returned to Holyhead, allowing the escort to proceed to Portland. For *Warrior* it was the beginning of another work-up to full efficiency.

After spending May 1868 in harbour, early the following month the seven ironclads put to sea for a four-week Channel training cruise. A flat calm during the first ten days was ideal for steam evolutions at five knots but economy dictated that sails must be carried whenever possible. To meet the current obsession that each ship must be in its correct station whatever the formation was never easy for ironclads. At two to three knots it must have been impossible, especially in poor visibility. A more realistic evolution exercised was 'tow ship', when *Warrior* towed *Royal Oak* from the after bitts for four hours at five knots. Channel squadron main engines were still not thought to be totally reliable.

As a man who probably owed his flag rank more to good luck than ability, Warden found it hard to assess the differing characteristics of his squadron. '*Minotaur*, *Achilles* and *Warrior* are three very noble ships' was all he could write to the Admiralty, but *Warrior* he believed least valuable 'due to her unarmoured ends, exposure of steering wheel and rolling propensities'.[17]

Boys reckoned that *Warrior* had been unfairly treated. 'We are keeping up the old name as far as sailing is concerned,' he wrote in a letter to Cochrane at the end of July but steam was a different matter. '*Warrior* lost a push when Mr Buchan left her. His successor (Cowan) is not a man to make the most of her . . . quite an average individual that is all.' Referring to the steam trial off Lisbon the previous November he pointed out that the ship was out of trim, deep laden with coal and stores and longest out of dock. Moreover 'to my horror the (chief) engineer told me he did not know we were on trial'. While admitting the weakness of the steering apparatus, he could 'not help feeling some disgust at the suppression of facts when any advantage is gained over the later ships'.[18] Clearly there was feeling between *Warrior* and *Achilles*.

Early on August 14 Admiral Warden set off from Portland on a cruise to Scotland and Northern Ireland. Sailing west with a southerly wind bringing frequent squally showers, the squadron was formed in two columns, ships in line ahead 800 yards apart. The port (weather) column consisted of *Minotaur*, *Bellerophon*, *Achilles* and *Defence*, the starboard column *Penelope*, *Royal Oak*, *Warrior* and *Pallas*. At 1.30pm *Warrior* hauled out of line to clear *Penelope*'s cutter picking up a man overboard; an hour later *Pallas* broke down and parted company. As darkness fell *Royal Oak* was much astern of her station, *Warrior* keeping about two cables (400 yards) from her.

●Captain and officers
of Warrior on the
quarterdeck circa 1869

1 Captain Nugent MacNamara,
  Marine Artillery
2 Commander Guy Twiss
3 Captain Henry Boys
4 Rev Jonathan Parkin
5 Staff Surgeon James Walsh
6 Assistant Surgeon Richard
  Mowll

At 9.30pm the Admiral in *Minotaur* signalled 'use steam to keep station'. This was received by *Penelope* and *Warrior* but not – as it later transpired – by *Royal Oak* for whose benefit it was intended. The signal caused *Warrior* to remain astern instead of passing *Royal Oak* and taking her place in the line. Both Boys and Inglis were on the bridge and they understood that with steam at her disposal *Royal Oak* could easily regain her proper station.

At 10.40pm *Minotaur* signalled 'reef topsails', firing a gun to draw attention. This was correctly received in *Royal Oak* but the combination of lights so confused *Warrior* and *Penelope* that both understood it to mean 'tack in succession'. Starting to reef her fore topsails *Royal Oak* turned into the wind and lost way as she came across *Warrior*'s bows. Sensing a collision Boys ordered, 'back the mizzen topsail', then 'back the main topsail' and finally 'full astern' on the engines. It was too late to stop the ship and at 10.55pm *Warrior*'s port bow touched *Royal Oak*'s starboard quarter, smashing her cutter. At the same time *Warrior* carried away her own jib-boom, figurehead, bumpkin and anchor stock. Within a minute Boys had dropped his ship clear and later rejoined station under steam informing the Admiral by signal of the incident.[19]

In worsening weather – it was blowing a strong gale – all hands in *Warrior* spent the rest of the night and part of the next day clearing the wreckage forward. On reaching Loch Foyle Rear Admiral Ryder, squadron second-in-command in *Penelope*, came aboard to hold an enquiry over the collision. In the absence of *Royal Oak* he was unable to make a definite report.

While *Warrior* continued the cruise to Belfast Lough and Greenock, news of the collision caused some unflattering press criticism which may have influenced the Admiralty to order a court-martial on Boys which was held in *Royal Adelaide* at Plymouth. The charge read '. . . did on or about the 14th day of August 1868 negligently or by default, damage and hazard the loss of Her Majesty's Ships *Royal Oak* and *Warrior* by running foul of . . . *Royal Oak*'.

Captain Robert Hall, superintendent of Pembroke dockyard, was to act for the defence but could not get away at the time. He advised Boys to get a solicitor. The suggestion was not accepted. 'I have not availed myself of legal assistance,' said Boys in court, 'as this is entirely a nautical question.' President of the court was Admiral Sir William Fanshawe Martin, Commander-in-Chief, Plymouth. The court sat for four days.

A well-handled defence was undoubtedly assisted by a letter of appreciation of Boys from Admiral Warden. The charge was not proved and Boys was acquitted. According to *The Morning Post*, 'when intelligence of the acquittal of Captain Boys was known on board the *Warrior* three tremendous cheers were given him by the crew . . . Seldom has an officer come out of a court-martial more thoroughly exculpated.' Letters of congratulation poured in from all directions, including one from the First Sea Lord. The efficiency of Colomb's flashing night signals in poor visibility came in for considerable criticism and a demand was made for a better qualified yeoman of signals. What did not come out publicly was that the collision showed the inability of ships in company to manoeuvre safely at night under sail.[20]

From mid-October *Warrior* underwent repairs for two months in Plymouth, decidedly unpopular with the ship's company as they were basically Portsmouth-manned. After Admiral Martin inspected the ship he had helped to conceive ten years earlier, an unsuccessful search was made in *Royal Oak* for the head of the famous figurehead seen to fall on her quarterdeck. It later transpired that it had been captured by some midshipmen who had hidden it in the gunroom behind a false bulkhead. So James Hellyer of Portsmouth was commissioned to carve a new one.

Morale on board was never higher as the flag of Vice Admiral Sir Thomas Symonds, appointed to command the Channel squadron, was hoisted in *Warrior* on December 12. Sailing south the ship ran into a force ten gale, shipping quantities of water over the bows and causing minor damage to the upper deck; but the experience of heavy weather was invaluable. During the first three months of 1869 the 'Lisbon squadron', as it was sarcastically called by the wives in England, made four cruises off the Portuguese coast.

Admiral Warden had allowed the squadron 'to fall into a very slack and undisciplined condition' according to an officer serving at the time. Captains were allowed to do pretty much as they pleased and to chaff the Admiral by signal. The story goes that on one occasion Warden had asked why a ship was out of station, to which the captain replied that a woodcock had flown across the bows distracting the officer of the watch. Son of the former Surveyor of the Navy, Symonds soon put a stop to all that. "Old Tom', as he was called, was a stickler for discipline and a born ship-handler with an iron nerve. After many trials of his ships under sail he realised that sail power in a battleship was doomed and that steam power must be used for manoeuvring at higher speeds than hitherto employed, a decision not welcomed by an Admiralty intent on economy.[21]

During the early months of 1869, regular sail drill and target firings in varying degrees of weather helped to bring *Warrior* to the standard expected by a captain who was both a gunnery expert and a practical seaman. Officers of the watch were kept up to the mark as illustrated by the case of Lieutenant Hayes, reprimanded by the Admiral for allowing the ship to get a mile astern of station. In harbour the log recorded a two-day admiral's inspection, the arrival of the new ironclad *Hercules*, dressing ship overall with flags

for George Washington's birthday, the 'flogging of David Prince, Boy 1st Class, with 24 cuts of the cane', the lowering of colours to half-mast on the occasion of the death of Captain Dew of the *Northumberland*, and the reprimand of Mr Maxwell, boatswain, for not having the yards square when the Admiral passed in his barge.

On April 20 the squadron sailed for England. Among official letters waiting in Portland was one confirming an unusual task for *Warrior* – to tow a floating dock to Bermuda. Because the local stone at the Bermuda naval base was unsuitable for a dry dock the Admiralty ordered a floating dock, large enough for ironclads, to be built by Campbell Johnstone on the Thames. Launched in 1868 and completed the following year it was almost as long as *Warrior* and displaced more than 8,000 tons, the biggest floating dock in the world. In view of its cost – two thirds that of *Warrior* – considerable care was taken to ensure its safe arrival, the first occasion that such an unwieldy vessel had to cross an ocean. *Northumberland* and *Agincourt* in tandem escorted by the large paddle frigate *Terrible* would tow the dock from England to Madeira where *Warrior* and *Black Prince* would take over. Coal consumption would be critical.

On *Warrior*'s arrival in Portsmouth dockyard on May 31 all hands were needed to get on board the long and heavy 26in circumference towing hawsers and the shorter chain cables and towing slips. Artificers had to modify the stern ports and

fit special gear aft on the main deck. Particular attention was given to the point of tow in *Warrior* and measures to avoid chafing, all of which played havoc with the captain's quarters.

The upper deck armament having been landed *Warrior* took on extra coal in sacks to sail for Madeira on June 17, 1869. Off Plymouth *Black Prince* joined company, *Warrior* being senior ship for the operation. As such Boys reported direct to the Admiralty emphasising in his first letter their efforts to conserve fuel. Coal lighters were awaiting them in Funchal Roads, each evolution of coal ship being rewarded by the popular pipe, 'hands to bathe'. The paddler *Helicon* brought a despatch from Captain May of the *Northumberland* describing how the tow behaved in the Bay of Biscay and recommending 'an additional 150 tons of coal'. On July 3 *Warrior*, *Black Prince* and *Helicon* moved round to Porto Santo to await the dock's arrival next day.

Next morning Boys boarded *Northumberland* which, with *Agincourt* and the paddle frigate *Terrible*, anchored at 3pm close enough to *Warrior* to allow the two big towing hawsers to be transferred. At 5pm *Warrior* weighed anchor, going ahead 'easy' with the dock in tow. At 7.45pm *Black Prince* was towing from ahead while *Helicon* was ordered to England, her place being taken by the twin-screw gun-vessel *Lapwing*. To assist steering *Terrible* was secured astern of the dock with towing hawsers but opinions differed as to

● Campbell's patent
floating dry dock adapted
for HM Dockyard,
Bermuda, and launched
September 3, 1868,
length 381ft, width 123ft,
height 74ft

her value. Headsails hoisted, *Warrior* set course for Bermuda at four to five knots, initially steering WSW to pick up favourable trade winds. The operation had started – 2,700 miles to go.

Under the command of Staff Commander William Hains, H M Floating Dock *Bermuda* had been officially commissioned to obviate problems in case weather necessitated shelter in a foreign port. Officers included a surgeon, boatswain, carpenter and an Admiralty overseer, with accommodation for a ship's company of nearly 80. Two 90ft wooden bridges spanned the sides and there was a binnacle, semaphore apparatus, Colomb's lights and, of course, a white ensign. Ship routine was strictly observed – scrub and wash decks, defaulters, grog at seven bells and constant communication with *Warrior*, sometimes by boat but more often by semaphore. Assistant Paymaster Dixon from *Warrior* was sent over to assist with the accounts and on another occasion a hindquarters of mutton arrived for Hains with Captain Boys' compliments. On the last Saturday evening the dock's wardroom officers performed 'the Cobbler's Dance' described by an onlooker as 'a marvel of agility and grotesqueness'. When *Warrior*'s band played for them from her quarterdeck they reckoned it was better than the music from *Northumberland*.[22]

Although its twin-rudder steering was largely ineffective the dock yawed only a few degrees and 'dock towing steady' was recorded in *Warrior*'s log every four hours. Hands on deck were fully occupied setting, furling and trimming sails to eke out the precious fuel. At no time did the wind exceed a strong breeze or the captain have qualms about bad weather. On July 18 *Terrible* exchanged positions with *Black Prince* allowing *Lapwing* to be towed astern as she was running short of coal. Six days later she had conserved enough to go on ahead to warn Bermuda of the flotilla's imminence.

Staff Commander Frank Inglis sighted Bermuda's Gibbs Hill light just after midnight on July 28; by dawn land was well in sight. According to the *Bermuda Royal Gazette*, 'two huge ships, the *Warrior* and *Black Prince*, were seen towing the immense structure towards the east end of the island, with the *Terrible* acting as rudder . . . every height commanding a view of the North Channel was crowded with carriages and people and the water was well covered with boats of all descriptions.' They were due for a disappointment because the two ironclads were too long and drew too much water to negotiate the dock through The Narrows.

Honours for the final stage were passed to *Terrible* whose 800 hp and churning paddles proved insufficiently powerful to control the tow, so *Warrior* took the strain ahead of the dock first with a 10in then a 13in hawser, putting *Lapwing* astern. By that time Captain James Wainwright, formerly of *Black Prince* and now naval officer-in-charge of Bermuda, came out to help. Both he and Boys were angry at the lack of suitable towing power. Apparently the local commander-in-chief had promised to send all available paddlers but none had arrived.

Next day *Warrior* anchored before transferring her tow to the local tug *Spitfire*. At 11am the dock was ready to go with *Terrible* and *Spitfire* ahead, the gunboats *Viper* and *Vixen* on each side and *Lapwing* astern. Despite an abrupt turn in the Channel that nearly put the dock aground, the flotilla came to rest in Grassey Bay to the resounding cheers of spectators – 36 days out from England. 'The whole town of Hamilton', wrote an officer ashore had 'come out to stare at the strange monster – the most wonderful craft that ever made voyage since Noah's Ark went cruising.'

Task completed, *Warrior* re-embarked her working party of seamen, filled her bunkers and prepared to leave. When the bullock boat came alongside the butcher went down to select four healthy specimens to be hoisted aboard for the passage home. On July 31 the two ironclads sailed for Plymouth.

The two captains could now afford to relax as the ships spread to a mile or so apart racing for home. Frederick Ouslie, captain of the foretop, fell overboard from aloft as *Warrior* heeled to a strong breeze. An alert quartermaster by the wheel threw him a rope's end which he grabbed before disappearing in the wake and was hauled aboard. After stopping briefly in Plymouth Sound *Warrior*

●HM Floating Dock
Bermuda in tow of
Warrior and Black Prince
(ahead) with Terrible
astern, leaving Porto
Santo, Madeira

fetched up in Spithead.

At evening quarters on August 25 all hands closed aft on the quarterdeck so the captain could read a letter from the Admiralty. 'The reports of the successful towing of the dock to Bermuda having been received . . . my Lords desire to place on record their marked appreciation of the zeal and skill displayed by captains, officers and men employed . . . The navigation of the Bermuda dock over a distance of 4,000 miles of ocean was an operation without precedent in the British or any other navy.'[23] For the next two nights the public houses of Queen Street by Portsmouth Hard were full of happy *Warriors* as each watch celebrated the ship's achievement.

Henry Boys was also delighted to learn of his immediate appointment to command the *Excellent*, a plum job. A strict and competent officer and greatly respected by officers and men, Boys' leadership had the human touch as illustrated by the following story, recounted by his grandson Commander Frank Boys. Soon after he joined *Warrior* Midshipman John D P French was found to suffer from a fear of heights although he stuck to his duties manfully. Realising that he would never adjust himself to the Navy, Boys sent for him, discussed his future and eventually arranged his discharge with a favourable report on his ability. French joined the army, commanded the British Expeditionary Force in France in 1914 and ultimately became Field Marshal the Earl of Ypres.

Warrior's new captain was Frederick Stirling appointed, for some reason, for only six months. The ship went in to have the bottom scraped, hoist in the upper deck guns and fasten the new, much-admired figurehead, its arrival delayed by the towing operation.

Ordered to join the Channel squadron in Milford Haven *Warrior* returned to fleet routine once more and towards the end of October 1869 sailed south to Lisbon. From then until May 1870 *Warrior's* programme resumed the familiar pattern, cruising to the Canaries, Gibraltar and the Azores when not at anchor in the Tagus off Lisbon. On March 2 Stirling was relieved by Captain Henry Glyn.

On leaving Corunna the squadron sailed for England and on May 21 met the two turret ships *Monarch* and *Captain* at a rendezvous off Cape Finisterre. The latter had more recently commissioned and the former in 1869 had crossed the Atlantic to make a tremendous impression on the United States. With her greater freeboard and displacement *Monarch* had gained the edge in comparative sea trials and according to Ballard, 'in the supreme question of combatant efficiency during heavy weather conditions . . . while the *Captain's* decks were swept by the sea and her turret ports frequently flooded in a moderately fresh breeze . . . the decks of *Monarch* remained bone dry.'[24]

It was a memorable occasion for the Black Battlefleet, this meeting between the first and second generations of broadside ironclads and the world's first seagoing turret battleships. Steering north Symonds formed his ships into two columns with *Captain* stationed on the admiral's weather beam. Off Ushant they ran into strong gales from which *Captain*, under close reefed main topsail and storm staysail, emerged satisfactorily. Cowper Coles regarded this as proof of her seagoing capability but Admiral Symonds' instinct was less sure.

At Portsmouth Symonds relinquished command prematurely, the result of his uncompromising views on the ships under his command and criticism of the Controller's department in their attempts to build ships that combined steam and sail. His outspoken reports were less than popular with the Admiralty which sent him a telegram before leaving Lisbon 'Will you accept Good Service Pension (£300 per annum) conditional on resigning command of the Channel Squadron?' Resolute to the end Symonds replied, 'I am proud to accept the honour you propose to confer on me.'[25]

Early in June 1870 *Warrior* went into dock coming out six weeks later with a new commander, Alfred Markham, and a new watchkeeper Lieutenant Harry Keith Murray, delighted to be back in his old ship. *Warrior* then sailed to join the Mediterranean fleet at Gibraltar and the

● Impression of HMS
Captain in the Bay of
Biscay, 1870

combined force sailed northward on August 19 under Admiral Sir Alexander Milne, Commander-in-Chief, Mediterranean. The fleet organisation in divisions and sub-divisions comprised *Lord Warden, Royal Oak, Captain, Prince Consort, Caledonia* (Rear Admiral Cooper Key), *Monarch, Bristol, Bellerophon, Minotaur* (Vice Admiral Yelverton), *Northumberland, Hercules, Agincourt* (Admiral Chads), *Inconstant* and *Warrior*. According to Ballard 'many of the 7,000 officers and men present had not seen the *Captain* at sea and her behaviour was under critical observation from the fleet'. Undoubtedly the old sailors shook their heads when they saw her close-hauled with her lee rail awash.

After briefly visiting Vigo the fleet continued the cruise with steam evolutions off Cape Finisterre in fair weather although *Warrior's* log recorded that the long, heavy swell caused considerable rolling. Until then Admiral Milne had been too busy to inspect *Captain* at sea but on the morning of September 6 he went aboard to witness target practice and walk round the ship.

That afternoon wind and sea increased as the glass fell. About an hour before sunset Milne signalled *Lord Warden* to close and send a cutter for him as an ugly swell set in from the west. Pressed to stay on board for the night by the *Captain's* commanding officer, Hugh Burgoyne, the admiral decided his place was in the flagship. The fleet hove to, the cutter came alongside and with

some difficulty Milne followed his flag lieutenant into the boat.

From *Warrior's* bridge Captain Glyn watched first *Lord Warden* and then *Captain* resume station as the squadron steered WNW in two columns. He ordered a second reef to be taken in the topsails, warned the engine room of the need for steam for station-keeping and warned the commander to ensure that the ship was well secured. It was going to be a dirty night.

By 11pm the heavy and confused sea combined with south-westerly winds gusting to gale force made station-keeping impracticable and frequent rain squalls reduced visibility to a few hundred yards. At midnight Lieutenant de Hoghton fought his way to the after conning-bridge to take over the watch. The ship was steaming north west at three knots, with *Minotaur* somewhere to the west and *Agincourt* ahead.

At about 00.15am the wind strength suddenly increased to storm force and either split or blew clean away no fewer than 23 sails in the fleet. *Warrior* lost her main and fore topsails but as always came through under total control.

In *Captain* the situation was quite different. When the middle watchmen were called at 11.45pm the watch on deck were trying to clew down the topsail yards on the cramped superstructure. The halyards had been let fly but the ship was already heeling too much to allow the spars to come down by their own weight. As the

●Lieutenant Henry Keith Murray (below) served in Warrior from July 16, 1870 to June 20, 1871

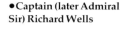

●Captain (later Admiral Sir) Richard Wells

relieving watch mustered on the foc'sle the squall struck, throwing the *Captain* over to the maximum angle of safety and beyond. For a few moments she lay on her beam ends until the inrush of water through funnel and superstructure destroyed her buoyancy. Then she rolled over and disappeared 20 miles west of Cape Finisterre. Ignorant of the tragedy *Inconstant* passed over the spot ten minutes later. And saw nothing.[26]

When Lieutenant Keith Murray came up for the morning watch at 4am he found the wind had veered to the north west and that all effort was concentrated on regaining station. By the half light of the dawn, ships were gradually identified but when Glyn enquired the position of *Captain*, Murray replied laconically, 'Sir, she has not yet been sighted.' At noon Admiral Milne ordered ships to spread out in line abreast reversing course along the tracks of the previous night. In *Warrior* lookouts were posted at yard arms and mastheads as the weather slowly improved. The despatch vessel *Psyche*, joining from the south, reported seeing two cutters, bottoms upward. *Inconstant* sighted boxes and *Monarch* picked up part of a topgallant yard. At midnight, laying-to under steam, ships had boats away picking up wreckage.

Next morning *Warrior* lowered her cutters four times to recover boat's gear, a hatch ladder and part of a hammock netting, all identified as being from the *Captain*. At noon Milne signalled, 'Admiral is sure all will sympathise with regard to dreadful disaster that has occurred'.

On September 9 *Monarch* came up over the horizon signalling 'one officer and 17 men saved from HMS *Captain* in launch.' These were the only survivors of 472 officers and men. They had succeeded in making a landfall on the coast of Spain where they were picked up by *Monarch* and transferred to *Volage* for passage to Plymouth.

That was the end of fleet exercises. When the news reached England the nation was aghast at the loss of a ship and her crew which had been so much in the public eye. On September 15 *Warrior* returned to Portland with the squadron where she remained for three months. During that period *Minotaur* sailed into the roads with yet another change of flag, this time that of Vice Admiral George Wellesley (whose flag captain, Richard Wells, was the author's grandfather). When it came for *Warrior*'s wardroom to pay a call on their opposite numbers in the flagship, Lieutenant Keith Murray was delighted to meet Paymaster John de Vries and recall memories of the first commission over a glass of brandy and soda. Later *Warrior* went to sea with *Minotaur* and *Northumberland* for a day's prize firing at targets, perhaps the first indication of competitive gunnery practice in the Channel squadron. 'On these occasions', according to Ballard, 'it was not uncommon for a ship to be so completely enveloped by her own smoke for appreciable periods that nothing was visible from anywhere but the mastheads'.

In December, 1870, *Warrior* sailed for Portsmouth to give leave over Christmas before returning to Portland for another three months stint of sail, boat and gun drill, target firings and inspections; on one occasion Captain Boys brought a party of gunnery lieutenants from the *Excellent* to watch the experimental firings of the new pebble powder charges. At this stage the number of punishment warrants increased noticeably indicating that either Commander Markham was stricter than his predecessor or ship's company were wearying of routine. The fact that Lieutenant C J Wise was placed under arrest – later to be court-martialled – at the same time as a 'search for stolen articles' spelt laxity in the wardroom. In the gunroom midshipmen were kicking over the traces and breaking out of the ship, necessitating stern disciplinary action. Midshipman Frederick Fisher, younger brother of Jackie, recalls, 'we had a chaplain on board who was much too fond of the bottle and finally he distinguished himself by falling down a hatchway when conducting divine service. After that his services were dispensed with by the navy.'[27]

An interesting aspect of the second commission was the number on the sick list, well below that of the first commission. Better ventilation, food and medical facilities obviously made for a healthier life below decks. Yet, for some reason, men's teeth were neglected, surgeons leaving the business of extraction to sick berth stewards who received next to no training. Writing later a staff surgeon revealed, 'when in 1870 I was serving on board HMS *Warrior* I was one day horrified by the sick berth steward producing two of Lazenby's pickle bottles – one of which was full and the other two thirds full of teeth which, the man said, he had extracted in ten months without the knowledge of the medical officers of the ship, and he was not a little proud of the achievement.'[28] All of this must have caused a great deal of pain to the patients who presumably bore their suffering with Victorian stoicism. In March when *Warrior* arrived in Plymouth for docking, the entire ship's company mustered for vaccination against smallpox; at that time the disease was rampant in Gosport and parts of Portsmouth.

Early in May 1871 *Warrior* joined the squadron at Bearhaven, Ireland, for the summer cruise and en route to Madeira 'observed an English merchant brig . . . flying a signal of distress.' Shortening to topsails *Warrior* hove to and sent boats over to what transpired to be the *Hannibal* with two mutineers on board. Captain Glyn had them transferred first to *Warrior*'s cells and then to the British Consulate in Madeira.

Vice Admiral Wellesley came aboard soon after arrival to look round the ship, witness muster by open list and, a few days later, watch the men at general quarters. 'Capital ship you have, Captain Glyn,' was his parting remark. Just to show there was life in the old girl yet *Warrior* was pitched against *Hercules* and *Inconstant* to 'try a rate of sailing'. When running before the wind it was *Warrior* that surged ahead and only when close hauled did *Inconstant*, reputedly the fastest sailer in the navy, gain a narrow lead.

Following a short spell in Gibraltar the squadron sailed for Tangier on July 1. Formed in two columns in line ahead *Warrior* was stationed two cables (400 yards) astern of *Agincourt* leading the lee column, flagship of Rear Admiral Eardley Wilmot, second in command. It was a beautiful calm day without a ripple on the surface but on clearing Gibraltar Bay and steaming at six knots the squadron encountered a contrary four-knot current. It was unusual for the junior admiral's column to be positioned nearer the land with a current setting them towards danger, a fact grasped by both Captain Glyn and Staff Commander May on *Warrior*'s bridge. 'I don't like this,' exclaimed Glyn to Lieutenant de Hoghton, the officer of the watch, 'steer a point to port. Keep leadsmen sounding.' Within seconds *Agincourt* ran aground on the clearly charted Pearl Rock, so gently that those on board scarcely felt it. 'Helm hard-a-starboard. Stop engines. Full astern,' ordered Glyn. Slowly *Warrior* swung round, clearing *Agincourt* by the narrowest of margins.

The squadron closed in round the stranded ship. Anchors were laid out without success so

●**Hercules about to tow Agincourt off the Pearl Rock, July 1, 1871**

efforts were made to lighten her. By the time lighters arrived from Gibraltar the boats of the squadron, including *Warrior*'s, were alongside *Agincourt* to relieve the ship of anchors, cables, shot and shell – in fact everything movable. Still the ship would not shift so out came the heavy guns. When this measure failed the situation became critical: a change of weather could have broken her up. On the fourth day *Hercules* was given the job of towing her off. Carefully positioning his bower anchor Captain Lord Gilford backed his ship until the stern was close enough to *Agincourt* to pass two chain cables. Then 'heave round the capstan' and 'full speed ahead' on the telegraph. Off came the stranded ship to squadron cheers for masterly seamanship.[29]

On return to Gibraltar *Warrior*'s working parties were again employed, this time in recovering anchors while Glyn, May and de Hoghton were sent home as witnesses for the inevitable court-martial. *Agincourt*'s captain and staff commander were severely reprimanded and admonished to be more careful in future. Both admirals were superseded, Admiral Wellesley's departure from *Minotaur* causing 'a very great commotion amongst his crew, all of them greatly disappointed. The gallant offcer left us deeply regretted.'[30] In fact he went on to command the North America and West Indies station – taking Richard Wells as his flag captain – and became First Sea Lord in 1877.

Although *Warrior*'s time was running out it was not quite the end. In mid-July she sailed for Vigo, to rendezvous off Ushant with ships from the Channel, Reserve and Flying squadrons together with the Mediterranean fleet – 17 iron-clads, four large frigates and two corvettes. On August 12 the most powerful British fleet ever seen formed three lines of columns of divisions in line ahead under the command of Vice Admiral Sir Hastings Yelverton in *Lord Warden*. After carrying out evolutions in ideal weather conditions for 48 hours they dispersed, a fitting swan-song to *Warrior*'s service as a first line warship.

Calling briefly at Queenstown, when a party of midshipmen visited Blarney Castle, *Warrior* sailed first for Plymouth and then Portsmouth where the ship was dismantled and destored. On Friday, September 15, 1871, *Warrior* was paid off, Midshipman Eeles recording in his log at 1.25pm, 'Finis'.

The second commission was over.

CHAPTER NINE
Coastguard and Reserve

WARRIOR WAS BUILT to meet a threat from France; it seemed only right that her departure from the active fleet should coincide with the eclipse of a naval challenge that in retrospect should never have been mounted by a country so inferior in material resources. *Warrior*'s new and subservient role marked a decade of ironclad shipbuilding, in which 30 ships of 20 different designs and almost as many armament layouts were constructed. A third of the ships had wooden hulls, most had rams and sails remained their primary method of propulsion. Controversy continued over the merits of more powerful, heavier muzzle-loading guns – an attempt to introduce breech-loaders in 1868 failed – versus tougher armour. Whereas the French strove for uniformity the Royal Navy, ever confident of superiority, believed in experimentation; and although in 1864 Spencer Robinson had foreseen the dangers ahead little was done to standardize or classify armour-plated ships in the fleet, causing problems in operations, logistics and administration. Luckily there was no major war.

After designing *Monarch* Chief Constructor Reed produced a smaller class of belt-and-battery ironclad with a platform stable enough to satisfy gunnery specialists. First came *Audacious* and *Vanguard*, then *Invincible* and *Iron Duke* to join the fleet in 1871.

In 1873 *Devastation* appeared – as innovative as *Warrior* had been in 1861, *Royal Sovereign* in 1864,

and *Monarch* in 1869 – to become the fourth milestone in capital ship evolution. Designed by Reed and modified by his successor Barnaby, *Devastation* was the first ocean-going, mastless turret ship in the world. Four 35 ton guns were mounted in twin turrets on top of, instead of inside, the hull while a turn of speed combined with a 4,700 mile cruising radius. But ungainly appearance and lack of sails led to public outcry. After commissioning few were surprised when a notice fixed anonymously to her gangway stated, 'letters for HMS *Captain* may be posted on board'. However, she and her sister ship *Thunderer* vindicated their unusual design.

As a youthful constructor, Nathaniel Barnaby had been a member of *Warrior*'s design team. Against his advice and that of the Committee on Design, the Admiralty astonishingly reverted in 1873 to sailing battleships, instructing Barnaby to design *Alexandra*, the last British central battery ship, and *Temeraire*, known as the Great Brig. Then came the lean years when the economies of successive Liberal and Conservative governments became known as the 'dark ages of the Victorian navy'. By 1880 the French navy claimed parity with the British.

Ten years of service without major modification made *Warrior* obsolescent. Capable of reasonably hard-hitting support, her speed unimpaired and her hull in excellent condition, she had to face relegation to second-line strength.

For this purpose her second refit in Portsmouth from 1872 to 1875 entailed overhauling main engines, fitting Penn's new pistons and trunks into re-bored cylinders and installing new boilers able to burn a wider variety of fuel together with superheaters and improved funnel draught arrangements. Upper deck planking was relaid and a poop constructed extending some 48ft from the stern to provide quarters for an admiral; to balance the extra weight aft a new bowsprit was fitted. On the main deck the forward capstan was converted to steam and the rudder head repaired after damage caused when entering dry dock. The armament was unaltered, the guns remaining in the ship until she was finally disarmed. To her steam launch was added a steam pinnace.

Chief Engineer Matthew Kidd supervised the refitting work helped, later, by a gunner, boat-swain and carpenter, following an Admiralty instruction that 'everything should be done to advance the completion of Warrior'. The ever-growing cost of the fleet caused raised eyebrows in Parliament when it was learned that £125,245 had been expended on Warrior since 1862, a third of her original cost.

As a unit of the First Reserve in the Coastguard service and 'for Royal Naval Reserve duties', Warrior was commissioned in Portsmouth on April 1, 1875 by Captain William Whyte. Her executive officer, Commander William Scott, was assisted by four watchkeeping lieutenants in a wardroom of 27 and a ship's company of 320, mostly from Achilles.

Admiralty's decision to take over the Coastguard service from the Commissioner of Customs was based on the need to defend the coast against French invasion, man the fleet in emergency and stamp out smuggling. To cover the coast from Bournemouth to the Scilly Isles nine commanders were appointed to Warrior 'additional for Coastguard service'. In theory every part of the coast was patrolled from sunset to sunrise 'to prevent collusion with smugglers'. In practice it was all a bit of a farce.[1]

The captain of Warrior's job was to inspect his stations once a year and visit reserve drill ships and batteries at larger stations. Coastguard service ships went to sea only once a quarter to fire their allowances of ammunition; and each summer there was a four to six weeks cruise when extra officers and men joined to complete the comple-ment. Routine was easy-going, a cushy job for the older men. For officers it did not count for seatime and was unpopular because of so many changes in the wardroom. Inevitably Warrior was to earn the derogatory epithet of 'gobby ship', meaning a soft number.[2]

Warrior's full power trial on May 3 recorded 14.15 knots, slightly better than in 1868. From Spithead Warrior sailed for Portland to take up her station at anchor in the Roads now enclosed by breakwaters with two entrance channels.[3] At the end of July the First Reserve squadron assembled for their annual cruise.

Vice Admiral Sir John Tarleton, Admiral Superintendent of Reserves, hoisted his flag in Warrior on July 26, 1875, the first flag officer to occupy the new suite on the poop. Following complaints in Parliament that Ireland did not see enough of the navy, the admiral was ordered to take his seven ironclads round the island, calling in at several ports before finishing at Kingstown in Dublin Bay. There Admiral Tarleton was told to take four ships to Queenstown (Cork). On September 1, Warrior, Hector, Vanguard and Iron Duke sailed in single column, shaping course to the east to clear Kish Bank before turning south. A signal was made to form divisions in line ahead disposed to port. This meant that the two rear ships had to move up on the port beam of the two ahead by increasing speed from seven to eight knots, an evolution that would take 30 minutes and permitted captains to go below for a meal. Ten minutes later the squadron ran into dense fog. Within a few moments the ships lost sight of each other.

Then followed a series of human errors. On regaining his bridge the captain of Iron Duke was astonished to find his officer of the watch had altered course outwards to port on losing sight of Vanguard. So the captain sheered back to starboard to regain station, increasing engine revolutions. Meanwhile Vanguard had reduced

● Boats from Iron Duke
closing on the stricken
Vanguard to embark
survivors, Sept 1, 1875

speed and altered course to port to pass astern of a sailing ship crossing her bows. At 12.45pm came a thunderous crash as *Iron Duke* rammed *Vanguard* port-side amidships, piercing the engineroom close to the vital transverse bulkhead next to the stokehold. Both compartments flooded quickly and after failing to control the damage *Vanguard's* Captain Dawkins had to order abandon ship. Eighty minutes after the collision she sank in 16 fathoms; efficient rescue operations by *Iron Duke* ensured that no lives were lost. Oblivious of the disaster *Warrior* and *Hector* sailed happily on for Queenstown where the admiral received a telegram from *Iron Duke* now in Dublin describing what had occurred. He must have been a worried man.

Warrior returned to the scene off Kish Light and sighted *Vanguard's* topmasts at low water. On arrival at Portland Admiral Tarleton was ordered to strike his flag and the country was staggered as the news broke of the avoidable loss of a battleship costing half a million pounds. When the First Lord tried to point out that valuable experience had been gained both Parliament and the press objected strongly to his reasoning, as well as the way in which the 16-day court-martial was handled by senior officers. *Vanguard's* captain was severely reprimanded, dismissed his ship and never employed again; yet nobody in *Iron Duke* was brought to trial.[4]

In 1876 *Warrior's* coastguard duties were disturbed by Russia making warlike gestures in the Balkans following Turkish atrocities in Bulgaria. The Reserve squadron was ordered south to Gibraltar to reinforce the Channel squadron. With her old rival *Achilles* and the smaller *Valiant*, *Warrior* sailed from Spithead on June 13. Tension soon subsided and by the end of August all three veterans were back in England. It had been a useful exercise for the 'gobby squadron' with consequent uplift in morale at the thought of tasting action.

In 1877 *Warrior* continued coastguard administration, the log recording in red ink the daily raising of steam in the launch to run stores and personnel to and from Weymouth. After divisions and prayers came cutlass and rifle drill, heavy gun drill, school and gymnasium. Forty-eight hours leave was given periodically to 'natives'. Because life on board lacked incident the 'melancholy affair' of the senior medical officer sent a tremor of excitement through the ship. Fleet Surgeon Jacob Dyas had not been himself for some days, possibly due to domestic troubles. One morning early in June he retired to his cabin saying he was unwell. When the captain sent a midshipman for him the cabin door was locked with not a sound from inside, despite frequent knocking. The door was broken open to find the surgeon lying on his bunk insensible. Application of a stomach pump in the sick bay '. . . was to no avail' reported the *Army and Navy Gazette*. 'Dyas died that evening from the effects of an overdose of morphine.'

For the annual sailing regatta at Cowes, normally attended by the *Victoria and Albert*, the Royal Navy traditionally provided a guardship and this year *Warrior* was chosen. Freshly painted and dressed with bunting she looked a picture moored in Cowes Roads. Then followed five days of punctilious ceremonial and festivities that meant continuous running of boats to and from the steps of the Royal Yacht Squadron. While the Prince of Wales was to be seen racing in his cutter *Britannia*, the Queen preferred to view the activities of 'Bertie's yacht in the Solent through a telescope on the terrace of Osborne House, not perhaps amused by the bevy of pretty ladies accompanying him.'[5]

Among the junior officers appointed temporarily to *Warrior* for the occasion was Sub-Lieutenant Percy Scott whose enterprise was later responsible for building the *Excellent* gunnery school on Whale Island. On Sunday, July 22 he was instructed to take a dispatch to Osborne House. Landing by steam launch at Osborne Bay Scott walked to the house bearing a leather folder and 'feeling very proud of entering the portals'. To his surprise the equerry told him that Her Majesty might wish to see him. 'A minute or two later he was conducting me to the lawn, where the Queen was looking through a pile of correspondence.' Scott stood at attention until the Queen looked up. 'Well, young man, how is the

●Warrior entering
Portsmouth harbour,
late 1870's

Warrior?' Scott explained that he had joined only a few days before but that she was in 'capital state'. 'Now, Mr Scott, tell me, how is John Hyde getting on? He used to live here you know.' Scott again explained that due to the short time he had been on board he had not had the pleasure of meeting him. The audience was at an end, leaving Scott uncomfortable but curious.

In the gunroom he roused John Hyde from a nap to hear a strange story. During the final stages of the war in Crimea in 1855 the naval brigade were re-embarking when they stumbled on the scene of a massacre of several men, women and children. All lay dead except two 'dreadfully wounded' young boys who were taken aboard where they gradually recovered. The Queen then directed the refugees to be sent to England for accommodation at Osborne. Called Hyde after the name of the captain of the ship that brought them back, the Queen had them educated at the Royal Naval School at New Cross, enabling the pair to join the navy as clerks. Subsequently John and George Hyde became assistant paymasters, although neither stayed long in the service.[6]

After Cowes *Warrior* joined the Reserve squadron for a month's cruise to Spain. In company with her contemporaries *Black Prince* and *Minotaur* it was quite like old times to make all plain sail, set studsails and form columns of divisions in open order, using special cones and helm signals. Her log records the thorough

training then given to the Royal Naval Reserve ratings in seamanship and gunnery.

A young ordinary seaman, Charles Alexander, wrote in November 1877 to his father on *Warrior* notepaper, 'I never thought of going round to Portland just yet . . . when I was on *Victory* they told me that we was going to China . . . I like the ship very well . . . she is a coast guardship till next April and then . . . we expect to go round to Portsmouth and be done up to go on her summer cruise to Gibraltar and Vigo.'

Early in 1878 Captain Whyte was succeeded by Captain R Gordon Douglas, who had recently commanded the screw frigate *Newcastle*. After hostilities broke out between Russia and Turkey in 1877 the British government feared Russian forces would attack Constantinople, the Dardanelles or the Suez Canal. In the spring of 1878 anti-Russian war fever swept the country and by June all available coastguard and reserve ships were mobilised in Portland. Under the command of Admiral Sir Astley Cooper Key they formed a Particular Service squadron of 19 second-line warships; should war break out this unhandy, incongruous force would proceed into the Baltic. The best news for *Warrior* was to be selected as flagship, this time for a second-in-command, and on June 5 she welcomed back Henry Boys, now a Rear Admiral.

The presence of a powerful British fleet in support of the ailing Ottoman Empire turned the

● **First Reserve Squadron
at Portland June, 1878.
Warrior's stern is in line
with bow of the old
two decker Boscawen**

● Charles Stapleton, Petty Officer 1st class Gunner's Mate served in Warrior 1878-80 and later became Superintendent of Gosport Ferry Service

scale and the Russians backed down. The Particular Service squadron remained in Portland until the Berlin Congress put an end to all thought of war. With his flag in *Hercules* commanded by Captain J A Fisher, Cooper Key took his older ironclads for an evolutionary cruise in Irish waters leaving the more modern turret division exercising in the Channel. A few days in Bantry Bay, followed by a week of gunnery and tactical steaming soon worked them up to a reasonable standard. As a reward for responding so well to a national emergency the 'special service fleet of masted ironclads, turret ships and gunboats' under Cooper Key assembled in Spithead for a review by the Queen.

August 13, 1878 was marked by wretched weather, a heavily clouded sky, wind and rain. The fleet consisted of 26 ships anchored in two lines, with *Warrior* number five in the starboard division. 'At half past three Her Majesty, accompanied by the Prince and Princess of Wales' and several members of the Royal family 'embarked on board the royal yacht *Victoria and Albert* in Osborne Bay' while others went aboard various vessels that would comprise the procession. In deference to the Queen's dislike of gunfire the royal salute was fired at some distance and soon after four o'clock she reached the fleet. Led traditionally by the Trinity House yacht the 'procession was of considerable length' as it passed sedately through the lines greeted by

tumultuous cheers.[7] Rain fell at intervals from a black sky.

Next day she received flag and commanding officers on board *Victoria and Albert*. Before the ships dispersed Captain Douglas read out a letter to *Warrior*'s company from the Queen complimenting the 'chief officers and men of the Coastguard . . . while temporarily employed afloat.' At sunset on August 16 Admiral Boys' flag was hauled down. It was *Warrior*'s last review.

Returning to Portland *Warrior*'s cutters were sent away to demonstrate firing Hale's rockets for a visit by the Duke of Cambridge; a day later ships in port exercised placing collision mats. Since the *Vanguard* disaster all ships had been instructed to make mats of canvas 'thrumbed' with rope on the side to be placed over a damaged hull. *Warrior*'s mat was 12ft square, fixed in position by chains rove round the bottom of the ship. When leave was given after the fleet review Chief Engineer Edward Brown of *Warrior* successfully sued the Great Western Railway for expenses incurred in hiring a waterman to take him off to the ship because a late train to Weymouth caused him to be stranded.[8] He would not have been so fortunate today!

Mid-19th century naval strategy was based on the concept of a battle fleet guarding home waters while cruisers and gunboats protected British interests overseas. With the enormous expansion of trade routes and the threat from unfriendly

powers the need for more effective cruisers was paramount. In war an equally important role for these vessels was to act as scouts ahead of the main fleet to detect and report enemy movements. Endurance and speed were therefore important characteristics.

In 1877 the first British armoured cruiser *Shannon* was commissioned but due to Admiralty's muddled planning she was a failure, too slow for cruiser duties and unsuitable for line of battle. Until more effective ships could be built the situation called for a stopgap; initially the plan was to convert *Warrior*, *Black Prince*, *Minotaur*, *Northumberland* and *Agincourt* into protected cruisers. To save fuel compound engines would be installed and, in the case of *Warrior* and *Black Prince*, armour protection for the steering gear. Discussions started in August 1879 and continued inconclusively into the following year.[9]

In that year, as Ballard reported, *Warrior* was fitted with steam steering gear; probably during the April docking, after which she joined the Reserve squadron for the summer cruise to Spain and returned to Portland mooring buoys. Over Christmas and into 1880, leave had been given to each watch in turn, mostly to go on drinking sprees in Weymouth judging by the number of men punished by warrant. Life in the wardroom had also seen better days, the older officers affronted by the unseemly behaviour of the youngsters. Matters reached a head in January

● **Warrior in No 10 Dock, Portsmouth**

when Assistant Paymaster Gabriel Beer was 'placed in arrest for his conduct in the wardroom and being drunk.' To set an example Captain Douglas applied for court-martial and the miscreant was duly reprimanded and dismissed his ship.

After docking in Portsmouth *Warrior* spent ten days in Portland for various harbour drills, including the firing of torpedoes from the launch. On sailing for Plymouth she turned to pass the breakwater; either the steering gear failed or a mistake was made in conning because the ship struck the fort at the end of the inner breakwater with a glancing blow. As a diver reported no damage, Douglas decided to press on to Plymouth where a dock was made ready. *The Western Daily Mercury* (July 5, 1880) reported that 'one of the bilge keels' was found turned up and that 'composition was also scraped off part of her bottom by contact with the breakwater piles.' It was nothing serious and easily repairable, allowing the ship to undock and join the First Reserve squadron assembling in Torbay for the summer cruise.

Command had now passed to Rear Admiral the Duke of Edinburgh who, as Prince Alfred, had visited *Warrior* when she was building at Blackwall and frequently since. With *Hercules* (flag), *Lord Warden, Hector, Valiant, Belleisle, Audacious* and *Defence* they called in at Beerhaven to join *Minotaur, Agincourt, Northumberland* and

Achilles of the Channel squadron. *Warrior* was in good company and it was quite like old times when the combined squadrons sailed for Vigo on July 22.

Throughout the nine-day passage the admiral put them through every evolution in the book – hard going for the gobby ships but such was the stimulus of competition that they were soon able to compete on equal terms with their Channel squadron sisters. After a spell of heavy weather on July 29 one of Warrior's *coastguardsmen, John Scadden, fell down a hold and died soon afterwards. Next day* Warrior *hauled out of line and stopped ship. On top of the bulwarks just forward of the quarterdeck was a wooden platform on which rested the body, sewn up in canvas and weighted at the feet with three unserviceable 32pdr shot. After a brief service attended by the captain, officers and many of the ship's company a section of Royal Marines brought their Martini-Henry rifles to the shoulder to fire three volleys of blank as the body slipped overboard. Married with six children, Scadden's uniform was later auctioned by the master-at-arms, a generous sum being forwarded to his widow with a letter from his divisional officer explaining the unfortunate circumstances.*[10]

The rest of the year was spent at Portland. In September the ship was visited by a local man, Henry Wheeler, whose *Sketches in, about and round Weymouth* describes scrambling up the gangway to reach the upper deck whose 'planks were as clean as the pavement of a Dutch street.' The freshly painted ship impresses, as does the sight of eight 7in guns 'in their coats of sober black'. He regards with awe the foc'sle sentry armed with 'carbine and cutlass', evidently a seaman and not a marine. Down to the main deck where a large enough ship's company could be observed 'joking, smoking, eating, drinking, sleeping, cooking, brushing and scrubbing'. With all the noise about, the landsman marvels at the ability of a man off-watch to sleep – 'Fast as a rock, sir'. It is an art that generations of sailors have had little difficulty in acquiring. In the hold he sees the donkey engine, the condensing apparatus, the coal bunkers and the propeller shaft 'that is turned every day'. Regaining the upper deck he watches a topgallant yard being sent down. 'What do you call that?' asks Wheeler. 'Discipline' comes the laconic reply.[11]

Early in 1881 Captain Douglas was succeeded by Captain Algernon Charles Fiesche Heneage. Nicknamed 'Pompo', Heneage was an appalling snob in an era when eccentricity and affectation by senior officers were not uncommon. Dress was his fetish and before emerging on deck in the morning his valet would inspect the tall thin figure to remove the minutest speck of dust. His speech was affected, some said, with a German accent, but behind his exaggerated elegance lay a razor-sharp brain. Moreover, he was a first class seaman who hated steam and the engineers who produced it. The following story may or may not have occurred when he was in *Warrior* but it gives

●Captain (later Admiral Sir) Algernon Heneage, better known as Pompo

●Lieutenant Walter Hailstone

some indication of the remarkable character who commanded the ship from January 7 to April 30.

Warrior was secured alongside a jetty prior to docking, the captain walking the quarterdeck. That chief engineers were worthy of a salute from the seamen was bad enough but when Pompo observed the marine sentry presenting arms to Chief Engineer Edward Eckersly he boiled over and summoned the major of marines for an explanation.

Major: 'The chief engineer is entitled to a salute, sir.'

Pompo: 'But not to a Present?'

Major: 'Yes, sir. It's laid down in the regulations.'

Pompo: 'That a chief engineer should receive the same mark of respect given to his commanding officer?'

Major: 'Yes, sir.'

Pompo: (Utterly defeated, then suddenly brightening) 'I haf it! Take away the sentinel's musket.'[12]

During April while in dock at Portsmouth *Warrior* exchanged officers and ships' company with *Hercules*. Her new station was Greenock and her captain Samuel Townsend, with Commander Ernest Rolfe as executive officer. Among the wardroom officers was Lieutenant Thomas Cochrane, first cousin of Arthur (now Admiral) Cochrane. While in dock *Warrior*'s plates and frames were surveyed, their lordships later expressing satisfaction 'at the creditable solution in which the ironwork was maintained'.[13]

Making full use of close relationships with the royal families of Denmark, Russia and Germany, the Duke of Edinburgh hoisted his flag in *Hercules* to take his squadron including *Warrior* to the Baltic in the summer of 1881. On June 17 they anchored off Heligoland, then British. When weighing *Repulse* was found to be aground but floated off on the next tide and all was well by the time they reached Copenhagen.

Here the King of Denmark called on the flagship before the squadron sailed for Cronstadt. The current in the harbour must have been strong because when John Mullin, captain of *Warrior*'s foretop, was rigging a torpedo boom from the port heads he fell overboard, was swept away in the tide and drowned. Able Seamen Toomey jumped in to rescue him followed by Lieutenant Walter Hailstone and two other seamen. Despite every effort Toomey was also lost but Hailstone's gallantry was later rewarded with the Humane Society Medal (worn on right breast).

Following a four-day stay in Kiel a German ironclad squadron joined company for two hours of evolutions. By the end of July *Warrior* was back in Spithead. Anchoring at Plymouth to top up her complement, the ship sailed for Greenock to take up the station recently vacated by *Hercules*. Calling in briefly at Loch Ryan and Lamlash *Warrior* moored at the Tail o' the Bank off Greenock on October 3. Then at the end of April 1882 came her last test of heavy weather. En route to Portsmouth, *Warrior* was steaming to round Longships lighthouse off Land's End with minimum sails set. Shortly after noon she was struck on the starboard bow by a squall. The fore-topmast staysail sheet carried away, the sail split and all canvas fell to the deck including two trysails. Rolling heavily the ship rounded the Lizard and next day off Portland sighted the merchant ship *Salamander* flying distress signals. *Warrior* closed, lowered a cutter with a towing hawser but in passing it the *Salamander* grazed *Warrior* on the starboard quarter, slightly damaging the boats and superstructure. The cutter was hoisted and the tow started at slow speed in improving weather. An hour later the towing hawser parted, so *Warrior* bore up again and lowered the cutter with a four and a half inch steel hawser. This time it held. At 11pm they passed the Nab, slipping the tow at Spithead. With a small complement, admittedly of experienced men, it was a fine feat of seamanship.

For the summer cruise of 1882 the Duke of Edinburgh took his ships to the Spanish coast and on passage to Gibraltar in line ahead signalled all ships to turn together four points to starboard. The officer of the watch on *Warrior*'s bridge was Lieutenant (later Admiral) Lewis Bayly. 'Owing to my brain not acting or acting imperfectly', Bayly said later, 'I turned *Warrior* to port. Captain Townsend came on the bridge, put matters straight and asked why I had done it. To which I replied that I thought the Commander-in-Chief had made a mistake. It was the only occasion that our Captain was ever known to smile.'[14]

At Gibraltar the Duke inspected *Warrior* and he complimented Townsend on the *Salamander* salvage. Next day Midshipman George Ballard joined *Warrior* for the passage home. The squadron had a roughish time across the Bay and reefing topsails one evening after quarters a man fell overboard from the flagship. In Ballard's words written in 1941, 'engines were stopped by general signal and the man was seen to reach the lifebuoy, but the seas were breaking heavily enough to make boatwork decidedly risky and he had drifted some distance astern before the flagship lost way, nor could we see any signs of her boat being lowered though we were her next astern. Our captain – Townsend – resolved to try a rescue, and called away the seaboat's crew, who were all coastguard men holding the coastguard rating of "boatman", which mean special

qualification for boatwork (including lifeboats) while a lieutenant named Galloway – who was to reach flag rank – volunteered to take charge. Lifebelts were quickly put on and the boat lowered. They made the finest job of a rescue in a rough sea that could ever be seen, and, though the boat shipped a lot of water, got back safely with the man. A highly complimentary signal from the Duke of Edinburgh followed, and the squadron resumed course.' On passing Ushant the squadron dispersed, *Warrior* stopping at Portland to explode a torpedo from the fore end of the lower boom – torpedoes were currently popular weapons – then returning to her station off Greenock. Marking the end of *Warrior*'s sea service Ballard concludes, 'and so now in my 80th year I find myself the last remaining of all the many who ever stood a sea watch on the bridge of the first armoured battleship of the Royal Navy.'[15] Admiral Ballard died in 1948 at the age of 86.

On November 27, 1882, Townsend was relieved by Edward S Adeane – her last captain as a seagoing ship. After target practice in March, 1883 *Warrior* was ordered south for what was an uneventful passage down the west coast to anchor in Spithead on May 11. Up harbour *Warrior* went first to the coaling jetty in the Tidal Basin and thence to the South Jetty where she disembarked guns, stores and equipment.

The evening of the old navy was drawing to a close. Overtaken in performance by newer, better

armed and protected ships, *Warrior* had reached
the end of her allotted span with the fleet. On May
31, 1883 Charles Rowley, flag captain to
Commander-in-Chief, Portsmouth in the old
Duke of Wellington, came aboard to pay off *Warrior*
for the last time. At sunset the log simply
reported, 'hauled down the pendant'.

In the Admiralty discussions were still under
way over the possible conversion of the old
ironclads to cruisers. A new personality had
entered the scene in the shape of Captain George
Tryon, appointed Secretary to the Board of
Admiralty. To the Director of Naval Construction
and First Sea Lord, Tryon stated that '*Warrior,
Achilles* and similar vessels possess great
structural strength, well tried and well recognised
seagoing qualities, and are of practically unlimited
durability while they are of a form capable of being
propelled at a very high rate and of maintaining a
high speed in a seaway'. There was no question as
to where his sympathies lay. He continued, 'they
have a great future before them. To convert
Warrior into a double-screw vessel with new
engine and protected steering arrangements
would cost £120,000. She would then be unsurpassed as a cruiser . . . she should carry 40 guns in
all, exclusive of machine guns . . . a good 16 knot
speed might be expected . . .'

Cooper Key, the First Sea Lord, agreed,
emphasising the need for 'compound engines,
coal storage to be increased, masts should be

●Dolphin striker and
whisker poles secured
for entering dock
circa 1875

removed, etc.' The Director of Naval Ordnance concurred. '*Warrior* and *Minotaur* would make magnificent cruisers . . . *Warrior* with 40 good BL guns, with cutwater and as much of the stern as possible taken off . . . would hold her own against any cruiser afloat . . .'. The Admiral Superintendent, Portsmouth, confirmed that *Warrior* 'is in a very good condition'. A model of *Warrior* was tank tested by R E Froude in the Admiralty Experimental works at Torquay in 1884 in connection with proposed modernization. And so it drifted on until 1887 when a Sea Lord questioned whether old ironclads such as *Warrior* might not be 'relegated to the Coal, Store, Ammunition and Transport Department for war purposes'.[16]

In the event nothing happened and *Warrior* remained unmutilated by conversion plans, moored head and stern in the tidal stream off Portsmouth dockyard. Chief Engineer Eckersley and three warrant officers were succeeded by Chief Engineer Sheave and three staff engineers in 1885. From 1887 *Warrior* was classified as a 'screw battle ship (ie not *battleship*), third class, armoured and reduced to a single staff engineer.[17] In the event of war and heavy fleet casualties the old veterans might have been called out to fill the breach. But there was no war.

In May 1892 she was designated a first class armoured screw cruiser – the nearest she ever got to conversion. A sketch of her in Portsmouth harbour shows three lower masts, two stump

● Warrior as a hulk, 1899

funnels and seven forlorn looking derricks. During 1894 'it was suggested that *Warrior* be modernized and re-armed to act as guardship at one of the coaling stations abroad, but it was decided that she was not worth it.'[18] Sadly she had missed the great Jubilee naval review of 1897 – in which *Black Prince* featured – which instilled in the country a spirit of pride and confidence.

The Army and Army Illustrated (January 7, 1899) described the ships of 'Rotten Row' as 'the last refuge of the time-expired and cast-off men-of-war. It is, so to speak, the condemned cell of the navy for ships that are past service, where vessels that have hauled down their last pennants at their last mooring await the final fiat of the Admiralty that will hand them over to the tender mercies of the shipbreaker. D Reserve is the official designation of the class found in Rotten Row – aptly named indeed the Reserve of the Damned.' Nostalgically the writer stresses the appeal of these 'time expired veterans of the Legion of the

Lost; these old time men-of-war whose names for the most part figure only on the "Vessels for Sale" pages of the Navy List. Gone is the joyous day of launching with its flutter of flags and patriotic music and re-echoing cheers of the crowd. Gone are the happy commissions . . . when the now deserted decks were alive with well ordered activity and stir of naval life. No more manning of yards . . . all that is over and done with and nothing remains to recall the past but the name.' All that was said of *Warrior* was that she was 'the very first ironclad ever built and as such has a peculiar interest.' But at least she was spared the fate of *Resistance* 'pretty well knocked to pieces during the last ten years as a target ship to test the power of modern shells.' There is no evidence that *Warrior* was offered for sale.

A rather different point of view was published in another periodical entitled 'Our Paper Fleet', in which the writer took the Admiralty to task for falsifying a statement on the strength of the fleet.

His case was that of the 53 battleships and 17 armoured cruisers '16 of the former and eight of the latter are totally unfitted to go to sea with the prospect of meeting a modern French or Russian squadron. Amongst these are a number of craft which could not be fitted for service in six months and that when fitted would prove death traps to the men who fought them.' Among the eight cruisers were *Achilles, Agincourt, Black Prince, Minotaur, Northumberland* and *Warrior*. Captioned 'HMS *Warrior*: one of Britain's bulwarks', a photograph appears with the following note, 'this interesting antiquity is entered . . . as an armoured cruiser. She is in her 40th year and would be about as useful against a French or Russian warship as an Isle of Man steamer. She is said to be armed with 32 muzzle-loading guns and . . . four and a half inch armour. She has now lain derelict in Portsmouth Harbour for some years and it will be noted that she has shed her masts and generally presents the appearance of a coal hulk.' The writer

concludes, 'yet my Lords of the Admiralty include this remarkable curio in the most recent return of the British Fleet. Perhaps Mr Goschen (First Lord) or some of the permanent officials will explain.'[19]

At 11.45pm on Sunday, December 31, 1899, Portsmouth harbour was crammed with warships, many berthed alongside or in the basins. Seasonal leave had been granted to one watch while part of the other was ashore celebrating the end of the 19th century. Gathered on each quarterdeck round the ship's bell was a small group of officers and men awaiting midnight. Just before the hour was struck the youngest person on board stepped forward to seize the bellrope. 'Twelve o'clock, sir' called the quartermaster, the youngster rang sixteen bells in traditional fashion and everyone shouted 'Happy New Year!' It was a momentous occasion.

At the head of Fareham creek there was one ship where no bells were struck, simply because there was no one on board. Empty and discarded she lay at her moorings with little hope of being employed again. Warrior was at the end of her tether.

CHAPTER TEN
Hulked

AS *WARRIOR* DETERIORATED the turn of the century saw an upsurge in the navy's strength and popularity. The huge shipbuilding programmes of 1894 and later enabled Great Britain to maintain a two-power standard - her fleet numerically equal to the combined fleets of any two other nations. The man to make this possible was about to become the sole survivor of the three outstanding officers in *Warrior's* first commission. Tryon lost his life in an accident which marred an otherwise unblemished career of skill and enterprise. In 1893 when commanding the Mediterranean fleet his flagship *Victoria* was sunk in collision with the *Camperdown* and Tryon was drowned. Cochrane had been Commander-in-Chief in the Pacific in the 1870s and until late in life had been mentally active, especially about new ideas for the navy, such as self-heating tins of soup for men in boats.[1] Every year on his birthday he climbed to the top of St Paul's Cathedral in a space of time that would have put many a younger man to shame. Unmarried, he died at the age of 81. That left the dynamic Fisher who, as Controller of the Navy (1894-1897), had often visited Portsmouth so might well have been responsible for placing *Warrior's* figurehead at the dockyard's main entrance where it attracted considerable attention. As Commander-in-Chief, Mediterranean, Fisher wakened the naval profession and the country to what was meant by efficient administration and preparation for war.

From the moment he returned to become Second Sea Lord in 1902 the wind of change started to blow for *Warrior*.

Recognised as a naval weapon of potential strength but still in its infancy, the torpedo had been mounted in small, nimble vessels called torpedo boats. The threat of such craft in the hands of foreign navies led to production of the antidote in the shape of larger, faster vessels named torpedo-boat destroyers; by 1900 these 400 ton 30 knotters were commanded by youthful lieutenants needing guidance and support. Hitherto used as a store for torpedoes, *Warrior* was now chosen to fill the role of mother ship and headquarters for flotilla administration. Some of her machinery had already been removed but to become a repair and depot ship it was necessary to take out her engines, boilers and whatever armament remained, subsequently roofing over parts of the upper deck.[2] The ship took on a new lease of life.

On July 16, 1902 *Warrior* was commissioned in Portsmouth under Captain John de Robeck, as Captain, Portsmouth Flotilla. Seven officers and a ship's company of 100 provided stores, fuel and provisions for the flotilla as well as servicing their 19 knot torpedoes and four inch quickfiring guns. Alongside *Warrior* was berthed her brood of 27 knot miniature warships bearing the evocative names of *Fervent, Flirt, Lightning, Success, Syren, Wizard, Zebra* and *Zephyr*.

In 1903 de Robeck, later to command the naval forces at Gallipoli, was relieved, first by Arthur Dodgson, then Seymour Erskine and finally Edward Charlton. The last two had 24 torpedo-boat destroyers operating from Felixstowe and Devonport as well as Portsmouth. The eight-ship flotilla system was now well established.

Service with small craft, however, was short-lived and on March 31, 1904 *Warrior* was paid off and the ship prepared for another task. In June she was towed to Southampton to be converted into an auxiliary workshop for *Vernon*, the floating torpedo school in Portsmouth harbour. The work was carried out by Day Summers of Northam; because of *Warrior*'s 21ft draught it was not possible to take her up the River Itchen so she was berthed in Southampton's Outer Dock.[3]

Six Belleville-type water tube boilers were installed together with four electricity generators. A single funnel was erected, new fore and mizzen masts stepped in their original positions and two thirds of the upper deck roofed to accommodate offices, classrooms and a gymnasium. On the main deck a small chapel was built; below were workshops and stores. *Warrior* was also to be a wireless telegraphy trials and instructional ship, for which her iron hull was well suited.

After separating from *Excellent* to become an independent command in 1876, *Vernon* joined the hulks *Actaeon* and *Ariadne* in Fountain Lake, Portsmouth. In 1895 the school was moved to

Portchester creek and by the end of 1904 consisted of *Vernon* (ex-*Donegal*) and *Vernon II* (ex-*Marlborough*), while moored between them and connected by catwalks was *Vernon III* (ex-*Warrior*).[4]

Warrior must have been pleased to have as shipmates vessels she had known from her youth. Loss of official identity was a blow to pride but the veteran ironclad can have had few regrets when her name was transferred to a new *Warrior* emerging from Pembroke Dockyard. A four-funnelled twin-screw armoured cruiser of 13,550 tons armed with six 9.2in and four 7.5in guns, she was soon at sea with sister ships bearing the names of previous vessels in the Black Battlefleet.

Who was responsible for deciding that *Warrior* should form part of *Vernon* is not known; but it is significant that Fisher, who conceived the torpedo branch and was its greatest supporter, had been Commander-in-Chief, Portsmouth, from 1903 to 1904 before becoming First Sea Lord. Almost daily he would have passed *Warrior*'s figurehead as he made his way to and from the main gates to his residence in the dockyard. At a time when the 'all-big-gun' fast battleship *Dreadnought* was being planned it is possible he spared his old ship more than a casual thought. Like *Warrior*, *Dreadnought* made her predecessors obsolete, marking another stage in capital ship evolution.

With gunnery and torpedo branches firmly established it was now the turn of signals to gain

the limelight, particularly as the standard of visual signalling with flags, lights, semaphore and even carrier pigeons had reached its zenith. When wireless telegraphy came on the scene it was logical that it should be handled by *Vernon* to whose responsibilities for mine and torpedoes had been added ships' electrical installations. The Royal Navy's new wireless department was officially established in 1901 to undertake development work and the instruction of selected signal ratings. The man who pioneered the introduction of radio telegraphy into the navy, Henry Jackson, was not only in command of *Vernon* when *Warrior* joined the school but also supervised the setting up of Marconi equipment in box-like compartments on *Warrior*'s upper deck. In 1908 a telegraphist branch was formed and one of the first trainees to take a leading telegraphist's course in *Warrior* was Charles Cutler. Previously qualified as a W/T operator in basic Marconi gear, Leyden jars, coherers and magnetic detectors, Cutler commented wryly, 'the early sets were rough and exposed; if you touched them the shock would throw you off your chair'. He rose to chief petty officer to serve with distinction in both world wars before retirement.[5]

With the approach of war torpedo and wireless telegraphy training intensified and from 1914 thousands of officers and men passed through *Warrior*'s classrooms to qualify in various courses before joining the fleet. Although not on the scale of World War II, Portsmouth was subjected to sporadic bombing raids, notably on September 25, 1916, when a zeppelin came over the naval base shortly before midnight. According to an anti-aircraft gunner, 'she was first picked up by *Vernon*'s searchlights', instruments powered by and possibly mounted in *Vernon III*. 'Guns from all directions began to fire at her, a lovely target she made'. The new battle-cruiser *Renown* was in dock and 'the first bomb to be dropped pitched in the fairway between the *Renown* and the *Vernon* . . . After releasing several bombs the Zep made off to the east.'[6] In *Warrior*'s searchlight's crew was AB Arthur Ferrett who in 1986 was alive and well aged 90.

However, in the North Sea her successor, the armoured cruiser *Warrior*, with her sister ships *Black Prince* and *Defence*, took part in the battle of Jutland. Briefly engaging enemy light cruisers they proved no match for the German battle-cruisers. *Defence* blew up, *Warrior* was hit five times and only saved by *Warspite* circling her with jammed steering gear, thereby drawing enemy fire. *Black Prince* sank that night and next morning *Warrior*, towed by *Engadine*, was barely afloat and later had to be abandoned before scuttling. So ended the third *Warrior* and her sister *Black Prince*.

Late in 1918 Sir John Heffernan, an engineer of *Warrior*'s first commission who had risen to the top of his branch, wrote to his old friend Fisher congratulating him on victory. In characteristic fashion Fisher replied concluding, 'I often enjoy the remembrance of our ancient days when dear old Buchan in the *Warrior* so delighted me with his promises for "malleable iron".' Apparently when serving together in the first commission Buchan had told Fisher that 'he had arranged for his monument at death to be of "malleable iron". No cast-iron for him, he said. It played you such pranks.'[7]

When requirements outgrew *Vernon*'s capacity, the mining school was first moved into the Gunwharf near the dockyard, before the whole establishment settled ashore in 1923. As soon as Captain Derwent Allen hoisted his pendant in the Gunwharf, *Warrior* was commissioned as a tender to accommodate the Whitehead torpedo department. *Vernon* and *Marlborough* had been broken up leaving *Warrior* in solitary state, wearing a white ensign for the last time. Serving on the experimental staff in the Whitehead torpedo office on board was Lieutenant Allan Bickford-Smith; on his wedding day, February 11, 1924, the old naval tradition of hoisting a garland between the masts could be observed. But *Warrior*'s time was running out and Fisher was no more. On August 31, 1924, *Warrior* was again paid off, the *Engineer* stating that, 'she must be sold to the shipbreakers unless a means of preserving her can be found'. At that time many ships were going to the scrapyards and in 1923 *Black Prince* had been sold to Dover Shipbreaking Co.

●Warrior's berth for
50 years

●Bickford-Smith
wedding day, 1924 with
traditional garland aloft
between the masts and
in close-up

But due to the excellent state of her hull the Admiralty had a better idea for *Warrior*. In 1926 she was placed on the sales list as an 'oil fuel pontoon hulk' and saved from ignominy by the fortuitous need for a floating jetty off the Llannion fuel depot near Pembroke Dock. For that she was taken in hand by Portsmouth on October 22, 1927, for another conversion. Boilers and generators apart, all equipment was removed above and below decks and two diesel-driven pumps supplied for emergencies. While in dry dock she was visited by Electrical Fitter Apprentice John Barrett whose grandfather William had served in *Warrior* as an engine room artificer in 1876 when the Reserve squadron was mobilised. William drew his pension for 55 years before dying a centenarian. Equally important to the old ship's memory was the protection of her figurehead, now seriously decayed. Following the precedent of charging the preservation of *Victory* to Navy Votes the Admiralty was persuaded to expend £300 to repair *Warrior*'s figurehead, placing it under cover near the dockyard fire station. Thus *Warrior*'s presence in the naval base was maintained.[8]

Early on March 13, 1929, *Warrior* was towed out of Portsmouth by Admiralty tugs *St Clears* and *St Mellons* for a two-day passage into Milford Haven; one of the crew of 13 aboard *Warrior* was Gilbert Plumridge, late AB RN, who remembers the tow, 'running into a gale and only just making

St Ann's Head in time'. Stopping briefly at Pembroke Dock the hulk was towed up the Cleddau river to the wooded shore of Llannion Pill by Waterloo Point.[9] There she was secured fore and aft with heavy cables, bows down river, port side against sturdy wooden dolphins in eight fathoms of water. From the sponson amidships came a gangway that rested on the short metal pier so as to move up and down with the 24ft rise and fall of tide. In view of the strong stream, size of berth and depth of water, vessels coming alongside were restricted to minor warships and Royal Fleet Auxiliaries not exceeding 550ft in length. This well-sheltered berth was to be *Warrior*'s home for the next 50 years.

As a ten year old Frank Denzey can remember, 'seeing her being towed past Pembroke Dock when dawdling back from school. My father was a foreman of works with the naval store officer in the dockyard and his duties often carried him to the *Warrior* . . . we boys loved to play amongst the cavernous, rust-encrusted decks, a gloomy but thrilling environment for adventurous youngsters.'[10]

To accommodate a shipkeeper and his family *Warrior*'s poop had been converted to make two bedrooms, a living room, kitchen, lavatory and bathroom. Water was piped in but lighting was by oil lamp and both cooking and heating by coal. The first shipkeeper was Bill James, an ex-Royal Navy chief petty officer, whose job was to look

●Warrior figurehead,
by Main Gate,
Portsmouth dockyard

●Old Warriors under the
figurehead June 22, 1914
(below)

after the ship, watch the moorings, check the
draught marks on stem and stern and make
rounds of the ship at regular intervals. After her
husband's death Mrs James wrote, 'the 29 years
we spent on board *Warrior* I recall as the happiest
of my life. Even though I am 90 years young the
memories are still very clear to me.' There was one
other family living on board the after main deck
quarters – the stoker harbourman who worked at
the fuel depot. This was connected by a 1200ft
tunnel cut in the hillside which contained the oil
fuel hoses. When ships came alongside *Warrior* he
tended hawsers and connected hoses, events that
occurred about 10 to 15 times a month. Mrs James
continued, 'Both my children were brought up in
Warrior – and my daughter Brenda was married
from the old ship . . . those happy days when my
husband used to catch bass, mullet and skate by
line or spear, very often through the bedroom
windows and even by torchlight. The children
went to school by bicycle and at weekends would
cycle round and round the upper deck . . .'[11]

Warrior's uneventful piscatorial existence in
the twilight of her days was abruptly broken by
the outbreak of World War II.

Many more ships arrived to take or discharge
fuel causing *Warrior* to note with some interest the
lightweight characteristics of wartime destroyers,
sloops, corvettes and minesweepers as they
bumped against her armour plated sides. Many
were allied warships and Mrs James 'often

● The best fishing in
the Cleddau river

wondered what country we did live in listening to all the different languages being spoken'. At one of the ship's periodical dockings by the Milford Haven Dry Dock Company the far from sound upper deck was covered with a thick layer of cement and soon *Warrior* was in use as a base ship for coastal force craft, mainly motor-launches. In 1942 she was redesignated 'Oil Fuel Hulk C77' (by Admiralty Fleet Order 4182/1942) to make way for a new *Warrior*, a light fleet aircraft carrier, building in Belfast for the Royal Canadian Navy. Once more the old ship was not too concerned at losing her name, this time to a new breed of capital warship.

Under the mistaken impression that Pembroke Dock was a major naval base the Germans subjected the town to heavy air attacks. On one occasion oil tanks were hit and the resultant fires burned for three weeks. Tucked in under the shore line *Warrior* was unscathed despite near misses. In 1945 Sub-Lieutenant John McGivering RN was appointed to *Skirmisher II* which meant serving aboard a motor-launch based alongside *Warrior*. An office for coastal forces was set up in a Nissen hut on *Warrior*'s upper deck where McGivering remembers, 'having tea with Mr and Mrs James in the cabin and meeting their pretty daughter, Brenda, who occasionally washed the odd shirt for the ML officers'.[12]

After the war Mr Colley took over as stoker harbourman bringing his wife and daughter, soon to become Mrs Waitimus, whose wedding reception was held on board. According to the local press Mrs Waitimus said that 'on May 27, 1950 while we were still living in *Warrior* our daughter Jennifer arrived' the first and only child to be born in the ship.

While preparing at Devonport in 1953 for service in the Far East, the light fleet aircraft carrier *Warrior* sent a dozen officers and men to visit their ship's namesake at Llannion. They returned greatly impressed.

Hugh Griffiths took over as shipkeeper in 1958, after a career as an Admiralty stores assistant, bringing his wife and three daughters. The youngest was Rita who described 'living conditions as far from ideal but . . . I loved every minute of it. The long walk from Pembroke didn't distract friends from coming to play. The *Warrior* was always a great attraction and we had many hours of fun playing hide-and-seek. There were hundreds of places to hide and some were quite creepy being dark, damp and musty smelling. Two families lived on board at one time, one in our quarters and one on the second (main) deck . . . Best of all I used to sunbathe on the flat roof of our quarters in the stern.'

Rita Griffiths - later to become Mrs Desjardins - recalls that 'it was always exciting when a tanker came alongside for refuelling or unloading. We did sway a few times due to bumps from incoming ships - some of them were quite big - but it was

never anything the *Warrior* couldn't stand up to.'[13] Although berthing alongside was limited to vessels of less than 16,000 tons not all came alongside as gently as intended. The *British Maple* was approaching *Warrior* one summer morning in 1959 when her captain remarked to the pilot, 'I'm going slow. We don't want to damage the old ship.' 'It's your ship you should worry about,' replied the pilot, 'you won't damage *her*.' Thirty seconds later the deep-laden *British Maple* berthed a little too fast so that *Warrior*'s bow neatly carried away every one of the tanker's forward stanchions. *Warrior* was unmarked.[14]

At the end of 1958 the light fleet carrier *Warrior* was sold to Argentina and renamed *Independencia*. This meant that *Warrior*'s name became available again, a fact that did not escape Admiral Sir Charles Madden commanding the Home Fleet, who in 1962 was the first C-in-C to be permanently stationed at the RAF establishment in Northwood, Middlesex. 'Before taking up my appointment I found that we had no ship name and no proper cap ribbons, etc. So I wrote to the First Sea Lord (Admiral Sir Caspar John) proposing that we should be called *Iron Duke*. I did this partly because she was Jellicoe's flagship in World War I and my father was his Chief-of-Staff, and partly because it was my first ship. But Caspar John feared that the press might make disparaging comparisons between the status of the C-in-C, Home Fleet, in World War I and that occupied by

me. So he offered me various ship names of which I chose *Warrior*.

'Someone then discovered that *Warrior*'s figurehead was at Portsmouth. They painted and gilded it most beautifully and put it up in the large circular drive in front of Admiralty House, Northwood. Unfortunately they hadn't restored its timbers and the very severe winter of 62-63 caused it to split in various directions.'[15] The figurehead was just presentable for the commissioning ceremony in April 1963 but the elements had taken their toll and, according to the admiral's coxswain, Chief Petty Officer Dynes, 'the order was given to me to demolish poor old *Warrior*. It was pretty rotten inside and came to pieces quickly'.[16]

Throughout her time at Llannion *Warrior* was administered by the Director of Stores (Navy) while Devonport dockyard was responsible for periodical surveys. The yard's mooring officer paid regular visits with a team of divers to check the moorings; and every five or six years the ship

was towed away for docking, usually at Pembroke Dock but sometimes at Devonport. In 1958 Mr A W Cullicot and three shipwright colleagues were instructed to survey her while she was in dock to 'determine the future life years' of the vessel. Their opinion was that 'after close examination of the plating, rivets and frames, the very good condition of the hull structure coupled with the excellent standard of construction left no doubt that *Warrior* would outlive a lot of warships built today'.[17] High praise indeed!

Apart from the curiosity shown in her by the crews of some of the ships that berthed alongside and the local people who had some knowledge of her background, few appreciated *Warrior*'s significance. An exception was John Moore, then working for ICI, whose interest in British warships started in the 1930s. 'I was amazed to learn that she was still in existence at Pembroke and after our first exciting visit in 1952 I was, of course, . . . completely hooked on her.'

Of her sister ships *Defence* and *Hercules* had been scrapped in the 1930s, *Valiant* was broken up at Bruges in 1954 and *Agincourt* said goodbye on Trafalgar Day 1960 after 50 years as a Chatham coaling hulk. G A Osbon describes *Agincourt*'s passing 'while Her Majesty the Queen was launching Britain's first atomic submarine, a very tired old lady was gently coaxed up river to Ward's shipbreaking yard at Gray's and into her final berth.'[18] She fetched £50,000. Britain's first

ironclad was now the last survivor of the Black Battlefleet of 45 ships completed between 1861 and 1877. And as *Warrior* celebrated her 100th birthday, quietly confident that she still had a long way to go, *Vanguard* was towed out of Portsmouth to be scrapped. Thus *Warrior* became Britain's last surviving battleship.

On her next docking at Milford Haven in 1964 the *Evening Standard* (August 4) drew attention to the ship, 'once the pride of the Royal Navy that

had made her first voyage for seven years . . . for a four-week bottom scrape and anti-foul coating.' An Admiralty spokesman said, 'you could not call this buff down a noble gesture to preserve the ship for posterity. She still has a required life and a task to perform. This is necessary maintenance . . . so she can continue in service as a berthing stage.' Meanwhile Hugh Griffiths, the shipkeeper, after withstanding the severe winter of 1962, decided to take a council house in Pembroke

Dock; but he never failed to give the ship his undivided attention, going the rounds below decks and checking the for'd and after draught marks to ensure that she was still floating correctly.

On June 29, 1967 the *South East London Mercury* reported that Frank Carr, former director of the National Maritime Museum and, in conjunction with the Duke of Edinburgh responsible for saving *Cutty Sark*, had put forward 'an imaginative idea to bring the forgotten but famous *Warrior*' to the international yacht harbour planned for Thamesmead. 'A great deal of work would have to be done to restore her – but the hull itself is in excellent condition,' said Mr Carr. 'The whole project might cost something like £500,000 – but it would be worth it. *Warrior* could be used for Sea Scout Headquarters . . . I envisage a first class restaurant with excellent wines and waiters dressed as sailors of the 1860s. Imagine the atmosphere.' Thamesmead was the new town to be built between Woolwich and Erith with Greater London Council support. On August 21 the Ministry of Defence wrote to C in C Plymouth confirming this proposal and arranging for *Warrior* to be surveyed by Mr Sutherland of Lloyds Register of Shipping and Mr Archibald of the National Maritime Museum.

Early in 1968 a crucial meeting took place at Buckingham Palace. Chaired by the Duke of Edinburgh, a high-powered committee which

●Dry Dock, Milford
Haven, 1964 (below) for
bottom scrape and
anti-foul

included Sir Arthur Bryant, Sir Michael Cary of the Ministry of Defence, John Smith, MP for the Cities of London and Westminster, and Frank Carr met to discuss how *Warrior* might be preserved. Representatives from the GLC and the Town Clerk of Greenwich were also present in view of the Thamesmead scheme. John Smith and Frank Carr felt it was a pity to deal with *Warrior* only and suggested the formation of a National Maritime Trust to preserve historic ships in the same way as the National Trust preserved historic buildings. John Smith was asked by the Duke of Edinburgh to draft a constitution for the Trust which he submitted together with a promise of £350,000 to get it off the ground. Estimated to cost well over £1m the expensive part of the *Warrior/*Thamesmead operation was establishing a permanent berth between the marina and the Thames. Although it would have been cheaper to float her in the tideway, the Port of London Authority were understood to have raised objections.[19] In the Commons John Smith asked that *Warrior* be preserved, adding that a handful of such vessels still surviving could be 'a potent source of education and inspiration for our children, out of all proportion to the cost of keeping them'.[20]

After the Queen had opened the Gulf Oil Refinery at Milford Haven in August, Prince Philip visited *Warrior* with the Resident Naval Officer at Pembroke Dock and Laurence Phillips,

vice president of the Navy League.[21] From that moment *Warrior*'s preservation was never in doubt.[22] In October 1969 the Maritime Trust was established, its founder president the Duke of Edinburgh, John Smith was appointed one of the honorary vice-presidents, and later Vice Admiral Sir Patrick Bayly its director. A distinguished and influential appeal committee set about raising money to preserve Britain's maritime heritage.

When the Thamesmead plan evaporated Councillor Dance of the Borough of Newham proposed bringing *Warrior* to the Royal Victoria Dock to 'improve the environment, provide employment and bring about a radical change in London's dockland'. According to Patrick Duffy, Navy Minister, the alternative was to berth her at Plymouth. The arrival of SS *Great Britain* from the Falkland Islands heightened enthusiasm for preserving historic ships; so although the Maritime Trust would have preferred to start on a smaller vessel they invited a marine surveyor, Michael Willoughby, to inspect *Warrior* to establish if she was worth preserving.

Captain Willoughby reported in July, 1970 that 'the fabric of the ship, although of tremendous strength, has been sadly neglected for 40 years with the result that internally she is very far gone . . . The 100-odd manholes in the double hull have been opened for inspection from time to time and . . . at her last docking in 1964 . . . it is assumed that the hull was found of satisfactory thickness to be safe at her moorings. She has to be pumped out about once a fortnight, but I was assured that this is mostly rain water. In the event of the Trust taking the ship over it would appear that she will remain afloat for many years with only superficial care and maintenance.' There was as yet no indication that the Ministry of Defence would release the ship from her berthing duties and so the matter rested. Only Admiral Bayly and his colleagues realised what an immense and costly project reconstruction presented.

When *Warrior* docked at Milford Haven in July 1974 – the last docking before leaving the Cleddau river for good – she was inspected by the Maritime Trust council. Her underwater condition appeared first class, little being needed except to scrape off several tons of mussel shells and apply the usual bituminous coating. It was on this occasion that Commander Johnston, in charge at Pembroke Dock, signalled HMS *Warrior* at Northwood, 'Elder brother afloat again. Matthew, Chapter 13, Verse 30' ('But many that are first shall be last; and the last shall be first.')

Not until 1976 was Frank Judd, then Under-Secretary of State (Royal Navy), able to tell the Trust that the Ministry was likely to dispose of *Warrior* in 1978. This was followed by a letter on June 8, 1977 from Mr Pritchard of Fleet Support Co-ordination stating that the fuel depot would close in the spring of 1978 and asking if the Trust had any suggestions for *Warrior*'s future. Bayly

replied hoping that the iron hull would not be broken up unnecessarily but doubting if she could be restored immediately. 'Would the Trust be offered the vessel as a gift?' he asked. In August Pritchard replied that if no-one wished to take over the depot and ship the probable answer was 'Yes'.

For some time the Maritime Trust had considered how best to tackle the reconstruction of a large iron hull short of fittings and in need of considerable repair to her timbers. The task was part restoring and part rebuilding the ship as nearly as possible to the 1859 design. Fortunately both the National Maritime and Science Museums possessed many original plans of *Warrior*. With data obtainable from other sources and the use of the original Thames Ironworks builders' model, now in the Science Museum, there was sufficient information to provide a basis; but further research would be necessary.

In the Trust's view the logical way was to commission a feasibility study, preferably conducted by a major shipbuilding organization. Bayly concluded his memorandum of October 1977, 'this proposed project is many times larger than any yet attempted by the Maritime Trust. It is therefore all the more important that it should be approached with caution, taking the best advice available into consideration at each step.'[23]

Clearly the project was going to cost a great deal of money, far in excess of what the Maritime Trust had or could raise by appeal. Patrick Bayly's

estimate of restoration costs was of the order of £3m. In the hope that others would follow his lead John Smith said in September 1977 that the Manifold Trust, which he had founded in 1962, would underwrite this sum and provide whatever could not be raised from other sources. This magnificent offer not only gave fresh impetus to the project but put heart into those concerned with *Warrior*'s future. There remained an immense amount to do, not least to obtain assurance from the Ministry of Defence that the ship would become available to the restorers.

At the end of 1977 the Maritime Trust considered how much restoration would be needed, from keeping the ship at Milford Haven under care and maintenance to complete reconstruction in a shipyard. The scale recommended fell short of the latter but to prepare her for public exhibition would necessitate work on rigging, funnels and bridges, upper and main decks, officers' and crew's quarters and propeller gear.

And where would she be berthed? Portsmouth put in one bid, the Borough of Newham another. In the Commons the Secretary of State for Defence was asked, 'if he will take action to preserve the hull of HMS *Warrior*, Great Britain's first iron warship, until she can be reclaimed and refitted in a similar manner to other historic ships'. Mr Duffy replied that there was no question of disposing of her 'until the possibility of preserving her had been fully explored,, although there will be no defence requirement for the vessel . . . after next April'.[24]

In view of the navy's decision to release *Warrior* and John Smith's offer to underwrite the cost of restoration, Admiral Bayly felt the time ripe to inform his president. In January 1978 he wrote to the Duke of Edinburgh, emphasising the need for a year's feasibility study to assess the costs and time scale before starting reconstruction, assuming that the Ministry of Defence would give her to the Maritime Trust. Only a berth at London or Portsmouth, he thought, would attract the annual 400,000 visitors necessary for the ship to pay her way.[25]

One proposal for a feasibility study came from Kenneth Evans, a senior naval constructor. Following a survey of the ship another came from Burness Corlett and Partners, who had been involved with the restoration of *Great Britain*. Meanwhile two more personalities entered the scene from the Maritime Trust Council, one was Maldwin Drummond, the vice chairman, the other Lord Strathcona & Mountroyal.

By May, 1978 there were still two schools of thought as to how *Warrior*'s restoration should be tackled. John Smith favoured a developing pro-gramme as was successfully applied to the *Great Britain* project, supported by a small group of single-minded enthusiasts. Since in his view *Warrior* was a more formidable task than *Great Britain*, Patrick Bayly preferred a more cautious approach with preliminary studies on a com-mercial basis before committing the project to expensive reconstruction. Compromise was reached before the end of a decisive year and, with John Smith's support, the Maritime Trust put together a bid to the Ministry of Defence (Navy), indicating their desire to rebuild *Warrior* to her original condition and display her preferably in Portsmouth. It was thought that this would entail a five year programme, a good source of skilled and unskilled labour, assisted preferably by a Manpower Services Commission scheme. Owner-ship and responsibility for the ship would be vested in the Ships Preservation Trust Ltd, a company originally formed as a subsidiary to the Maritime Trust for another restoration now completed. Portsmouth City Council, mean-while, seized the initiative by proposing a detailed plan to install *Warrior* near the dockyard. But the Borough of Newham was keen to berth the ship in Royal Victoria Dock, making maximum use of a job creation scheme before putting her on display.[26] In the words of Portsmouth's leader, John Marshall, when the decision was eventually made for the ship to come south, 'Portsmouth 1 – Newham 0'.

Early in 1979 John Smith confirmed that the Manifold Trust would underwrite the whole cost of restoring *Warrior* estimated at between £4m and £8m on the understanding that other sources of income would be forthcoming.

Consideration was then given to an enthusiastic approach from Michael Satow, chairman of Locomotion Enterprises 75, to take on the *Warrior* project. His company had been set up in the Newcastle area in 1975 to work on steam railway engines and build replicas of famous old locomotives. Although lacking marine experience the company apparently had the potential to restore *Warrior*; so Satow and Bayly toured possible refit berths on the north-east coast. The most promising was Hartlepool, a development area. Skilled labour was at hand and office accommodation adjacent to what looked a suit-able berth. All this Bayly was able to report to John Smith, adding that there appeared to be scope for a joint Locomotion Enterprise/Ships Preservation Trust project. The feasibility study had been forgotten.

In June the Ministry of Defence announced that *Warrior* would be given to the Maritime Trust for restoration on the north-east coast and envisaging that work would continue for about five years when *Warrior* would be berthed at Portsmouth. The statement pointed out that reconstruction would 'give direct employment to about 100 people and would be eligible for MSC assistance.'[26] Meanwhile Maldwin Drummond agreed to act as chairman of the Ships Preser-vation Trust and Burness Corlett and Partners to advise on towing to Hartlepool. The necessary funding was put into operation.

Since 1929 *Warrior*'s starboard side had successfully withstood the impact of some 5,000 ships berthing alongside – usually giving more than she got – and it was only in the last year of operation as a floating jetty that a major accident occurred. On this occasion SS *Wadhurst* misjudged the approach, struck *Warrior* at speed across her bows, carried away the beak, tore the port after hawsepipe out of its frame, wrecked part of the jetty and retired in shame to anchor in the fairway. Divers recovered the beak and hawsepipe, reporting no underwater damage.[27] All was well.

After ownership of *Warrior* was formally transferred from the Royal Navy to the Maritime Trust on August 12, 1979 events moved fast. At Pembroke Dock *Warrior* was prepared for her 800-mile tow, her ballast adjusted, bottom scrubbed and openings checked by divers. Bilges were pumped out - only fresh water was found - and gun ports blanked off with marine ply. A towing bridle was led through the bower hawsepipe to the bitts so the tow could be picked up by tugs of the Alexandra Towing Company of Liverpool, direct descendants of James R Watkins, whose tugs took *Warrior* down the Thames from Victoria docks in 1861.[28]

Bad weather thwarted an attempt to start the voyage over the Bank Holiday and a week later the tug *Hendon* moored alongside *Warrior* pm on August 28. With a promise of fine weather a decision was made to sail on the next day with the Maritime Trust flag hoisted on the lamp post on *Warrior*'s upper deck. Just before departure Wing Commander Ken Lucas, deputy to Admiral Bayly and due to embark in the tug, fell down one of *Warrior*'s main deck hatches and broke his thigh. As soon as he was safely ashore *Warrior* was slipped and gently eased into mid-stream to proceed down river in what Ron Tovey, mate of the *Hendon*, described as a carnival-like atmosphere. Crowds of people had gathered at Cleddau Bridge and on shore to wave good-bye. Then in Tovey's words, '. . . *Warrior* was quite obstinate whilst negotiating the numerous bends and . . . when rounding Thorn Island buoy to enter the east channel *Hendon* had to tow for all she was worth to edge her round. It really was like dragging an old lady from the home where she was born and grew up to love.

'After clearing the Haven we lengthened our tow and proceeded on what was to be an uneventful voyage. Quite a number of ships called up on VHF to enquire if it really was the *Warrior* and some asked if they could come closer to take photographs. We arrived at Hartlepool with 12 hours to spare having averaged six and a half knots and docked on the noon tide of September 3 to what really was a tumultuous reception with film and TV cameras everywhere. It was 1700 hours before we finally tied up and everyone concerned felt a great sense of achievement.'[29] Berthing temporarily in the Union Dock the ship was moved to the Coal Dock on September 7, narrowly squeezing through the basin entrance.

What the mate did not mention was that on entering the channel at Hartlepool *Warrior*'s port side sponson, that took the gangway to the Llannion jetty, collided with a light buoy and – in Admiral Bayly's words – 'swiped the top off.'

In her old ebullient fashion *Warrior* had arrived.

CHAPTER ELEVEN
Restoration

THE SHIPS PRESERVATION Trust negotiated a five-year lease from the Tees and Hartlepool Port Authority of a 450 ft long ship's berth extending about 80 ft inland. Snugly secured alongside the Coal Dock in a non-tidal basin, her port side well fendered and the berth dredged to two feet below the keel, *Warrior* awaited repair and restoration. At first, access to *Warrior*'s upper deck was via scaffolding towers but soon Ray Hockey, Locomotion Enterprises' project manager, acquired a couple of gangways and erected fencing to form a secure compound on the jetty.[1]

Before work could start below decks electricity had to be connected and the ship made accessible for survey. Hatches were being fitted with guardrails, some ladder ways rebuilt and handrails provided for safe access by visitors and workmen. As well as running lighting circuits as far down as the hold, daylight was enhanced by replacing skylight covers with translucent corrugated pvc. Then under Stan Morrell's supervision a tiny labour force of two shipwrights and five labourers started to remove 50 years' rubbish – 80 tons in all. Everything had to be examined lest a valuable artefact should be discarded accidentally; however little came to light apart from small items of doubtful source and two of the early coal trams discovered in one of the bunkers. The only first commission mechanical equipment found in position were some Downton pumps and Brown's patent capstan. Abaft the screw well was a Victorian water closet of unknown origin.

In her role as *Vernon III* the after portion of *Warrior*'s main deck had been turned into classrooms with wooden partitions, which now had to be dismantled and kept for possible re-use. Covering the main deck was an inch of fire-resistant composition whose removal revealed old deck planking, much of it rotten, on iron plating. Near the gun ports at each end of the battery were the marks of racers set on an arc for training heavy muzzle-loaders. Although the forward magazine had disappeared, the after magazine and midships shell rooms were intact. With its adjacent handing rooms, cartridge hand up holes and lightrooms the after magazine shelves and bins carried clearly inscribed tally plates, the whole area apparently untouched since the second or third commission. However, there was precious little else that could be associated with a fighting warship and it needed only a tour of the ship to reveal the prodigious task that faced the Trust.

Aware of the need to establish an alternative commercial operation to recently closed steelworks and idle docks, British Steel and local authorities pledged their support. With unemployment higher than the national average local shipyard skills and their management were abundant. Thus Locomotion Enterprises' lack of maritime experience could be countered provided they seized opportunities. As a first step the labour force was confined to two main unions, reducing

● Alongside the Coal Dock, 1980. Note the poop structure aft and the danger warning white line painted on the stem to indicate an increase in draught

the possibility of industrial problems.[2]

Financial support would come mainly from John Smith's Manifold Trust, hopefully backed by grants from the Department of Industry and British Steel. Hartlepool Borough Council would also help by refurbishing and renting the old three-storied Custom House building only 200 yards from *Warrior*'s berth, an ideal shore base and design office with space for a small museum. Once there was something to show with which to impress prospective donors the plan was to launch an appeal for funds. Thus the 'Friends of the *Warrior*' was established to consolidate the interest of local volunteers anxious to help by selling souvenirs, guiding visitors round the ship and raising funds. Its first chairman was Colin Doram whose former secretary, Jean Bartram, was engaged as personal assistant and secretary to the Ships Preservation Trust directors. In fact Jean was the first *Warrior* employee, followed by two draughtsmen who set up a drawing office on the ground floor of the Custom House. Through Patrick Bayly copies of the original Admiralty drawings for 'Her Majesty's Iron, Iron Clad Ship *Warrior* of 1250 Horses Power' were acquired from the National Maritime Museum.

It was agreed that Locomotion Enterprises would contract with the Ships Preservation Trust to reconstruct *Warrior* as detailed by Burness Corlett who, as the Manifold Trust's naval architects and consulting engineers, would vet

the work. John Smith wished *Warrior* to be restored to a state as near as possible to her original first commission condition which necessarily entailed a high degree of historical accuracy. As a first stage Admiral Bayly engaged John Moore for six months as Research Officer (Historical), an ideal choice as it turned out since he combined an extensive knowledge of the ship with an ability to tap further sources of information. By that time the title 'HMS *Warrior* (1860)' had been chosen both to describe the project and differentiate it from HMS *Warrior* (Northwood), headquarters of the Commander-in-Chief Fleet of the Royal Navy.

In theory the restoration plan seemed feasible if cumbersome but by March 1980 when the Duke of Edinburgh visited the project there was little apparent progress. John Smith had already been

to Hartlepool to assess the situation and because he doubted Locomotion Enterprises' suitability for the task it was decided that the Ships Preservation Trust itself should undertake the restoration. The project manager, some office staff and a small labour force elected to transfer to the Trust, thanks to the good offices of Admiral Bayly. In April 1980 the new company got under way with Maldwin Drummond in the chair, supported by Patrick Bayly and later Tom Dulake from the Manifold Trust as fellow directors. Their second meeting on June 5 was attended by Ray Hockey as project manager, Ron Clark representing Burness Corlett as consultant naval architect and Jean Bartram as secretary. She reported that about 1,000 visitors had come aboard over the spring bank holiday. News of *Warrior* was spreading.

The first creative step was taken when Jack

Whitehead and Norman Gaches were approached to carve a new figurehead for the ship in their Cowes, Isle of Wight, workshop and another when J W (Bill) Stevenson and Keith Johnson were re-engaged as draughtsmen, their initial task being to plan the design work needed to get reconstruction started.

Meanwhile discussions ranged over Michael Willoughby's drawings of the rigging, the possible appointment of a project director to administer the work at Hartlepool and the ship's future when restoration was complete in about five years. At the invitation of John Smith, E V Gatacre had submitted a report on how the ship might be restored and displayed which questioned the viability of the Portsmouth berth and recommended that Warrior should go to the Thames in the vicinity of HMS Belfast, the sole occupier of the best berth opposite the Tower of London.[3] However, Admiral Bayly pointed out that the Portsmouth City Council was dedicated to Warrior's returning there and the matter was left open. Later when Michael Leek of the Bournemouth and Poole College of Art and Design announced that one of his students, Stephen Ortega, had completed a nine-foot by four-foot coloured illustration of Warrior, Portsmouth's offer to display it in the entrance of the civic offices in Guildhall Square was accepted. There it remained for the whole period of Warrior's restoration.

Towards the end of 1980 Admiral Bayly invited me to undertake research for Warrior with the help of a two-year Leverhulme Foundation grant. If my qualifications were slender, a deep-rooted interest in the Victorian Navy stemmed from my grandfather's service therein; and a commission in the light fleet carrier Warrior remained one of my happiest memories. My answer had to be 'yes'.

Because few grants had come through to supplement financing by the Manifold Trust the board of the Ships Preservation Trust decided to recruit a fund raiser. In May 1981 A G (Tony) Bridgewater was appointed, with the additional title of development officer, to negotiate with companies who might donate their products or services. Tony started work with the Manifold Trust team in their Westminster office.

The third new appointment was Walter Brownlee. After acquiring his master's ticket in the Merchant Navy he turned to teaching. Specializing in history and archaeology he became a warden at the Stockton Teachers' Centre where he developed an interest in Warrior. Fortunately for the project Walter was seconded to the Trust on a yearly basis by Cleveland Educational Authority and eventually on a more permanent contract. He soon made himself succinctly knowledgeable about the ship, initiating photographic records and acting as a guide to an increasing number of visitors who arrived during working hours.

Meanwhile at the Coal Dock the whole of 1981 was spent in getting the project under way starting with the arduous job of repairing the upper deck. After removing the poop structure there were lamp standards, huts and a jumble of pipe line equipment to get ashore before tackling the thick covering of cement. Two hundred tons were eventually removed to expose decayed planking and rusted wrought-iron plating perforated by numerous holes used to fix a variety of equipment when part of HMS Vernon. Rainwater poured through the exposed surface, necessitating replacement with steel plating, and had even found its way below decks to wing compartments and the after magazine, all of which had to be pumped dry. Examination of the bulwarks revealed that both wood and iron work would have to be completely renewed, leaving a strong suspicion that the teak timber between the ship's side plating and the armour might also have deteriorated. Alongside the ship a second-hand shed was erected to house wood and steel working machinery for shipwrights and joiners amongst the 26-strong labour force. Included were two apprentices and some from the Manpower Services Commission (MSC) scheme recently launched by the Government to alleviate unemployment and assist industry. Acquisition of a punt capable of supporting a scaffolding tower enabled a new beak to be welded on to the bow to replace that part broken off by Wadhurst.

information which could be provided only by co-ordinated research. Before producing working drawings for shipwrights and joiners the draughtsmen had to be satisfied that every source of evidence had been verified and for that reason it was logical to separate on-board research, that could best be performed by the man on the spot – Walter Brownlee – from support research. The latter required searches in museums, libraries and private collections to collect evidence from documents, photographs, drawings and books. Although my brief was slanted towards personnel, in particular the life styles of those who served in *Warrior*, it seemed best to concentrate on support research, using as a basis the 1980 report compiled by John Moore. This paid off when on the first of many visits to the Portsmouth Royal Naval Museum, the Director – Captain Ray Parsons – was able to produce a recent acquisition of a log kept by Midshipman H A K Murray of *Warrior*'s first commission, containing a sketch identifying the exact position on each deck of every item of main armament, small arms, stores and ammunition. As a prime historical source the drawing proved indispensable as a guideline for restoration, especially when HMS *Excellent* photographed and enlarged it.

Despite a search at the National Maritime Museum *Warrior*'s ship's cover, that traditionally incorporated documents relating to the ship, could not be found, nor could that of *Black Prince*.

On the development side Tony Bridgewater was actively pursuing options on pitch-pine timber with which to plank the upper deck, as well as investigating means of getting the ship's boats built with the help of a shipping industry training board. Through the chairman he also set up a planning group to consider methods of fund raising, the outline restoration programme and the choice of a final berth for *Warrior*.

After establishing the likely sources of historical data about *Warrior* by personal visits to many establishments, my next stage was to agree research priorities with Hartlepool. It soon became apparent that although the Custom House had obtained sets of *Warrior*'s original drawings and a copy of building specifications, reconstruction to original conditions above and below decks demanded a great deal more

Nevertheless, throughout the period of restoration a number of drawings, some supported by documents, progressively came to light showing sections of contemporary warships, weapons, masts and rigging, machinery and equipment, much of which had some bearing on *Warrior*'s needs. In some cases the drawing office was able to match the data produced with material evidence on board the ship; in others it was a matter for inspired guesswork. And because the Victorian mind possessed both ingenuity and common sense it became possible to understand the style of approach adopted by the designers, builders and those who manned *Warrior* in overcoming the many problems peculiar to a novel type of warship in those far-off days.

From museums, libraries and private albums there arrived in the Custom House a selection of photographs, some of *Warrior* and many of her sister ships depicting different aspects of upper decks, armaments and ships' companies grouped on the upper deck. By the 1850s, it is worth recalling, photography was no longer a scientific wonder but a lucrative business. Using glass negatives and paper prints the wet plate process was common practice, exposure times being reduced to a matter of seconds; even better results came with the invention of the dry plate. One cannot but admire the early photographers with their cumbersome complicated apparatus who produced pictures of such exceptional quality

● **Bill Stevenson, manager of the Warrior project**

capable of considerable enlargement, little realizing the immense value they would prove to researchers of the 20th century. Among the group photographs it is enlightening to note the staid self-conscious attitude of the older officers and ratings contrasting with the guileless expressions on the faces of the midshipmen and ordinary seamen; together they immortalize the image of those who served the Royal Navy a hundred years ago.

Successful research means avoiding the temptation of jumping to false conclusions – not always that easy – and it did not take the

Hartlepool team long to become expert in sifting solid evidence from hearsay. For example, we had been led to believe that the photograph on page 142 of *Warrior*'s officers referred to the first commission because the officer leaning on the binnacle was allegedly Lieutenant Fisher. For months the identity of the officers had puzzled me, particularly the captain and commander who did not look at all like Cochrane and Tryon. Not until the sharp eyes of draughtsman Keith Johnson detected that the guns in the background were 7-inch muzzle-loaders and not 7-inch Armstrongs did we realize it was a second commission photograph. But in some investigations there remained gaps which no research effort could fill and the agreed solution was qualified with what the assistant project manager, Bill Stevenson, termed 'defendable accuracy'.

During the first months of 1982 discussions took place on *Warrior*'s final destination. Apart from the need to prepare a berth for the ship it was important to establish SPT's credibility with potential donors by presenting realistic long term plans and at the same time maintaining good faith with Hartlepool. There were only two front runners for a berth afloat, Portsmouth and London, with Chatham as a possible outsider whose naval base possessed the original dock built for the construction of *Achilles* in 1862. It was finally recommended by SPT's planning group that Portsmouth offered the best opportunities.

Over a generation the city's image had changed markedly from a dockyard port, a pebbly beach, a roller coaster and Southsea landladies into a thriving industrial and commercial centre, possessing fast rail services from London, good motorway access and an expanding ferry port. These characteristics, added to a location for *Warrior* just inside the naval base adjacent to the naval museum and *Victory*, promised viability. Equally indispensable for this project was local authority and public support; here Portsmouth scored maximum points. In May John Smith and Tom Dulake visited Portsmouth informally to satisfy themselves that the choice was correct before a letter of intent was sent to the city council. Later in the year the first of many meetings took place to discuss berthing options with the Chief Executive, Richard Trist, and the Leader of the Council, John Marshall, an inveterate *Warrior* enthusiast. It was also decided by SPT that since restoration facilities at any display berth were almost certain to be unfavourable the move south should not take place until reconstruction was virtually complete.

Then came some bad news. Although it was known that he was far from well it was with a deep sense of shock that the Trust learned of John Moore's death on April 27, 1982. Over the previous year we had met occasionally and communicated frequently about the *Warrior*; John's notes will remain a fitting tribute to his profound enthusiasm and conscientious research.

In seeking further information on Captain Arthur Cochrane, *Warrior*'s first commanding officer, the late Earl of Dundonald, put me in touch with Richard Cochrane of Ballykelly, Northern Ireland, grandson of Captain Ernest Cochrane, Arthur's younger brother. After unsuccessfully courting Miss Mary Wake in 1867 Arthur never married and on his death bequeathed his possessions to Ernest, who kept them in his family property at Redcastle in Co Donegal. While working in Canada Richard Cochrane succeeded to the property in 1961, and returned to Eire; but ten years later moved with his wife, son and daughter to the Bridge House in Ballykelly, which they ran as a small hotel.

Early in July 1982 I paid my first visit to Bridge House where I found Arthur Cochrane's uniform, medals, swords and instruments together with documents, drawings, photographs, correspondence and newspapers spread all over the house in some confusion. As the Cochranes were reputed never to throw anything away the amount was considerable. By September, 'Cochranalia' – as the contents of numerous boxes and trunks were termed – had been sorted, listed and graded, with items relevant to *Warrior* separated from those relating to Cochrane's later naval career. When it came to purchasing the relics the Royal Naval Museum at Portsmouth stepped in with a substantial contribution and early in October Richard Cochrane and I brought a car and trailer full of Cochranalia to Portsmouth. Because of this rare stroke of luck it will be possible to associate many items of Arthur Cochrane's personal possessions with the restoration of his quarters, as well as providing invaluable primary source evidence of *Warrior*'s equipment and administration in her first commission. On leaving *Warrior* in November 1864 Cochrane was so attached to the ship that he took with him the captain's letter book, containing copies of more than 700 official 'out' letters written between 1861 and 1864, five *Warrior* signal logs and a host of personal letters, diagrams and drawings. Something exciting was always coming to light and just before leaving Ballykelly a last look round uncovered a torn coloured illustration of the midships section of *Warrior* thought to be dated 1861. The story has a sad ending in that although this unique collection is now safely housed in the RN Museum, Richard Cochrane always intended to use the proceeds of sale to set up house for himself and his wife back in Canada. After a long and painful illness he died in Ballykelly in 1985.

Restoration got into its stride on the upper and main decks in 1982. A start was made on the lengthy job of renewing the bulwarks while the upper deck was being prepared with red lead, studs and sealant to take 20,000 square feet of soft wood planking obtained from a demolished Bradford warehouse. At the same time the

●Midship section of
Warrior at after stokehold
showing boilers, bunkers,
coal trams, wing passages,
bag racks and 68 pdr guns,
circa 1861

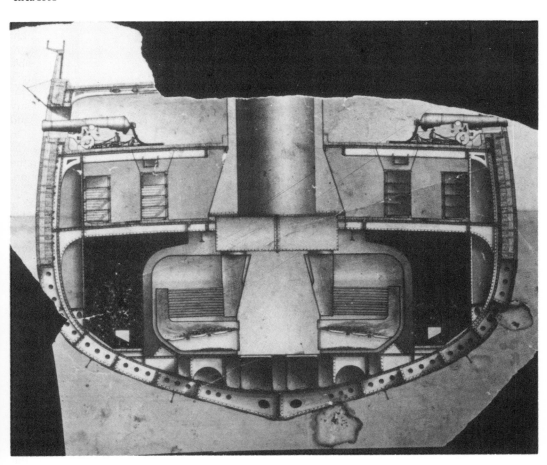

draughtsmen produced working drawings for the guns and carriages that would eventually be mounted on the main deck, the heart of the ship for display purposes. Conforming to the policy of constructing guns and equipment appropriate only to the first commission, relevant data was fed into the Custom House from various sources, including information volunteered by Ernest Slaymaker of Gosport whose lifetime hobby has been the study of 19th century naval ordnance. But to construct historically accurate reproductions of guns in fibreglass – casting in metal would have been prohibitively expensive – meant searching the country for exact specimens, there being no national inventory of vintage cannon. Early in the year I was able to confirm the existence of at least one 110pdr Armstrong at Fort Regent, Jersey; later Bill Stevenson and Keith Johnson discovered a 68pdr in the Museum of Artillery in the Rotunda at Woolwich, together with information on aspects of *Warrior*'s armament supplied by the curator, Major Stan Walter.

Starting with the 68pdr, both guns were later transported to Hartlepool where the work of making replicas was undertaken locally. Meanwhile the empty main deck was gradually fitted with wooden mess tables, stools and mess shelves, as well as wooden cooperage manufactured within the Custom House to supply the various receptacles associated with a broadside mess. In this respect and many others we were

●Starboard side
broadside messes and
battery on main deck
ready for inspection

●110 pdr Armstrong gun,
moulded in Hartlepool
and mounted on elm
carriage constructed in
project workshops

fortunate to secure the unstinted advice of R D (Bob) Ridding, an ex-Royal Marine officer and former executive in the naval victualling branch whose knowledge of Victorian naval food, stores, clothing and customs was unrivalled. Finally the *Warrior News*, first edited by Walter Brownlee, appeared three times a year as a four-page progress report on restoration. Illustrated by photographs and distributed widely, it attracted considerable attention and not a few cash contributions. In retrospect 1982 was a satisfactory year.

For the January 1983 National Boat Show at Earl's Court the *Daily Express* sponsored the display of the *Warrior* figurehead. Standing 12ft from the ground the yellow pine martial figure looked magnificient as Jack Whitehead and Norman Gaches put the finishing touches to their carving with mallet and chisel. Tony Bridgewater organized three panels of photographs behind the figurehead, together with a superb model of *Warrior* made by Ken Duckers for Cleveland County Council. The stand attracted unusual interest among a maritime-minded public as a volunteer staff handed out thousands of leaflets, collecting some £700 in donations. Further publicity was gained from the appearance of the figurehead on the Blue Peter BBC programme immediately after the Boat Show.

When the Leverhulme Trust research sponsorship ran out in April 1983, Portsmouth City Council generously stepped in to establish me as their liaison officer with SPT and to continue with research. The timing was about right since negotiations were under way to agree the positioning of the ship's berthing jetty which the council would build near the Victory Gate of the naval base. Sustained by the local press a growing surge of interest had sprung up among Portsmouth people for the return of *Warrior* to a port where she had spent much of her active life – and twenty years as *Vernon III*. When rumour suggested that the ship might go elsewhere, a TV interviewer asked a passer-by near the Guildhall what she thought of *Warrior* going to Chatham. 'Chatham?' asked the lady, 'Where's Chatham?'

Besides the MOD Naval Historical Library at Earl's Court – the old Admiralty Library – the target for investigation was the Public Records Office at Kew, the official repository of Admiralty documents including ships' books, logs and description lists. Equally important were Admiralty letters mainly relating to various aspects of *Warrior's* construction period and full credit for painstaking, professional effort goes to Antonia MacArthur who joined the research team in 1983 to build up *Warrior* archives in the Custom House.

Included in my research task was the pursuit of artefacts. An early discovery in the west country was the original stadiometer invented and owned by Henry Blakey, *Warrior's* first master. A search in Wiltshire resulted in the gift of the clock presented to Commander Tryon before he left *Warrior* in 1864. The Admiralty Compass Observatory at Slough found two Admiralty-pattern compasses of the 1850 period, the Tower of London armoury offered to lend cutlasses, boarding pikes and tomahawks and the Queen's Harbourmaster at Portland located an old 'stream' sized anchor. In a corner of the Naval Ordnance Museum was a ship's bell of similar dimensions to *Warrior's*, which nobody seemed to own or want, the Royal Clarence Yard at Gosport discovered a dozen old pattern hammocks while the Naval Store depot at Woolston in Southampton yielded

assorted lamps, including a set of copper navigation lights. From Portsmouth dockyard came Victorian cooking utensils and from a London militaria store 500 metal plates and bowls. After searching for steering wheels and wheel indicators as a pattern for the Trust drawing office, the best source of evidence was found in HMS *Vernon*'s wardroom mess, graced since 1928 by the poop structure of *Marlborough* and the wheels of the large frigate *Ariadne*, one of *Warrior*'s big frigate predecessors. As expected the Royal Navy did us proud in all transactions, particularly in the reproduction and enlargement of photographs.

When *Warrior* first anchored in Spithead, Portsmouth was enclosed within its own fortifications, as were Portsea and Gosport, the only completely walled towns in England. Whale Island was still a mud bank and the harbour could only be entered by large warships at high water. Since then the facilities of the dockyard have multiplied although its physical shape hardly altered during the many years spent by *Warrior* in the naval base. It was therefore more worthwhile to visit the two places that symbolized the beginning and end of her naval career: first to Blackwall where little trace of Thames Shipbuilding and Ironworks can be found on either bank of Bow Creek. Although the River Lea is now heavily silted one can still stand alongside an electricity pylon near where *Warrior* was built and visualize the amazingly narrow channel into which the great ship was

launched. Today Thames Ironworks Orchard Yard office by the waterfront is used by Trinity House Works Department while across the river at Deptford, John Penn's boiler shop is lettered Payne's Wharf. Further down river lies the vast expanse of Royal Victoria Docks, empty and awaiting redevelopment, but the basin where *Warrior* was fitted-out is still intact although her exact berth cannot be confirmed. *Warrior*'s success in the 1860s was reflected in Thames Ironworks full order book for British and foreign warships, the company

reaching its peak at the turn of the century when it amalgamated with the then ailing John Penn. Thereafter and despite the valiant efforts of their last chairman, Arnold Hills, the company went downhill in the face of stiff competition from northern shipyards, and closed in 1912. Arnold Hills left a 'legacy' in the shape of a works football team that grew into West Ham United, currently in the First Division, whose nickname, the Hammers, was derived from the old Ironworks badge.

Equally cheerless but more attractive was Llannion Cove visited early one summer in the Queen's Harbour-Master's boat from Pembroke Dock to find *Warrior*'s jetty looking sad and deserted under a thick belt of trees. The fuel depot had been dismantled and the real pleasure was to meet *Warrior*'s last shipkeeper, Hugh Griffiths, full of memories and delighted to know his old ship was in good hands. It is also worth mentioning that in 1983 I happened to be aboard the Gibraltar-Tangier ferry whose master knew all about the *Agincourt* incident in 1871 and altered course to pass close to the Pearl Rock, with its distinctive breaking water and strong current swirl. Under identical weather conditions one could imagine the enthralling scene on *Warrior*'s conning bridge as *Agincourt* grounded four hundred yards ahead when but for Captain Glyn's swift reaction *Warrior* might have suffered another collision; incredible, too, that *Agincourt* failed to avoid such a well identified mark.

Warrior's sound hull, confirmed to a limited extent by plate thickness test readings, was a contributory reason for selecting a berth afloat in Portsmouth after restoration; in any case there was no suitable dry dock available. By the summer of 1983 Portsmouth City Council had budgeted £1.5m and secured planning permission to build a jetty into the harbour near the Victory Gate.

In August Captain Colin McMullen and Associates agreed to act as consultants in the complex operation of mooring the ship.[4] Account had to be taken of several factors; the wind force on a large ship carrying top hamper by prevailing southerly and sou'westerly winds gusting at times to 70 knots, the thrust and drag effect of the daily tidal stream, the rise and fall of the tide that could exceed 13 feet and finally the state of the sea bed in which mooring cables would be laid. To accept *Warrior* at a draught of 24 feet – two feet less than in active commission – the berth alongside the jetty would have to be dredged to 26 feet below chart datum, the trench extending into the harbour a further 100 yards to provide an approach channel. Sixty yards to the south of the berth lay the Common Hard, its use by Portsmouth fishermen protected by Ancient Rights, while in the north the jetty penetrated the naval base boundary where the boat pound contained service and police craft. The Queen's Harbour-Master had to be satisfied that *Warrior*'s overall length did not interfere with the ever-increasing ship traffic in the fairway, including the daily ferry service to and from Gosport. For these reasons it was decided that *Warrior*'s stern resplendent with her red ensign, should face the fairway and not conform to the custom of securing HM ships with their bows pointing out of harbour. Bowsprit and figurehead at the head of the jetty would make an impressive visual impact on approaching visitors. Three times the displacement of *Victory* and twice her length *Warrior* would be highly conspicuous to thousands of people on the waterfront as well as to the considerable ship traffic. It was indeed a prime berth that Portsmouth had chosen.

Until Ron Clark, now Managing Director of Burness Corlett, expressed misgivings on the plan to fender *Warrior*'s armour-plated side on two jetty sponsons an alongside berth was favoured. Final agreement was reached early in 1984 to moor *Warrior* by eight heavy chain cables – four ahead and four astern – about five metres clear of the jetty and to use two angled brows for access to and from the upper deck.[5] Former commanding officers of *Warrior* would have been pleased to learn of the trouble being taken to provide their old ship with a secure berth, but perhaps censorious of the plan to bring one pair of cables through the after hawsepipes to bitts in the after cabin and another pair through the day cabin to bitts on the half-deck.

For some years Portsmouth City Council had built up the city's tourism industry on its wealth of maritime heritage. To the unfading *Victory* and the comparatively recent but popular RN Museum was added *Mary Rose* whose spectacular raising and placing in dry dock in 1982 was widely publicized. Not for nothing did a national Sunday newspaper describe Portsmouth as the 'saltiest show on earth'. At a high-level meeting in the naval base early in 1983, chaired by Mr Jerry Wiggin MP, Under-Secretary of State for the Armed Forces, it was made clear that action must start now in co-ordinating the requirements of space and facilities to accommodate *Victory, Mary Rose, Warrior, Foudroyant* and the RN Museum in one heritage project. Later the so-called 'Gang of Five' agreed the need for two reports, one to cover the heritage area of the naval base, the other the whole of Portsmouth, Gosport and the Isle of Wight. In April 1983 a retired flag officer and former Commodore of the Royal Naval Barracks, Vice-Admiral Sir John Lea, became chairman of the committee and wrote to the Ministry of Defence setting out the position between the parties involved in creating the maritime heritage area in the naval base. The outcome was that the English Tourist Board agreed to fund a development study to be undertaken by Ventures Consultancy Ltd to consider first the 'narrow' and then the 'broad' project. In October the Robinson Report – named after Ken Robinson, managing director of Ventures Consultancy – was received

●Warrior's figurehead
being lowered onto its
trolley for transport to
Naval Base, August 10,
1983

with acclaim and adopted as a blueprint of how the two projects should develop.[6] Pointing out that the concentration of *Warrior, Mary Rose* and *Victory* would provide greater financial benefit to each participant than if displayed in separate locations, it did not recommend the inclusion of the Sea Cadet training ship *Foudroyant*. The scheme envisaged public access to the naval base through 'a hole in the wall' in Queen Street to a reception centre in No 6 Boathouse – use of No 5 Boathouse had been pre-empted by a decision to give it to *Mary Rose* for its exhibition hall. Ticketing, the report recommended, should be on a combination basis to include a charge for entering the project; and, by setting-up a service company, the reception centre, catering and shops would also be handled jointly by participants. Although an imaginative report it had expensive implications. The plan allowed *Warrior* to develop the two-storey cell block – built against the Georgian dockyard wall in 1881 to accommodate inebriated sailors returning from leave – as well as a space to build a museum at some future date. One was also left with the impression that the heritage project would not get off the ground until *Warrior* arrived.

Following the 1983 Boat Show the word started to get around that the world's biggest maritime reconstruction project was heading for Portsmouth. Although Hartlepool remained the focus of attention it was felt that time was ripe to

● Working with the adze on Warrior's upper deck, November 1983

establish an organization based in the south to harness the many offers of assistance and goodwill. Indeed, this was in line with the wishes of John Smith to whom the idea of voluntary help with restoration had always made a strong appeal. And so in the spring of 1983 I was able to select a committee of volunteers to set up the Warrior Association, its aim to support the *Warrior* project through fund raising, manufacture of equipment, research and publicity. Essentially it would work in conjunction with the Friends at Hartlepool. Rear-Admiral Philip Higham was elected chairman and in November a presentation took place in the Guildhall when Maldwin Drummond and the Lord Mayor shared the honour of launching the Warrior Association to about 500 people. Simultaneously Portsmouth City Council produced 25,000 popular and attractive *Warrior* leaflets, which included the spectacular Tudgay portrait of *Warrior* and did much to publicise the ship world-wide.

In August *Warrior*'s figurehead was brought over from Cowes by Harry Spencer in his lighter, hoisted on to *Vernon*'s jetty and hauled along the Hard on its trolley by Portsmouth's Lord Mayor, Councillor Leslie Kitchen, and a team of willing volunteers. Once in the naval base it was positioned against the wall of No 5 Boathouse facing the Victory Gate, only a few yards from the site vacated by its predecessor 65 years previously. From that moment *Warrior*'s presence

in Portsmouth was re-established.

1983 was another good year for Hartlepool. The long and laborious task of laying the upper deck planking was all but completed. First the channel bars had to be shaped and fitted into place where the deck met the ship's side. Then centrally placed hatchframes, formed by solid timbers dovetailed together, were assembled. After fastening rows of bolts on the deck the 20ft planks were marked and drilled for bolting in position, then a patent compound was laid on the deck and the planking drawn to it. It was decided to caulk the seams in the traditional manner and although

a dying skill caulkers in Hartlepool were able to perform the same job as men from Thames Ironworks and *Warrior*'s ships' company some 120 years before. After hot pitch had payed the seams – with particular attention to the garboard seam known as the devil – the deck was planed. An equally long-winded, more laborious but less noticeable task had started below decks – descaling deckheads and bulkheads with needleguns. Often working deep in the bowels of the ship under cramped and irksome conditions a group of some 30 stalwarts led by George Wall systematically removed paint and rust from every

compartment in the ship. According to the Paints Division of Associated Lead, who had a factory at Millwall before 1860 and analysed *Warrior*'s paint chippings in 1981, some fragments consisted of 120 different coats ranging from dark brown to white. In particular the heavy lead content presented health and safety problems entailing protective clothing and decontamination. As soon as they were clean the iron surfaces were coated with preservative and finally white paint where a fresh, clean appearance was needed.

The year also marked the concentrated efforts of Bill Stevenson and Keith Johnson, who were now able to tackle working drawings for the various spars and rigging. A start was made in constructing the mizzen mast from a 28 inch diameter steel tube and the D-shaped mizzen top in wood and steel. In the same shed shipwrights and joiners had started the production line for elm gun carriages to match the fibreglass gun barrels moulded with great skill by E and F Fibreglass Products Ltd in Hartlepool. Because the idea had often been mooted, serious thought was then given to building a full scale working model of the ship's engines and boilers.

On arrival in Hartlepool a heavily-rusted Belleville water tube boiler plant was found in the forward stokehold, a relic of *Vernon* days when *Warrior* supplied electrical power to the Royal Navy's floating torpedo training school. When it was removed in 1982 and a section given to the

Science Museum there was left an immense void in the bottom of the ship that obviously had to be filled, if only to provide boiler casing support on which to build the two telescopic funnels. Advice was sought from Richard Tomlin, a retired marine engineer who had written a thesis (1972) on *Warrior* and possessed a deep knowledge of the ship's engines and boilers. His recommendations followed a visit to SS *Great Britain*, which was facing the same problems at Bristol. It was agreed that he would work with Dorothea Restoration Engineers Ltd who were commissioned to report how the engines and boilers could be constructed. Meanwhile work was started on flooring the large coal bunkers to take quantities of rail chairs for ballasting the ship from 21ft down to 24ft. Incidentally, *Warrior* needed no ballast during her active life.

Not all restoration work was carried out by the Ships Preservation Trust. In 1982 the students of Hartlepool College of Further Education produced steel replicas of iron fittings for guns and rigging, the pièce de résistance being the massive curved tiller yoke, later to be fitted on the lower part of the rudder head. Billingham Industrial Training Centre followed with two Rodgers-type stern anchors to the design of the drawing office and being plated in steel they weighed considerably less than the 2½ ton originals. North-East Training Association undertook to build a number of spars, Rolls Royce started on gunsights and for those wishing to contribute financially Tony Bridgewater launched a gun sponsorship scheme inviting individuals or companies to subscribe £3,000 towards a 68pdr gun and carriage.

The year 1983 also brought about significant changes in SPT organization. In September the Maritime Trust transferred its majority shareholding in Ships Preservation Trust Ltd to the Manifold Trust and Vice-Admiral Sir Patrick Bayly resigned as a director and company secretary of SPT. As a mark of appreciation of his long-standing and invaluable association with the project, the staff at Hartlepool presented him with a miniature steering wheel inscribed 'Princess is much pleased' on the brass rim. Lord Strathcona and Sir Peter Vanneck joined the SPT board and Ray Hockey resigned as project director because of ill health. Bill Stevenson remained as project manager, with Stan Morrell as ship manager, while David Walton joined to assist with administration, taking over the ordering of materials and services. To handle reconstruction work at a more detailed level than required by the board a ship committee was inaugurated in July under the chairmanship of Tom Dulake, to include planning and installation of ship's internal services.

With the ship's reconstruction past the halfway mark the first general meeting of 1984 set targets for the workforce now over the 100 mark, before giving thought to how *Warrior* might be displayed to the public. Tony Bridgewater and I

had previously prepared a discussion paper which was used as a basis for the display committee convened later in the year with Maldwin Drummond as chairman, meeting periodically at Dean's Yard. Michael Darby, deputy director of the Victoria and Albert Museum, initially agreed to help, bringing John Bancroft, an architect with experience of furniture design. It was agreed that the ship would be displayed in her 1861-1864 condition 'as if all the crew had unaccountably gone ashore', and that with the aid of a leaflet visitors would find their own way round the ship, from the upper deck down and through two decks to the engineroom, a route that would also satisfy Portsmouth fire authorities. To illuminate the ship below decks replica lanterns of 1860 were to be modified to suit visitors; it was also proposed to locate individual displays in the gundeck to create the atmosphere and environment of a mid-19th century warship. At the same time Bill Pearson was seconded from Burness Corlett and Partners as part time hull services engineer, his job to plan the installation of electrical power, telephones, water, sewage, heating, ventilation, public address, security and fire-fighting arrangements.

By the middle of 1984 a metal working shed had been erected on the jetty and on board a third of the main deck armament and all upper deck planking had been finished. September 25 was a great day. The mizzen lower mast with its top

fitted and the topmast lashed alongside was hoisted by a giant crane through upper and main decks to rest on the floor of the wardroom. Raked at four-and-a-half degrees from the vertical, the 13 ton 28 inch diameter steel tube was guided into position by a small team led by shipwright supervisor Arthur White. No time was wasted by the photographer in climbing up the steel ladder inside the mast to take the first shot of the upper deck from aloft. On November 19 the main mast and main topmast were lowered into position, the foot resting on the floor of the auxiliary machinery space, its overall length 120ft and its weight more than 30 tons. The 25ft wide top seemed enormous as it lay on the jetty, sufficient to carry 20 men with ease. Modern cranage accomplished the operation in an hour causing one to reflect on the efforts of Chatham yard riggers in 1861 with their sheer hulk, capstans and windlasses.

Not long after the ship's arrival in Hartlepool came letters from people claiming family links with officers and men who had served in *Warrior*. In 1983 Mrs Blackett-Jones, aged 96, arrived to see the ship in which her father – Assistant Engineer James Bedbrook – served from 1867-69. Walter Brownlee reported that 'she was vital and sprightly, climbing up and down ladderways . . . it was hard to believe that we were talking to someone whose father had served in the 1860s.' Even more amazing was to discover Chief Petty Officer Telegraphist Charles Cutler alive and well in Devon, aged 98. In a recorded interview he gave to Bob Ridding and myself, Cutler remembered his brief service in *Warrior* as *Vernon III* in 1908-1909 when he qualified leading telegraphist with top marks, and told us a lot more about the navy of that time. Regrettably neither he nor Mrs Blackett-Jones survived 1985 but thanks to the *Warrior News,* now edited and published by the Warrior Association, it was possible to collect particulars from more than 40 Old Warriors, ranging from grandsons of *Warrior* commanding officers to great-grand-nieces of former crew members, many contributing service certificates, artefacts and photographs.

The year 1984 was mainly one of consolidation, notable for the signing in September of a formal agreement between the Ships Preservation Trust and Portsmouth City Council, the former agreeing to bring *Warrior* to Portsmouth in 1986 to a berth provided by the Council.[7] Further legislation was enacted seven months later when it was felt that 'Ships Preservation Trust' was insufficiently descriptive of the project's role so the name was changed to Warrior Preservation Trust at a meeting saddened by news of Ray Hockey's death, following a long illness. By now Tom Dulake had assumed the highly important duties of project director that soon necessitated weekly visits to the ship from the south.

The beginning of 1985 marked a surge of activity in Portsmouth and Hartlepool. To secure

● Chief Petty Officer Telegraphist Charles E T Cutler, wearing the medals of two World Wars, outside his bungalow in Exmouth, Devon, June 10, 1984

Warrior in her berth the marine consultants had specified mooring equipment based on the City Engineer's drawings, recommending the Department of Transport as the best source of supply; in fact DOT produced most of the cables, shackles and sinkers, all tested and fairly new. The balance was found in Harry Pound's Portsmouth yard, including unused seven-ton mooring anchors. To construct *Warrior's* berth a contract was awarded to L A Dawson Ltd of Luton, Zanen Dredging and Construction being sub-contracted to dredge and lay part of the moorings. By March 1 work had progressed sufficiently for the Lord Mayor of Portsmouth, now Councillor John Marshall, to

inaugurate the jetty project, the first load of mooring equipment arriving at the end of the month. Working round the clock the dredger excavated *Warrior's* berth to a depth of 26ft, using laser beams for navigational accuracy and filling barges with soil to be dumped off the Nab Tower. The most obstinate obstructions encountered proved to be the foundations of the old railway viaduct between Portsmouth Harbour Station and South Railway jetty, built in the 1870s so that Queen Victoria could embark in comfort in her yacht en route for Osborne House, Isle of Wight.

At the end of January Portsmouth said 'au revoir' to *Warrior's* figurehead when it was transported to Hartlepool in company with a 6pdr brass cannon for the ship's upper deck armament; a week later the figurehead was mounted on the beak. On February 20 the fore lower mast was positioned followed by the bowsprit which fitted neatly into a new wooden step. First stage of masting was now complete, allowing fife rails to be set up either side of each mast by the mast partners – thick curved deck planking to steady the mast. The plan was then to set up lower mast shrouds and stays complete with dead eyes, channels, chain-plates and rods, using ship's labourers supervised by Rigger Brian Metcalf. In April Harry Spencer, with his exceptional experience of rigging sailing ships was called in to advise. Finally, as its first fund raising effort the Warrior Association launched an appeal for £750

● John Marshall, Lord
Mayor of Portsmouth,
inaugurates the Warrior
jetty, March 1, 1985

● John Marshall, Lord
Mayor of Portsmouth,
inaugurates the Warrior
jetty, March 1, 1985

to pay for the fore topmast. Such was the response from members in the UK and overseas that a cheque for £2,000 was sent to Hartlepool within three months, together with a list of 92 donors to be inscribed on a scroll and placed inside the topmast for posterity.

During the summer months the ship bustled with activity, reminiscent of *Warrior*'s fitting out in 1861. On one side of the main deck steering wheels were stacked ready for assembly while on the other the whole broadside of guns had been moved fore-and-aft so that shrouds could be set up for stretching and serving. Further aft marines' rifle racks were fitted on either side of the half deck; down below two wardroom cabins were furnished to John Bancroft's specifications, noticeably larger than similar single accommodation in the modern navy. Forward and below the figurehead Richard Barnett from Devon was installing his wooden carvings, joiners were completing the last of the upper deck skylights, shrouds were going up on the mizzen lower mast and the elliptical roofless armoured tower, complete with rifle apertures, was lowered into position. Over the stern men were working on the ornamental gallery from staging on a pontoon.

Early in 1985 a decision had been made to set up an engineering department to provide *Warrior*'s steam propulsion machinery. Possessing a wealth of practical experience and plenty of initiative C J (Jim) Wilson was appointed project engineer with a small team of draughtsmen and a further 15 men for plant construction and installation. By the end of the year ten boiler frames, the main condenser, two main engine cylinder frameworks and the side valves were on board. Because steam was the first technology under man's control and is still relatively easy to understand, *Warrior*'s engine room

is expected to hold a particular fascination for visitors. One day they may be able to see the funnels being raised and lowered as well as the massive engines turning slowly, accompanied by suitable sound and vapour effects.

After more than a hundred years as a dormant, unlovely hulk *Warrior* was now looking like a real ship eager to start another career. To celebrate her new lease of life a naval helicopter of 707 Squadron from Yeovilton rose to the occasion in September with a spectacular set of coloured photographs. It was opportune because viewed across the basin at ground level one could detect for the first time since arrival in Hartlepool the strength, character and beauty of the great ship's lines as she lay at her berth high out of the water wearing the red ensign as she did in her first commission. Easy to understand, too, why a youthful lieutenant in 1864, later to become a distinguished admiral, described *Warrior* and *Black Prince* as 'stately and noble vessels' and why 'their long hulls and yacht bows, the vast expanse of flush wooden decks, their solidity and grace, set them among the finest ships ever built'.[8] Tribute was paid at that time to the men who built *Warrior* as credit must be given today to those who restored her. Walking round the ship, discerning visitors are invariably struck with an impression of a job well done; under the direction of Bill Stevenson and the leadership of Stan Morrell, the 140-strong Hartlepool workforce had developed a

●Lowermasts, bowsprit
and armoured tower in
position, September 11,
1985. Note the scale of
infrastructure in the
compound needed to
support the work on board

capability and craftsmanship never previously imagined and were now in top gear as the ship entered her sixth year of repair and reconstruction. By the end of 1985 the Manpower Services Commission had contributed £1m in the wages of the majority of those employed, a commendable example of government support for a worthy cause.

Regrettably the opportunity to record on TV a stage-by-stage progress of restoration was missed but later in the year the BBC went some way to make up for it with an entertaining 30-minute programme for national coverage. In the spring of 1986 BBC's Blue Peter presented another programme and articles about *Warrior* started to appear in several national newspapers and magazines. By now Bob Davis of the Friends of Warrior was fully employed showing visitors round the ship.

Since 1984 a Government-funded community project, organized by the Cleveland Council of Churches, had been set up alongside the Custom House to manufacture various artefacts and projectiles – *Warrior* had an outfit of more than 3,000. Although correctly shaped their composition in cement was below the specified weight so it was fortunate that apprentices of the Royal Ordnance Factory at Patricroft, Manchester, had already started casting in metal a number of 68pdr, 110pdr and 40pdr projectiles to be displayed in *Warrior*'s ready-use racks. Then in

1984 Royal Ordnance, Nottingham, successfully refurbished a 20pdr Armstrong gun generously loaned by the Maritime Command Museum in Halifax, Nova Scotia, which was flown over from Canada by the Royal Air Force; unfortunately it turned out to have a land service and not a sea service barrel. With equal enthusiasm the Nottingham apprentices tackled a 40pdr Armstrong, ex-Woolwich Rotunda museum, which lacked a breech screw and vent piece. These and a wooden carriage were skilfully made in their workshops so that the gun could form part of the Royal Ordnance stand at the Royal Naval Equipment Exhibition at Whale Island in September 1985. With an attendance of 30,000 visitors, the Warrior Association staff were hard put to compete with demands for breechworking demonstrations by a technically-minded public, many of whom had never heard of *Warrior* and still less an Armstrong gun. Thanks to Royal Ordnance and BMARC (British Manufacture and Research Co Ltd) who exhibited one of our 110pdr Armstrongs, the exhibition attracted good publicity for *Warrior.*

Although plans were agreed to complete the *Warrior* jetty early in 1986, ready for the ship's arrival in the following September, the Portsmouth Naval Heritage Trust project could report only limited headway during 1985. On the positive side a Property Trust had been created to handle certain buildings in the south-western area

of the dockyard, such as boathouses, storehouses and No 3 Dock containing *Mary Rose.* Having been endowed with sufficient government funds to maintain them for 99 years the Property Trust would then lease the buildings to the Heritage partners. The experiment of closing the Victory Gate for vehicle access during most of the day, coupled with the placing of temporary barriers for visitors had been successful, which augured well for the permanent erection of a security fence around the Heritage area and the release of further buildings no longer needed by the dockyard. This in itself is a considerable achievement within a nationally important operational naval base of which the Ministry of Defence is the freeholder.

Despite the appointment of Marc Mallam in 1984 as project director, who worked with great zeal to co-ordinate planning of essential infrastructure and to get the show on the road, the Heritage Trust found the going difficult. Quite simply the Heritage partners, particularly *Mary Rose* and *Warrior*, were unable to subscribe to the estimated £2m costs needed to finance the joint service company to develop the project. In the case of *Warrior* John Smith pointed out that his Manifold Trust was providing all funds, except those available through the MSC scheme and grants from English Heritage, to restore *Warrior* and could not extend itself further. Not until November 1985 did the Heritage Trust seek

commercial participation when a number of interested developer/operators were invited to meet Admiral Lea and his management committee, supported by the English Tourist Board, to learn about development prospects. The response was encouraging.

During the summer in Portsmouth the Royal Marine Band of Naval Home Command played the Warrior March before the Queen, a stirring tune composed by the Director of Music to celebrate the ship's restoration; in Gosport the Maritime Trust's Manpower Services Youth Training project, now called the Maritime Workshop, put finishing touches to *Warrior's* jolly-boat and copper punt, the latter rescued from the Hilsea moat where it had lain for many years. As 1985 drew to a close *Warrior's* passage south and procedure for taking up moorings were discussed but by far the most important event was the announcement that Captain Colin Allen, RN, had been selected to command *Warrior* on arrival in Portsmouth. Currently Director of Fleet Supply Duties in the Ministry of Defence he had recently been Chief Staff Officer to Flag Officer, Portsmouth, and was no stranger to the Heritage Project. One of his first jobs would be to handle the applications for the ship's display staff, including many from the Hartlepool work force.

Early in January 1986 it became all too evident that the rate of work and spending on the ship would have to be stepped up if *Warrior* was to

come south in September as planned. However John Smith felt that the Manifold Trust just could not increase further its contribution of £90,000 per month. Although this news came as a disappointment to some, Portsmouth City Council took it in their stride because the proposed delay of six months would bring certain advantages. First it meant that virtually all the work could now be completed in Hartlepool, in particular the rigging where progress had come to a standstill in the bitter winter weather, and in the engineroom. Secondly, *Warrior's* new arrival date in the spring of 1987 at the start of the tourist season would not only be more beneficial to the ship but to the Heritage Project, the facilities of which would be more advanced to receive a principal partner.

Finally, there was the bonus to Hartlepool where an extra six months employment would be highly popular, especially as there were now good prospects for a project to restore the paddle steamer *Wingfield Castle* – and possibly the small World War I monitor *Minerva* currently in Portsmouth harbour – starting in 1987.

At the Hartlepool meeting late in February Bill Stevenson, the project manager, listed the tasks outstanding to complete restoration, still formidable but hopefully within reach if current progress above and below decks was any yardstick. *Warrior's* berth by the Hard was ready in September, 1986. Supervised by the City Council's engineer David Clubb, the contractors did well and the 590ft long, 23ft wide concrete jetty, with two sponsons, guardrails, bollards, lifebuoys and lamposts, has become a prominent Portsmouth harbour landmark. Throughout the year my research efforts included cutlery and chinaware for the wardroom and seaman's uniform for the ship's staff. These culminated in the RN College, Dartmouth loaning a quantity of silver, Royal Worcester Spode contributing plates with 1862 naval crown engraving, Olney of Luton making hats and caps and Blair of Portsmouth jackets, frocks and trousers. Gieves and Hawkes made Captain Allen's frock coat, the first to be cut for 45 years. Largely through the Warrior Association artefact contributions included a telescope, glassware, ditty boxes, a sandglass, cat-o'-nine

tails, clay pipes, family photographs and numerous 19th century Victorian knick-knacks for officers' cabins.

By April 1987 visiting the ship had become a stimulating experience; *Warrior* was now alive with features typical of a Victorian warship in final stages of preparation for active service. Viewed across the Coal Dock basin the great ship lay truly ataunto, ie fully masted up to the royals with gaffs in position and lower, topsail and top gallant yards hoisted and crossed, their sails neatly furled. Although lacking reef points and cringles the canvas was cut to correct size by Alf Readman, late RN and now a period sailmaker of Whitby, who used, for example, 600 yards of Duralon three feet wide to make the main course. A longer bowsprit of early 1861 dimensions has replaced the shorter 1862 bowsprit originally fitted, extending the ship's overall length – jib boom to stern – to 500ft. The impression of power and sheer size is further enhanced by the two telescopic funnels, complete with steam pipes, erected over the casings either side of the fore conning bridge. Painted buff they match the spars.

Approaching *Warrior's* port bow the ornate wooden carvings below the figurehead catch the eye as do the gunport lids held horizontal by chains and purchases inboard. Right aft the stern gallery with wooden scrollwork sets off *Warrior's* nameplate freshly gilded on the stern. On the upper deck 110pdr bow and stern chasers are mounted on 14ft revolving slides, 40pdrs amidships on wooden carriages and further forward the 20pdr boat guns and 6pdr brass cannon. Standing on the after conning bridge one can visualize how the captain might have handled his ship and how the officer of the watch would have moved from the after standard compass to the engine room telegraph in the wings. Both would have had a clear view along the ship's side despite the bulwarks interspersed with shrouds and dead eyes. So easy, too, to give orders to the quartermaster and helmsmen on the wheels by the mizzen, the helm position shown by pointer on a circular indicator. From the maintop the view was breathtaking – as was the ascent by ladder inside the mainmast. Looking down 64 feet to the upper deck the thought of barefooted upper yardmen racing up the ratlines over the futtock shrouds to take a brief spell on the top before ascending the topgallant and finally the royal, stretches the imagination to its limit.

Starting aft on the maindeck the captain's quarters contain his coffin-shaped cot slung fore and aft in the sleeping cabin while a dining table with 12 chairs, two easy chairs and a desk occupy his day cabin; on the bulkhead hangs a picture of *Driver*, Cochrane's previous command in the Baltic. Captain Allen will take over the commander's cabin as his own; the paymaster's office contains control gear for the ship's electrical/electronic

●Upper deck steering
position at the foot of the
mizzen, October 1986

equipment; and for security reasons the master's cabin displays the barometer, chronometer and tell tale overheard campass loaned by the National Maritime Museum. A specially-collected set of 1860 navigational publications fills the cabin shelves. Forward two massive armoured doors mark the entrance to the citadel where the visitor is confronted with another steering position under the armoured tower which has the unique double steering compasses made recently in the Admiralty Compass Observatory to the specifications of Commander Tony Fanning. Warrior's bell is hung amidships by the main mast, its clapper adorned by one of the many bell ropes presented to the ship. Further forward is Brown's patent capstan beautifully refurbished, and the galley with cooking utensils ready to feed 700 officers and men. Either side of the gundeck the sweep of shining black guns and scrubbed mess-

tables leaves a lasting impression. Right forward on the cable deck are the bitts and deck fitments as well as two lever-operated controllers to the bower cables. A glance through the forward ports reveals the ship's company heads on either side of the beak. The lower deck has come to life; officers' cabins, wardroom and gunroom are painted in gleaming white, some with furniture fitted; issue room, slop room and dispensary are ready while nests of racks have been installed either side of the marines', seaman's and engineers' flats for kit-bags. The last space also includes baths and a washing machine. However, it is the stokehold and engine room that undoubtedly arouse the greatest interest. All ten boilers are installed with furnace doors and draught plates that open onto the central firing aisle; in the engine room the trunk engine connecting rods have been joined to the crankshafts and on the port side in one large casing Jim Wilson's men have connected the two jet condensers that supplied feed water to the boilers. Initially no auxiliary machinery or propeller shaft between the stern tube and engine turning gear is to be fitted.

Earlier in the year an announcement that Warrior's departure south would be mid June, 1987 preceded a visit to Hartlepool by the Duke of Edinburgh. Having played no small part himself in initiating what amounted to the greatest maritime reconstruction project ever undertaken Prince Philip was able to assess the degree of

courage, skill and effort demanded and to congratulate all concerned on a job well done. Meanwhile preparations for Warrior's homecoming moved into top gear as Portsmouth realised the tremendous impact the ship would make on a city that will soon boast a truly unique collection of distinguished warship's spanning over 400 years of naval history.

Captain Allen and his executive officer Graham Salt set up office within the Heritage Area, now surrounded by fencing, to coordinate arrangements for handling the public, as well as recruiting permanent staff and volunteers in support.

It was a sad day for Hartlepool when the ship moved out of the Coal Dock and started her 384-mile passage south. Most appropriately Warrior was towed by two of Alexandra Towing Company's latest tugs, their Voith-Schneider propulsion contrasting with the diminutive paddlers Punch and Uncle Sam which were paid £20 apiece for attending the ship when she left Victoria Docks for Greenhithe on August 8, 1861.[9]

When Warrior left Portsmouth in 1929 the harbour was packed with warships, including the new 35,000 ton battleship Nelson bristling with 16inch guns, which had recently joined the fleet at a cost of £6M. The Royal Navy then was still the world's largest with responsibilities that stretched throughout the Empire. A single destroyer in 1929 could be built for about the same as Warrior,

£377,000 equivalent today to £8¾M.[10] On her return 56 years later the harbour looks much the same but with far fewer warships and only *Victory* recognizable. Although fully operational a once thriving dockyard is now reduced to a fleet maintenance base, *Excellent* and *Vernon* have been paid off and the role of capital ship passed to the nuclear-armed submarines whose standard displacement (7,000 tons) and length (420ft) are similar to those of Britain's first ironclads. Home at last *Warrior* has started a third career, this time as a famous historical ship – not bad for an old lady of 126.

* * * * *

When France launched *Gloire* in 1859 she challenged England not so much to fight as to adapt to a new pattern in naval warfare. Our response was *Warrior*, by no means the first iron ship or the first with screw and sail propulsion or even the first armoured ship; but by combining all these features and more in one hull *Warrior* initiated the greatest leap forward in capital ship design for 300 years. As the most formidable warship in the world *Warrior's* place in naval history was as significant in 1860 as the original nuclear submarine nearly a century later. Both demonstrated the value of seapower to deter war and both brought about such a flood of innovation that they soon became obsolescent.

Warrior's active career in the age of Pax Britannica was unspectacular but a study of her personality reveals certain notable characteristics:

her feminine capriciousness in refusing to budge from the launching ways on that bitterly cold day in December 1860; her awkwardness in steering which meant that her officers never knew when she was going to disobey the helm in confined waters or broach to when running before a full gale; and her lucky streak when she escaped with only minor damage following collision or grounding – a streak that embraced her crew who possessed that indefinable spirit which binds a ship's company, enabling them to face any predicament with the sure knowledge that they will come out on top.

As a hulk *Warrior* owed her survival not only to being built of wrought iron in an era when ships were made to last but also to the care bestowed on her by the Royal Navy. And luck did not desert her at the end. Although *Warrior* was never offered to scrap dealers she came perilously close on at least one occasion.

Her final stroke of good fortune was in catching the attention of John Smith. When asked why, single-handed, he took on the tremendous task of restoration he replied, 'because *Warrior* is a beautiful, unique and powerful object, a monument to the enterprise, skill and toughness of the Victorians – and because nobody else apparently could be found to foot the bill'. John Smith's dedication and contribution to national heritage has been considerable; perhaps his own service in the Royal Navy inclined him towards historic ships. As he wrote,

'. . . in the past important ships have been lost to posterity because there was not enough time, once their disposal had been announced, to organize their preservation. I was quite sure that with *Warrior* it was essential to make arrangements in advance so that when the time came the authorities could be swiftly convinced that a viable scheme for her restoration existed. The Maritime Trust, of course, was the obvious body to undertake this task. However, when it was formed, its committee, not unnaturally, was daunted by the amount of money necessary to preserve *Warrior* and I felt that an appeal for funds to guard against a future event – when she was no longer required – stood no chance of success. To get things moving I said that the Manifold Trust would provide whatever money which could not be raised from other sources for her preservation. I hoped that we would not have to provide anything like the whole lot, nor envisaged that we would become involved with the actual work of restoration. However, when tackling an unfashionable, neglected or desperate cause nothing will be done unless you do it. So the present state of affairs has its compensations; at least it can be said that it is *we* who have brought *Warrior* back from the dead and that she is *our* present to the nation. If every warship in the whole 19th century still existed – and was available for preservation – *Warrior* would still be my first choice.' A sentiment that will be shared by all who really care for our naval heritage.

A typical day at sea

2.45 am Course south by east. Wind sou'west. Gentle breeze. Sky clear. Sea smooth. Ship proceeding 3 kts on starboard tack under headsails, topsails and courses. On bridge watch Lieutenant Wilson and Midshipman Grenfell. At the wheel Quartermaster Hetherington and two helmsmen from the watch on deck.

3.10 am Able Seaman Cole, starboard lookout, reports 'Light on the starboard bow, sir'. Wilson orders seaman gunner of watch to burn blue light to warn passing ship to keep clear.

3.45 am Pipe 'All the starboard watch and idlers – rouse out, rouse out, lash up'. Watch on deck take up ropes and prepare gear for washing down. The stir and murmur of a ship becoming awake.

4.00 am Morning watch of seamen and idlers mustered by their officers. Scrub and wash upper deck. Idlers man pumps below decks, (boilers not alight). Midshipman of the watch heaves log to record last hour's distance run.

4.20 am Midshipman Grenfell calls Mr Blakey to take star sights to fix ship's position.

4.30 am Sudden appearance of Commander Tryon stimulates the hands on deck to greater energy.

6.00 am Officer of watch calls captain in his sleeping cabin, 'Six o'clock, sir. Daylight. Decks dried and ropes down, sir. No ships in sight.' 'Thank you, Mr Parker, pass the word for my coxswain.'

6.15 am 15 boys second class muster in waist under Petty Officer Tanner who sends them over the mizzen masthead, coerced by responsible topmen. Last boy down is touched by Tanner's rope's end.

6.45 am All hammocks brought up from below and stowed in upper deck hammock nettings under supervision of duty midshipmen. Pipe 'Cooks to the galley'. Upper deck clean and all gear neatly stowed.

6.50 am Captain Cochrane arrives on bridge, looks aloft. 'Mr Parker, if you paid more attention to the headsail sheets the ship would move faster.' Parker gives orders; hands on deck move rapidly about their duties, ashamed to have been caught off balance.

7.00 am Six bells. Pipe 'Hands to breakfast' provides welcome break to morning's work. Ships Cook Holding supervises issue of cocoa from galley. By habit older men tap biscuits on messtables since weevils still prevalent. Sun well above horizon and with it a stronger breeze to put fresh vigour into ship's movement. Master gives officer of watch new course. Officer of watch 'Starboard ten.' 'Steady' – 'Steady sir, course sou' sou' east.' Sails are trimmed to new course.

7.15 am With screw up and funnels down steam department concentrate on maintenance, brushing through fire tubes and hoisting ash to upper deck for discharge overboard. Fires lit under cupola and blacksmith's forge.

7.45 am Forenoon watchmen in white frocks and trousers inspected before relieving deck at eight bells (8 am).

7.55 am As midshipmen sit down to breakfast Captain's Steward Hunt appears at door of gunroom, 'Captain's compliments and will Midshipmen Murray and Coddington take breakfast with captain at half past eight?' This puts the midshipmen in a quandary since both have been taking sights with the master since 4.30 and to wait another half hour is too much strain on their appetites.

8.30 am Marine drummers forward and aft beat two rolls on drums for 'quarters clean guns'. Each gun is a source of pride to crew who burnish metal parts while others sand down staves of rammers, worms and sponges. Small arms are cleaned and oiled for inspection by gunner. Gunnery lieutenant and captain of marines walk down the battery.

9.00 am Two bells. Pipe 'Hands to divisions with hammocks'. Holding hammocks washed and dried ship's company are paraded on upper deck for inspection. Each division is reported correct by its officer to the commander who says a few words to assembled company. Then hats are removed for prayers taken by Chaplain Jackson.

9.35 am Tryon orders 'Sound off action'. Marine drummers beat one long roll on drums to call attention. Two taps on drums galvanise every officer and man into activity as they rush to general quarters throughout the ship. Crews close up on upper deck guns and cast loose. Riflemen collect their weapons go aloft and man the tops. Quartermasters man wheel positions with action helmsmen. Signalmen fetch cutlasses and pistols before hoisting battle ensign. From the maindeck comes deafening clatter with hoarse shouts as crews cast loose the guns, open gunport lids, stow mess tables overhead, pass mess gear below and carry out preliminary drill. Gunner draws keys to open up magazines and handing rooms for crews. Idlers stand by to provide ammunition. Gunnery lieutenant is everywhere urging men to move faster, then mans voice pipe on maindeck under conning bridge. Officers take charge of respective quarters and await orders. Fire brigade musters in marines' flat, carpenter assembles his wing passage men and surgeons set up first aid centres in sick bay and wardroom. Steam department go to full steaming stations and prepare to hoist funnels and lower propeller. Master-at-arms releases cell prisoners under escort. Tryon reports to Cochrane

on after bridge 'Ship at General Quarters, sir, time taken four and three quarter minutes'. 'That's better, Commander, proceed with training.'

9.50 am Pipe 'First division – repel boarders.' Upper deck guns crews collect rifles and cutlasses and some man the armoured tower. Idlers rush up on deck arming themselves with pikes and tomahawks. Gunnery lieutenant and chief gunner's mate take them to drill. Main deck guns to individual instruction under gunner's mate and officers of quarters.

10.20 am General quarters secure and disperse. Resume ship's work.

10.45 am Gunner's mate Partridge takes midshipmen to cutlass drill in starboard after waist. 'Now, gentlemen, cutlass scabbard in left 'and and close to left 'ip. At the order draw – seize the 'ilt smartly with the right 'and and draw the cutlass smartly to the right shoulder, right forearm 'orizontal. Everybody understand? *Draw!* … As you were, as you were. One after the other, just like a peal of bells. *Return swords.* Now, sirs, we'll try it again. Take that smile off your face, Mr Duthie. Cutlass work is no laughing matter.'

11.00 am Warrior is hove to by counterbracing yards (in opposite directions) to reduce headway to half a knot. Supervised by Chief Quartermaster Williams five seamen take sounding with deep sea lead, finding bottom at 91 fathoms. Layers of sand adhering to tallow on base of lead indicates nature of sea bed.

11.55 am Sextant in hand the master observes sun's

altitude. Blakey then reads off, makes brief calculations and informs officer of watch.

12.00 pm Officer of watch to Cochrane, 'Twelve o'clock, sir, please. Latitude 49 degrees 51 minutes north, sir.' 'Thank you, make it so' says Cochrane. Eight bells are struck. Hands are piped to dinner. Salt pork, cabbage and oatmeal soup.

1.15 pm First class boys to drill with Second Captain-of-Mizzentop Moore in furling and sending up and down topgallant and royal yards.

2.00 pm Chief Bandmaster Hope conducts band practice on cable deck with four violins, cello, clarinet, viola and euphonium.

2.15 pm Followed by Boatswain Beaton and Midshipman Pugh Commander Tryon starts tour of the ship. On deck and aloft afternoon watchmen are occupied splicing ropes, strapping (strengthening) blocks and whipping ropes' ends. Quartermaster on watch teaches ordinary seamen the art of steering. In the booms Chief Carpenter's Mate Kingstone contemplates the gash in the bow strakes of the second launch, the result of a recent grounding off Weymouth. Up forward Able Seaman Sewells is cleaning out the pen which houses two fat ewes destined for the wardroom table while Captain of the Focs'le Turrell is tending a line secured to Ordinary Seaman Jannaway working over the side re-lashing the best bower anchor. On the cable deck Tryon finds the carpenter's crew at work on their benches; he stops to speak to Carpenter Davidson about a leak in the captain's cabin skylight. Passing aft through the messdeck he sees men off watch, washing, mending and making clothes; Leading Seaman Giddy teaching Ordinary Seaman Juggins the art of sennit plait to make a hat; Leading Stoker Pinckneys is starting to roll a prique of tobacco, others are writing letters, taking advantage of the fleet mail arrangements entitling the lower deck, but not officers, to free postage. Those who notice the commander are quick to rise to their feet but Tryon waives them to be seated as he makes his way to his cabin aft, where Captain Mawbey is waiting anxiously to see him about a marine sentry found absent from place of duty.

3.00 pm Consulting his journal Surgeon Wells writes his quarterly report to the Physician of the Fleet, wondering how he is going to explain the numbers on the sick list that compare unfavourably with other ships in the squadron.

3.16 pm Paymaster de Vries and Yeoman of Storerooms Wright investigate the source of unpleasant odour emanating from the port side of the provision room. Discover two casks of putrid salt beef.

3.30 pm 'Clear up decks'. Ropes coiled down and decks swept.

4.00 pm At the change of watch on deck ship is braced round onto port tack.

4.15 pm Lieutenant Perceval on watch orders Boatswain's Mate Mounsey to pipe 'Hands to supper.' Cocoa and biscuits.

5.00 pm Drums beat to evening quarters. Amongst reports to commander are

– Divisional lieutenants – 'Men sober, properly dressed, quarters cleared for action.'
– Master – 'Wheel ropes and relieving tackles correct.'
– Surgeon – '34 on sick list.'
– Paymaster – 'Storerooms secure.'
– Master-at-Arms – 'Two prisoners in cells.'
– Gunner – 'Magazines manned, guns cast loose, lifebuoys correct.'

5.15 pm Pipe 'Clear lower deck – each watch own side.' Commander orders evolution 'Shift topsails.' Three masts in competition send sails down to deck and back again. Mizzen topsail – 15½ minutes; fore topsail – 17½ minutes; main topsail – 20 minutes. This does not satisfy Tryon and main-topmen are required to repeat evolution, this time in 18 minutes.

5.30 pm In his cabin Chief Engineer Buchan receives Assistant Engineer Baldwin's report on the state of the fire tubes in the forward stokehold. Buchan congratulates Baldwin on his efforts.

6.00 pm Lamps are placed on main deck allowing men to light up their pipes for two hours. Spitkids are placed.

7.00 pm Captain Cochrane writes his night order book 'Course north west by north a half north. Look out for Lizard light on lee bow and call me when it is sighted. Call me at 2 o'clock and on any material change of weather.'

7.15 pm Officer of the watch reports to Cochrane 'Sunset, sir, lookouts placed and lights lighted.' 'Very good, Mr Phillimore, please take the night order book.'

7.30 pm Pipe 'Down hammocks.' Ships company collect hammocks to sling them on main deck.

8.00 pm Eight bells. Out ship's company lights.

8.30 pm Commander Tryon goes night rounds of the ship led by Master-at-Arms Hendlay carrying a lantern and followed by First Lieutenant Owen, Midshipman Fortescue and Ship's Corporal Chapman. Receives report from Assistant Engineer Swiss at top of engine room hatchway that steam department rounds are correct. Reports to Captain on completion.

10.00 pm Out wardroom lights.

10.20 pm Ship comes to the wind on port tack. Main yard is squared and course resumed.

11.50 pm Midshipman on the watch heaves the log to record distance run in past hour – 3½ knots.

Midnight.

1858

Nov Admiralty decide to build armoured frigate

Dec Admiralty approve iron-hulled armoured frigate

1859

Jan 18 Parliament approve construction of 'two iron-cased vessels'

Jan 28 Admiralty invite tenders for design of armoured frigate

Apr 29 Surveyor's design approved. Building tenders called for

May 11 Thames Ironworks & Shipbuilding Co win contract

May 16 Tender from J Penn to build engines

May 25 Laid down. Penn's tender accepted

Oct 5 Name *Warrior* announced

1860

Apr 11 *Warrior's* contracted launch date

Dec 29 Launch. Secure to buoys in Thames

Dec 30 Shift to Victoria Docks for fitting out

1861

Mar 1 Trials of engines and boilers

Mar–May Rigged with masts and spars

Aug 1 Captain Cochrane commissions ship

Aug 3 Bulk of ship's company join

Aug 8 Navy accepts *Warrior*. To Greenhithe to embark guns, stores etc.

Sept 19–20 Passage to Spithead with First Sea Lord

Sept 21–

Oct 4 In dock, Portsmouth

Oct 14 Preliminary machinery trials

Oct 17 Full power trial over measured mile

Oct 25 Reduced power trial

Oct 31–

Nov 23 First experimental cruise, Portland to Queenstown, with *Revenge*

Dec 2–31 Plymouth–Spithead. Portsmouth harbour for maintenance

1862

Jan 18–

Feb 4 Spithead–Plymouth–Lisbon on second experimental cruise

Feb 4 Lisbon. Joined by RY *Osborne*. Royal and ambassadorial visits

Feb 7 Lisbon–Gibraltar

Feb 9–19 Engine room repairs in Gibraltar, thence Plymouth

Mar 5 Hamoaze for refit

Mar 22 To and from sheerhulk to exchange bowsprit

Jun 6 Post refit trials. Anchor in Hamoaze

Jun 10 Plymouth to Queenstown

Jun 20 Depart Queenstown with *Revenge*, *Emerald*, *Chanticleer* for launch of *Triumph*, Milford Haven

Jun 26–28 Milford Haven–Spithead. Royal visit

Jul 10 Enter harbour for docking

Jul 11–15 Dock. More royal visits. Thence Portland

Aug 12–16 Cruise in company RY *Osborne* (Admiralty Board)

Aug 23–30 Training cruise off Scillies

Oct 1–16 Portland–Lisbon–Gibraltar with *Edgar*, *Black Prince* and *Liffey*

Nov 20–

Dec 3 Lisbon and cruise with *Revenge*, *Black Prince*, *Defence* and Resistance

Dec 3–20 Lisbon. Target firing with Martin's shell

Dec 20– Lisbon–Madeira with *Revenge*, *Black Prince*, *Defence* and *Resistance* – Lisbon

Jan 4, 1863

1863

Jan 29–

Feb 3 Cruise in company Channel squadron

Feb 16–21 Lisbon–Portsmouth with *Revenge*, *Defence* and *Resistance*

Mar 2 Downs to Flushing with Channel squadron

Mar 5 Escort HRH Princess Alexandra of Denmark to Margate Roads

Mar 6–7 Escort *Victoria and Albert* to Nore and Gravesend

Mar 8–13 Spithead. Exchange part RMA for RMLI

Mar 14 Hamoaze for annual refit. Embark Renton's hydraulic steering gear

Apr 1 Fisher joins

Jun 2 Hydraulic steering gear sea trials

Jun 17–

Jul 3 In dock, Portsmouth

Jul 11– Leave Spithead to join Channel squadron

Oct 9 in Downs for Round Britain Cruise, Yarmouth–Sunderland–Leith–Forth–Cromarty–Kirkwall–Inganess–Loch Foyle–Greenock–Carrick Fergus–Liverpool–Dublin–Plymouth

Nov 12–27 In dock, Portsmouth

Dec 22– With Channel squadron, Plymouth–

Feb 27 1864 Funchal Bay–Madeira–Teneriffe–Gibraltar–Lisbon

1864

Feb 4–5 Inspection by Rear Admiral Dacres

Mar 5 Portland. Garibaldi's visit

Apr 30 Portland–Spithead. Fisher leaves to join *Excellent*

May 13–20 Arrive Plymouth, Queen's dock, Keyham

Jun 17 Commander Tryon leaves to command *Surprise*

Jul 18– Cruise Torbay–Queenstown–Bearhaven–

Sept 1 Plymouth

Sept 2–16 Gibraltar and back. Thence Portland and Spithead

Nov 3 Secure alongside in Portsmouth harbour

Nov 22 Pay off under superintendence of Admiral Dacres

1864–1867 First major refit, Portsmouth dockyard

1867

Jul 1 Captain J Corbett assumes command

Jul 8   Anchor Spithead in review berth with Channel squadron
Jul 17   Queen Victoria reviews fleet
Jul 25   Captain H Boys assumes command
Aug 21   Run measured mile off Stokes Bay
Sept 24–26   Spithead to Queenstown
Oct 8–15   Depart Queenstown with Channel squadron, *Minotaur* (flag), to Lisbon
Oct 25–
Nov 8   Lisbon and back for training cruise with Channel squadron
Nov 20–
Dec 2   Lisbon and back with Channel squadron
Dec 14–19   Lisbon–Plymouth–Spithead
Dec 28   Cowes Roads as guardship. Queen Victoria in Osborne House

1868
Feb 24–
Mar 30   Portsmouth harbour, including 12 days in dock
Apr 1–3   Full power trials
Apr 14–27   Escort *Victoria and Albert* with Prince of Wales from Holyhead to Kingstown (Dublin Bay) and back to Portland
Jun 4–
Jul 4   Cruise in company *Minotaur* (flag), *Royal Oak*, *Prince Consort*, *Bellerophon*, *Defence* and *Achilles*
Jul 31   Portland, joined by *Pallas* and *Penelope*
Aug 14   Cruise to Northern Ireland and Scotland. *Warrior* collides with *Royal Oak*
Aug 21–
Sept 1   Moville, Lough Foyle, thence Belfast– Greenock–Plymouth
Oct 1–6   Court martial of Captain Boys
Oct 9   Hamoaze to moor off Keyham
Oct 13–
Nov 25   Dock
Dec   Hoist flag of Vice Admiral Sir T Symonds
Dec 17–28   Plymouth–Lisbon and then first training cruise

1869
Jan 21–
Feb 3   Lisbon and back for second training cruise
Mar 4–13   Lisbon and back third training cruise
Apr 5–9   Fourth training cruise off Lisbon

Apr 20–28   Lisbon–Portland with Channel squadron
May 6-7   Portland–Spithead
May 31   Secure dockyard jetty to fit ship for towing
Jun 17–21   Spithead–Madeira in company *Black Prince*
Jul 3–29   Funchal Roads–Bermuda *Warrior*, *Black Prince* and floating dock with *Terrible* astern
Jul 31–
Aug 23   Bermuda–Plymouth in company *Black Prince*
Aug 25   Spithead, then dockyard
Aug 28   Captain Stirling assumes command
Sept 8–20   In dock. Fit new figurehead
Sept 27–29   Spithead–Milford Haven to join Channel squadron
Oct 19–25   Milford Haven–Lisbon
Nov 8–21   Cruise, Madeira–Teneriffe–Gibraltar– Lisbon

1870
Jan 20–21   Inspection by Rear Admiral Symonds
Jan 24–
Feb 6   Lisbon and back with Channel squadron
Mar 2   Captain Glyn assumes command
Mar 7–
Jun 6   Depart Lisbon with squadron, Fayal– Lisbon–Vigo–Corunna–Spithead
Jun 11–18   In dock, Portsmouth
Aug 4–15   Spithead–Gibraltar with *Minotaur, Hercules* and *Captain*
Aug 19–27   Gibraltar–Vigo with combined fleets
Sept 2   Depart Vigo for cruise off Iberian coast
Sept 6–7   *Captain* capsizes, search for survivors
Sept 15   Arrive Portland Roads
Nov 28   To sea for target practice with *Minotaur*
Dec 18   Spithead

1871
Jan 7   Spithead–Portland
Jan 30   Experimental firing
Mar 15–16   Portland–Plymouth with *Agincourt* and *Northumberland*
Apr 6–24   In dock, Devonport
Apr 30–
May 2   Plymouth–Bearhaven

May 6   Depart Bearhaven, Bantry Bay with *Minotaur, Agincourt, Hercules, Northumberland, Inconstant, Monarch* and *Helicon*
May 19–30   Funchal Roads, Madeira
Jun 11   Arrive Gibraltar
Jul 1   Gibraltar–Tangier with squadron. *Agincourt* grounds on Pearl Rock. Anchor in Getares Bay
Jul 11–20   Gibraltar–Vigo with *Hercules, Monarch* and *Northumberland*
Aug 6–28   Depart Vigo with 23 major warships for Queenstown
Aug 28–30   Queenstown–Plymouth
Sept 1   Enter Portsmouth
Sept 15   Pay off into 4th division reserve
1871–1875   Second major refit in Portsmouth dockyard

1875
Apr 1   Captain Whyte assumes command of *Warrior* in Portsmouth as coastguard service unit and for RNR duties
May 3   Run measured mile (14.079 knots)
Jul 26   Vice Admiral Sir J Tarleton, Ad Supt Naval Reserves, hoists flag
Jul 29–
Sept 9   Portland and back with *Iron Duke, Vanguard, Hector, Penelope* and *Defence* when Tarleton strikes flag

1876
Apr   Portland–Portsmouth for docking
Jun 13–17   Spithead–Gibraltar to join Channel squadron ('Bulgarian atrocities')
Jul 18–23   Gibraltar–Portland

1877
Jan 1   Portland
May 14–20   In dock, Portsmouth
Jul 18–23   Cowes Roads for Cowes Week
Aug 2–31   Portland–Vigo–Corcubion –Torbay– Portland with *Black Prince* and *Minotaur*

1878
Jan 1   Portland
Mar 15   Captain Douglas assumes command
May 5–16   In dock, Portsmouth

Jun 5	Rear Admiral Boys hoists flag as Second in Command Particular Service squadron	
Jun 13	Spithead–Portland to join Particular Service squadron	
Jul 3	Cruise, Portland–Bearhaven–Portland	
Aug 7	Portland–Spithead for review of Particular Service squadron by Queen Victoria	
Aug 16	Rear Admiral Boys hauls down flag	

1879

Jan 1	Portland
Apr 16	Secure to jetty, Portsmouth and fit steam steering gear
Apr 21–May 6	In dock
Jun 22–Aug 7	Cruise, with 1st reserve squadron Falmouth–Torbay–Portland–Gibraltar–Lagos–Vigo–back to Portland

1880

Jan 1	Portland
May 3–19	In dock, Portsmouth
Jun 18–29	Portland
Jun 29	On leaving Portland hits breakwater. Return to harbour for divers' inspection. Plymouth for docking
Jul 7–Aug 11	Depart Torbay with 1st Reserve squadron Rear Admiral the Duke of Edinburgh
Jul 10–22	Crookhaven–Bearhaven–Bantry Bay
Jul 31–Aug 6	Vigo Bay–back to Portland

1881

Jan 1	Portland
Jan 3	Captain Heneage assumes command
Mar 21	To sea for target practice
Apr 22–May 5	In dock, Portsmouth
Apr 30	Captain Townsend assumes command. Exchange crew with *Hercules*
Jun 15–Jul 29	Depart Downs with 1st Reserve squadron to Heligoland–Copenhagen–Cronstadt–Kiel–Lieth–Osborne Bay
Aug 1–Sept 22	Slip jetty, Portsmouth

Sept 27–Oct 3	Plymouth–Loch Ryan–Lamlash–Greenock, to take up new station

1882

Jan 1	Greenock
Apr 27–30	Greenock–Spithead
May 10–19	In dock, Portsmouth
Jul 16–Jul 24	Depart Portland in company with 1st Reserve squadron. Arosa Bay–Gibraltar–Portland–Spithead
Jun 29	Inspection by Rear Admiral the Duke of Edinburgh
Aug 49	Return Greenock
Nov 27	Captain Adeane assumes command

1883

Jan 1	Greenock
Mar 20	To sea for target practice
May 8–11	Greenock–Spithead
May 14	Enter Portsmouth harbour for the last time under own power
May 31	Pay off under superintendence of Captain Rowley. Remains on Effective List

1902

Jul 16	Captain de Robeck commissions *Warrior* as depot ship for Portsmouth Torpedo Boat Destroyers

1904

Mar 31	Captain Charlton pays off *Warrior*
June	Towed to Southampton for conversion
Dec	Forms part of Torpedo School ship and commissioned as *Vernon III* in Portsmouth

1914–1918 World War I

1924

Mar 31	Pay off as *Vernon III*

1927

Oct 22	Convert to oil fuel pontoon hulk in Portsmouth

1929

Mar 13	Depart Portsmouth under tow
Mar 16	Arrive Pembroke Dock. Secure to jetty at Llannion Cove

1939–1945 World War II

1958 In dock, Devonport

1964

July	In dock, Milford Haven

1968

July	Visited by Prince Philip, Duke of Edinburgh

1969

October	Establishment of Maritime Trust

1974

July	In dock, Milford Haven

1979

Feb	John Smith agrees to underwrite cost of restoration
June	Given to Maritime Trust for restoration
Aug 29	Depart Pembroke Dock under tow for Hartlepool
Sept 3	Arrive Hartlepool for repair and reconstruction in Coal Dock

1987

Feb	Visited by Prince Philip, Duke of Edinburgh
June	Depart Hartlepool. Arrive Portsmouth

Operational Data. Between 1861 and 1871 Admiralty deployed its most modern ships in the Channel to deter the French naval threat. Apart from the dock tow to Bermuda *Warrior* was confined to the home station, extending from northern Europe to the eastern Atlantic seaboard bounded by the Canaries, Gibraltar, and Spain. Service in the First Reserve squadron restricted *Warrior*'s movements to the British Isles, except for training cruises to the Baltic and Spain. When in port between 1861 and 1987 *Warrior* spent her time mainly at Portsmouth (60 years), Portland, Plymouth, Llannion Cove (50 years) and finally Hartlepool (7½ years).

Between 1861 and 1869 *Warrior*'s distance run in nautical miles reveal an interesting contrast in modes of propulsion typical of a Channel squadron ironclad.

Year	Steam	Steam/sail	Sail	Mileage
1861	655	216	497	1368
1862	1712	3657	1288	6657
1863	2381	2401	998	5780
1864	2225	3043	564	5832

Total first commission	Steam	Steam/sail	Sail	Mileage
	6,973	9317	3347	19,637
1867	556	1785	—	2341
1868	2905	841	1569	5315
1869	3111	4985	5132	13,228
Total second commission	6572	7611	6701	20,884
Total 1861–69	13,545	16,928	10,048	40,521
Percentage	33	52	25	

Not too much credence should be paid to the high steam/sail figures because *Warrior* frequently used her engines to keep station or manoeuvre while sailing.

To estimate total distance covered during *Warrior's* active service career an annual figure of 6000 miles has been added when in full commission and 4,500 when in coastguard reserve. Thus 1861–69, 40,500, 1870–71, 10,500 and 1875–83, 36,000 to a total of 87,000 miles.

Best performances during first commission were – under steam 14.354 knots, under sail 13 knots and under steam and sail 17.2 knots.

Official designations 1859 to 1987. On Admiralty building drawings the ship was designated 'Her Majesty's Iron, Iron clad ship *Warrior* of 1250 horses power'. Thereafter as No 532 in the *Navy List* she was described as a 40gun screw ship, iron (when first built); as a 32gun iron screw ship, armour-plated (after her 1864–67 refit); and from October, 1887 as a 32gun screw battle ship, 3rd class armoured. From May, 1892 she was listed as a 32gun screw cruiser, 1st class armoured.

From early 1900 she appeared among non-effective vessels as '32gun screw cruiser, 1st class, armoured (only considered available as a hulk).' From July 16, 1902 to March 31, 1904 she was a depot ship for torpedo boat destroyers, and from April 1, 1904 a Torpedo School ship as *Vernon III*. After October 1, 1923 she was omitted from *Navy List* until August 27, 1942 when she became oil fuel hulk C 77. From 1980 she was designated HMS *Warrior* (1860).

Personnel   Appendix II

In 1863 HMS *Warrior's* crew comprised 50 officers, 12 chief petty officers, 51 petty officers 1st class, 30 petty officers 2nd class, 25 leading seamen, 416 seamen, stokers and boys, 6 sergeants and corporals RM, and 116 drummers and privates RM. (Total 706).

In the 1864 *Addenda to QR and AI* (1861) *Warrior* was shown as complemented for a third rate ship of the line during Channel squadron service. For coastguard and reserve duties (1875–1883) her complement was approximately halved, except when fleetmen were embarked for summer cruise training.

Ship's establishment (1863). *Officers* One Captain, Commander, Chaplain, Master, Naval Instructor, Paymaster, Surgeon, Second Master, Boatswain, Carpenter, Gunner. Two Assistant Surgeons, Master's Assistants, Assistant Clerks. Three Assistant Paymasters and Clerks. Five Lieutenants. Six Naval Cadets. Ten Sub-Lieutenants & Midshipmen.

Chief Petty Officers: one Master at Arms, Chief Gunner's Mate, Chief Captain of the Forecastle, Chief Quarter master, Chief Carpenter's Mate, Seaman's Schoolmaster, Chief Bandsman, Ship's Steward, Chief Boilermaker, Ship's Cook, Founder.

First Class Petty Officers: One Armourer, Blacksmith, Captain's Coxswain, Coxswain of the Launch, Captain of the Hold, Plumber, Ropemaker, Sailmaker, Yeoman of the Signals.

Two Captains of the Afterguard, Foretop, Maintop, Forecastle, Carpenter's Mates, Caulkers, Gunner's Mates.

Four Ship's Corporals. Seven Boatswain's Mates, Quartermasters.

Second Class Petty Officers: One Caulker's Mate, Cooper, Coxswain of the Barge, Coxswain of the Pinnace, Musician.

Two Captains of the Mast, Captains of the Mizzentop, Coxswains of the Cutter, Sailmaker's Mates, Second Captains of the Forecastle. Three Signalmen.

Four Second Captains of the Afterguard, Second Captains of the Foretop and Maintop.

Seamen and Boys: One Armourer's Crew, Barber, Blacksmith's mate, Captain's Cook and Assistant, Captain's Servant, Captain's Steward. Commander's Servant. Cooper's Crew, Lamp Trimmer, Second Captain of the Hold. Ship's Steward's Assistant and Boy, Sick Berth Attendant, Assistant and Steward, Tinsmith, Ward Room Cook's Assistant, Warrant Officer's Servant, Warrant Officer's Cook.

Two Butchers, Cook's Mates, Engineer's Servants (or Cooks), Shoemakers, Tailors, Painters, Ward Room (or Gun Room) Cooks and Stewards, Ward Room Servants, Gun Room Servants.

Three Sailmaker's Crew, Yeoman of Store Rooms.

Five Shipwrights; Nine Carpenter's Crew; 15 Bandsmen; 25 Leading Seamen, Boys 2nd class; 44 boys 1st class; 199 Able or Ordinary Seamen.

Steam Department: two Chief Engineers, ten Assistant Engineers (1st or 2nd class), Leading Stokers (First Class POs); 18 Second Class Stokers/Coal Trimmers; 48 Stokers/Coal trimmers.

Marines: one Captain, two Lieutenants, Drummers and Buglers, three Sergeants, Corporals, 114 Privates (RMA or RMLI).

First commission officers and senior rates. This list of officers and senior ratings who served from 1861 to 1864 differs from the establishment because men were not always available to fill complement billets and there were changes due to promotion, drafting and sickness.

Officers

Captain the Hon A A Cochrane. Commander G Tryon, W Codrington, Lieutenants H B Phillimore, J E M Wilson, G F H Parker, H L Perceval, N S F Digby, J A Fisher, C G Jones.

Master (later Staff Commander) G H Blakey. Second Master J B Doyle

Sub Lieutenants D E K Grant, W H M Molyneux, F C Brown, F J Pitt, E B P Kelso, W E K Cockell, F R Boardman, R B Croft

Midshipmen J H E Parker, R J Fortescue, A H Duthie, H A K Murray, F R Brown, T H Coddington, H J M Pugh, W Neilson, W Marrack, R P Humpage, H T Grenfell E P Statham, W Hailstone, J H Owen, C P G Hicks E T Le Vert, R Voysey, C W Dickenson
Masters Assistants C B Franks, G W Balliston
Captain Marine Artillery H Mawbey, E R Horsey
1st Lieutenant Marine Artillery H Everitt, F H Owen
2nd Lieutenant RMLI J L Maccall
Chaplain Rev R N Jackson, Rev J Harrison
Surgeon S D Wells, Assistant Surgeons W J Asslin, R Grieve, E W Coleman, F B Hurley, W Grant
Paymaster J de Vries, C S Giles, Assistant Paymasters N J Aaron, H H Wyatt
Clerks G F Mathews, W T Fencock, A H Carylon
Assistant Clerk G B Townsend
Chief Engineer W Buchan, Assistant Chief Engineer W Glasspole
Engineer W T Fry, J Heffernan, J P Taplin, R W Jones
Assistant Engineers 1st Class W Milln, P Baldwin, G Hosteys
Assistant Engineers 2nd class H Swiss, T G Punnett, E Comley, W Jones, J Melrose
Gunner D Colinburn, W Dore. Boatswain C Beaton. Carpenter J Davidson

Chief Petty Officers
Master at Arms G Hendlay. Chief Gunner's Mate J Pearce, A Johnson. Chief Captain of the Forecastle W Percival. Chief Quartermaster J Adnams, J Williams. Chief Carpenter's Mate G Kingstone. Seamen's Schoolmaster F Adams. Chief Bandsman J Hope, A Strauss. Ship's Steward W Cheeseman, J Good. Ship's Cook C Holding.

1st class Petty Officers
Armourer C Hyde. Blacksmith T Watling, J Ellis. Captain's Coxswain P Kingsley. Coxswain of the Launch E Griggs, R Bone. Captain of the Hold G Gladman. Ropemaker S Hobday. Sailmaker J Roper. Yeoman of the Signals J Beaver, W Williams. Captain of the Afterguard J Durham, W Surman, J Wynn. Captain of the Foretop J Miller. Captain of Maintop T Roberts, T Miller. Captain of the Forecastle W

Pill, R Turrell. Carpenter's Mates J Radford, H Allen. C Hatchard.
Ship's Corporals T Tull, W Chapman T Ellis. Boatswain's Mates C Caunter (Chief), J Redcliffe, J Ryder, J Scott, J Gibson J Fellon, G Olive, J Mounsey Quartermaster J Hetherington, R Smith, J Tozer, C Earle, W Jones, H Kendall, E Bryan.
Steam Department
Leading Stoker J Turrell, W H Bearne, J Lawton, H Martin, E Coulston, R Ryall, S Bishop, T Howard, W Wiley, T MacFarlane, A Emery.
Marines
Sergeant RMA G Jackson, T Tetley, E Pratt. Corporal R. Nichols, J Nye, J Newman.

Flag, commanding and executive officers. These officers hoisted flags in *Warrior*:
Rear Admiral S Dacres (31 x 1864–1 xi 1864)
Vice Admiral T Symonds (12 xii 1868–23 xii 1868)
Vice Admiral Sir John W Tarleton (26 vii 1875– 9 ix 1875)
Rear Admiral H Boys (5 vi 1878–16 viii 1878)

Captains of *Warrior*
The Hon A Cochrane (1 viii 1861–22 xi 1864)
J Corbett (7 vii 1867–24 vii 1867)
H Boys (25 vii 1867–20 viii 1869)
H Stirling (21 viii 1869–21 ii 1870)
The Hon H C Glyn (22 ii 1870–15 ix 1871)
H Wyte (11 iv 1875–14 iii 1878)
R G Douglas (15 iii 1878–7 i 1881)
A C F Heneage (7 i 1881–30 iv 1881)
S P Townsend (1 v 1881–26 xi 1882)
E S Adeane (27 xi 1882–31 i 1883)
J M de Robeck (16 vii 1902–29 v 1903)
A Dodgson (30 v 1903–29 viii 1903)
S E Erskine (30 viii 1903–31 xii 1903)
E F B Charlton (1 i 1904–31 iii 1904)

Executive Officers as Commander:
G Tryon (10 viii 1861–10 viii 1864)
(Lieut) J E M Wilson (11 viii 1864–9 ix 1864)
W Codrington (10 ix 1864–22 xi 1864)
G Twiss (30 viii 1867–7 vii 1870)

A Markham (7 vii 1870–15 ix 1871)
W G Scott (1 iv 1875–25 ix 1877)
F Rougemont (26 ix 1877–25 ix 1879)
R Watts Davies (26 ix 1879–30 iv 1881)
E N Rolfe (1 v 1881–1 i 1882)
C E Gissing (2 i 1882–31 iv 1883)
No executive officer was borne during the brief commission of July 1, 1867, nor during the ship's service as depot ship in Portsmouth until Feb 10, 1904 when Commander H Skipwith served until ship paid off on March 31 that year.
Shipkeepers of *Warrior*: Mr W James (1929–1958) and Mr H Griffiths (1958–1978).
Captain of *Warrior*: Captain C G Allen 1987

* * * * *

During first commission 1861–1864
• approval was given for five midshipmen promoted to sub lieutenant to be borne in lieu of naval cadets
• due to drafting changes 65 officers and 1550 ratings and other ranks served in *Warrior*

When in 1859 it was decided to invite tenders for the design and construction of an armoured frigate this Admiralty letter was sent on January 28, 1859 to leading commercial shipbuilders and Royal dockyards. '. . . having had under their consideration the subject of shot- proof vessels, their Lordships would be glad to receive designs and suggestions for vessels of this description, observing that if you furnish a design not in accordance with these conditions, but which in your opinion would be better calculated to answer the intended purpose, their lordships would be glad to receive it also.

The design is to be for a frigate of 36 guns, cased with 4½in wrought iron plates from the upper deck to five feet below the water line. She is to be capable of carrying the weights specified in the accompanying list, in addition to the machinery, boilers, water and coals for full steaming for at least seven days; the height of the midship port is to be at least nine feet above the water, and she is to possess stability sufficient to enable the guns to be worked effectively both when she is full laden and when coals and stores are expended.

As iron appears to be the most suitable material . . . the design should be for an iron ship; but if . . . a more satisfactory arrangement could be made with wood than iron, a plan . . . of a wooden ship may be forwarded; observing that the armour plates must . . . extend from stem to stern, whereas in an iron ship it might be considered advisable to limit their extent to about 200ft of the middle part of the vessel, separating the parts cased by strong athwartship bulkheads, covered with 4½in plates . . . to about five feet below the plates on the sides. If this arrangement be adopted, the ends of the ship not cased should have as great a number of water-tight compartments as can be constructed to afford strength in running down or ramming and securing the armour plates, which in the case of an iron ship should have a bed or backing of timbers and planks of hard wood placed between them and the ordinary plating of

the ship, equal in substance to the timbering and planking of the top sides of a ship of the line, and the edges of the armour plates should be planed and closely fitted.

The main deck to be of 4in Dantzic oak, with beams sufficient in number and strength to bear the guns and other weights. The upper deck to be of iron ⅝ inch thick, and to be covered with Dantzic fir three inches in thickness.

The ship to be masted and rigged as a 80-gun ship, and to have sufficient steam power to give a speed of at least 13½ knots under steam alone, when fully equipped with all stores on board, as per list annexed.

The horse-power of the engines to be stated, and the space for them and the boilers to be shown in the drawing.

As it is important that their Lordships should know the probable expense of such a vessel, I am to request that you will furnish an estimate of her cost, and that you will state the time required for building her, forwarding this information with your design on the 1st March next.

W G Romaine.'

Weights to be received on board	Tons
Water for six weeks for 550 men	124
Provisions and spirits for four months	105
Officers' stores and slops	14
Wood, sand and holystones	16
Officers' men and effects	75
Masts and yards, including spare spars, booms, etc	119
Rigging blocks and sails	70
Cables and anchors	121
Boats and warrant officers' stores	92
Guns and carriages, main dk, 34 68pdrs	215
upper dk, 2 68pdrs	
Small arms and ammunition	8
Powder, 550 cases	42
Shot and shell, 100 rounds, as solid shot	109
Grape and cannister shot	14
Galley and condensers	10
Engineers stores	15
Spare screw, etc	12
Equipment total	1161
Weight of hull	4500
Weight of armour plates	950
Engines and boilers complete with spare gear	950
Coals for seven days at 10lbs per nominal hp	1000
	8561

In April 1859 some 15 proposals were submitted to the Board with the Surveyor's criticisms. None was entirely satisfactory, but Watts' design was preferred and since Thames Ironworks and Napier were judged as most nearly suitable these two yards were later selected to build *Warrior* and *Black Prince*.

Design Features. When *Warrior* was designed *Gloire* had not been launched and the Chief Constructor had to ensure that Britain's response was superior, the starting point being the number of guns in the broadside. Watts was aware of the waveline theory which pre-disposed him to use fine ends, believed then to be necessary for good sea keeping and which led to a length that he knew from *Mersey* experience was too great for a wooden hull; also he must have learnt from Brunel and Scott Russell's *Great Eastern*. As a result his first ocean-going iron warship was designed with a longitudinally framed structure of the most advanced practice of the day but with no innovative characteristics.

Warrior was initially planned for a 19gun main deck broadside requiring a battery length of 285ft. Stem to stern armour might have caused excessive pitching in heavy weather so only 13 guns each side were centrally protected by a 210ft long armoured citadel from the upper deck to six feet below the waterline. Thus, although 65% of the armament was behind armour impenetrable by guns of the day, only 42% of the total target above the waterline was protected. This was acceptable, emphasis being laid on the buoyancy strength of her unarmoured ends subdivided by four transverse bulkheads before the armour and two abaft. Flooding both ends would have admitted 1070 tons of water increasing draft by 26in barely affecting fighting efficiency, although flooding one end might have been awkward.

The armoured citadel contained seven of the 16 main watertight compartments extending from the hold to the lower deck including magazines, engine room, stokeholds, auxiliary machinery, bread, spirit and shell rooms. Above the magazines were watertanks and separating either ends of the forward magazine and the after end of the after magazine from their respective bulkheads were two foot wide water spaces. Abaft the engine room was the watertight shaft tunnel extending to the stern gland, known as screw alley.

Hull shape was formed by frames and main longitudinals encased by skin plating and set in at seven feet below the waterline to provide a recess and ledge for the armour. At its midships cross section the hull was

given a shallow vee-shaped floor which turned through a large radius four feet below the waterline to form the sides which rose with a 10° tumble home to the gunwhale. A light beak structure was added to the stem post to enhance appearance and provide support for figurehead and bowsprit. Abaft the beak the vee-shaped entrance extended 140ft to the rounded cross section of the parallel body – 170ft long – and was followed by a 103ft parabola-shaped run. Beyond the run was a counter stern.

The keel structure was made up of flat keel plates – which acted as doublers for the garboard strake – and a 3½ft vertical keel plate topped by a 1¼in keelson, which

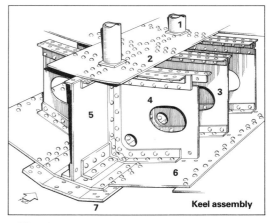

Keel assembly

1	Wrought iron pillar	5	Vertical keel plate
2	Keelson	6	Garboard strake
3	Intermediate floor plate	7	Flat keel plates
4	Transverse floor plate		

1	Wing passage space	3	Transverse frame
2	Lower deck beam	4	Intermediate frame

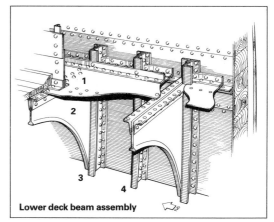

Lower deck beam assembly

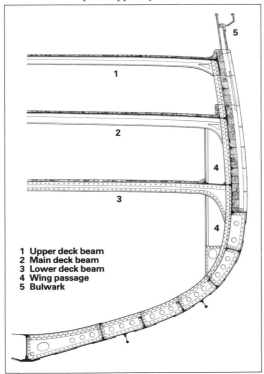

1 Upper deck beam
2 Main deck beam
3 Lower deck beam
4 Wing passage
5 Bulwark

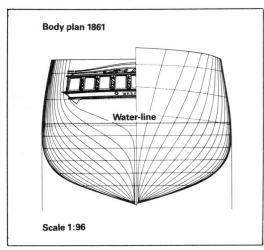

Body plan 1861

Water-line

Scale 1:96

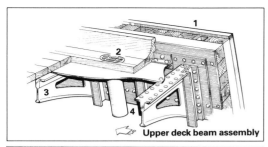

Upper deck beam assembly

1st Longitudinal frame assembly and lower front of armour plating

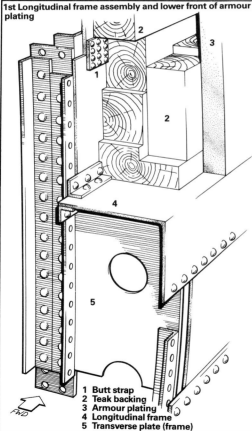

1 Butt strap
2 Teak backing
3 Armour plating
4 Longitudinal frame
5 Transverse plate (frame)

FWD

acted as a doubler for the ceiling plates of the double bottom. The double bottom was 20ft wide and ran for 287 ft between the two inner longitudinals. The 30ft stem post was forged in one piece, weighing some 17 tons and was shaped to form a ram at the waterline. The stern frame comprised the stern post, the rudder post and a sole piece forged into frame 42ft high and weighing 43 tons.

The 95 riveted main frames, fabricated from angle bars and one inch plate, varied in depth; frame spacing was at 44ins except in the way of the gunports where it was increased to 54ins. Including intermediate half frames there were 125 numbered frames. Upper and main deck beams, which completed the transverse framing, were made by Butterley of rolled wrought iron, moulded to give a camber, split at the ends and completed with a filler plate to form a knee. These two iron decks of one inch plate were further strengthened against buckling by timber planking, while the lower deck was timbered but not plated. Between-deck pillars were fitted around openings where decks had been pierced for hatchways and funnel casings.

The ten longitudinals, five each side of the keel, were made from 1¼in plate riveted to angles to give an I-shaped girder. Two 2½ft long longitudinals were set 10ft each side of the keel to form the cellular structure of the double bottom. The remaining longitudinals were set at five feet centres, the second, third and fifth being 1¾ft deep. The fourth longitudinal was 2½ft deep, its top flange riveted to the lower edge of the longitudinal bulkhead in the machinery spaces, thus completing the watertight integrity of the central body of the hull.

The novel feature was the armour which consisted of 4½in thick hammered wrought iron plates, between 10 and 15ft long by 3ft wide, tongued and grooved around the edges to ensure interlocking over an area of 210ft by 27ft wide on the sides; similarly the citadel was completed by athwartships armour on the fore and after bulkheads extending from the upper deck down 27ft. Behind the plate were two layers of teak the outer layer standing vertically, the inner laying horizontally on the skin plating; inboard of this was a 9in timber lining on the main deck. The layers of armour were secured to the

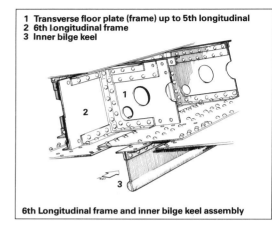

6th Longitudinal frame and inner bilge keel assembly

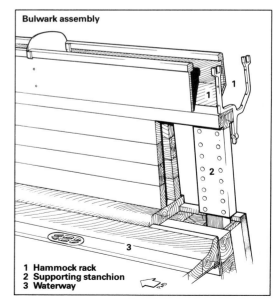

Bulwark assembly

1 Hammock rack
2 Supporting stanchion
3 Waterway

hull by 1½in bolts at 12in centres, fitted with a tapered head flush with the outside surface and fastened inboard with two nuts.

Support for the engines and boilers was provided by longitudinal box girders laid on frames, three forming seating for the engines and five under each stokehold. The floor plates on top of the box girders gave a bilge depth of 4½ft.

The skin plating was double riveted and set on frames up to the armour recess, the bottom plates being one inch thick at the garboard strake and ⅞in adjacent to armour recess. Behind the armour the skin plating was ⁹/₁₆in. *Warrior* was amongst the first ships to be given two bilge keels on each side, both 14in deep bulb plates attached to the hull by double angles. The upper keel was 89ft and the lower 136ft in length, their purpose to reduce rolling.

Watertight bulkheads divided the lower deck into 16 compartments, mainly flats whose only access was through hatches from the main deck; the orlop deck before and abaft the main machinery spaces was similarly compartmented. In addition to 35 watertight compartments in the hold there were a further 57 in the double bottom under the machinery spaces and the watertight wing compartments which gave *Warrior* some protection against grounding or collision. Providing an inner skin paid off when *Great Eastern*, with a complete double bottom, tore a hole 80ft long on grounding, also when *Agincourt* ran onto the Pearl Rock; in neither case did water enter the hold. Similarly the wing passage compartments proved their value when *Bellerophon* and *Minotaur*, also *Hercules* and *Northumberland*, were in collision. In *Warrior* some bulkheads were pierced for watertight doors low down and it cannot be certain that the sub-division would have been effective after damage.

Warrior's immensely strong hull can best be summarized as a box girder formed by the sides, double bottom structure and the upper and main decks. The bottom plating was stiffened by the vertical keel and five continuous longitudinals on each side, further support to the plating being given by intercostal plate floors which carried the partial inner bottom. Side and deck

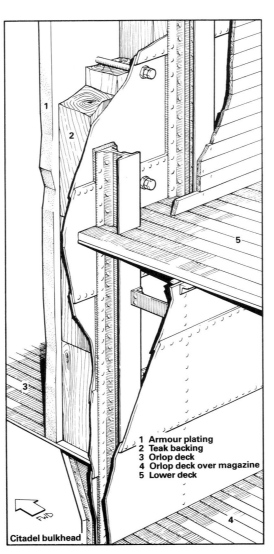

1 Armour plating
2 Teak backing
3 Orlop deck
4 Orlop deck over magazine
5 Lower deck

FWD

Citadel bulkhead

plating were stiffened by transverse frames and beams while continuous longitudinal bulkheads abreast the machinery spaces added further strength.

However, certain features suggested that *Warrior's* design was partly based on wooden ship lines, eg the multiplicity of transverse frames, the method of fastening the rigging chains to the ship's side and the fitting of diagonal tie plates above the wooden deck. Such plates were required by Lloyd's regulations in wooden ships for strengthening the hull but served no useful purpose in an iron ship.

It may be argued that because Watts erred on the side of caution in designing a hull heavy in relation to dimensions he did not fully understand the characteristics of an iron hull. But this in no way detracts from a remarkable architectural achievement.

Specification. The Admiralty approved *Warrior's* design on April 29, 1859 and supplied the contractors with a set of drawings, similar to those shown in Plans A to H, together with a specification. Length overall was 418ft and between perpendiculars 380ft 2ins. Maximum beam was 58ft 4in. Length to beam 6. Depth of the main deck was 7ft 11in, of the lower deck 9ft 2ins, of the hold 21ft 1in and the double bottom 3ft 6in. When rigged overall length from ensign staff to flying jibboom was 500ft. Mean draught loaded was 25ft 11ins, midships immersed cross section loaded was 1219sqft and the wetted surface loaded 28,704sqft.

In tons the weight of the hull was 3925, the armour backing and fastenings 1300, the machinery and fuel 1745, armament and stores 1690, masts, rigging and sail 192, making a total displacement loaded of 8852. By Builders Measurement the tonnage was 6038 85/94. The displacement rate loaded was 45 tons/in and the metacentric height at 9035 tons was 4ft 8ins. *Warrior* carried no ballast.

The hull was built in wrought iron – iron in its commercially purest form – notable for its toughness and ductility, resistance to corrosion and ready weldability requiring only simple blacksmithing.

Armour. Although the Admiralty decision in 1850 to cease iron hulled warship construction may have been precipitate the *Excellent's* conclusions after the *Ruby* trials (1846) and *Simoon* trials (1850) were valid. Iron plating, then of variable quality, could break up shells and some shot but left problems over the splinter effect from projectile impact as well as jagged holes difficult to plug. There were further trials:

- mid-1854 at Vincennes to test iron plate backed by timber for the French floating batteries
- September, 1854 at Portsmouth to test 4½in wrought iron plate backed by 4in fir for British iron and wooden floating batteries
- December, 1856 and April–June 1857 at Woolwich to test 4in plates of different manufacture against 68pdr projectiles. Wrought iron proved superior to cast iron shot and all iron plates resisted shot at 600 but broke up at 400 yards
- October, 1858 at Portsmouth to test wrought iron plate on the hulk *Alfred* confirmed superior punch of 68pdr against armour especially when firing wrought iron projectiles
- October and November, 1858 at Portsmouth to test effect of 32 and 68pdr projectiles against floating batteries *Erebus* (iron hull) and *Meteor* (wooden hull), both with 4in armour. The *Meteor*'s iron plates, fastened by bolts passing through thicknesses of oak timber, remained undamaged whereas bolts and nuts flying about in *Erebus* were lethal.

Sufficient evidence was now forthcoming from the Special Committee on Iron Plates and Guns for Isaac Watts to design *Warrior*'s armour and in August, 1859 Thames Ironworks were instructed in general terms, 'the armour plates to be made of such quality of iron, in such a manner and by such parties as the Surveyor of the Navy should approve'. Although by May, 1860 production had reached 50 tons weekly the first of five plates was condemned as unsatisfactory. Thames

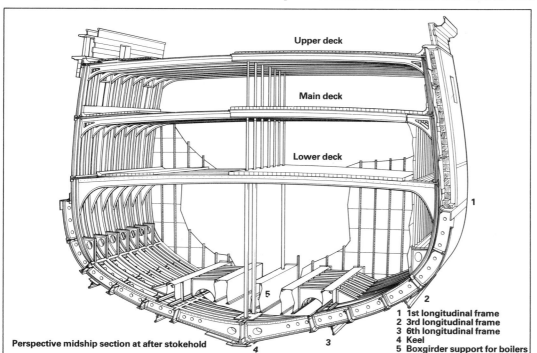

Perspective midship section at after stokehold

1 **1st longitudinal frame**
2 **3rd longitudinal frame**
3 **6th longitudinal frame**
4 **Keel**
5 **Boxgirder support for boilers**

Upper deck

Main deck

Lower deck

● **Impression of *Warrior* target moored off Shoeburyness (above)**

● **Probably the original *Warrior* target at Shoeburyness circa 1861 (below)**

Ironworks emphasized that they had complied with instructions and regarded trials results as 'conflicting'. However their overall record was better than those built for *Black Prince*, *Defence* and *Resistance*, the main problem being the length of time needed to tongue and groove the plates whose fitting was further delayed by Penn's engineers needing the port side for machinery installation.

In July, 1860 the *Excellent* tested Thames' armour plates fastened to the side of the hulk *Sirius*. At 200 yards the plates were impervious to 68pdr shot even on the tongue and groove join, except when hit twice in the same position. Captain Hewlett recommended clothing '*Warrior* with them as being the best to resist shot that is at present known.'

In January, 1861 the War Office set up a Special Committee on Iron to investigate the composition, manufacture and resistance qualities of iron plate. A replica of *Warrior*'s armour was mounted as a target at Shoeburyness – 20ft long, 10ft high with a gunport in the middle – and tested in October, 1861. The 4½in plates, made by the Thames Ironworks in the same way as those for *Warrior*, were bolted to two layers of 9in teak beams laid crossways and behind them was a ⅝in plate and frames representing the ship's side. The armour was attached by through bolts with countersunk heads and two nuts spaced about 18ins apart, inside.

The target was hit by 29 projectiles weighing from 68 to 200lbs and totalling 3,229lbs. None penetrated and only one bolt was damaged. Other targets, with less timber backing were unsuccessful and the Committee concluded, 'this target has sustained a greater amount of firing with less injury than any other tried'. However, they criticized the tongued and grooved connections between plates as likely to damage neighbouring plates, making repair difficult.

The failure of targets with thin wood backing or no wood at all was probably due to fracture of the bolts which held the armour in place. The French identified the problem before *Gloire* was built and her armour was secured by screws driven into her timber hull. Timber backing caused problems when it got wet. The armour in front of the wood prevented its drying out and rot

inevitably followed. During *Warrior*'s reconstruction test bore holes through the ship's side plating confirmed timber decay.

In 1984 samples from *Warrior*'s hull plating and armour were tested at Admiralty Research Establishment, Dunfermline, who reported that the overall properties were typical of good wrought iron, confirming the 1861 Shoeburyness test results but indicating that the strength in the direction perpendicular to the plane of the plate, important in projectile resistance, was low and variable. Impact strength was also temperature sensitive, falling off rapidly below 20°C, thus showing why wrought iron was shot resistant in warm climates but failed its brittle tests during an English winter.

Today *Warrior*'s iron armour is as sound as when fitted 125 years ago, reflecting the skill of both designers and builders.

Accommodation. In comparison to earlier, wooden steam ships *Warrior*'s deck space and accommodation was spacious. Comparative lack of tumble home gave her more than 22,000sqft of largely uncluttered upper deck for seamanship evolutions while the main deck accommodated the entire ship's company with mess tables between guns and hammocks above, arrangements that did not differ from those of Nelson's day or for that matter much from World War II – but *Warrior*'s crew had more space than either. Bag racks were situated below the messdecks in lower deck flats.

Cabins for the captain, commander and master were in the half deck, the remainder of wardroom officer's cabins adjacent to what was little more than a wardroom mess on the lower deck. Further forward was the gunroom mess with adjacent flat for washstands; under the wardroom was the midshipman's chest room. Only the warrant and engineer officers lived forward.

Sub contractors to Thames Ironworks. Besides Butterley who supplied iron beams there were more than 20 sub contractors involved in *Warrior*'s construction, ranging from iron pillars and galvanizing to dredging, pilotage and towage. It is probable that Stone's of Deptford supplied a number of fittings, including the ship's bell and the water closets.

Building costs

	as published *The Engineer* **March 7, 1862** £	as recorded in *Ships Book* £
Hull	251,646	282,284
Machinery	71,875	74,409
Masts and yards	18,536	3,756
Rigging boats and stores		15,952
Engineers stores		891
Fittings and additions	12,828	
TOTAL	354,885	377,292

- May 11, 1859 the contractor's tender was accepted at £31.5 per ton BM or £190,225 for the hull complete. To this was added £20,000 for authorized extras and a further £3518 to the dockyards for unfinished work, to make a total of £255,164
- Admiralty waived the penalty clause of £50,000 for late delivery and later paid Thames Ironworks a further £12,000 over the contract price, to save it from liquidation
- Reed states that *Warrior* cost £379,154 but the Ships Book cost figure of £377,292 has been taken as the most nearly correct (£8,738,000 in 1987 terms).

Built by John Penn the steam propulsion plant was basically ten coal-fired sea water filled boilers (four in forward stokehold and six in after stokehold) supplying steam to a horizontal trunk engine driving a single propeller.

Boilers Box type of rivetted, wrought iron construction with brass smoke tubes. Maximum steam pressure 22 psi. Main features of each boiler as fitted in 1861 were

Dimensions   14ft 7in (W) x 12ft 7in (L) x 12ft (H)
Smoke tubes   440 tubes (20,755sqft heating surface)
Weight   3.35 tons
Weight of water 1.72 tons
Furnace grates 4 per boiler each 7ft 3in (L) x 3ft (W)
Flues and furnace 2628 sqft heating surface

A telescopic funnel of 7ft 7in diameter, extending to 55ft 3in above furnace grate level, was fitted to the bank of boilers in each of the forward and after stokeholds.

During the 1872–75 refit in Portsmouth new boilers to the same design, but with marginal differences in some dimensions, were fitted. Superheaters were added at the base of each funnel (1022 sqft of heating surface in forward funnel and 1533 sqft in after funnel) and the extended height of the funnels increased to 88ft 6in above the furnace grate level.

Furnace ash was raised from the boiler firing aisles to the upper deck in buckets attached to a vertical chain hoist driven by the donkey engine through gearing and layshafts. At upper deck level the buckets were transferred to fixed rails and disposed over the ship's side.

Main propulsion engine A 1250 nominal HP double acting twin cylinder, single expansion horizontal trunk engine with two jet condensers. Each piston was connected to an air pump and a 7.5in diameter plunger which served as a boiler feedwater pump at the outboard end and at the inboard end as a bilge pump, discharging overboard through the condenser water boxes. Boiler feed water was drawn from each condenser hotwell, any excess being returned to the condenser through spring-loaded valves. With main engines stopped boiler feed water was supplied by two small horizontal single acting pumps situated in the auxiliary machinery space.

Engine movements ahead and astern were controlled by two separately operated link mechanisms each connected to double ported slide valves deriving their motion from ahead and astern eccentrics on each end of the crankshaft. The link motion permitted steam cut off to each cylinder to be varied up to ⅝ piston stroke. Each valve chest was also fitted with a throttle valve for control of engine power in conjunction with link setting.

Principal engine dimensions were cylinder bore 112in, effective piston area 8532 sqin, stroke 48in and trunk diameter 41in. Engine and condensers weighed 248.5 tons.

Shaft and propeller Engine power was transmitted to a Griffiths two-bladed bronze propeller, fitted in a frame, through a wrought-iron propeller shaft running in four plummer bearings. Propeller thrust was taken on seven collar thrust bearings. The raising frame and stern tube bearings were lined with self lubricating lignum vitae.

The 17in diameter shaft was 108 ft long and the weight of shaft and bearings estimated at 54.75 tons. The 24.5ft diameter propeller had a pitch range of 27ft 7in to 33ft. rotated left handed and its estimated weight was 26 tons. The raising frame weighed 8 tons.

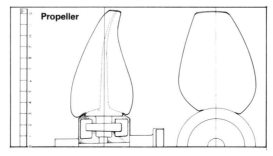

Propeller

Operation and performance By 1861 principles for the operation and maintenance of steam propulsion machinery had been established at sea. Readings were taken regularly, from hourly to daily of parameters and events covering propeller rpm, steam pressure, bearing temperatures, coal expenditure, boiler water condition, temperatures of machinery spaces, use of donkey engine, times of lighting up and shutting down boilers, maintenance carried out and stores consumed.

During reduced power trials 12.174 knots was recorded with six boilers and 11.04 knots with four. The first real test of the plant came in the first full power trial, when at a displacement of 8852 tons a speed of 14.354 knots was achieved at 54.25 propeller rpm. At that trial the more significant parameters were

Boiler steam pressure 22 psi
Estimated steam flow to engine 184,500 lbs per hour
Engine power 5469 I HP
Propeller pitch 30 ft
Estimated coal consumption 8.67 tons per hour
Estimated boiler efficiency 67%
Estimated engine thermal efficiency 7%
Condenser vacuum 25 in mercury
Engine mean effective pressure 24.37 psi

At the post 1872–75 refit trial, 14.158 knots was recorded at 56 rpm with a propeller pitch of 27ft 8½ in.

Examination of 1861–62 engine room logs show that the steam plant was in use from 75% of the time underway, mostly under cruising conditions, with a majority of the entries being between 20–30 rpm, giving a ship's speed of 6 knots (330 IHP) to 8.5 knots (900 IHP) under steam alone. When cruising common practice was to use four or six boilers, the operation of all boilers being limited to full power trials, trials against other vessels and, very occasionally, when leaving or entering harbour. Coal consumption was 2 to 3 tons per hour. Initially the plant operating procedure was to maintain boiler steam pressure as close to 22 psi as coal quality would allow and control engine power by a combination of throttle valve opening and link setting. Subsequently it became practice to control engine power by varying boiler pressure and engine link setting alone. When cruising boiler steam pressure varied between 12 and 17 psi, with 15 psi and engine levels set to give cut-off at half stroke being usual. Condenser vacuum varied between 25–28in mercury, with the preponderance of log entries being 26in mercury.

Consistent attention was paid to boiler water condition, maintained at hydrometer readings of 15–17, the upper limit being set at 20. The condition was presumably maintained by blowing down.

Operating conditions Records of the 1861 full power trial reveal average temperatures of 84°F (engine room), 85°F (forward stokehold) and 108°F (after stokehold), with a maximum 129°F at the latter's after end. Under steam or sail/steam conditions were little better with 70°F–89°F (engine room) and 85°F–95°F (after stokehold). And each stoker on watch was required to handle up to a ton of coal per hour!

Coal Furnace design and the need for economy caused the RN to be particular about the quality of coal and the efficiency of stokehold crews. Inferior coal and/or inexpert stoking caused extra expenditure and volumes of smoke that dirtied the upper deck and clouded visibility while reducing steam power. Prior to passage to Portsmouth in September, 1861 Warrior was bunkered with Aberdare Valley steam coal from the Nixon Duffryn colliery, as successfully used in the Royal Yacht. It was thought that its relatively high cost would be compensated by its superior quality although on passage the log recorded 'engines performed well, steam could not be maintained owing to inexperienced stokers'. For full and reduced trials Warrior was again bunkered with Aberdare coal subsequently to be used by all HM Ships undergoing measured mile trials. Stoking techniques must have improved because the results speak for themselves.

During Warrior's first commission she was bunkered from South Wales, North Country and Scottish collieries, the latter two being found unsatisfactory, although combustion techniques improved during later commissions. It is evident that Welsh steam coal, with its low ash content, fast combustion and light coloured smoke best suited Warrior. At this period the cost of coal at Admiralty depots depended on distance from coalfields and varied between 60p per ton at Plymouth to £1.40 at Madeira.

Bunker capacity Warrior had six large and two small coal bunkers (coal boxes) providing a storage volume of 40,931 cuft which held 853 tons of coal. This capacity gave an endurance of 1410 miles at 12½ knots and 3500 miles at 6 knots (steam alone). In the 1872–74 refit capacity was reduced to 789 tons.

Coaling ship This laborious, dirty and sometimes hazardous evolution often involved fraud, damage or loss of equipment and the risk of fire damp explosion. During the first commission Warrior coaled ship 12 times; on only three occasions did the tonnage exceed 400 and at the rate of about 24 tons per day the evolution was spread over many days.

Coaling was a whole ship evolution. Seamen and marines manned the collier, filling 2cwt bags and manhandling them through the gunports. On the gun deck stokers emptied the bags down the chutes and manned the bunker. Deck and engineer officers played a full part and the ship's band performed. Hot fresh water was provided for men to wash themselves before meals and, in special circumstances, Admiralty permitted commanding officers to authorize an extra allowance of grog on completion. Subsequent cleaning ship was in itself an evolution, the careful ventilation of bunkers an on-going routine.

Ancillary machinery and systems Warrior's hull was subdivided into 16 watertight compartments necessitating an extensive pumping and flooding system; this subdivision, restricting air circulation between decks, led to the introduction of mechanical ventilation systems. Machinery was also fitted to distil fresh water, operate anchor cables and, by means of a cupola, to heat molten metal for the filling of Martin's 68pdr shells.

The main donkey engine's original purpose was to operate the double acting plunger pumps, which could be used independently to pump sea water into the firemain system or pump out bilges or both. The 'as fitted' engine was modified to include a belt drive for the ventilation fans and with an extended crankshaft to provide a gear and longshaft drive to the ash hoists. The engine, which developed 30ihp, had a steam cylinder bore of 24in with an 18in stroke. There were two pumps each of 6in bore with an 18in stroke; the flywheel's diameter was 8ft.

Flooding, pumping and firemain systems Admiralty specification required sea cocks to be fitted for flooding compartments, with sluice valves on each side of bulkheads and 'levers for opening and closing them'. Compartments could be pumped out by a combination of main engine and donkey engine bilge suctions and manually-operated Downton and lift pumps. The Downton pumps could be connected to the main suction lines, which ran fore and aft port and starboard under the lower deck; practice became to leave pumps 4–7 connected. When used for pumping bilges the donkey engine and Downton pumps discharged into the port and starboard sewer (common waste discharge overboard) system.

Eleven hand-cranked Downton pumps, each with a three-throw crankshaft driving superimposed plungers working in series, were spaced throughout the citadel. Nine of the pumps were fitted on the lower deck and two (nos 1 and 11) on the main deck. To provide for additional man effort pumps 4–7 were also fitted with extended operation on the main deck.

Pump	Size ins	Compart-ment	Location	Deck for crank drive	Men on crank*
1	9	5	Centre	Main	16
2	9	6	Port	Lower	9
3	9	6	Stbd	Lower	9
4	9	8	Port	Main and lower	30 and 5
5	12	8	Stbd	Main and lower	30 and 5
6	12	10	Port	Main and lower	30 and 7
7	9	10	Stbd	Main and lower	30 and 7
8	9	11	Port	Lower	12
9	9	11	Stbd	Lower	10
10	7	13	Centre	Lower	3
11	9	14	Centre	Main	16

*estimated

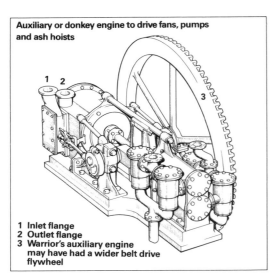

Auxiliary or donkey engine to drive fans, pumps and ash hoists

1 2

3

1 Inlet flange
2 Outlet flange
3 Warrior's auxiliary engine
 may have had a wider belt drive
 flywheel

Five 4in lift pumps were fitted, one each in compartments 6 and 12 to pump out bilges, double bottoms and water spaces, two in compartment 4 to pump out store rooms and in compartment 14 to pump out chest room. The firemain was supplied, when steam was up, by the donkey engine sea water pump, which had discharge points on the main and upper decks and in compartments 6 to 14. When cold, Downton pumps 1 & 11 could connect to sea suctions to supply the system.

Ventilation system Natural ventilation was ducted through 24 pipes round the circumference of the upper deck to the main deck, thence through pipes to provision, bread, spirit and shell rooms; those for the chest room, for example, being shafts under the half deck bitts. Magazine ventilation was provided by manually operated air pumps in the lower steering compartment and engineer's flats. Machinery space ventilation was supplied from upper deck cowls.

Mechanical ventilation was provided by two fans, driven by the donkey engine, which drew air from upper deck ventilators and through a common header exhausted into port and starboard ventilation ducts running fore and aft under the deckhead of the lower deck. Air from these ducts was then piped to main and lower deck accommodation spaces outside the armoured citadel. The system also provided air for the coal chutes (thence to bunkers) and cupola.

At General Quarters armoured bulkhead citadel doors, upper deck hatches and skylights were closed, as well as the shutters in the coal chutes on the lower deck. By opening the shutter and covering the coal chutes on the main deck with a solid lid it was possible to ventilate the bunkers, although it is not known how often this was necessary. When guns were fired pressurized air was diverted to clear the gundeck of smoke through the open gun ports. Evidence suggests that the fans were little used for messdeck ventilation, other than in November/December 1862 when the ship was at Gibraltar and Lisbon.

Fresh water stowage and Grant's distillers 100 tanks fitted adjacent to the forward and after magazines and in the chest room provided a capacity of 104 tons. Ready use tanks, topped up daily from the storage tanks through flexible hoses, were on the main and lower decks for washing, drinking and cooking purposes. Fresh water consumption was about 5 tons per day, with replenishment from shore by lighter and ship's boats or 'made-up' from two Grant's distillers installed in the water tank compartments above the forward magazine. Each of the simple water-jacketed multi-tubular steam condensers with natural circulation condensing water (later modified to pumped circulation) had an output of ¾ ton per hour. The engine room logs record daily production between 4 and 20 tons.

Capstans and crab engine In addition to main deck capstans was a small steam crab winch in the cable locker flat for hoisting cable from the lockers to range on the main deck. During the 1872–75 refit the Brown's capstan was converted to steam operation from engine and reduction gear also fitted in the cable locker flat.

Cupola Essentially a 2ft diameter cylinder lined with fire bricks and associated fan, was installed in the forward stokehold with exhaust into the funnel uptake. A molten metal fill for a 68pdr shell was 26lbs and the capacity of the cupola was 500 lbs/hour. Briefly, the practice was to heat the cupola until molten metal started to run out and then plug the tapping hole. The cupola was then fed alternatively with iron and coke until full of molten iron, care being taken not to allow the level rise above the blast hole. When ready the molten metal was drawn off into ladles to fill the shells through a funnel, additional iron and coke being fed into the cupola to produce a continuous process. The engineer and stokers involved wore protective clothing and a sand bed was available to prevent molten metal escaping from the cupola when the ship rolled.

Steam department complement and watchkeeping 95 officers, chief and petty officers and junior ratings comprised

Chief Engineer– Head of department and referred to as the 'Chief'

Chief Engineer – Asst Chief Engineer responsible for the daily supervision of the department and referred to as the 'Senior'

Three Engineers – Primarily, first engineer officers of the watch

Three Asst Engineers 1st class – Second engineer officers of watch. Stationed in engine room

Four Asst Engineers 2nd class – Third engineer officers of the watch. Stationed in stokehold. Under training.

When not watchkeeping subordinate engineer officers were employed on ship's work as artificers afloat and when in harbour used shore facilities.

Chief Petty Officers – 1 boilermaker, 1 founder.

1st class Petty Officers 1 blacksmith, 1 plumber and 9 leading stokers.

Steam Department ratings – 48 stokers and coal trimmers, 18 second class stokers and coal trimmers.

Seamen ratings – 1 blacksmith's mate, 1 tinsmith and 2 engineers' servants and cook.

When under steam the department was in three watches, except at general quarters or when entering or leaving harbour. The two chief engineers would divide their responsibilities to suit the occasion.

The complement of each watch was probably one engineer, asst engineer 1st class, leading stoker and stoker in the engine room and one asst engineer 2nd class, two leading stokers, nine stokers and eight coal trimmers in the stokeholds.

The assistant engineer 2nd class and stoker not on watch operated auxiliary machinery as required, issuing stores and, along with the artisans, attending to maintenance. The number of stokers and coal trimmers was occasionally below complement and seamen then helped trim coal. Stokers were trained at 68pdr gun drill to replace casualties in action.

Stores, spare gear and machine tools *Warrior* was intended to be self-maintaining and workshop machinery included anvil and block, drilling machine, screw cutting lathe, punching and shearing machines with associated tools. Spare gear provided for maintenance and repair for every contingency, including a spare propeller blade. Sufficient stores were carried for six months, the inventory containing 1500 separate items ranging from hand tools and raw materials to sufficient canvas and fearnought to make a frock and trouser suit for each stoker.

Stores consumed were typically

Year	Oil (gal)	Tallow*	Oakum	Cotton waste
1862	2302	7970	3625	212
1863	1716	6370	2582	172
1864	1416	4897	2480	298

*The allowance of tallow for Penn trunk engines was 50% more than that allowed for other engine designs.

Tallow, oakum and cotton waste figures are in lbs.

Spars, sails and seamanship   Appendix V

In designing *Warrior* Isaac Watts argued a policy for her masts, '. . . the fewer the masts on which a given amount of sail is spread, the more effective is that sail; in light winds lofty sails are better adapted for propelling and also for checking rolling, than low sails. In long ships with fine lines, it is desirable to place the masts as far from the extremities as they can be, consistent with proper regard to tacking and wearing. Except in very short vessels the custom is to distribute the sail on three masts which, moreover, would leave the sides of the ship more clear of shrouds and rigging than a greater number of masts and thus afford more space for broadside guns on the upper deck. The sails on them would be quite clear of the funnel; and the main mast, like the foremast, could step on the keelson without in any way interfering with the machinery, or in time of action, rendering it liable to receive injury by the fall of mast gear into the engine room. Ample room is also afforded for the stowage of boats and booms between the main mast and funnel, and the boats can be readily got in and out by the usual means. It was thought that iron masts might ultimately be placed in vessels of this class; but it was considered advisable to try one or more of them in the first instance with wood masts as they were of a class usually kept in store.'

The naval square ship rig was officially standardized not only in spar dimensions and cut of sails – proportioned to the size of ship – but for the lead, reeving and fitting of every individual rope of the standing and running rigging, as indicated by dockyard rigging models. A rigging warrant authorized the ship's boatswain to draw from the dockyard the exact quantity of each size of rope to enable her to be rigged to plan.

Warrior and her engines were contract built and installed but she was rigged by Chatham dockyard as an 80 gun ship of the line in approximately ten weeks. The size of her masts – very similar to those of *Victory* – was determined by her beam where the masts were stepped and since the mainmast was approximately amidships it followed that the ship's beam gave the shrouds the

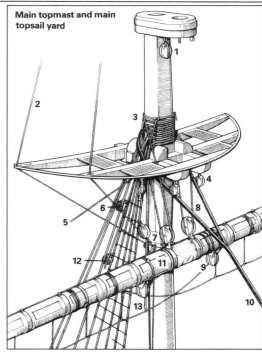

Main topmast and main topsail yard

1 Block for topmast stunsail halliard
2 Topgallant shrouds
3 Standing part of ties
4 Block for buntine
5 Topsail lift
6 Block for mizzen topgallant brace
7 Block for fore topgallant brace
8 Block for topsail tie
9 Double quarter block forward sheave: topsail clewline
   after sheave: topgallant sheet
10 Main topmast stay and preventer stay
11 Truss parrel
12 Block for mizzen royal bowline
13 Burton pendant

greatest spread and the mast the greatest height. The foremast was taller than the mizzen as the former had better lateral and backward support. To achieve correct sailing balance the foremast was placed just abaft the stempost and the mizzen between the main and stern, which explains why there is a larger gap between foremast and main than main and mizzen. Unlike later ironclads *Warrior's* bowsprit had plenty of steeve – angle between bowsprit and horizontal – to allow for pitching in a seaway.

Lower masts were built up of lengths of yellow pine, scarfed and dowelled together with iron hoops driven in and screwed up; lower yards were usually built up of pine while the remaining spars were made of one length of timber selected from Chatham dockyard. Trysail masts were fitted on the after sides of lower masts for trysail gaffs and the spanker to work on.

Around the holes in the upper (spar) deck through which each mast passed was an area of thick planking or partners, which supported the mast wedges as well as the framework of bitts fitted with sleeves. Ropes were also belayed on fife rails, cleats and belaying pins.

As recommended by the scientist Wm Snow Harris, copper strip lightning conductors were let in to all masts from truck to keelson, as well as bowsprit and jib boom.

Warrior's spar dimensions conformed to current usage for wooden masts, the fore and mainmasts being similar in length and diameter while proportionately larger than the mizzen. However, the main lower mast was two inches thicker at 40 ins than the fore lower mast and six feet longer at 66ft from deck to trestle trees. Fore and main topmasts were 65ft, topgallants and royals 53ft while the mizzen equivalent were 50 and 39ft. Fore and 2ft thick lower yards were 105ft (crossjack 71ft) and royal yards 33ft (mizen 25ft). The spanker boom was 70ft long and the lower and topmast stunsail booms 53 and 37ft respectively. Fore, main and mizzen masthead heights from the upper deck were 169, 175 and 138ft, while from the waterline were 190½, 196½ and 160ft.

In 1861 the original 3½ft thick bowsprit of 49ft carried a 49ft jib boom and a 52ft flying jib boom. In 1862 the new bowsprit was cut to 25ft with a 42ft jib boom and a 45ft flying jib boom. The jackstaff measured 18ft and the

Jib boom and flying jib boom

1 Jib stay	7 Flying jib boom guy P + S
2 Footropes P + S	8 Back ropes P + S
3 Jib martingale stay	9 Flying jib stay
4 Fore topgallant stay	10 Flying jib martingale
5 Topping lift P + S	11 Fore royal stay
6 Jib boom guy P + S	

Main topgallant mast head and topgallant yard

1 Main royal mast	6 Double quarter-block forward
2 Main topgallant stay	sheave: topgallant clueline
3 Topgallant tie	after sheave: royal sheet
4 Block for buntline	7 Topgallant shrouds
5 Truss parrel	8 Backstay

ensign staff 45ft. Masts and spars weighed 107 tons.

Standing rigging was used to support masts, yards and bowsprit, lateral support being provided by shrouds and backstays. *Warrior's* lower shrouds (nine each side) improved the angle of support, similarly the topmast shrouds were spread by the width of the top and topgallant shrouds by the topmast crosstrees. Additional backing was provided for lowermasts and topmasts by pendants shackled to purchases. Masts were supported forward by stays named for the masthead they supported and used for bending on stay sails. Foremast stays were led to the bowsprit, which was held down by the bobstay shackled to the ship's stem, similarly the fore topmast and fore topgallant were stayed to the jib boom and flying jib boom and held down by martingale stays led via martingale or dolphin striker. Laterally the bowsprit was supported by shrouds and the jib boom by guys led via whiskers either side of the bowsprit. Shrouds and stays were parcelled, served and blacked down with tar.

The weight of each yard was taken by lifts, its centre secured to the mast by a truss or parrel, loose enough to allow it to be turned to the wind by braces. At intervals along the yard stirrups supported the footropes below and parallel to the yard to provide a foothold for men.

Warrior's masts were progressively raked from forward to aft, the foremast by 2½°, the main by 3½°, and the mizzen by 4½°. The crossjack yard on the mizzen existed only to spread the foot of the mizzen topsail. Lower mast, topmast and topgallant shrouds and stays were of iron wire, as was the royal mast stay, all other standing rigging being of tarred hemp. No chain was used except for the slings and trusses to the lower yards, the crosstree necklaces, the bobstay and the martingale stay. Yard fittings such as parrels, jackstays, lift and brace block strops were of wire while yard tackle pendants, footropes and stirrups were of hemp. All blocks, hearts and deadeyes were of wood, tye blocks of the topsail halyards and the jib and fore topmast staysail halyards were iron stropped.

Running rigging was used for handling sails and hoisting or striking yards. Fore and aft sails were hoisted by halyards and trimmed to the wind by sheets. Topsail, topgallant and royal yards were hoisted by tye (runner) and halyards (tackle), the falls being led either side of the upper deck. Each yard had two braces referred to as 'port' or 'starboard' and 'lee' or 'weather'. Each squaresail was trimmed by sheets. Running rigging was hawser laid, three stranded tarred hemp with the Admiralty yellow thread, denoting manufacture in Chatham ropeyard. Fore and main tacks and sheets were tapered rope for ease of handling. No left-handed rope was used aloft.

Wire was measured by diameter, rope by circumference and the following dimensions were typical of *Warrior*'s standing and running rigging, those for the fore and main masts being identical and those for the mizzen relatively smaller. Lowermast wire shrouds were 2¼in (mizzen 1½in), the stays 3¼in (mizzen 2¼in), topmast wire shrouds 1³/₁₆in and stays 1½ while topgallant wire shrouds and stays were ⅞in and ½in respectively. Lower yard horses were 5in rope, the braces 4½in (mizzen 2½in), topsail halyards, lifts and braces 3½in (mizzen 2½in), while the sheets were 8in. The royal yard tye was 4in (mizzen 3ins), lifts 2½in and sheets 4ins. According to the rigging warrant of her sister ship *Achilles* there were 25 miles of cordage, 660 blocks and 80 hearts and deck eyes on board.

Sails *Warrior*'s sail wardrobe comprised two sets or suits of those sails regularly worked and one set of those less frequently used. Made in Chatham it comprised

- two sets – fore and main course, topsail, topgallant sail, topmast studding sail and topgallant studding sail; fore staysail, topmast staysail and lower studding sail; mizzen topsail and topgallant sail
- one set – flying jib; fore and main gaffsail, trysail and royal; mizzen royal, trysail and gaff topsail; spanker.

With the introduction of steam the number of fore and aft sails increased since they could often draw when steaming on a course too near the wind for square canvas to remain full however sharply braced up. Initially 'gaffsails' they were set on the fore and main trysail masts and, although later called trysails, they differed from the storm canvas trysails.

Jibs and flying jibs travelled on lacings, the foretopmast staysail being hanked onto the stay.

Topsails had four sets of reef points fitted with lines and earrings with two reef tackles each side. In reefing the earrings were passed round the yard and the reef line secured by beckets along the jackstay; with a close-reefed topsail the yard was right down on the lower cap. The spanker had three reefs and the trysails had one reef at the foot and were not laced to the trysail mast on the luff. Courses were pierced for two reefs but only the upper were ever fitted. Maintopmast studding sails were abolished in the 60's but the others remained.

In harbour sails were normally furled on their yards, the remainder being stowed in the sail rooms forward and the sail bins on the lower deck. The area of the main course was 5755 sqft, that of the mizzen royal 410 sqft and the total sail area, without studding sails, was 37,546 sqft. The total weight of sails embarked was about 12 tons.

Performance Under canvas *Warrior* was one of the four fastest ironclads, her 13 knots under plain sail and weather stunsails being exceeded only by *Royal Oak* and equalled by *Royal Alfred* and *Monarch*. Despite the advantage of a hoisting propeller her performance underlined the value of fine lines since it compared favourably with contemporary three deckers although *Warrior* displaced an extra 3000 tons and spread slightly less sail area. Being stiffer she held her canvas for longer, her masts and spars being stouter and heavier than comparable wooden ships. At the end of 1864 Captain Cochrane logged her best sailing trim for draft marks as 25½ft forward and 26¼ft aft, commenting that in moderate gales under sail the ship was remarkably easy and that under steam and sail she achieved 17.2 knots.

Warrior was at her best with the wind abaft the beam, although with the wind on the starboard quarter blowing a strong gale crossing the Bay of Biscay on March 2, 1864 she scudded (broached to at right angles to her course); signalled later by Admiral Dacres for the reason Cochrane replied, 'Helm to port ten minutes; ship did not answer helm'.

In common with all square-rigged ships *Warrior* could sail close-hauled to within six points (about 70°) of the wind's direction. When sailing to windward and requiring to tack the ship was steered to keep the sails

full as speed gathered. The helm was then eased down slowly, the headsail sheets let go and the spanker hauled amidships to aid the turn into the wind. Steerage way was checked as the square sails were taken aback on coming head to wind and the turn assisted onto the new tack by hauling round the after square sails. When the turn had filled the after sails those forward were also swung to the new tack and the ship forged ahead. When tacking *Warrior* in smooth water the whole operation from 'Ready all' to 'haul the bowlines' occupied about seven minutes – quicker when the crossjack yard was swung round when easing the helm. To wear ship (turning the stern into the wind) was a safer but longer manoeuvre that took *Warrior* from 15 to 30 minutes, although on more than one occasion it took nearly an hour. Undoubtedly *Warrior*'s great length made her unhandy for sailing manoeuvres; moreover she tended to ship water by dipping her stern to a heavy following sea after she had been trimmed down aft.

Seamanship By experience aloft, on deck or in boats an officer or man acquired seamanship and the knowledge that on his personal skill depended not only his own safety but that of his shipmates. At sea the essence of watchkeeping was strict and continuous attention to the trim of the yards and set of the sails, with a glance at the sky and a feel of the wind to determine the future weather pattern. And as he grew up he also learnt to understand men, because an emergency brought out the best and worst in human character and he had to know how to meet every reaction.

Boys 1st and 2nd class learnt basic seamanship in training ships before joining *Warrior*, when they gained further experience before being rated ordinary seamen. The next stage was able seaman – the ability to 'hand, reef and steer', heave the lead, knot and splice, strop a block, row a boat, use palm and needle and turn in rigging. To pass to leading seaman or petty officer required a proven record and power of command while midshipmen also learnt the hard way by going aloft daily at top speed, sea and harbour watch keeping, running boats under oars or sail and keeping in close contact with the men they would later command. It was the ambition of every youngster to be a top midshipman and when their batch was examined for lieutenant failure to pass was little short of disgrace.

Warrior's station bill was precisely detailed for every evolution ranging from loosing or furling sails to shifting topsails. Each man knew exactly what to do and what gear to handle, the upper yardmen on each mast, for example, being numbered like a gun's crew. Constant competitive training produced results and it was not uncommon for a worked-up ship to make all plain sail in four minutes or, with all square sails set, to shift three topsails in less than ten minutes. Training continued in harbour, royal and topgallant yards being crossed daily at 8am and lowered at sunset as routine by the watch on deck.

In addition to chief captains and captains of tops, who were the best petty officers, *Warrior's* seamen specialists included the sailmaker, the ropemaker and captains of the mast.

Armament   Appendix VI

The purpose of *Warrior's* great gun armament was to discharge maximum weight of metal in broadside fire. Inside the citadel were 26 68pdrs and four 110pdrs, before the citadel were two 110pdrs and abaft it were four 68 and two 110pdrs. The upper deck included two 110pdrs mounted forward and aft, able to fire on either side, as well as four 40pdrs mounted in pairs able to fire on one side only. Total projectile weight of one broadside to port or starboard was 1624lbs.

The 68pdr 8.1in calibre cast-iron gun was designed in 1846 by Colonel Dundas as a bow/stern chaser, saw service in the Russian war and more recently had been mounted in *Mersey* and *Orlando*. Evolved from the long 32pdr the 68pdr was reliable, effective and equivalent to the fire of two 32pdrs. Although a 68lb shot could just be handled by one man the six ton gun and carriage was as much as a crew of 18 could manage, the average rate of fire being one round per 55 seconds. Although having fitted sights its trajectory was erratic and being smooth bore effective range was limited to about 2,000 yards.

The 68pdr wooden carriage originated from the common four-truck carriage, being built with a rear chock instead of a rear axle tree which rested on a directing bar whose head block was coupled by iron

straps to a pivot bolt in the gun port lower sill. During construction the original square gun ports were reduced to 3ft 7in high and 2ft wide, strengthened and shaped to allow guns to be trained up to 29° off the beam while pivoted on the lower sill. With the stool bed installed the gun could then be elevated to 12° and depressed to 7° using a quoin, provision being made for an elevating screw in lieu. Recoil was about six feet.

The 110pdr 7in calibre gun was designed by Wm Armstrong in 1855, weighed 4.1 tons and was built at Woolwich and Elswick by shrinking wrought iron coils onto an inner tube rifled by the polygroove system. Fitted with a breech screw, vent piece and breech screw lever for loading from the breech end and manned by a crew of 18 men it could fire one round about every 50 seconds to a maximum of 4500 yards. Aimed by tangent elevation sights adjusted for range and deflection it was far more accurate than any smooth bore gun. With minor modifications, such as shortening it to allow unrestricted operation of the breech lever, the 110pdr rear chock carriage was similar to the 68pdr's.

The bow and stern chaser 110pdrs had wooden carriages fitted with revolving slides which could be transversed from centre line across deck to bow, quarter

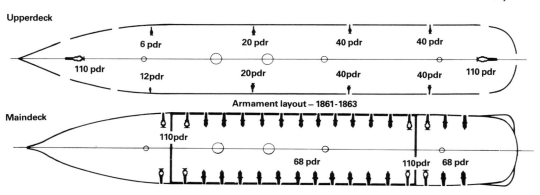

Upperdeck

6 pdr   20 pdr   40 pdr   40 pdr

110 pdr   12pdr   20pdr   40pdr   40pdr   110 pdr

Armament layout – 1861-1863

Maindeck

110pdr

68 pdr   110pdr   68 pdr

or broadside ports by pivoting at each end around deck pivot bolts, an operation requiring skill and team work. In 1863 a proportion of main deck guns had their rear chock carriages exchanged for sliding carriages and slides fitted with pivot bars.

The 40pdrs of 4.7 calibre were similar to the 110pdrs, intended as secondary armament and could be used for saluting. Initially weighing 1.6 tons they were replaced by a slightly heavier improved gun, manned by a crew of 12 and capable of firing every 45 seconds with a range of 4500 yards. The 40pdr common wooden carriage was converted from a 32pdr carriage, modified to provide clearance for the breech lever.

Projectiles 68pdr projectiles were mainly spherical, of varying weights and comprised

- solid shot, diameter about 7.9in, made of cast, chilled or wrought iron. After heating in ship's furnaces, red hot shot were carried to the guns in special bearers and loaded after ramming wet grommet and junk wads on the charge
- cylindrical case shot filled with 90 iron balls
- cylindrical shot filled with 15 large iron balls in three tiers separated by discs (grape shot)
- common shell filled gunpowder fitted with time fuze
- shrapnel shell containing 340 balls separated from bursting charge by metal diaphragm and fitted with time fuze
- Martin's shell filled with molten iron from cupola, carried to gun in bearer and loaded as for red hot shot. Introduced to replace the latter they were safer to handle, load and fire and more effective.

110pdr/40pdr projectiles were cone-headed, lead-coated and comprised

- solid shot, weight about 110/40lbs and 12/10ins long
- common shell fitted and fuzed with a bursting charge and 18/14ins long
- segment shell, about 14/10ins long lined with iron segments and a bursting charge
- case shot, similar but smaller than that used for 68pdr.

Solid shot was used against armoured targets and fortifications, common and Martin's shell against unarmoured wooden ships – the latter intended to spill molten iron and ignite combustible material on striking

the target – while case, grape, shrapnel and segment were anti-personnel at close range.

Propellants The object of the gunpowder charge was to produce a low, continuous pressure on gun and projectile and give a high muzzle velocity. As calibres increased smallgrain powder developed into pebble powder producing almost instantaneous combustion and dense smoke.

68pdr powder charges comprised distant (16lbs), full (12lbs), and reduced (8lbs), made up into flannel cartridges and brought to the guns in cylindrical leather cases. When firing shot or shell distant charges would be used at long range (up to 2500 yards), full at medium range (500 to 1500 yds) and reduced at close range.

110pdr charges comprised distant (14lbs but withdrawn in 1863), full (12lbs) in flannel cartridges carried in leather cases marked to distinguish them from 68pdr cases. 40pdr charges weighed 5lbs. Muzzle velocities in feet/second were approximately 68pdr – 1500, 110pdr – 1125 and 40pdr – 1170.

Ammunition outfit and stowage The original ammunition outfit was based on a 36 gun 68pdr armament with 100 rounds per gun shot and shell, a total of 3600 rounds. Additionally 17 rounds per gun of grape and cannister (case) projectiles were to be supplied, together with approximately 4000 rounds gunpowder cartridges in 550 metal cases containing charges of varying weights.

When Armstrong guns were introduced the outfit was adjusted and by the end of the first commission the probable number of rounds per gun were

	Shot	Total	Shell	Total	Total s & s
68pdrs (26)	90	2340	15	390	2730
110pdrs (10)	33	330	40	400	730
40pdrs (4)	35	140	40	160	300
		2810		950	3760

Up to 820 cases of powder propellant for all calibres of gun were stowed in the magazine.

Stowage of projectiles with distinguishing markings embraced all decks in the ship. 1200 rounds of 68pdr shot were stowed on the maindeck (339), lower deck

(393) and hold (468) the balance of 1140 rounds being mainly in shot lockers. Most of 68pdr shell (390) were stowed on the main deck (144), lower deck (35 Martin and 16 grape) with 120 Martin shell in the after hold, the remainder in the shell room.

In action crews could expend the following rounds per gun before re-supply

- 48 shot from each upper deck 110pdr and 36 shot from each 40pdr
- 13 shot, one grape and 4 to 5 common shell and case from each 68pdr
- 20 shot and 8 shell from each maindeck 110pdr.

68pdr shells were fitted with wooden bases and supplied fuzed in boxes; Armstrong time fuzes were not screwed in shell until just before firing.

To replenish ammunition on main and upper decks during a lull in action additional shot could be hoisted up from below, mainly from the cable locker flat where the port and starboard shot lockers were sited. Each locker was a vertical shaft to the hold that housed 68pdr shot hinged on shelves. As each shelf was emptied starting from the top it folded upwards to expose the next layer beneath, access to the locker being down an iron ladder on one side. Shot was hoisted in canvas bags and brought to the guns in two-man shot bearers.

Additional shell could be hoisted up from the cable locker flat in turn replenished by the shell rooms sited in the hold either side of the auxiliary machinery space and fitted as for a magazine with light rooms.

Forward and after powder magazines were of equal size and well protected at each end of the citadel, the after magazine being constructed in two separate compartments either side of the shaft passage. Each magazine had its adjacent handing room, both compartments being illuminated by lamps sited by glass port holes in adjacent light rooms running fore and aft each side. Strict precautions were employed not only in the construction of compartments – the crown of each magazine was lead-covered – but in the handling of powder. Manual air pumps ventilated each magazine.

Approximately 410 brass pentagon cases of powder were stowed in each magazine on wooden shelves and marked according to weights of charges. In general a higher proportion of distant to full and reduced charges were supplied by the ammunition depot.

Before going to action the leaden flooring of handing rooms was covered in water, leather aprons let down on scuttles, magazine and handing room crews closed up to await orders passed by voice pipe from the main deck. Selected charges were inserted in leather cartridge cases, passed horizontally through a supply scuttle into the handing room, thence upwards through orlop and lower deck flashtight scuttles in handing compartments to the main deck where powdermen took them to the guns. Empty cases were dropped down an adjacent canvas chute back via the handing rooms and through the return scuttle into the magazine. Thus the rate of supply from two supply scuttles at each magazine of 15 to 18 cartridges per minute would require 60 charges per minute at each end of the gun deck, drill that had to be carefully monitored by the officer of quarters. A form of manually-operated telegraph was probably installed between gun deck and magazine to select powder charges.

Magazines and shell rooms were opened and inspected by the gunner daily at evening quarters and when not in use kept locked, their usage govered by

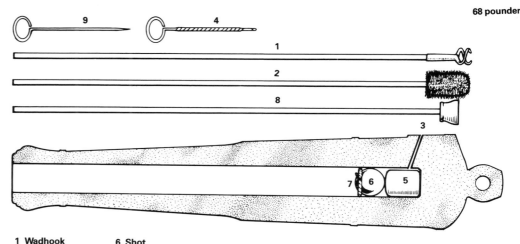

68 pounder

1 Wadhook
2 Sponge
3 Vent
4 Vent reamer
5 Cartridge
6 Shot
7 Grommet wad
8 Rammer
9 Priming iron

110 pounder

1 Breech screw
2 Vent piece
3 Saddle
4 Vent
5 Vent piece primer
6 Projectile
7 Rammer
8 Lubricator
9 Cartridge
10 Tin cup
11 Cleaning rod

strict regulations, with keys in the captain's custody.

Numbering and manning of guns The 34 main deck guns were numbered and designated with a purpose in mind. Contrary to Ballard's assertion that *Warrior* was the first ship to have a 'quarterbill . . . drawn up on the principle of a full gun crew to each gun in place of a full crew to every pair of truck guns' the complement did not stretch to such arrangement. Guns were numbered from 1 to 17 on both sides of the main deck. The even numbered guns on the port side and the odd numbered to starboard were designated LEFT guns. Similarly the odd numbered port guns and even numbered starboard guns were called RIGHT guns. Thus a full gun's crews was provided for each pair of guns from 1 to 17 with odd numbered crews taken from starboard watch and even numbers from port watch.

When ordered to 'man the port guns' each gun's crew manned its corresponding numbered gun on the port side, thus number one gun's crew manned P1, number two gun's crew manned P2 and so on. Similarly for the starboard side. Hence the ship could mount a fully manned broadside port or starboard sides when engaging a single target.

In both 68 and 110pdr guns the crew was numbered from 1 to 18 and crews were drilled to fire a gun with half a gun's crew. When the ship was required to engage targets on either side odd numbers in the crew manned the *left* guns and even numbers the *right* guns. Manning both sides with reduced crews was used not only when engaging targets on two sides but also when closing up at General Quarters and when securing the guns. Manning port, starboard or both sides formed the basis of gun drill with emphasis on the supply of charges to keep the guns in continuous action even when casualties occurred. On the upper deck the same principle was adopted in manning the 40pdrs but the 110pdrs at bow and stern retained full crews at all times.

Duties of guns crew Main battery gun's crews numbered 18 men, their duties being similar for 68 and 110pdr guns. One and two were Captains and Second Captains of Guns respectively, both Seamen Gunners. Three and four in the 68pdr were loaders and spongers with five and six as their assistants. Three and four in the 110pdr were required to handle the 136lb ventpiece while five and six were loaders. These formed the nucleus, the remaining duties included handspikemen, assistant and roller handspikemen, rearmen, stationary powderman and powderman.

Loading and firing the 68pdr Gun is cast loose, rear chock raised with roller handspike and gun run in with the train tackle, adjusting the breeching so that the gun muzzle is one foot clear of the gun port sill. Gun is scoured with the *wadhook* (1) and cleaned with the *sponge* (2). *Vent* (3) is reamed with the *vent reamer* (4); to ensure that it is clear the *sponge* is passed up bore so Captain of Gun can check draught of air being expelled. Gun is now ready for loading and firing in following sequence,

- Captain of Gun serves vent, by stopping it with a vent plug
- Cartridge (5) is entered seam sideways and bottom first to full extent of loader's arm, followed by shot (6) and grommet wad (7)
- all three are rammed home with rammer (8)
- priming iron (9) is passed through vent to prick cartridge
- train tackle released, rear chock raised with roller

handspike and gun run out with side tackles
- gun is now primed by placing tube in vent, putting detonating hammer (percussion firing) or firing lanyard (friction firing) to half cock
- while Captain of Gun holds trigger line or firing lanyard the gun is pointed for training by levering over the rear of carriage with handspikes and hauling on side tackles, either to left or right
- gun is elevated to required elevation with handspikes and adjustment of quoin or elevating screw under the breech
- when Captain of Gun is satisfied that gun is correctly pointed he gives order 'Ready'. Two cocks the detonating hammer or casts off half cock loop of firing lanyard and the side tackles are released
- when sights are on Captain of Gun fires by jerking trigger line or firing lanyard. As gun recoils the slack of train tackle is hauled in and held by choking the luff
- Captain of Gun serves vent, then gun is sponged out with wet sponge to dowse smouldering residue (8).

Loading and firing the 110pdr Gun is cast loose and run in with roller handspike and train tackle, tompion removed, *breech screw* (1) slackened and *vent piece* (2) lifted out and placed on *saddle* (3). Captain of Gun checks that bore is clear, vent piece is replaced and breech screw tightened. Gun is then run out with side tackles and roller handspike, *vent* (4) is reamed and then cleared by inserting and firing a tube. Gun is now ready for loading and firing in this order.

- breech screw is slackened, vent piece is removed, placed on saddle and primed with *vent piece primer* (5)
- projectile (6) entered and rammed home with *rammer* (7)
- *lubricator* (8) is screwed on to *cartridge* (9) and both entered into chamber, lubricator in front
- *tin cup* (10) is placed, the primed vent piece is replaced and the breech screw tightened
- gun is primed by placing tube in vent and firing lanyard put at half cock
- while Captain of Gun holds firing lanyard gun is pointed for training by levering over the rear carriage with handspikes and hauling on side tackles, either to left or right

- gun is elevated to required elevation by adjusting the elevation screw assisted if necessary by handspikes
- when Captain of Gun is satisfied that gun is correctly pointed he gives order 'Ready'. Two casts off half cock loop of firing lanyard, and simultaneously the side tackles are released
- when his sights are on Captain of Gun fires by jerking firing lanyard. As soon as gun has recoiled the side tackles are manned and gun run out
- vent piece is removed, placed on saddle and primed tin cup extracted, the loading and firing sequence is repeated.

On completion of firing gun is secured with tompion out, vent piece removed and gun is left for 12 hours to soften residue in the bore. It is then cleaned out with *cleaning rod* (11) wrapped with tow.

Organization and methods of firing The maindeck battery was divided into fore, centre and after quarters and the upper deck into a further quarter. Each quarters or division was in the charge of a lieutenant known as the officer of quarters. Once the ship had worked up to full efficiency guns could be fired,

- independently of each other, each captain of gun firing on opportunity
- in succession, dependent on wind direction, to produce continuous steady fire, for example at an approaching target
- quick, rapid independent when at close range
- in broadsides or by quarters simultaneously by order from officer of quarters
- in concentration.

Normal point of aim was gundeck level of enemy's hull but when the target could not be seen at night or in bad visibility the broadside had to be concentrated or converged on to a pre-determined point of aim. Concentrated or director firing was achieved by training a master sight, mounted on the upper deck amidships over the directing gun in the centre of the battery, onto a point at a pre-determined range known as the point of concentration. When the target was aligned with the director and all guns converged the broadside was fired. Guns were converged on the deckhead beams which were marked for four ranges – 200, 300, 400 and 600 yards – and five bearings – abeam as well as 1½° and 2½° before and abaft the beam. To set gun elevation it was necessary to allow for angle of heel which was measured by pendulum or Moorsom's director. Range of target was estimated, or measured by sextant angle.

Training captains of gun Mounted on a wooden carriage a 6pdr brass smooth bore gun was sited on the upper deck for training captains of gun in aiming and firing on the roll. 1000 rounds of shot were kept in the hold aft for this purpose.

General quarters Exercised frequently by day and quarterly at night the ability of a ship to close up at general quarters was regarded as a measure of fighting efficiency. On special occasions and before battle a full scale evolution was carried out that exceeded the customary four or five minutes. This would include sending down royal and topgallant yards, rigging preventer stays, frapping down rigging, clearing boom boats for hoisting out, sending down below all combustible material from main deck including cabin partitions on half deck, distributing shot plugs, rigging fire engine and fire pumps and manning the lower deck steering position (the fighting wheels).

In addition to gun's crews the organization was probably

Magazines, handing rooms and cartridge supply, 30
Shell rooms and cable locker flat, 14
Wing passages and store rooms, 18
Conning bridge and helm, 12
Relieving tackles, 8   Signals, 3
Attending surgeons, 5   Fire brigade, 20

Great gun performance The rear chock carriage with directing bar was not an unqualified success because it required considerable effort to train a gun carriage from side to side; when firing under heel gun would run out before slack of train tackle could be taken up (causing carriage to hit directing bar head block, often shearing the pivot bolt) and it took too long to cast loose from housed position.

Originally called the 100pdr Armstrong the gun was exhaustively tested in 1861, 'the remarkable strength of this gun is very satisfactory' when firing a 110lb proof shot. Re-designated a 110pdr in February 1862 every

endeavour was made to improve the vent pieces and ships were warned to fire shells jambed in the barrel and not try to drive them back after cessation of firing practice. In 1863 another Admiralty circular drew attention to the reporting of accidents with Armstrong guns. To the Select Committee on Ordnance enquiring on 110pdr performance Cochrane reported

- slightly higher rate of fire than 68pdr
- great advantages of accuracy and range
- danger from cartridge explosion while loading
- dense smoke from slow combustion powder and lubricating wad
- delay after pulling trigger before gun is fired causing bad aiming
- unsatisfactory for riccochet firing
- accidents and jamming of vent pieces
- misfires.

Landing parties, boarders and ramming Current war experience proved the value of ship's landing parties, either independently in aid of civil power or with other ships in support of the army. In addition to marines *Warrior* was expected to land three companies of 80 seamen with three petty officers, each company commanded by a lieutenant with sub lieutenants or midshipmen. Carrying a rifle, cutlass bayonet and 60 rounds of ammunition the company would be organized in sub divisions (platoons) and sections, together with pioneers, stores and all that went with a

mobile landing force. Details of boat armament are included in Appendix VIII.

Ship versus ship engagements envisaged closing the enemy and either sending or repelling boarders. In *Warrior* three divisions of boarders were organized, the first division from upper deck quarters, the second and third from even and odd numbered guns on the maindeck. At each main deck gun were stowed four cutlasses, and revolver for the captain of gun, while at each end of the citadel 124 rifles were located for use by gun's crews and in the half deck a further 68 for the marines. The organization for boarders included marksmen in the tops and armoured tower, idlers armed with pikes and tomahawks (for cutting away rigging and clearing wreckage) and all upper deck personnel armed with revolvers and either swords (officers) or cutlasses (chief and petty officers).

When ordered to prepare for ramming broadside guns on both sides were trained 30° before the beam and laid horizontal, gun's crews lay flat on deck fore and aft, bow chaser was run in and stern chaser run out.

Small arms and weapons In 1858 the navy adopted a .55in calibre rifle very similar to the Enfield muzzle loader so that there was one cartridge for all muzzle-loading musket rifles for Line, Marines and Navy, the bullet having a wooden plug in base and a charge of 2½ drachms. The rifle weighed 8½lbs, was 4¾ft long, sighted to 900 yards and was fitted with a cutlass

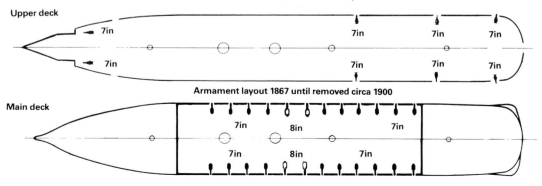

Upper deck

7in   7in   7in   7in
7in   7in   7in   7in

Armament layout 1867 until removed circa 1900

Main deck

7in   8in   7in
7in   8in   7in

bayonet. *Warrior* was supplied with 350 rifles, including 68 for marines who fixed a bayonet with serrated blade.

Warrior was also supplied with about 70 Navy Colt revolvers (with six shot chambers and weighing 2½lbs), 200 pattern 1855 cutlasses with scabbards, 50 seven foot pikes stowed on the upper deck and ten tomahawks.

Gunnery personnel and training Qualified in the *Excellent* the gunnery lieutenant was responsible for the efficient gunnery performance of the ship, in conjunction with the gunner whose instructions filled Chapter 48 of *QR and AI (1861)*. The *Excellent* produced gun drill books and also trained the chief gunner's mates, two petty officer gunner's mates and the seamen gunners 1st and 2nd class. Amongst *Warrior*'s guns crews were petty officers and leading seamen qualified as gunner's mates, also men trained in Armstrong guns. A qualified armourer maintained the armament. Throughout the commission instruction was given to qualify 'trained men' (a penny per day allowance) to prepare young seamen for a gunnery career.

Gunnery responsibilities and stores *Warrior*'s diving apparatus, stowed in the cable locker flat, was probably Siebe's equipment which enclosed the diver, except his hands, in an airtight dress complete with metal helmet and manually operated air pumps. One pump could take diver to 17 fathoms, two to 30 fathoms. *Warrior* carried at least one diver – a penny per day allowance – employed mainly on hull, rudder and propeller gear, and operating under the gunner's supervision from a cutter rigged as a diving boat.

There were two types of lifebuoy,
- Kisbie's lifebuoy – a circular ring of painted canvas filled with cork and distributed round the upper deck and at the ends of conning bridges
- common service lifebuoy – a light metal framework floated by two copper balls designed to support four men. Secured to the ship's quarters on a holder it was launched by trigger release by the lifebuoy sentry and was illuminated at night.

For night signals and supply to boats the Gunner was responsible for stowage and issue of signal rockets, signal lights, long lights, port fires, blue lights and short lights. Regulated by establishment Gunner's stores were mainly stowed in the Gunner's storeroom right forward. Included were percussion and friction tubes, pyrotechnics and small arms ammunition.

Re-arming of *Warrior* 1865–1867 During her refit between first and second commissions *Warrior* was re-armed with,
- 28 seven inch 6.5ton rifle muzzle loaders on iron sliding carriages, 20 on the maindeck inside the citadel and eight on the upper deck
- four eight inch 9ton rifled muzzle loaders on iron sliding carriages
- four 20pdr Armstrongs as saluting guns
- two 12pdr Armstrongs for launches and one 9pdr Armstrong for the pinnace.

Warrior's navigation arrangements were standard for a third rate, except that special provision was made for the magnetic effect of a large iron hull on standard compass deviation.

Conning bridges About ten feet above the upper deck were two identical athwartships conning bridges of light metal and wood construction, the after bridge being ideally situated for communicating with the steering positions, while the foward bridge had a light charthouse amidships. The wings of both bridges provided good fore and aft visibility. To furnish the command with instrumentation and communication there were

- standard compass binnacles amidships on each bridge
- a ladder to the third standard compass binnacle between the mizzen mast and steering position
- on the wings of both bridges manually operated telegraphs and voice pipes to transmit orders to the engine room
- voice pipes from after bridge to main deck steering position and amidships for gunnery control
- helmsman's telegraphs either side of fore bridge to enable quartermaster to receive helm orders when after bridge was not manned.

Manned by officers and men on watch it seems probable that the forebridge was used under steam, the after bridge under sail or when sail/steaming and both in bad visibility, close company or at general quarters. In action the ship was conned from the after bridge, possibly with small portable rifle towers in the wings to protect the telegraphs. The after bridge was also manned by the signalman in harbour.

Compasses In 1861 compasses were sited where deviation was smallest and *Warrior's* eight comprised

- a standard compass on both fore and after bridges. When the armoured tower was fitted the after standard was moved to a binnacle on a platform above the upper deck between the mizzen mast and steering position

- compass at head of mizzen lower mast
- two steering compasses, port and stbd, for upper deck steering position
- two steering compasses in dwarf double binnacle stand for maindeck steering, the only pattern of its kind ever fitted in a warship (probably early 1862)
- hanging (tell tale) compass, probably in captain's cabin.

Standard compasses were mounted in column-shaped or vertical pillar binnacles fitted with conical brass covers and oil lamp illumination; spare cards, glasses and equipment were kept in the compass and chronometer closet. There were also boat compasses for cutters (2) and launches (2).

Because deviation caused a major problem in iron-built ships attention was given to measuring it by swinging the ship and then either allowing for or reducing it. When the ship was swung through 360° deviation was observed every point (11¼°) or two points and tabulated so it could be applied, together with variation, to every compass course or bearing to convert into true course or bearing.

After a compass check by Master Superintendent of Compasses F J Evans in August, 1861 as *Warrior* went down the Thames, the ship was first swung at Greenhithe and subsequently at Spithead in October, 1861. Maximum deviation of after standard was then 28°, the fore standard 14° and the masthead 1¾°. In September 1862, after further swing at Portsmouth, Evans wrote to Cochrane expressing satisfaction with fore standard results but concern about the deviation in main deck steering compasses which he had designed and for which he recommended further experiment. At Lisbon in January, 1863 *Warrior* was artificially heeled 7½° to port and starboard to investigate compass heeling error and in a paper on the magnetic character of *Warrior* Evans emphasized the magnetic influence derived from the direction of the ship's head when building. In her first commission *Warrior* was swung six times.

On *Warrior's* upper deck recesses were cut adjacent to the binnacles to fit magnets to reduce steering compass deviation, which differed from the standard compass deviation causing standard and steering compass courses to vary, often by several degrees. When altering standard compass course the helmsman was conned on to the new course and ordered to 'steady', when he reported his new steering compass course. Helm orders were given differently from today by a procedure that lasted until after World War I. For example, when ordered to 'port the helm' the wheel and rudder were moved to starboard, the tiller to port and the ship's head to starboard; conversely when the quartermaster was ordered by the officer of the watch 'to starboard the helm' the ship's head moved to port.

Time was regulated by three Arnold chronometers stowed in chronometer closet, recorded and wound daily to set the master's deck watch, officers' watches and the ship's time. Apart from the engine room clock and possibly the captain's it is not known what other clocks were fitted. Half hour sand or watch glasses were provided for timing the striking of the bell, adjusted to the flagship's noonday gun in harbour and the master's observations at sea.

Sextants or quadrants were carried by executive and subordinate officers who, in addition to the master, were expected to take sights when on passage.

Barometers of the mercurial column and aneroid pressure type were in service in 1861 but apparently *Warrior* carried only the former. Read and recorded in the log, with the thermometer, every four hours it was fitted in the half deck outside the captain's cabin, watched by the marine sentry and unshipped in action.

Charts, pilots, tide tables, light lists, notices to mariners etc appropriate to the Home and Western Station, including the west coasts of France, Spain and Portugal, were carried as well as nautical almanacs and Dr Inman's tables.

Depth sounding was performed by 14lb hand lead and

lines for depths to 20 fathoms, 28lb deep sea lead and lines for depths to 100 fathoms and Massey's sounding machine for depths up to 150 fathoms.

Speed and distance run was measured every watch at sea by the midshipman who hove the wooden 'log ship' over the lee quarter every hour to record ship's speed by noting the number of knots (per hour) that passed during the 28secs or 14secs elapse of time on the appropriate sandglass. The long (28sec) glass was used for faster and the short (14sec) glass for slower speeds. Speed was also recorded by Massey's Patent Log and *Warrior* may have had Walker's Harpoon log, patented in 1861, an improvement on Massey. Distance run was recorded at noon daily, together with ship's position.

Wind speed and direction was estimated and recorded; however *Warrior* alone in the Channel squadron carried an anemometer. Wind vanes were fitted on masts to aid sail trimming.

Navigation lights were exhibited as port and starboard bow lights and, if steaming, a fore masthead steaming light but not a stern light. To indicate her position *Warrior* had blue lights and rockets. When necessary she also hoisted an admiral's top light. At anchor in harbour an anchor light was displayed forward.

Fog signals were made on a whistle when under steam, but when under sail a foghorn indicated starboard tack and a bell port tack. In harbour in fog a bell indicated a vessel at anchor.

Navigational complement comprised a master, second master, two masters assistants, a chief quartermaster and seven quartermasters (first class petty officers).

* * * * *

Signals Naval signals were born when ships found themselves working together beyond shouting range. Flag signals were created primarily to convey instructions from the admiral to his squadron when in enemy contact; various flag officers introduced their own code of signals, initially using a numerary system, later by alphabetical flags. In 1816 was published Admiral Popham's signal code book comprising 14 letters, nine numbered pendants and a form of semaphore, the basis of signals that lasted into the 20th

century. *Warrior's* signalling outfit for service in the Channel squadron as a private ship included,

- a set of General Signal flags and pendants, including numeral, divisional, and single flags that were mainly used to manoeuvre the fleet in peace or war; a set of 21 Vocabulary alphabetical flags and three pendants to supplement General Signals. Flags and pendants were kept for ready use in upper deck lockers
- various sizes of ensigns and jacks for ship and boats; a set of foreign ensigns
- halyards for hoisting flags on fore, main and mizzen mastheads also halyards for ensign and jack staffs
- signal slates and fair logs to record messages transmitted and received
- pyrotechnics, eg blue lights, long lights and rockets
- night signal lights
- publications – *General Signals for use in Her Majesty's Fleet*, 1959, *Vocabulary Signals for use in Her Majesty's Fleet*, 1859, *Night and Fog Signals for use in Her Majesty's Fleet*, 1859, *Signals Book for use in boats in Her Majesty's Fleet*, 1859 and *Commercial Code of Signals* 1857.

The best colour combinations in flags were red and white or blue/black with either white or yellow. To simplify recognition at a distance all numeral flags were square, divisional flags for manoeuvring were triangular and vocabulary flags either square or triangular. Pendants were the most easily distinguishable and the firing of guns 'to secure prompt attention' to flag hoists was customary but its over-employment discouraged.

Warrior's ship's name flags, according to *List of Navy*, were SP with union jack inferior. *Warrior's* distinguishing pendants when addressed by another warship were 42. Signalling procedure was as follows: *Warrior* in harbour signalled to flagship MTR – PEM – QBN – PFB – VNQ – TVL with six three-letter flag hoists. The message read, 'may I postpone receiving powder until tomorrow morning?' Originated by the first lieutenant the message was written on the slate by the yeoman-of-the-signals who consulted the *Vocabulary Signals* book and ordered the signalman to hoist the flags. By hoisting the answering pendant close up the flagship acknowledged the signal and to indicate approval hoisted the affirmative flag superior to 42 –

Warrior's pendants. Although tried in 1853 mechanical semaphore did not reach the fleet until late 1860's. Confidential messages were sent by boat.

Night signals owed their development to Commander Colomb whose candle lantern apparatus produced flashing signals on the morse principle and were frequently exercised in the Channel squadron. Messages took up to 30 minutes to be acknowledged; the system was officially adopted in 1867 but the morse code was not fully effective until 1889.

Warrior was complemented for one yeoman-of-the-signals (petty officer first class) and two signalmen (petty officers second class). Watchkeeping officers took an active part in signalling and a subordinate officer detailed as signal mate.

* * * * *

Ceremonial Ceremonial in various forms based on tradition played a significant part in *Warrior's* life. For example, the boatswain's call with 22 different 'pipes' regulated both daily routine and evolutions enabling verbal orders to be reduced to the minimum, while marine drummers beat the ship's company to quarters and performed military honours. Although the bugle was used ashore it was not general in the fleet until 1865. Other examples of ceremonial included,

- ratings saluted officers by removing or touching the cap or hat. Similarly junior officers saluted senior officers.
- officers and ratings saluted when coming on the quarterdeck
- hats were removed at 'colours', divisional inspections (petty officers touching their hats), when reading *Articles of War*, by men receiving payment, by defaulters and when mustering by open list
- when in ship's boats juniors saluted seniors by tossing oars or letting fly sheets. Senior officers got into boats last and out first
- the boatswain's call was used to pipe the side when the sovereign, commanding or foreign naval officers came aboard
- in harbour, sunrise and sunset were marked by the flagship firing morning and evening guns. The

morning gun was accompanied by a 'volley of musketry' from marine sentries' rifles followed by the beating of reveillé on the drums. 15 minutes before the evening gun the tattoo was beaten and another rifle volley with evening gun fire

- when colours (ensign and jack) were hoisted in harbour at 8am (9am in winter) the marine guard and band were paraded, the guard presenting arms as the national anthem was played and the quartermaster piped the 'still'. Colours were lowered at sunset
- flag officers coming aboard were received by a marine guard at the present, the appropriate number of ruffles on the drums and the band playing a march. The guard was turned out and a similar procedure enacted when a flag officer passed in a boat with flag flying in the bows
- gun salutes, ranging from 21 guns for royalty to seven for a consul, marked royal visits and anniversaries as well as salutes to flag officers and diplomats visiting the ship or squadron
- merchantmen of all nationalities dipped their ensigns to British warships, who dipped to acknowledge
- on specified occasions in harbour ships were dressed overall with flags from jibboom to stern; at sea ships dressed with masthead flags only; on special occasions yards were manned by the ship's company
- when under plain sail a junior warship saluted a senior by dipping the royals
- half masting colours as a gesture of mourning.

After the 1851 Great Exhibition which featured anchors the Admiralty set up a committee to determine their relative merits. Trial results (1853) considered that Trotman's, Rodger's, Aylen's and Porter's anchors were superior in holding power to the Admiralty pattern anchor, which led to *Warrior* being supplied with a Trotman's anchor for trial (1862) and with Rodger's kedge anchors. However, the fixed stock Admiralty pattern anchor was still employed for many years.

Warrior carried nine achors, including the heaviest in maritime history to be operated manually. Apart from the stern anchors all were Admiralty pattern comprising

- two wooden stocked anchors of 5.6tons – although identical they were known as best bower (stbd) and small bower (port). Employed to bring ship to single anchor or to moor with two anchors
- two wooden stocked sheet anchors of 5.6tons – stowed well abaft the bowers on hinged iron crutches to throw them clear of ship's side on letting go. Sometimes called waist anchors they were used for additional holding power
- one iron stocked stream anchor of 1.4tons, used for holding ship temporarily in given direction. Stowed on upperdeck unstocked and lashed to mainmast
- two iron stocked kedge anchors of 0.4 and 0.8ton. By taking away in ship's boat could be used for warping ship. Stowed port and stbd abaft the mainmast
- two of Cdr Rodger's patent stern anchors of about 3 tons they were stowed on either quarter and used to hold stern, for example, when bombarding at anchor.

Capstans Two identical Brown and Harfield's capstans, each manually operated by 12 or 14 capstan bars, were installed abaft the mainmast on the upper and main decks and keyed to a common spindle. Replaced by two stronger capstans in 1862 their function was to heave in the bower cables via an endless chain messenger. Both capstan barrels could be fitted with whelps for hawsers and the upper capstan also used for heavy work aloft.

Brown's patent iron capstan, similar in size and operation to the other capstans, was installed before the mainmast on the main deck; it had sprockets which enabled the bower cable to be brought to it direct, the cable prevented from jumping out by transposable vertical rollers placed in sockets round the barrel. In event of total capstan failure the cable could be hove in by deck tackle.

Chain and hemp cables Naval length of cable was expressed in fathoms (one equals six feet) and a 'length' or 'shackle' of cable measured 12½fathoms. Chain cable was measured by the diameter of its links and hemp cable by its circumference.

Warrior was supplied with 600fathoms of 2⅜in studded cable, made up in lengths connected by joining shackles, the number of each length marked by wire either side of joining shackle. 250fathoms were used for each bower, leaving 100fathoms for one sheet cable. The other sheet cable was about 100fathoms of 18½in hemp, fitted with three lengths of 2⅜in chain ganger to keep the hemp cable being chafed on the bottom. To keep the bower cables clear of turns swivels were fitted.

Each stern anchor was provided with 100fathoms of 1⅝in iron cable while 12in, 11in and ½in hemp cables were supplied for the stream and kedge anchors. The messenger was 1⅝in studless cable, with oblong links alternatively short and long to fit the capstan sprockets, thence it was led either side of the main deck guided by a series of vertical rollers, through the armoured bulkhead, until it was joined by a shackle right forward on the cable deck. To weigh anchor the bower cable was secured to messenger by iron or hemp nippers, capstan turned and both messenger and bower cable hove in.

Bower, sheet and stern chain cable, the messenger and ganger were stowed in the four chain (cable) lockers in the hold either side of the mainmast. Bower (and sheet) cables were led from forward to the chain pipes amidships between the capstans, thence down to the cable lockers where the inboard ends were secured to slips. An 18½in hemp hawser was stowed in the midshipmen's chest room.

Anchor gear Starting right forward on the cable deck *Warrior's* anchor gear comprised,

- the manger with four hawse pipes for the bower and sheet cables, fitted with hawse plugs and bucklers to prevent entry of water
- two controllers for checking the bower cable
- two chain slips for temporarily holding the cable when bitting, unbitting or inserting a mooring swivel
- two small and two large mooring bitts for securing the riding cable at anchor and checking the cable when veering
- two rope stoppers for holding the cable abaft the bitts to share the strain and two ring stoppers to hold the cable should a compressor fail
- four tackle and lever operated compressors over the chain pipe amidships on the maindeck and in the cable locker flat to hold the cable.

Cable party Working with chain hooks, handspikes and strops the cable party was largely composed of forecastle seamen, although fore and maintopmen assisted in ranging cable and passing the nippers; the armourer traditionally handled the shackles with hammer, chisel and pellets and the gunners rigged the fish davit.

Letting go and weighing anchor To let go single anchor the cable deck was cleared away, bucklers and hawse plugs removed and sufficient cable ranged abaft the bitts to allow anchor to reach bottom without check. Bitt pin was shipped to prevent cable jumping off bitts. The cable was shackled to the ring of the anchor with aid of ring rope and buoy rope bent on to anchor crown. Keeping the anchor horizontal the inner fluke was eased off the bill board, the ring hung by the cathead stopper and the shank by the shank painter, both of which were fitted to go over the anchor tumblers on the upper deck bulwarks and the ends secured inboard. Approaching the anchor berth the order was given 'stream the buoy, stand clear of the cable' when the compressor was thrown back clear and the chock of the tumbler removed. Anchor buoy and rope running clear, the order 'let go' was given; the boatswain ordered 'one, two, three – let go' and the anchor tumbler lever was operated to allow the

Type	Length (ft)	Weight (tons)	Lifesaving	Oars	Sails	Armament
Launch (2)	42	8	140	18 DB	2 standing lug and staysails	20pdr
Pinnace (1)	32	4½	70	14 DB	2 standing lug and staysails	12pdr
Cutter gig (1)	20	—	19	4/6 SB	mainsail and staysail	-
Dinghy (1)	14	—	6	4 SB	foresail and mainsail	—
Cutter (2)	30	2	49	12 DB	dipping lug and mizzen	Rocket launcher
Galley (1)	32	¾	28	6 SB	2 lugsails	—
Gig (1)	30	¾	26	6 SB	2 lugsails	—
Cutter (1) (jolly boat)	18	—	12	4 SB	foresail/and mainsail	—

anchor to fall horizontally into the water. Cable was then veered and secured on the bitts when the ship had 'got' her anchor.

To weigh single anchor the cat head and fish davit purchases were prepared, bower cables held by slip before unbitting and the capstan rigged. If using the messenger it was brought to the cable, secured with one iron nipper before the bitts and its bight brought to the capstan sprocket. If using forward capstan the bower cable was brought to its sprockets. Hoses were rigged to play on cable and the anchor buoy recovered. On the order 'heave round' the capstan was turned and either the messenger brought the cable in, nippers being secured at the hawsepipe and taken off as these passed aft or the forward capstan brought it in direct. In either case the cable was fed into chainpipes down to the cable locker where it was stowed by cable party. 'Avast heaving' as soon as anchor was clear of water, then the cat purchase was hooked on, the cable surged and by hauling on the cat falls the ring of the anchor was brought to the cat head. Similarly by hauling away on the fish davit falls the anchor was brought up horizontally and the point of the fluke secured on the bill board. The cable deck was then secured for sea.

Boats The original allowance of boats for *Warrior* was appropriate to a two decker: two 42ft pinnace launches, one 32ft pinnace, one 32ft galley, one 30ft gig, two 30ft cutters, one 18ft jolly boat and one 14ft dinghy.

In April, 1862 Captain Cochrane asked that two 30ft cutters pulling 10 oars, one 20ft gig and the 18ft jolly boat should be replaced by two 30ft cutters pulling 12 oars, one 26ft gig and one 18ft cutter. He wanted boats with more oars for pulling in and out of harbour, complaining that 'the jolly boat of 18ft is so small as to be unable to bring the fresh beef off in ordinary weather.' As a result *Warrior's* outfit of boats became as tabled

- the establishment of boats bore less relation to the total lifesaving capacity (539) than to the requirements of boats for evolutions and transport of stores, water, and personnel
- although listed in the carpenters establishment of stores boats were an executive responsibility spread throughout parts of the ship
- larger boats were made of mahogany, smaller of elm or pine. Hull construction of pinnace and launch was diagonal (double planking), the remainder clinker-built (upper planking overlapping lower)
- oars were double banked (DB) or single banked (SB)

- although many rigs were experimental boats were sailed whenever possible
- anchors could be slung with strong back under a launch, pinnace or cutter to take away for evolutions
- boats maintained communication with *Warrior* using flags and *Boats Signal Book*.

Hoisting and stowage *Warrior* had two pairs of straight wooden davits for cutters (quarter boats), two pairs of curved iron davits for gig and galley and one pair over stern for the jolly boat. They were hoisted by tackles (falls) rove through standing blocks at davit head and moving blocks hooked on to chain slings at each end of boat. When a cutter rigged as a lifeboat was lowered a dangerous situation could develop if both falls were not unhooked simultaneously and the boat able to clear the ship. In the 1860's two types of quick release gear was fitted to seaboats – Cliffords (patented 1856) or Kynastons (patented 1857). It is probable that *Warrior*'s cutters had Clifford's gear. All other boats were stowed in the booms on the upper deck and adjacent to the funnels. On the port side were launch on crutches, with pinnace secured inside and on the starboard side were launch on crutches with cutter gig and dinghy stowed inside. Special tackles were used to hoist out boom boats, the main purchase being led to the main topmast head.

Man and arm boats The manning and arming of boats 30ft and over was a favourite evolution for admiral's inspections. The bows of both launches and the pinnace were strengthened to mount a gun and when the Armstrongs came into service the 25pdrs (3¾in calibre) were selected for the launches (in 1861 the 25pdr was redesignated a 20pdr as the weight of shell was reduced) and the 12pdr (3in calibre) for pinnaces.

Boat guns The 20pdr (0.7ton) and 12pdr (0.4ton) rifled breech-loading guns were similar to the bigger Armstrongs and both fired solid shot, case shot, common shell with bursting charges and segment shell with bursting charge and cast iron segments. Propellants for the 20pdrs and 12pdrs were 2½ and 1½ gunpowder charges respectively. Each gun was provided with a boat carriage and slide consisting of a sliding top carriage, a wooden boat slide and an undercarriage fitted with trucks (wheels) and a rear chock. A field marine carriage was used ashore with a field marine limber to house the ammunition. Each gun could be employed as a ship or a boat gun with a crew of five or as a field gun with a crew of 18 men to man the gun and limber drag ropes. The 20 and 12pdrs were secured in their boat carriages either side and forward on the upper deck adjacent to projectiles in ready use racks. Field carriages were stowed in the cable locker flat.

Rocket launchers Cutters (and possibly the gig/galley) were armed with rocket launchers to fire 24lb Congreve shot or shell rockets. The rocket launcher with rocket tube was mounted in the bow of the boat and at elevations between 18° and 45° could realise ranges of 1000 to 3000 yards. There is no evidence that rockets were considered reliable or effective, except as a weapon of surprise or for bombardment. Light in weight the launchers could be transported ashore.

Landing parties In one lift at short notice *Warrior* could land a total of 12 officers and 125 men comprising two launches each with three officers, 30 men and 20pdr gun; one pinnace with two officers, 23 men and a 12pdr gun; two cutters each with one officer, 15 men and a Congreve rocket launcher and two gigs each with one officer and 6 men. Sufficient ammunition, stores and provisions would be carried for seven days.

Miscellaneous A 10ft long wooden copper(ing) punt, constructed of two cylindrical floats supporting a platform with paddle propulsion, was introduced to enable artificers to repair copper sheathing on ship's bottoms. *Warrior* was supplied with one to clean and paint the waterline. Boom boats were painted black, davit boats were painted white with a black washstrake and the name *Warrior* painted on scroll on either bow.

Ships of the line were required to remain effective at sea for long periods in war; thus *Warrior* was victualled with provisions and spirits for three months, while the scale of various stores and spare parts enabled the crew to make good minor action or storm damage to hull or spars and repair machinery defects without dockyard assistance. Victualling included fresh, wet and dry provisions, clothing, shoes, bedding, soap, tobacco, vinegar and spirits. Provision rooms were located aft on orlop deck and hold; water tanks, spirit and bread rooms were within the citadel. To balance weights and assist identification certain items were traditionally stowed in port and starboard provision rooms.

Stowage and issue A limited quantity of fresh meat, poultry, eggs, fruit and vegetables was available in cattle pens or canvas-covered cages on the upper deck, fresh bread being kept in messes. 600 bags (30 tons) of biscuits were kept in the bread rooms, the newest at the bottom, while the spirit room held about four tons of rum in casks. The starboard provision room contained 19 tons (5,000 pieces) of salt beef in casks, 10 tons of flour, butter, suet, soap and tobacco. The port provision room contained 19 tons (10,000 pieces) of salt pork in casks, eight tons of sugar, six tons of peas, two tons of vinegar and lemon juice and several bales of tobacco. Amidships were eight tons of candles and two tons of raisins, tea, chocolate, tins of preserved meat and cheese. Slop clothing and materials were stowed in the slop room and included articles of uniform in large and small sizes for seamen and boys. Similarly marines uniform was in the marines slop room.

After initial provisioning by victualling yard periodical replenishments were hoisted in on the upper deck and struck down through gunroom flat to provision rooms. Similarly victuals were brought up for daily issue to cooks of messes from the issue room while slop clothing and tobacco were issued weekly from the slop rooms.

Water was stowed in iron tanks each containing up to 300 gallons; 9464 galls (45 tons) were stowed above the forward magazine, 9949 galls (47 tons) above the after magazine and, in reserve capacity, were 2520 galls (12 tons) in the midshipman's chest room. Tanks were stowed with holes adjacent to each other for ease of filling, spaces between tanks being filled with wood, bilge tanks being against the ship's side.

Scale of victualling *Daily* – 1¼lbs biscuits or soft bread, ⅛ pint rum, 2oz sugar, 1oz chocolate, ¼oz tea and when available, 1lb fresh meat and 1lb fresh vegetables. When the latter were exhausted the issue was 1lb salt pork and ⅓ pint split peas or 1lb salt beef, 9oz flour, ¾oz suet and 1½oz currants or raisins.

Weekly ¼pint each of oatmeal and vinegar, ½oz mustard and ¼oz pepper. Those not taking spirits were entitled to ¼oz tea and 1oz sugar; extra chocolate and sugar could be issued in severe weather to night watchmen and the sick were allowed lemon juice with sugar and medical comforts (App X). In addition to victualling allowance the captain's and officers' messes were supplemented by private purchases and traditionally the captain was entitled to a free cask of tongues on commissioning.

Candles Mainly for internal illumination, comprised police, fighting, signal, 'eights' and 'twenty fours'. Police candles were the biggest, burning for more than 12 hours, twenty fours burnt for only two hours. Eights were eight candles to the pound and three times the size of twenty fours (24 to the pound). Police candles went into magazine lightrooms when Argand lamps were found unsatisfactory but were intended for police lamps that illuminated important positions below decks. Fighting candles were used in wing compartments and storerooms but mainly in fighting lanterns between each pair of guns. Signal candles went into signal lanterns, while eights and twenty fours, mainly the latter, were found in hand lanterns, officer's cabins, messdeck sconces and in offices. Lamps and lanterns were stowed in the lower steering flat and tended by the lamptrimmer.

Mess traps, mess gear and meals On commissioning in 1861 each broadside mess was supplied with two mess kettles (five and four gallons) for hot or cold liquids or food, two meat dishes, two hook pots, three tin cannisters for tea, coffee and sugar, one pepper dredge, one salt jar, two soup ladles, one metal drinking cup for every four persons, and one metal basin, spoon and bowl for each man. All were marked with a broad arrow and subsequently with mess number; basins and plates were stowed in mess shelf, spoons in cutlery drawer. Men supplied their own clasp knives.

Cooperage items included bread barge (for biscuits), wash buckets, fire bucket, vinegar barricoe, spitkid and latrine bucket (shared between two messes). Nets, tallied with mess number, were provided for boiling vegetables and meat in galley coppers. Mess kettles or preserved meat tins (fannies) were used for collecting grog issue. Enamelware had not yet arrived in the fleet but some senior ratings may have acquired ceramic bowls and plates. Each mess table had a canvas table cloth and the whole mess was scrubbed out weekly for captain's inspection. Ditty boxes or ditty bags were stowed in the mess or in kitbags.

The galley fire was kept continuously alight, except when embarking powder and shell or going into action, to provide breakfast at 6 or 7am, dinner at noon and supper at about 4.45pm. Galley was ready by 4am to take food that required long cooking, vegetable nets by 7.30am. Coal galley at 3pm. Each day's menu was drawn up by the paymaster.

Complement The paymaster was the ship's accountant and from his office on the half deck controlled cash, victualling and clothing. He was supported by four assistant paymasters or clerks, one of whom was the captain's clerk, also two assistant clerks under training. The ship's steward was in charge of daily issues of provisions, assisted by the captains of the hold working in provision rooms. The ship's cook had two mates, with a butcher to handle the meat at the beef screen.

Departmental stores Forward were the gunner's, boatswain's and carpenter's stores, the master-at-arms store and the sail room. Amidships was the engineer's store and aft were wardroom, gunroom and captain's stores. Considerable quantity of departmental stores were stowed on the main and lower decks, including half a ton of holystones and sand.

Clothing soap and tobacco

Issued monthly from the sloproom

Pay Officers and men were paid in cash monthly by the paymaster in addition to victualling allowance.

1861 ANNUAL PAY
(1987 INFLATION EQUIVALENT FIGURES)

	£		£
Rear Admiral	1095 (25,350)	Master-at-arms	41 (950)
Captain in command	584 (13,520)	Ships cook	36 (835)
Captain	365 (8,450)	Gunners mate	36 (835)
Commander	301 (6,970)	Stoker	36 (835)
Lieutenant	182 (4,215)	Coxswain of the barge	33 (765)
Master	273 (6,320)	Able seaman	29 (672)
Engineer	164 (3,800)	Ordinary seaman	23 (535)
Boatswain	120 (2,780)	Boy Second Class	9 (210)
Midshipman	32 (740)		

- In 1861 beef was 3p per lb, beer 5p per gallon, a suit cost £1.25, a two-bedroom house £250 and a labourer's salary £39 pa. 1987 equivalent figures allow for an inflation figure of 23.15
- In 1987 and on promotion a rear admiral's salary was £35,350, a captain's £26,714, a lieutenant's £13,155 and an able seaman's £7665, victualling allowance having been abolished.

Medical and band   Appendix X

In the early 19th century the Admiralty paid insufficient attention to the basic causes of disease and sickness in the navy but later, particularly after the Russian war, the surgeon's status and the hygiene of the lower deck were improved. *QR and AI* (1861) devoted a chapter to the duties of medical officers, medical supplies and stores, living conditions, inspections and treatment of the sick.
Sick bay By 1860 sick berths (or bays) in major warships were reasonably equipped and ventilated to provide a combined consulting room, operating theatre and hospital. *Warrior's* sick bay on the lower deck had three scuttles each side, sufficient deck space for about ten iron-framed fixed cots, a curtained-off enclosure for consulting, a dispensary cupboard at the foot of the access ladder and a sick mess table that might have served as an operating table. Equipment probably included lockers and cupboards, a portable bath, a water tank, a commode for patients unable to use the heads on either side of the cable deck, a small library and a stove. A separate and larger dispensary was in the marines flat.
The surgeon and his staff What academic and practical knowledge the surgeon had acquired at medical school was considered sufficient qualification to join the navy and he was left to learn the special features of medicine and surgery afloat from hard experience. At his expense a surgeon was expected to provide a set of instruments.

In 1833 the fleet was directed to recruit sick berth attendants to staff the sick bay. Some ratings may have come from dispensaries or chemists shops but since qualifications besides physical fitness were the abilities to read, write and understand accounts, standards were mediocre. Afloat their duties with little or no training included administering medicines and diet to the sick, arranging beds and bedding, accounts, care and cleaning of equipment . Even when sent to naval hospitals for experience they were employed on 'labourer's duties' and there is no reason to suppose that *Warrior's* sick berth staff differed.

Warrior's surgeon was supported by two assistant surgeons, a sick berth steward and two attendants; in addition men on light duty were employed cleaning the sick bay, fetching meals and collecting stores.
Duties and routine Unlike his colleagues ashore the naval surgeon had to be physician as well as surgeon, a specialist in preventive medicine as well as a clinician; the restrictive circumstances aboard made it near impossible to acquire a wide field of knowledge. Daily the surgeon would present a sick list to the captain; once a quarter a nosological report had to be made to the Physician of the Fleet and he had to keep 'a rough and fair journal of his practice'. Men joining ship had to be examined, with particular regard to vaccinations against smallpox and venereal disease. The daily routine was probably

7am Sick bay inspection by surgeon or assistant surgeon

7.30am Dispensaries open for medicines

9am Report to captain with sick list and recording in log. In the first commission *Warrior's* sick list varied between 25 and 90, including those in hospital

9.30am Examination of fresh cases, minor operations, administration of sick etc

4pm-6pm After dispensary open for medicines, possibly attended by an assistant surgeon

The need for a special diet for the sick had long been recognized and medical comforts allowed to *Warrior* included preserved meat, concentrated soup, preserved potatoes, preserved rice, essence of beef, lemon juice, arrowroot and wine.
Medical organization for battle The forward first aid station was the sick bay, the after station being set up in the wardroom; the staff were divided so that each had an assistant surgeon in charge, with the surgeon probably forward to carry out emergency operations such as amputations. At each position medical staff would provide water, sponges, basins, towels, tourniquets, ligatures, anaesthetics (chloroform and ether), analgesics (opium), stimulants (ammonia), antiseptics

(carbolic acid), and surgical instruments. They would be assisted by paymaster's staff, naval instructor, chaplain and any civilians that might be on board. A position would be set aside as a mortuary and hammocks provided for sewing up corpses.

Surgeon's instruments

3 amputating knives
1 amputating saw
1 metacarpel saw
2 catlins
pair artery forceps
2doz curved needles
2 tenaculums
6 Pettit screw tourniquets
pair of bone nippers and turnscrew
3 trephins
saw for the head
lenticular and rugine
pair of forceps
elevator
2 trocars
2 silver catheters
2 gum elastic catheters
6 scalpels
small razor
key tooth instrument
gum lancet
2 pair tooth forceps
punch
2 seton needles
pair of probe scissors

curved bistory with button
long probe
pair of bullet forceps
scoop for extracting balls
2 probangs
½lb ligature thread
1 paper needles
case with lift-out
apparatus for restoring suspended animation
pocket instrument set
6 lancets
2doz bougies
2 pint pewter clyster syringes
6 small pewter syringes
2 sets splints
12 flannel/linen rollers
2 18-tailed bandages
20yds tourniquet web
60yds tape
cupping apparatus of scarificator and 6 glasses
Fahrenheit thermometer

Band 'Bands of music', resembling present day instrumental groups, started to appear unofficially in the fleet during the Napoleonic wars. In 1842 the Admiralty first gave limited approval to their existence by establishing the rating of musician, as a petty officer, 2nd class and allowing one to each ship, his main role as fiddler being at the capstan but also when hands were piped 'to dance and skylark'. In 1847 the rating of

bandsman was introduced, the entry open to foreigners since most unofficial bands included Germans, Spaniards, Italians or Maltese. *Warrior* was complemented with one musician and 15 bandsmen. In 1863 the rating of chief bandsmen and a uniform for bandsmen were introduced – blue braided tunic and trousers with a pill box hat. Until 1875 the captain and officers paid for the band instruments, greater importance placed on string than wind. This double handed ability was passed down to marine bands, a feature practically non-existent in the other services.

Warrior's band probably comprised,

Wind
1 piccolo/flute
5 clarinets
3 cornets
2 tenor
1 baritone
1 euphonium
1 bombardon
1 trombone

String
6 violins
2 violas
2 cellos
1 double bass

● *Gloire, Invincible* and *Normandie* were laid down between March and September, 1858, *Gloire* being launched in November 1859, some 18 months before the others. With a metacentric height of 7ft the class were bad seaboats, suffered from unsound timber and generally failed to come up to expectations. They were broken up in the 1870's. In contrast *Couronne*, with an iron hull and ordered the same day as *Gloire* but not launched until late March 1861, lasted well. After service as a training ship she was broken up in 1932.

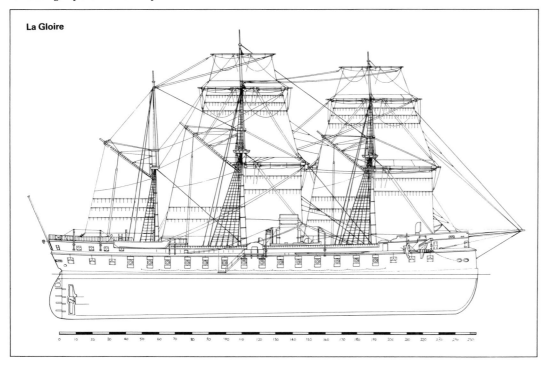

La Gloire

Although the threat of war hovered during her first commission and intermittent war scares occurred later *Warrior* never fired her guns in anger. Her impact on the maritime scene led some writers to credit Britain's first ironclad with the capability of defeating any number of ships single-handed while others were less confident of her prowess. The truth will never be known but it is interesting to examine the strength of potential opponents and assess how *Warrior* matched up to them.

The function of each ship in an engagement was to strike the enemy with more effective blows than those received in a given time. Hitting power depended on

● number, calibre and layout of guns
● stability of gun platform and height of port sill above waterline
● effective range of engagement and rate of fire
● weight, terminal velocity and nature of projectiles
● efficiency of guns' crews in loading and firing.

Only by developing maximum gun hitting power could decisive range be reached when the fire of one ship could overwhelm an opponent. Russian war experience showed that decisive range had grown to about 800 yards, a fact confirmed in 1864 when the Danes defeated the Austrians off Heligoland at ranges decreasing from 1200 to 500 yards using smooth bore and rifled guns. Again when the unarmoured American steam sloops *Alabama* and *Kearsage* engaged in a duel off Cherbourg in June 1864 victory went to the superior training and gunnery of the Federal *Kearsage*, at ranges between 900 and 600 yards.

Equally important was tactical mobility – the need for a ship to be handled to bring maximum guns to bear on the enemy whilst presenting a small or difficult target. Speed was advantageous for overtaking a slower opponent and choosing the range at which to fight. At close ranges speed was less significant than the ability to turn more quickly and tightly than the opponent.

While hitting power contributed both offence and defence the protection afforded by armour and watertight sub-division in an iron hull was superior to that in an unarmoured wooden hull. In addition, passive protection was augmented by personnel efficiency in controlling damage.

Although ironclads were built with rams the technique of ramming was a hit-or-miss affair as hazardous to the attacker as the defender. More likely the natural instinct when closing a stricken enemy would be to board and capture. Finally, the deciding factor in battle was more often the state of morale and the use which personnel made of ships and weapons than the statistical strengths of opposing forces.

Warrior's fighting qualities In terms of gun hitting power the combination of Warrior's armament of 75% 68pdrs and 25% 110pdrs, steady gun platform and good seakeeping qualities conferred theoretical superiority over any other warship in the world. Being a long ship with small rudder and inefficient steering gear the tactical advantage gained by unrivalled speed was offset by a large turning circle (760 yards at 12 knots) and sluggish reaction to the helm. Ramming was obviously inadvisable. But as Spencer Robinson pointed out 'the most vital defect of Warrior, one which absolutely forbids that the design is repeated, was the want of an armour-plated belt at the waterline round the bow and stern'. Warrior could not afford to expose her stern to an enemy broadside.

The opposition Early in 1863 the Controller reported that the French ironclads, Gloire, Normandie, Invincible and Couronne were numerically superior in armament – 148 guns of which 130 were behind armour – to the Warrior, Black Prince, Defence and Resistance with 80 protected and 36 unprotected guns. The superior speed of Warrior and Black Prince was offset by the slower Defence and Resistance. In the Atlantic the higher gunport sills of the British ironclads would have the edge but this would disappear in calmer seas and the French would enjoy complete end-to-end protection and handiness in turning. However, only Couronne had an iron hull and the French 55pdrs were inferior to British guns in armour penetration.

The French squadron was later reinforced by the wooden-hulled Magenta and Solferino of 6700 tons displacement armed with 50 guns on two decks and a partially protected armoured belt. To match these the wooden-hulled Royal Oak and the iron-hulled Hector joined the Channel squadron but it was considered that in a fleet action the six French ships would have an advantage in average speed, manoeuvring, lightness of rig and protected guns. While admitting that individual power was on the RN's side the Controller emphasized 'the compactness and homogeneous qualities of the French ships'.

During the American Civil War the situation became sufficiently serious for either Warrior or Black Prince to reinforce the North American squadron. In the event the Federal government backed down but had either ship been despatched they could have coped quite easily with Monitor, Merrimac and any of the Federal frigates.

Comparison between Warrior and French ironclads

	Gloire	Couronne	Warrior
Displacement (tons)	5630	5983	9210
Length (ft)	252	262	380
Beam (ft)	56	55	58
Draft (ft)	28	27	26
Height of port sills (ft)	6	6	9½
Armour	4½in iron belt on timber	17in teak and iron	4½in iron 18in teak
% of guns protected	100	100	75
% of target protected	75	75	42
Armament	36x6.4in RML	40x6.4in RML and 10x55pdr SB	26x8.1in SB 10x7in RBL 4x4.7in RBL
Weight of broadside (lbs)	1045	1100	1624
Distance between guns (ft)	11½	11½	15
Indicated horse power	2500	2900	5269
Speed (knots)	12	12	14
Complement	550	570	705

Training for war 'As you train so you fight' has been a naval dictum for generations and Warrior was brought up in the élite Channel squadron to operate in all weathers with emphasis on seamanship. That is not to say that gunnery was neglected because drill and firing featured regularly in her programme. However, instead of experimenting with new formations adapted for ironclads flag officers conservatively conducted steam tactics at six knots in open order based on signal books written for a sailing line of battle; but accurate stationkeeping helped concentrate broadside fire.

The outcome In event of war between Britain and France Warrior could have been involved in the Channel area, in a multi-ship action or single-ship duel. Only in the latter can Warrior's probable course of action be visualized, assuming her opponent to be Gloire or a sister ship. Disregarding the critical factors of weather and visibility, it is likely that Cochrane would have used his superior speed to gain the weather gauge and open fire initially with the bow chaser and subsequently turn on a parallel course to fire single broadsides, while trying to keep out of Gloire's range. He would certainly protect his stern. As soon as a favourable opportunity occurred Warrior would have closed to decisive range but – as Nelson remarked – 'nothing is certain in a sea fight above all others' and it is left to the reader to determine what the outcome might have been.

Major warships The *first* was a third rate of 1621 tons (BM) and 74 guns. Launched at Portsmouth on October 18, 1781 she fought at the Battle of the Saintes (1782) under Captain Sir James Wallace, at the Battle of Copenhagen (1801) and in Calder's action off Ferrol in 1805 under Captain Linzee. On December 3, 1805 Lieutenant Henry Lloyd of the *Warrior* wrote to his friend Captain George McKinley of the *Roebuck*, 'we have now in tow *Victory* with the remains of the Immortal Nelson and are proceeding to Spithead which we hope to reach tomorrow. On Friday last the Fleet made Falmouth, the first division got in on that day, the second was to follow in the next day and we being in the third, was to go in also in our turn but the wind shifted to the Northward and held us out. On Sunday the *Belleisle* and *Bellerophon* passed us and made the signal for the *Victory* being in distress to the Southward and it fell to our lot to be sent in pursuit of her which we effected yesterday and took her in tow being short of water – and ourselves also we were put to a pint and a half of water but now thank God the wind is fair and we shall get over it . . .' In 1809 *Warrior* was employed in the Mediterranean and in 1818 became a receiving ship. From 1840 she was used as a convict ship at Woolwich and was broken up in 1857.

The *second Warrior* is the subject of this book and the *third* was an armoured cruiser displacing 13,550 tons, with triple expansion engines of 23,500 hp giving speed of 23 knots. Armed with six 9.2in and four 7.5in guns and three 18in torpedo tubes she was launched from Pembroke Dock on November 25, 1905 and numbered 531 in the *Navy List*. After serving in the Home Fleet she joined *Duke of Edinburgh, Defence* and *Black Prince* at the outbreak of war to become First Cruiser squadron under Admiral Arbuthnot in the Grand Fleet. Although protected by 6in side armour *Warrior* and her sisters had been made obsolete by fast, heavy armed battle cruisers, as Jutland demonstrated on May 31, 1916 when the squadron came under their fire. *Defence* blew up, *Warrior*

● **The first *Warrior*, 1781 to 1857**

was hit repeatedly and was saved only by *Warspite* – her steering jammed – steaming between *Warrior* and the enemy to draw their fire; *Black Prince* sank later by which time *Warrior* was under tow by the seaplane tender *Engadine*. At 5am on June 1 the tow was abandoned and *Warrior* was scuttled 160 miles east of Aberdeen. Captain V B Molteno and all but 70 of her company survived; until 1980 the Old Warrior Dining Club foregathered

annually at HMS *Warrior* (Northwood) to celebrate Jutland.

The *fourth Warrior* was a 13,350 ton light aircraft carrier launched at Belfast on May 24, 1944 and commissioned by the Royal Canadian Navy in 1946. Capable of 25 knots (just) and armed with light AA weapons she could carry 40 aircraft. In 1948 she was handed back to the Royal Navy who used her for rubber-deck landing trials. In 1950 she was re-commissioned for trooping service to the Far East followed by limited modernization prior to a commission in the Far East at the end of the Korean War (1953–54). After further modernization gave her an angled flight deck and steam catapult *Warrior* was commissioned in 1957 as flagship of the special service squadron and headquarters for Britain's hydrogen bomb tests at Christmas Island. Finally in 1958 *Warrior* was sold to Argentina where she was renamed *Independencia*, and was scrapped in 1971.

Battle Honours *Warrior*'s were The Saints, 1782; Copenhagen, 1801; and Jutland, 1916.

Minor warships

1 Built in 1898 a 236ton trawler to be called *Warrior* was hired by the Admiralty in 1914 to operate with a 6pdr gun on the Kingston patrol between the Mull of Galloway and Wicklow Head. She was returned to her owners, Anchor Steam Fishing Co, in 1918.

2 Between August 1914 and October 1919 the 192ton tug *Warrior* was requisitioned and employed as a rescue work based on Queenstown.

3 Designed by G L Watson the 1,266ton yacht *Warrior* was built by Ailsa Shipyard, Troon in 1904 for Vanderbilt, director of New York Railroad. Her 284ft long steel hull, fitted out with every luxury, was capable of 14 knots and had a crew of 50. Hired by the Admiralty in 1915 she served on the American and West Indies station. In 1921 she was bought by Sir Ramon de la Sota, renamed *Giozeka Isarra* (Morning Star), and served in the Spanish Civil War. In 1937 she was sold to Sir Hugh Cunliffe Owen, renamed *Warrior* and requisitioned by the Royal Navy in October 1939. Armed with two 12pdrs she was commissioned as *Warrior II* and employed as a tender to *HMS Dolphin*. On July 1, 1940 she was sunk off Portland Bill by heavy air attack.

4 During World War II a 41 ton motor boat *Warrior* was requisitioned and operated as an auxiliary patrol vessel between Shoreham and Newhaven. In 1934 she became a training tender to *HMS King Alfred* until laid up in 1945.

● The fourth *Warrior*, 1944 to 1971

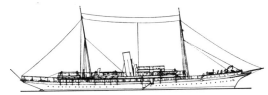

● HM Patrol Yacht *Warrior*, 1904 to 1940

Crests and badges After figureheads disappeared from later ironclads in the 1860's the ship's emblem, whether in badge or crest form, was not only an adornment but a means of emphasizing the dignity and tradition of the ship's name. In *Warrior*'s first commission *princess is much pleased* featured on wardroom notepaper and in the second commission different forms of a warrior appeared to identify the writer with a ship of distinction. Not until the third *Warrior* was a badge formally recorded and in 1945 Captain George Miles RCN chose a new badge in the shape of a Viking warrior with the motto 'Haul together'.

● The third *Warrior*, 1905 to 1916

● Crest circa 1905   ● Crest, 1945 to 1958

243

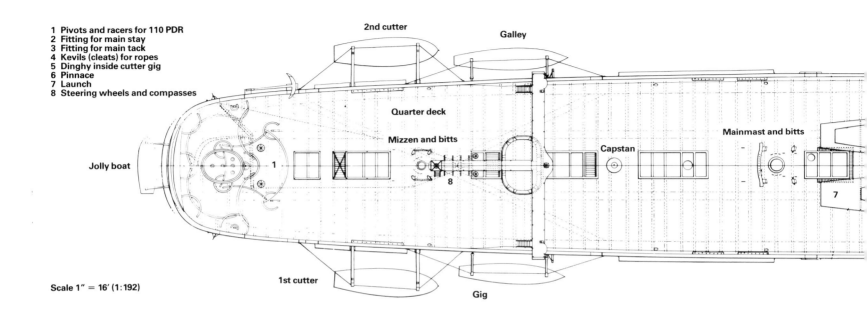

1 Pivots and racers for 110 PDR
2 Fitting for main stay
3 Fitting for main tack
4 Kevils (cleats) for ropes
5 Dinghy inside cutter gig
6 Pinnace
7 Launch
8 Steering wheels and compasses

2nd cutter

Galley

Quarter deck

Mizzen and bitts

Mainmast and bitts

Capstan

Jolly boat

1

8

7

Scale 1" = 16' (1:192)

1st cutter

Gig

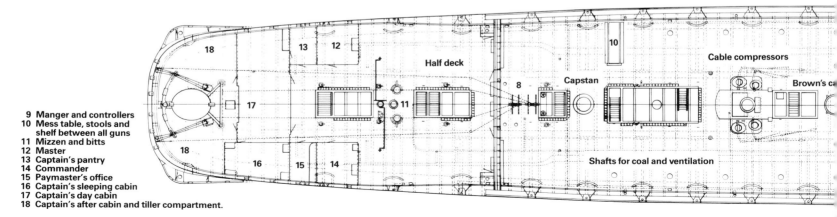

18

13

12

10

Half deck

Cable compressors

Capstan

8

17

11

Brown's ca

9 Manger and controllers
10 Mess table, stools and
   shelf between all guns
11 Mizzen and bitts
12 Master
13 Captain's pantry
14 Commander
15 Paymaster's office
16 Captain's sleeping cabin
17 Captain's day cabin
18 Captain's after cabin and tiller compartment.

18

16

15

14

Shafts for coal and ventilation

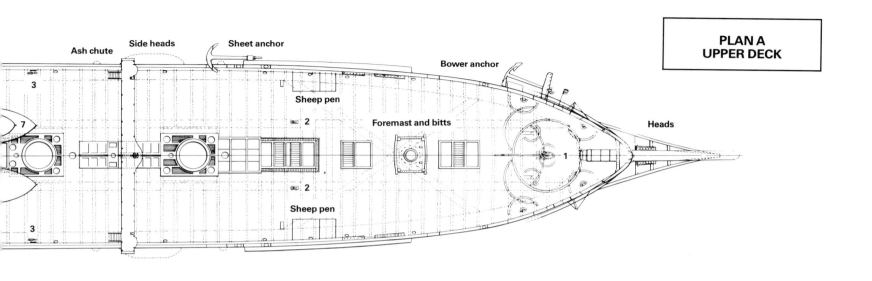

Ash chute   Side heads   Sheet anchor

Bower anchor

Sheep pen

Foremast and bitts

Heads

3

7

2

1

2

3

3

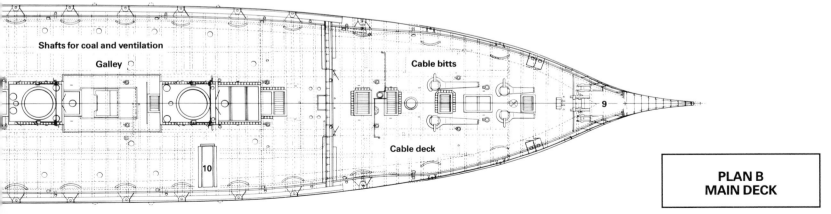

Shafts for coal and ventilation

Galley

Cable bitts

9

10

Cable deck

MESS DECK

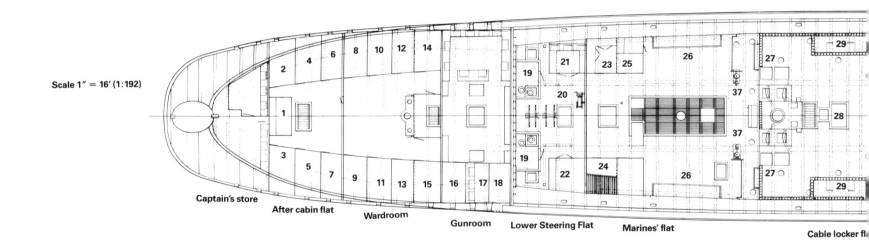

1	Wardroom pantry	6	Chaplain	11	2nd Lieutenant	16	Asst Surgeon	21 Issuing room
2	2nd Marine officer	7	Surgeon	12	3rd Lieutenant	17	Clerks office	22 Slop room
3	Asst Surgeon	8	Captain of Marines	13	4th Lieutenant	18	Pantry	23 Dispensary
4	1st Marine Officer	9	1st Lieutenant	14	Paymaster	19	Handing scuttles	24 Marines' slops
5	Asst Chief Engineer	10	5th Lieutenant	15	Chief Engineer	20	Magazine ventilator	25 Chronometers and band instrum

Scale 1″ = 16′ (1:192)

Captain's store

After cabin flat

Wardroom

Gunroom

Lower Steering Flat

Marines' flat

Cable locker fl

26 **Bag racks**
27 **to Shot and cable lockers**
28 **to Spirit room**
29 **Sail bin**
30 **Bathroom**

31 **Cells**
32 **Sail room**
33 **Boatswain**
34 **Carpenter**
35 **Gunner**

36 **Engineers' mess**
37 **Downton pump**

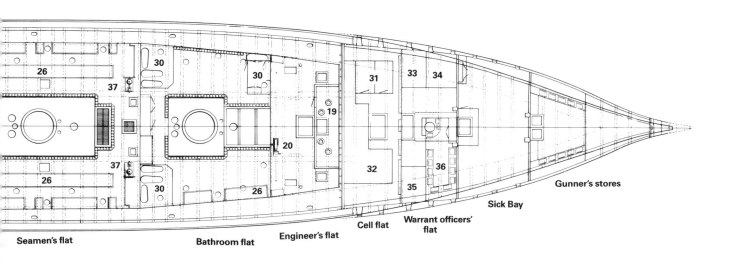

Seamen's flat

Bathroom flat

Engineer's flat

Cell flat

Warrant officers' flat

Sick Bay

Gunner's stores

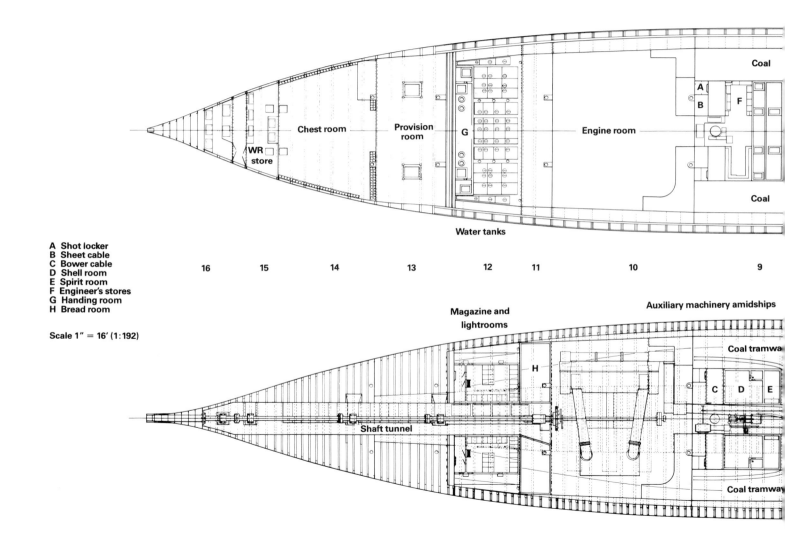

Coal

A
B
F

Chest room

Provision
room

G

Engine room

WR
store

Coal

Water tanks

A Shot locker
B Sheet cable
C Bower cable
D Shell room
E Spirit room
F Engineer's stores
G Handing room
H Bread room

Scale 1″ = 16′ (1:192)

16   15   14   13   12   11   10   9

Magazine and
lightrooms

Auxiliary machinery amidships

Coal tramwa

H

C D E

Shaft tunnel

Coal tramway

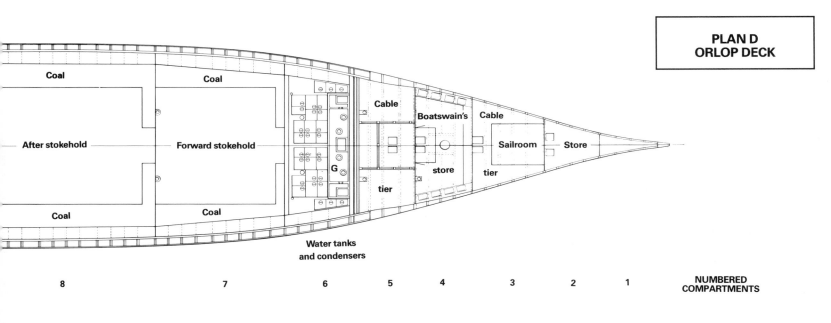

Coal

Coal

After stokehold

Forward stokehold

Coal

Coal

G

Cable

tier

Boatswain's

store

Cable

Sailroom

Store

tier

Water tanks
and condensers

**NUMBERED
COMPARTMENTS**

8   7   6   5   4   3   2   1

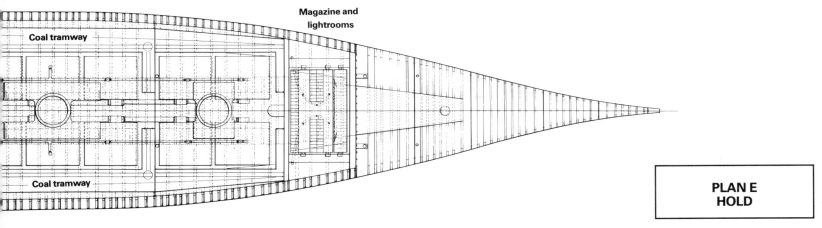

Magazine and
lightrooms

Coal tramway

After stokehold

Coal tramway

**PLAN E
HOLD**

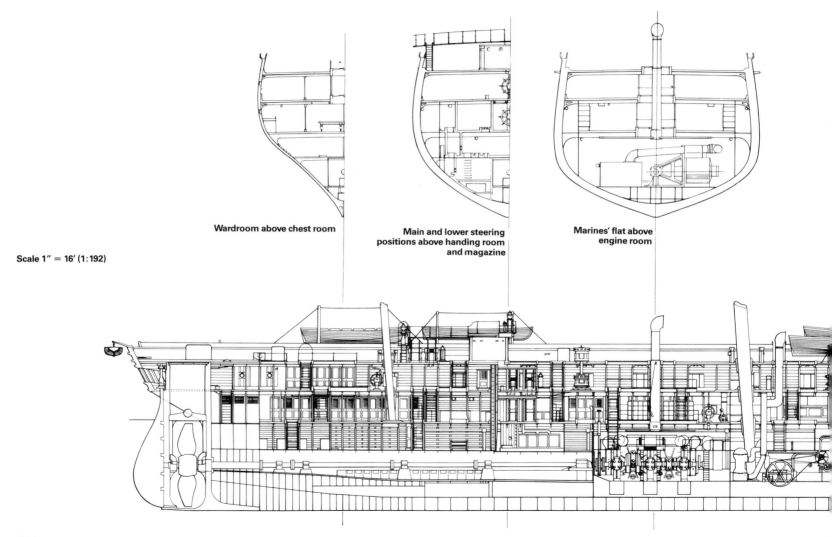

Wardroom above chest room

Main and lower steering
positions above handing room
and magazine

Marines' flat above
engine room

Scale 1″ = 16′ (1:192)

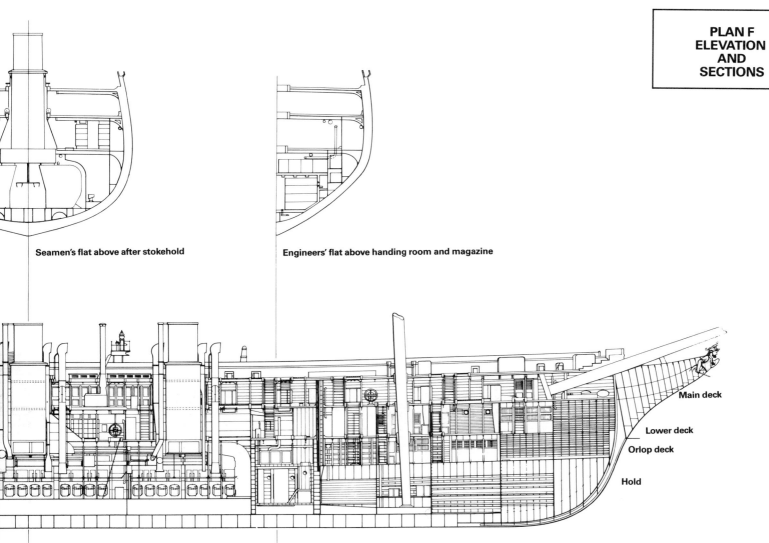

Seamen's flat above after stokehold

Engineers' flat above handing room and magazine

Main deck

Lower deck

Orlop deck

Hold

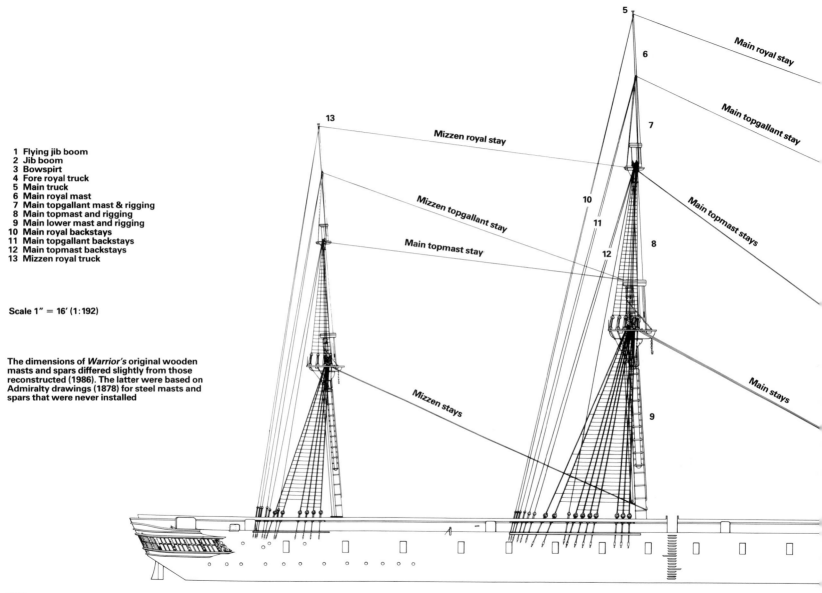

1 Flying jib boom
2 Jib boom
3 Bowspirt
4 Fore royal truck
5 Main truck
6 Main royal mast
7 Main topgallant mast & rigging
8 Main topmast and rigging
9 Main lower mast and rigging
10 Main royal backstays
11 Main topgallant backstays
12 Main topmast backstays
13 Mizzen royal truck

Scale 1" = 16' (1:192)

The dimensions of *Warrior's* original wooden
masts and spars differed slightly from those
reconstructed (1986). The latter were based on
Admiralty drawings (1878) for steel masts and
spars that were never installed

5

6

7

Main royal stay

Main topgallant stay

13

Mizzen royal stay

10

Mizzen topgallant stay

11

Main topmast stays

Main topmast stay

8

12

Mizzen stays

9

Main stays

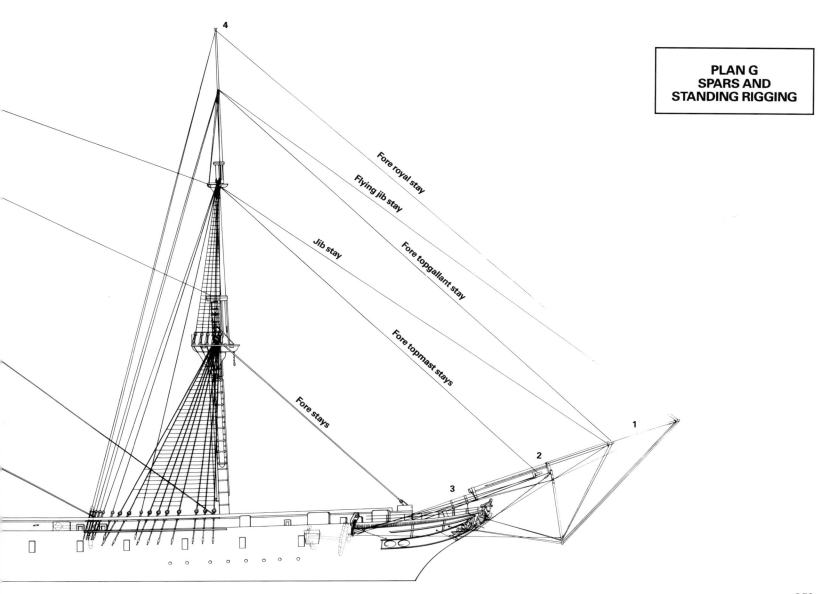

PLAN G
SPARS AND
STANDING RIGGING

Fore royal stay

Flying jib stay

Fore topgallant stay

Jib stay

Fore topmast stays

Fore stays

4

1

2

3

253

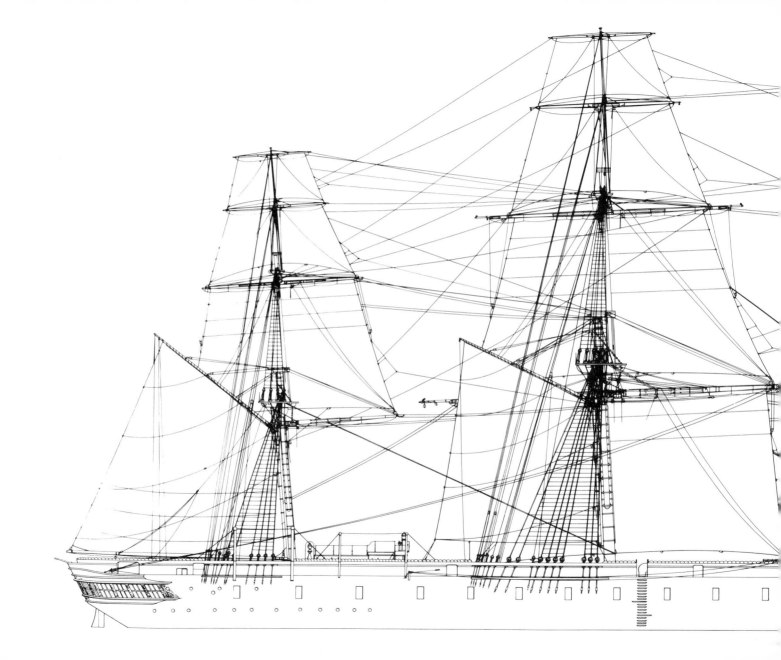

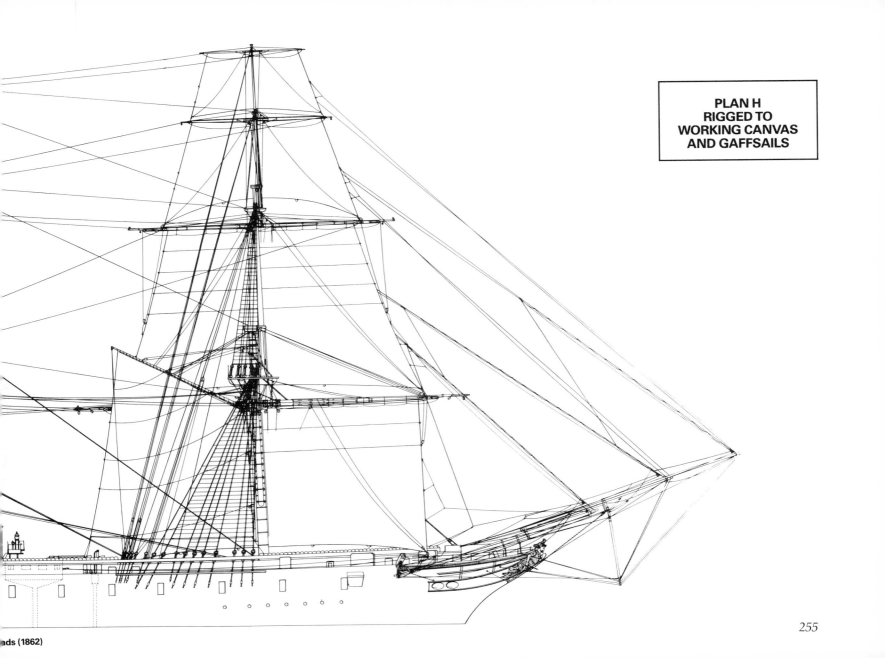

ads (1862)

References and bibliography

Research sources of unpublished papers and published documents include Admiralty correspondence in Public Records Office (ADM); MOD Naval Historical Library, London (NHL); National Maritime Museum, Greenwich (NMM); Royal Naval Museum, Portsmouth (RNM); Baldwin Walker collection in the University of Capetown Libraries (BWC); Arthur Cochrane collection in RN Museum, Portsmouth (Cochranalia); Captain's Letter Book, *HMS Warrior* 1861-4 (CLB); Naval Ordnance Museum, Priddy's Hard, Portsmouth (NOM); *Army and Navy Gazette* (ANG); *Mariners Mirror* (MM); *Transactions of the Royal Institute of Naval Architects* (TRINA); *Queens Regulations & Admiralty Instructions 1861* (QR & AI); The Maritime Trust (TMT); Portsmouth City Council (PCC); Support Research Papers by J G Wells in *Warrior* Archives (SRP) and private collections (Pr).

Chapter 1   Concept

1   Castlereagh, 1817 *Hansard* Series 3 XCVII, 779–80
2   J G Wells *Whaley – story of HMS Excellent* 1980, p4 et seq
3   D K Brown, Nemesis, first iron warship, *Warship* No 8, 1978; Experiments in *HMS Excellent* 1832–1854, p233 et seq ADM 12/461
4   Report of Select Committee on Board of Admiralty 1861 Minute 2334 (NHL)
5   R Murray *Shipbuilding in iron and wood* 1863, p22
6   D K Brown, Thomas Lloyd CB *Warship* 20 1981
7   N Barnaby *Naval development in the century* 1904, p63
8   *Hansard* Series 3 XLIX, col 915
9   A Lambert *Battleships in transition* 1984, p63
10 G S Emmerson *John Scott Russell* 1977, p160–161; R Murray ibid pp24–25
11 Capt W Moorsom *Remarks on construction of ships of war and composition of war fleets* Pamphlet, Sept 1857 (NHL); R Murray ibid p25; J P Baxter *Introduction of the ironclad warship* 1933, pp118–9
12 Report of Treasury Cttee on Navy Estimates 1852–1858 (NHL)
13 H & R Pakington *The Pakingtons of Westwood* 1975, p153 (Pr)
14 Pakington to Baldwin Walker Sept 5 & Oct 26, 1858 (BWC)
15 Select Cttee on Board of Admiralty 1861 Minute 1417–1418 (NHL)
16 J P Baxter ibid p120
17 Select Cttee on Board of Admiralty 1861 Minute 1696-1706 (NHL); J P Baxter ibid p123
18 J P Baxter ibid p124; ADM 12/653
19 D K Brown, Developing the armour of *HMS Warrior* Warship 40, 1986
20 Report of Treasury Cttee on Navy Estimates 1852–1858, pp 15–21 (NHL)
21 L M S Pasley *Memoir of Admiral Sir T S Pasley* 1900 pp246–249; P Fitzgerald *Memories of the sea* 1913, p187; W G Don *Reminiscences of the Baltic Fleet of 1855* 1894, p43
22 Select Cttee on Board of Admiralty 1861 Minute 1707 (NHL)
23 A Temple Patterson, Capt Cowper Coles and Palmerston's Folly *MM* Vol 51 p22
24 J P Baxter ibid p121 footnote No 3
25 H T L Corry to Board Nov 22, 1858 ADM 1/5698; J P Baxter ibid p127
26 Board to Surveyor Nov 27, 1858 ADM 1/5729–03292
27 Surveyor to Board Dec 1, 1858 ADM 1/5698; J P Baxter ibid p128
28 O Parkes *British battleships* 1970, p12

Chapter 2   Characteristics

1   Report of Cttee on Navy Estimates 1852 to 1858, pp18–19 (NHL)
2   *United Services Magazine* March 1861, pp342–3
3   Report of Commissioners to inquire into best means of manning navy (1859) (NHL)
4   Uniform and personal equipment of officers and men in *HMS Warrior* (1863), SRP 7, Feb 15, 1985
5   Walker's emphasis on speed later summarized for Admiralty, Sept 28, 1860 (ADM 87/77)
6   Report of Commissioners inquiring into control and management of naval yards (1861), evidence of Watts Minutes 10001–10009 (NHL)
7   Ibid. Evidence of R Admiral Sir B W Walker, Minute 341
8   *Thames Ironworks Gazette* 1899, p43 (NMM)
9   Mare to Admiralty March 1 1859 ADM 87/70 56516
10 Surveyor to Admiralty Jan 27, 1859 ADM 1/5729–039292; Report of Commissioners inquiry into control and management of naval yards (1861) evidence of Walker, minutes 343 and 349 (NHL)
11 Ibid p341
12 J P Baxter *Introduction of the ironclad warship* 1933, pp131–132
13 Surveyor to Admiralty May 10, 1859 ADM 1/5729 6588; ADM 87/6 39951
14 Report of Commissioners inquiring into management of HM Yards (1861), evidence of Watts 9943–9946 (NHL)
15 Surveyor to Board June 17, 1859 ADM 12/669
16 G S Emmerson *John Scott Russell* 1977, pp170–171
17 J Crighton *Contributions to maritime history of Great Britain* 1950, pp41–42
18 P Banbury *Shipbuilders of the Thames and Medway* 1971, p268
19 P Barry *Dockyard economy and naval power* 1863, pp209–215; *Jnl of the Institution of Municipal & County Engineers* Feb 7, 1928 pp989–1028

Chapter 3   Building

1   G S Emerson *John Scott Russell* 1977, p164
2   *Thames Ironworks Gazette* March 1899–Sept 1900 p255 (NMM)
3   Ford's speech based on P Barry *Dockyard economy and naval power* 1863, pp216–220; specifications of iron screw steam frigate to be cased with armour plates (NMM)

4 H & R Pakington *The Pakingtons of Westwood* (Pr)
5 *Hansard* Series 3 c/v col 657
6 Thornton to Capt Superintendent, Deptford and Surveyor, June 10, 1859, ADM 87/71–56526
7 Copy of correspondence between Admiralty and *Warrior*'s builders (non-fulfilment of contract within stipulated time), May 1, 1861 (NHL)
8 G Ballard *The black battlefleet* 1980, p51
9 J P Baxter *Introduction of the ironclad warship* 1933, pp155–157
10 *Excellent* to CinC Portsmouth, Dec 15 & 20, 1860 ADM 1/57 2
11 O Parkes *British battleships* 1970, p14
12 Report of Select Cttee on Ordnance, 1863 page v (NHL)
13 Bascomb to Surveyor ADM 87/33 39551
14 J Ford, Manufacture of armour plates *TRINA* Vol 2, pp144–7
15 *The Times* March 31, 1862
16 *Thames Ironworks Gazette* March 1899–Sept 1900 p4 (NMM)
17 Ford to Walker Sept 28, 1860 (BWC)
18 C Paget *Autobiography* 1896, pp194–5
19 *ANG* Dec 1, 1860
20 *Annual Register* Dec, 1860
21 Pakington to Paget accepting invitation Dec 20, 1860 ADM 3/268
22 H & R Pakington ibid p 180 (Pr); R Aldrich *Pakington*, London Univ Institute of Education pp13–14 (Pr)
23 Ford to Walker Dec 27, 1860 (BWC)
24 For *Warrior*'s launch see *ANG* Jan 5, 1861; *Naval Chronicle* Feb 1, 1861; *The Engineer* Jan 4, 1861; *Annual Register* December 1860; *Naval & Military Gazette* and *United Services Gazette* Jan 5, 1861; *The Times* Dec 31, 1861; *Chatham News* Jan 5, 1861; *Illustrated Times* Jan 5, 1861; *The Times* July 27, 1915
25 A Shewan *The Great Days of Sail* 1973, p80

Chapter 4   Fitting Out

1 Docks Board, W White *History and directory of Essex* 1863
2 Admiralty Board minutes on Armstrong guns Feb 26–28, 1861 ADM 3/269; Controller's minute Feb 26,

1861 ADM 1/5769
3 Surveyor to Board May 10, 1859, ADM 12/672–91/2
4 P Banbury *Shipbuilders of the Thames and Medway 1971*, p224–229
5 J H Briggs *Naval administrations 1827-1897*, p137
6 C Williams, Construction of marine boilers *TRINA* Vol 3, p101
7 O Parkes *British battleships* 1970, p23; N Barnaby, On the steering of ships *TRINA* Vol 4 pp56–61
8 Correspondence between Admiralty and *Warrior*'s builders ref non-fulfilment of contract within stipulated time May, 1861 (NHL).
9 W H White *Manual of naval architecture* 1877, p.66; E J Reed *Our ironclad ships* 1869, pp134–163
10 O Parkes, ibid p20
11 Watts to Controller March 27, 1861 ADM 1/5774; S Robinson to Board April 5, 1861 ADM 1/5774
12 G Ballard *The black battlefleet* 1980, p18
13 Admiralty Circular 35, Aug 5, 1864 (NHL)
14 HMS *Warrior*'s lighting SRP No 4 May 24, 1983
15 Briggs to Baldwin Walker, June 5, 1861 (BWC)
16 Moore to Cochrane, May 31, 1861 (Cochranalia)
17 Cochrane to Lady Dundonald, June 3, 1861 (Cochranalia)

Chapter 5   Commissioning

1 A Cochrane *The fighting Cochranes* 1983 pp381–384
2 Cochrane from Lord Dundonald Sept 6, 1847 and Lady Dundonald Sept 21, 1847 (Cochranalia)
3 Report of Commissioners to consider UK defences 1860, App 1 (NHL)
4 O Parkes *British battleships* p17; Controller to Board May 10, 1861 ADM 1/5774; G Ballard *The black battlefleet* 1980, pp26–27
5 Order in Council, April 5, 1852
6 *ANG* July 6, 1861
7 *Warrior* organization based on Admiralty's watch, station, quarter and fire bills, 1859; R Grenfell, Notes on sail in 19th c *MM* Vol 19 pp88–116; A C Corry, Executive officer's orders, 1888; A Fordyce *Naval routine* 1837
8 Ships Book (ADM 136/2) records August 8, 1861 building completion and acceptance

9 Fraser and Carr-Laughton *The Royal Marine Artillery 1930*, p518; Col Field *Britain's sea soldiers 1924*, p225; *ANG* July 20, 1861
10 *Warrior* Description Book 1861–1864 ADM 38/9310
11 *The Times* Aug 9, 1861; *Army & Navy Gazette* Aug 10, 1861
12 G Lowis *Fabulous admirals* 1957, p38
13 *ANG* Jan 10, 1861
14 *Naval & Military Record* March 15, 1900
15 The case of the missing horseshoe, Rutland record No 6 p205 (Pr)
16 Hood to Cochrane June 25, 1861 (Cochranalia)

Chapter 6   Trials

1 *The Times* Sept 21, 1861; *Stratford Times* Sept 28, 1861
2 *ANG* Sept 28, 1861; *Hampshire Telegraph* Sept 21, 1861
3 *Hampshire Telegraph* Sept 28,1861
4 *Surrey Comet* Sept 28, 1861
5 D Gieve *Gieves and Hawkes 1785–1985* pp16–17; Harvey and Sons *Record of ships supplied 1836–1873* (Pr)
6 *The Times* Oct 16, 1861; *The Engineer* Oct 18, 1861
7 *The Times* Oct 18, 1861; *Naval & Military Gazette* Oct 19, 1861
8 *The Engineer* Oct 25, 1861
9 *Naval Chronicle* Nov 1, 1861; *ANG* Oct 26 and Nov 2, 1861
10 *ANG* Nov 2, 1861
11 Smart to Admiralty Nov 5 1861 ADM 1/5757; Journal of R Admiral Smart Oct 1–30, 1861 ADM 50/529; *The Engineer* Nov 15 & 22 1861; CLB pp25–30
12 *Cork Examiner* Nov 6, 1861; *Hampshire Telegraph* Nov 9, 1861
13 Cochrane to CinC Portsmouth Nov 23, 1861 CLB p36; Controller to Admiralty Dec 12, 1861 ADM 1/5774
14 Cochrane to CinC Portsmouth Nov 25, 1861 CLB p35; *ANG* Dec 28, 1861
15 Palmerston to Prince Consort Oct 7, 1861 Royal Archives Windsor
16 G Ballard *The black battlefleet* 1980, pp70–1
17 Cochrane to CinC Portsmouth, Dec 1861 CLB pp46–57

18 Robinson to Cochrane Dec 28, 1861 (Cochranalia); *Naval & Military Gazette* Jan 4, 1862

19 Robinson to Cochrane Jan 2, 1862 (Cochranalia)

20 *ANG* Jan 21, 1862; Digest correspondence Jan 20 and 23, 1862, ADM 97/259

21 Admiralty to Cochrane Jan 15, 1862 (Cochranalia); Cochrane's letter of proceedings March 13, 1862 ADM 1/5784;; CLB pp73/79

22 CinC Plymouth to Admiralty March 1, 1862 (with defect list) ADM 1/5784

23 Cochrane to CinC Plymouth March 13, 1862 (CLB p79) enclosing indicator diagrams covering *Warrior's* performance

24 Briggs to Walker Sept 28 and Oct 5, 1861 (BWC)

Chapter 7   Operations

1 Cochrane to Smart June 30, 1862 CLB p127; *ANG* May 3 & June 6, 1862

2 Cochrane to Admiral Supt May 13, 1862 CLB p106

3 Cochrane to CinC Plymouth May 13, 1862 (two letters) CLB pp 107–108

4 Description of flogging based on W Don *Reminiscences of the Baltic Fleet of 1855*, 1894 pp 62–63

5 Cochrane to CinC Plymouth, May 14, 1862 CLB p109

6 Cochrane to Smart, June 25, 1862 CLB p125

7 P Fitzgerald *Life of Sir George Tryon* 1898, p69

8 C Gavin *Royal yachts* 1932, p142; *Warrior* signal log vol 2 (RNM)

9 Smart to Cochrane March 6, 1863 (Cochranalia); P Magnus *King Edward VII* 1964, p92; Cdr Owen to author, Aug 29, 1985 (Pr)

10 Report of Select Committee on Ordnance 1863 Minutes 2231–2295 (NHL)

11 Digest of correspondence March 17, 1863 ADM 12/731

12 R Bacon *Lord Fisher* vol 1, 1929, p29

13 Channel Fleet visit to Liverpool 1863 (Pr)

14 R Bacon ibid pp27–28

15 NMM Library, reference log n/27, 1863 (NMM)

16 Dacres to CinC Portsmouth Oct 20, 1863 ADM 1/5812

17 Letters from Cochrane to CinC Portsmouth etc CLB pp267–297

18 A Cochrane to E Cochrane Nov 21, 1862; August 19 & Oct 19, 1863; March, April 22, June 30, Oct 22, 1864 (Cochranalia)

19 R Mackay *Fisher of Kilverstone* 1973, p34

20 Lord Fisher *Memories* 1919, p148–149

21 Cochrane to Dacres Jan 23, 1864 CLB p309

22 Dacres to Admiralty April 26 1864 ADM 1/5867; R Bacon ibid p31/32

23 Letters from Cochrane to Dacres CLB 394–486

24 H & R Pakington *The Pakingtons of Westwood* p158 (Pr); Pakington to Cochrane Oct 25, 1864 (Cochranalia)

25 *Sailors Home Journal* and *Naval Chronicle* Dec 1, 1864

Chapter 8   Second Commission

1 E Archibald *The metal fighting ship* 1971, pl

2 Walker to Dundas Nov 13, 1860 (BWC)

3 *The Times* April 2 and 3, 1862

4   *Hansard* Series 3 clxvi, col 440

5 Journals of Admiral Smart ADM 50/329; Smart to Admiralty Nov 5, 1861 ADM 1/5757

6 Dacres to Admiralty on performance of *Edgar, Black Prince, Warrior* and *Defence* March 5, 1864; Dacres to Admiralty on seagoing and other qualities of Channel squadron ironclads, Nov 5, 1864, ADM 1/5867

7 Surveyor (Controller) to Admiralty on rig, armament of iron-cased ships Feb 2, 1863 ADM 1/5840; Controller to Admiralty on Dacres' report Nov 19, 1864 ADM 1/5867; Controller to Admiralty on classification, distribution and construction of armour-plated ships Dec 13, 1864 ADM 1/5892 pl and appendices; Performance of ironclads, Report to Parliament March 30, 1867 (NHL)

8 *The Artizan* Nov 1, 1866 p262

9 Barnes Centre of gravity of three ironclad ships *TRINA* Vol 7 p209; Ships Book ADM 136/2

10 *Boats of men of war, Maritime Monograph* 15, p19 (NMM); Stapleton *Steam picket boats* 1980, p1

11 Controller to Admiralty June 18, 1867 ADM 1/6018

12 Memoir of Admiral Boys, 1913, p33 (Pr)

13 Boys to Cochrane Aug 25, 1867 (Cochranalia)

14 Report of proceedings of Channel squadron Oct 16, 1868, ADM 114/1

15 Ibid Dec 3, 1867

16 Memoir of Admiral Boys p34 (Pr); A Florance *Queen Victoria at Osborne* pp43–4

17 Channel squadron memorandum by Warden to Controller May 26, 1868, ADM 114/3

18 Boys to Cochrane Aug 25, 1867 (Cochranalia)

19 Memoir of Admiral Boys p35–36 (Pr); G Ballard *The black battlefleet* 1980, p134

20 Memoir of Admiral Boys p37 (Pr); *ANG* and *Western Morning News* Oct 6, 1868; *Naval Chronicle* Nov 1, 1868

21 Admiral Sir R Harris *From naval cadet to admiral 1913*, p106; P Fitzgerald *Memories of the sea 1913*, p267–8

22 'By one of those on board' Narrative of the voyage of HM floating dock *Bermuda* from England to Bermuda, 1870 (NHL)

23 Accounts of towing of floating dock: Boys to Admiralty June 28, July 3 & 4 1869 ADM 1/6099; Memoir of Admiral Boys p40 (Pr); *Shipping wonders of the world* pp1047–1049; *Bermuda Royal Gazette* Aug 2, 1869; F Whymper *The sea* 1875, pp191–193

24 G Ballard ibid p106–111

25 Admiral Sir R Harris ibid p110

26 G Ballard ibid p110–113; Sept 17 & Oct 1, 1870; A Hawkey *HMS Captain* 1963

27 F W Fisher *Naval reminiscences* 1938, p69

28 'Original Communications' *Jnl of the RN Medical Services* (date unknown)

29 G Ballard ibid p73; P Fitzgerald ibid pp299–302; *ANG* July 29, 1871

30 Journal of Writer James Seymour p36 (Pr)

Chapter 9   Coastguard and Reserve

1 L Yexley *Inner life of the navy* 1908, Ch 11

2 E Freemantle *The navy as I have known it*, 1904 p282

3 Royal Navy in Portland p4 (Pr)

4 G Ballard *The black battlefleet* p184–188; *ANG* Sept 25, 1875

5 A Heckstall Smith *Sacred Cowes* 1955, p32

6 P Scott *Fifty years in the navy* 1919, p23

7 *ANG* Aug 17, 1878

8 *The Times* Nov 28, 1879

9 Precis of discussions on future of *Warrior* and early ironclads, Forwood papers Hampshire Records

Office 19762 No 42

10 G Ballard ibid p45; Miss Kelly Laing to author, letters Aug–Oct 1985

11 H Wheeler *Sketches in about and around Weymouth* 1881, p39–42 (Pr)

12 G Lowis *Fabulous admirals* 1957, pp32–33

13 Admiralty to ACR May 27, 1881 (Pr)

14 L Bayly *Pull together* 1939, p49

15 Some recollections of service in a mid-Victorian flying squadron *Naval Review* vol 29, p61–2

16 Discussions on future of *Warrior* and early ironclads ibid; R Gawn Historical notes on investigations at Admiralty Experiment Works Torquay *TRINA* Paper 3, 1941 pp18–20

17 *Navy List* 1887

18 *Ships and ship models* May 1936, pp265–267

19 *Black and White* Feb 24, 1900

Chapter 10   Hulked

1 A Cochrane to E Cochrane Apr 29, 1904 (Cochranalia); *Daily Mirror* Sept 24, 1904

2 *Hansard* Public Accounts (Navy Votes) March 24, 1903

3 *Southampton Times* June 4, 1904

4 G B Sayer *History of HMS Vernon* p32

5 Charles Cutler biography (Pr); *RN Barracks Portsmouth and its history* 1932, pp48–49 (Pr)

6 J G Wells *Whaley* 1980, p80

7 Fisher to Heffernan Dec 18, 1918 (Pr); J A Fisher *Memories* 1919, p101

8 Admiralty to First Lord Aug 13, 1928, ADM 1/8733; *Illustrated London News* June 4, 1932

9 *Naval & Military Record* March 20, 1929; G Plumridge to author May 10, 1986; *Warrior* hulk berth, DG Supplies and Transport to author May 3, 1982

10 F Denzey to author Oct 2, 1985 enclosing his father's article in *Navy works* 3, Dec 1949

11 Mrs James to author, Apr 5 1982 (Pr)

12 J H McGivering to author, May 14, 1984 (Pr)

13 Mrs Desjardins to author Feb 20, 1982 (Pr)

14 R P Holbrook to author Oct 5, 1981 (Pr)

15 Admiral Sir C Madden to author July 31, 1983 (Pr)

16 CPO A O Dynes to author July 7, 1983 (Pr)

17 A W Cullicot to author, Nov 1, 1981 (Pr)

18 G A Osbon, Postscript on battleship C109 ex-*HMS Agincourt, MM47*, p215

19 *Times* diary, Feb 17, 1968

20 *Sunday Times* Feb 21, 1968

21 L Phillips *The last battleship*, letter to *The Times* Sept 4, 1968

22 *Daily Telegraph* Sept 6, 1968

23 Admiral Bayly's memorandum to Council of Maritime Trust Oct 30, 1977 (TMT)

24 *Hansard* oral answers Dec 6, 1977 p1103–1104; *Daily Telegraph* Dec 6, 1977

25 Admiral Bayly to Lt Cdr D Blackburn, Equerry to Duke of Edinburgh, Jan 17, 1977 (TMT)

26 Maritime Trust press releases June 12, Aug 10 & 20, 1979 (TMT)

27 Report of QHM Pembroke Dock to author, May 1982 (Pr)

28 Alexandra Towing Company 150th anniv pamphlet 1983 (Pr)

29 Report of *Warrior* tow Aug 1979, Alexandra Towing Company to author (Pr)

Chapter 11   Restoration

1 N R Botterell and Roche to V Admiral Sir P Bayly July 30, 1979 (TMT); Bayly to Ian Campbell-Gray re-*Warrior* insurance Oct 4, 1979 (TMT)

2 M Drummond to J Smith Oct 11, 1979

3 Report by E V Gatacre July 7–Sept 3, 1980 (TMT)

4 Admiral Weir, Capt C McMullen et al, to WPT Aug 18, 1983

5 Minutes of meeting, Feb 22, 1984 Civic Offices, Portsmouth to plan *Warrior's* berth (PCC)

6 Portsmouth historic naval base and ships, Development study October, 1983; both by Ventures Consultancy, Hampshire (PCC)

7 Agreement between Portsmouth Council and Ships Preservation Trust relating to *HMS Warrior's* display in Portsmouth Sept 19, 1984 (PCC)

8 Admiral Beresford *Memoirs* 1914, p42

9 Cochrane to Cdre Nicholson, Sept 17, 1861, CLB p12

10 B C Cooper, Archivist Drummonds Branch of Royal Bank of Scotland, to author, Jan 8, 1986

APPENDICES

Sources common to most appendices include *Queen's Regulations & Admiralty Instructions 1861*; Ship's Book ADM 136/2; Captain's Letter Book *HMS Warrior* 1861–1864; Account and weight of stores, provisions etc received Jan 1, 1862 (Cochranalia); Midshipman H A K Murray's 1862 journal sketch of *Warrior* detailed deck plans; G Ballard *The black battlefleet* 1980; Captain J Boyd *Naval cadets manual* 1860.

● Appendix I–Chronology. Ship's logs ADM 53/8097 to 8102A; 8849 to 9850; 11401–3; 11840–1; 31953. Logs of Midshipmen H A K Murray (RNM 149/81); F C Brown (NMM–M584/042); C G Eeles (Pr). Contemporary *Navy Lists*.

● Appendix II–Personnel. Victualling and description lists ADM 38/7372–5 and 9310. Contemporary *Navy Lists*.

● Appendix III–Construction. Commissioner's report on control and management of HM Yards (1861) Minute 341 (NHL). Specification for iron screw steam frigate cased in armour plates (NMM). J Grantham *Iron shipbuilding* (5th ed) 1868. E J Reed *Shipbuilding in iron and steel* 1869. W H White *Manual of naval architecture* 1877. N J McMermid *Shipyard practice as applied to warship construction* 1911. W J Macquorne & C E Rankine *Shipbuilding theoretical and practical* 1866. E J Reed *Our ironclad ships* 18699. J Brough *Wrought iron*. D K Brown, Developing armour for HMS *Warrior* Warship 40, 1986. Treasury to Thames Ironworks Dec 20, 1861 ADM 1/5773. Establishment of Carpenter's Stores 1868 (NHL).

● Appendix IV–Marine engineering. J Bourne *Treatise on the steam engine* 1851. N P Burgh *Practical treatise on modern screw propulsion* 1869. R Sennett & H J Oram *The marine steam engine* 1898. J G Liversedge *Engine room practice* 1918. G L Overton *History and development of marine engines* 1935. E C Smith *Short history of naval and marine engineering* 1937. J H Morris & L J Wilson *The South Wales coal industry* 1958. *The Engineer* 1860–1864. Ship's logs ADM 53/8097 to 8100. Admiralty Regulations for management of machinery and boilers, 1868. Report on Nixon Duffryn coal ADM 1/5774. Instructions for cupolas Admiralty memo No 6, Dec 18, 1861. Report of committee on marine engines, 1859 (NHL).

Parliamentary papers 360, 364, 442, 212 and 246 Reports on coal 1862–1871 (NHL). Table of coal consumption and results of steam trials (Cochranalia). Establishment of engineers' stores 1868 (NHL).

- Appendix V–Spars, sails and seamanship. Watts to Controller March 27, 1861. ADM 1/5774. Snow Harris to Controller June 17, 1862, ADM 1/5774. Captain's remarks on performance in ship's logs ADM 53/8102A, 9847 and 9850. J Lees *Mastering and rigging of English ships of war 1626-1860* J Harland *Seamanship in the age of sail* 1984. G Ballard, Trysails *MM* Vol 29 p167 and *Naval Review* Feb 1940 p81. H D p Cunninghamn, Rig and sails of steamships of war *TRINA* Vol 2 p98. G S Nares *Seamanship* 1865. C Burney *Boys manual of seamanship and gunnery* 1871. T Walker *Captain Alston's seamanship* 1894. Establishment of Boatswains' stores, 1868 (NHL).
- Appendix VI–Armament. Capt W Moorsom Remarks on construction of ships of war and composition of war fleets, Pamphlet Sept 1857 (NHL). Gunport sizes *Excellent* to CinC Portsmouth Dec 15, 1860 and ADM 87/77. Quarterly list of changes of military equipment and stores (NOM) *Warrior* signal log 5, 1864 (RNM). *Excellent's* gunnery instructions 1864 (Pr). J W Nookes Gunnery notebook, 1858 (Pr). J Wood's Notes on naval guns, stores and fittings 1866 (NHL). Admiralty memoranda and circulars 1861-64 (NHL). Select Cttee on ordnance 1863 (NHL). H A Baker What went wrong with the Armstrongs *Journal of Arms and Armour* vols 7 & 8, 1973-74. H Douglas *Treatise on naval gunnery* 1855. H Garbett *Naval gunnery* 1897. N Barnaby *Naval developments of the century* 1904. R H Davies *Deep sea diving and submarine operations*. E F Slaymaker *The guns of HMS Warrior* 1984. F Robertson *Evolution of naval armament,* 1921.
- Appendix VII –Navigation, signals and ceremonial. Paper to Royal Society by A Smith & F J Evans *The Times* April 19, 1861. W E May, Compasses at International Exhibition of 1862 *RNSS* Journal. Evans to Cochrane Sept 13, 1862 (Cochranalia) Evans's character of RN armour-plated ships ADM 1/6019. A E Fanning *Steady as she goes* 1986. Hydrographic Dept's chart catalogue 1864. Development of nautical log 1976 (NMM). *Warrior's* signal logs (RNM). Establishment of Boatswains' stores,

1868 (NHL). J K Dempsey *Evolution of signalling at sea by flags* (*HMS Mercury*). Colomb & Bolton *Flashing signals* 1868 (Cochranalia) T Wilson *Flags at sea* 1986. L E Holland *Development of signalling in RN,* 1974 (NMM). Bugle and bugler in RN *MM* vol 10, p295. Admiral G A Wells *Naval customs and traditions* 1930.

- Appendix VIII–Anchors, cables and boats. Report of Committee on anchors 1853 (NHL). I G Aylen, Anchors and early trials *Naval Review* vol 72, 1984. Diagram Brown and Harfield's patents July 1, 1863 ADM 1/5890 M. G S Nares *Seamanship* 1865. W Henderson *Seamanship* 1907. Establishment of carpenters' stores 1868 (NHL). The boats of men of war 1974 (NMM) *Admiralty signal book for use in boats* 1865.
- Appendix IX–Victualling, stores and pay. T. Walker, *Captain Alston's seamanship* 1894 ch 8. The lighting of *HMS Warrior* SRP 4 May 24, 1983. Mess utensils Admiralty circular 399, Dec 21, 1859. Admiralty Instructions for Paymasters, 1854. C Burney's *Seaman's manual and rigger's guide* 1876. *Navy list* June 20, 1863, p247. H Priestly *What it cost the day before yesterday.*
- Appendix X–Medical and band. Lloyd & Coulter *Medicine and the navy* 1963 vol 4. Bennion *Antique medical instruments* 1979. A life on the ocean wave *Nursing Mirror* July 1, 1981. Medical officers' journals *HMS Marlborough,* 1858; Lord Warden 1870–1871 & 1873–1874 ADM 101/209. J T Trendell *Operation music maker* 1984.
- Appendix XI–*Warrior* in battle. Admiral Sir R Custance. *A ship of the line in battle* 1912. H W Wilson *Ironclads in action* vol 2, 1897. Anon *The revolution in naval warfare* 1867. Ironclads of the Channel squadron, remarks of Controller on Dacre's report, Nov 19, 1861. ADM 1/5892. Capt E A Inglefield, Naval tactics, Royal United Service Institution, June 29, 1868. *La Gloire* (1858) *Neptunia* March 1, 1958. Figuier *Les merveilles de la science* 1959 ch 9 comparison *Warrior & Gloire.*
- Appendix XXII–HM Ships named *Warrior.* Lt Lloyd to Capt McKinley Dec 3, 1805 (Pr). M Jackson, The Warrior Story *MM* 70, p427.

FURTHER READING
In addition to publications already mentioned the following are recommended:

E H H Archibald *The wooden fighting ship* 1969; *The metal fighting ship* 1971; R Bacon *A naval scrapbook* 1925; C S Bartlett *Great Britain and sea power* 1963; H Baynham *Before the mast* 1971; T Brassey *The British Navy* vol 1, part 1, 1882; H D Capper *Aft from the hawsehole* 1929; W Laird Clowes *The Royal Navy–a history* vol 7, 1903; P H Colomb *Memoirs of Admiral Sir A Cooper Key* 1898; W Cresswell *Close to the wind* 1965; S Eardley Wilmot *Our fleet today* 1900; J Fabb & A C McGow *The Victorian and Edwardian Navy* 1976; H L Fleet *My life and a few yarns* 1922; W Glascock *Naval Officer's manual,* 1836; L Gardner *The British Admiralty* 1968; I Hogg *Coast defences of England and Wales* 1974; R Humble *Before the dreadnought* 1974; E H Jenkins *History of the French Navy* 1973; P Kemp *Oxford companion to ships and the sea* 1976; H Keppel *A sailor's life under four sovereigns* vols 2 & 3 1899; J Laffin *Jack Tar* 1969; M Lewis *Navy in transition* 1965; T S Lyne *Something about a sailor* 1940; P Macdougall *Royal Dockyards* 1982; M Miller *USS Monitor* 1978; A Moore *Sailing ships of war 1800–1860* 1926; S Noble *Autobiography* 1927; J Pack *Nelson's blood* 1982; P Padfield *The battleship era* 1972; *Guns at sea* 1973; *Rule Britannia* 1981; G Penn *Snotty* 1957; N A M Rodger *The Admiralty* 1973; L T C Rolt *Victorian engineering* 1970; E Seymour *My naval career and travels* 1911; W H Symthe *Sailors' word book* 1867; L W M Stephens *History of Royal William yard* 1978; G Taylor *The sea chaplains* 1978; A T Patterson *Portsmouth, a history* 1976; J E Tennent *The story of the guns* 1864; J Winton *Hurrah for the life of a sailor* 1977.

Warrior Archives
Associated with and located close to the ship's berth at Portsmouth are the *Warrior's* archives which comprise:

- copies of most papers and official documents mentioned in the references
- copies of Admiralty collection of ship plans (NMM) associated with *Warrior* and her sister ships
- copies of detailed drawings by *Warrior* Preservation Trust draughtsmen of equipment and work carried out during reconstruction
- photographs of *Warrior,* contemporary ships and life afloat in the Victorian Navy (Imperial War Museum, Service Museum, NMM and private collectors)
- photographs of *Warrior's* reconstruction
- miscellaneous information about the ship.

Index